Economic Analysis of Accident Law

# Economic Analysis of Accident Law

Steven Shavell

Harvard University Press
Cambridge, Massachusetts
London, England
1987

This book is printed on acid-free paper, and its binding materials
have been chosen for strength and durability.

*Library of Congress Cataloging in Publication Data*

Shavell, Steven, 1946–
  Economic analysis of accident law.

  Bibliography: p.
  Includes index.
  1. Torts—Economic aspects—United States. I. Title.
KF1251.S53  1987            346.7303          86-29498
ISBN 0-674-22525-2 (alk. paper)     347.3063

*To my parents, Lillian and Henry*

# Preface

Accident law is the law determining when the victim of an accident is entitled to recover losses from the injurer. Scholarly writing on this important branch of law (as on most others) has traditionally been concerned with describing the state of the law and with examining it for consistency with general legal principles and felt notions of fairness. In the last two decades, however, a group of legal scholars and economists has undertaken a systematic theoretical study of accident law that focuses on identifying the law's effects on behavior. The approach of these writers is often called "economic" because, as in the discipline of economics, simple models are employed to predict the manner in which "rational" parties would act in the face of various incentives, such as the prospect of liability, and outcomes are evaluated with respect to carefully articulated social goals.

My aim in the present book is to offer a comprehensive analysis of accident law from this new perspective. To do so, I have had to restate, integrate, and extend the economically oriented literature on the subject, including my own contributions. Thus, I devote much attention to the issue the literature has emphasized, the influence of accident law on precautions taken to avoid harm and, consequently, on the incidence of accidents. In addition, I develop an analysis of topics that have received less consideration, particularly the role of the insurance system and how ownership of insurance alters the behavior of parties and the distribution of accident losses. I also analyze the costs of operation of the liability system and study alternatives to the system, such as governmental regulation of safety.

In an effort to make the book accessible to a wide audience, I have limited the use of terms of art, both legal and economic, and have defined those I do employ. For the professional economist I have included after each chapter a mathematical appendix presenting a complete formal version of the text. I hope, therefore, that the book will serve as a general reference on the theory of the functioning of the liability system and that it will provide a helpful framework for evaluating the current system and proposals for reform.

A number of individuals and institutions have aided me in writing this book. I especially thank Lucian Bebchuk and A. Mitchell Polinsky for their generous and valuable advice on the manuscript, David Rosenberg for numerous discussions about tort law, and Richard Posner for his encouragement and for an ongoing exchange of ideas throughout the years that I have been interested in economic analysis of law. I also want to thank Michael Faure, Marcel Kahan, Louis Kaplow, Lewis Kornhauser, William Landes, Robert Prichard, Samuel Rea, Gary Schwartz, Warren Schwartz, and Michael Trebilcock for their comments; and I am grateful to Michael Aronson and Kate Schmit of Harvard University Press for their editorial assistance. I acknowledge as well the financial support that I received as a Guggenheim Fellow in 1983–1984 and, at various stages, support from the National Science Foundation, the John M. Olin Foundation, the Eli Lilly Foundation, and the University of Chicago Law School, where I was a visitor in 1984–1985. Finally, I would like to express my gratitude to my wife, Catherine, and to my children, Amy and Robert, for being so accepting of the time I spent writing the book.

# Contents

**1. Introduction**        1

*Use of Models to Examine Two Types of Theoretical Questions*      1
*Organization of the Book*      3


**2. Liability and Deterrence: Basic Theory**      5

*Levels of Care the Only Determinant of Risk: Unilateral Accidents*      6
*Levels of Care the Only Determinant of Risk: Bilateral Accidents*      9
*Levels of Care and Levels of Activity the Determinants of Risk: Unilateral Accidents*      21
*Levels of Care and Levels of Activity the Determinants of Risk: Bilateral Accidents*      26
MATHEMATICAL APPENDIX      32


**3. Liability of Firms**      47

*The Case Where Victims Are Strangers to Firms*      48
*The Case Where Victims Are Customers of Firms*      51
MATHEMATICAL APPENDIX      64

**4. Factors Bearing on the Determination of Negligence**      73

*Differences among Parties*                                     73
*Prior Precautions*                                             77
*Uncertainty, Error, and Misperception*                         79
*Implications of Findings of Negligence*                        83
MATHEMATICAL APPENDIX                                           86


**5. Causation and the Scope of Liability**                    105

*Accidents Caused by Injurers*                                 105
*Coincidental Accidents*                                       110
*Uncertainty over Causation*                                   115
MATHEMATICAL APPENDIX                                          118


**6. The Magnitude of Liability: Damages**                     127

*The Level of Losses*                                          127
*The Probability of Losses*                                    128
*Courts' Uncertainty about the Level of Losses*                131
*Pecuniary versus Nonpecuniary Losses*                         133
*Economic Losses*                                              135
*Particularistic Elements in the Computation of Liability*     140
*Victims' Opportunities to Mitigate Losses*                    144
*Liability in Excess of Losses*                                146
MATHEMATICAL APPENDIX                                          151


**7. Other Topics in Liability**                               164

*Multiple Injurers*                                            164
*Injurers' Inability to Pay for Losses*                        167
*Vicarious Liability*                                          170
*Limited Liability of Shareholders for the Losses Caused by
   Corporations*                                               175
MATHEMATICAL APPENDIX                                          177


**8. The Allocation of Risk and the Theory of Insurance**      186

*Risk Aversion and the Allocation of Risk*                     186
*The Theory of Insurance*                                      192
MATHEMATICAL APPENDIX                                          199

**9. Liability, Risk-bearing, and Insurance: Basic Theory**      206

*Risk Aversion and the Socially Ideal Solution to the Accident*
   *Problem*      206
*The Accident Problem in the Absence of Liability*      208
*The Accident Problem Given Liability Alone*      208
*The Accident Problem Given Liability and Insurance*      210
MATHEMATICAL APPENDIX      215

**10. Liability, Risk-bearing, and Insurance:**
   **Extensions to the Basic Theory**      228

*Nonpecuniary Losses and Insurance*      228
*Awards Optimal for Compensation versus Awards Optimal*
   *for Deterrence*      231
*Victims' Collateral Insurance Benefits and Injurers' Liability*      235
*Injurers' Inability to Pay and Liability Insurance*      240
*Structure of a System of Pure Accident Insurance*      243
MATHEMATICAL APPENDIX      245

**11. Liability and Administrative Costs**      262

*Factors Determining Administrative Costs*      262
*The Private Motive to Make Claims versus Their Social*
   *Desirability*      265
MATHEMATICAL APPENDIX      270

**12. Liability versus Other Approaches to the Control of Risk**      277

*The Different Approaches to the Control of Risk*      277
*Factors Bearing on the Appeal of Ex Ante versus Ex Post*
   *Approaches*      279
*Factors Bearing on the Desirability of Privately Initiated*
   *versus State-Initiated Approaches*      283
*Factors Bearing on the Appeal of Nonmonetary, Criminal*
   *Sanctions*      284
*Concluding Observations*      285
MATHEMATICAL APPENDIX      286

**13. Critical Comments**                                        291
   *Predictive and Normative Analysis*                    291
   *Purpose and Future of Accident Liability*          297

   *References*                                                   301
   *Index*                                                            309

# Economic Analysis of Accident Law

# 1 | Introduction

The subject of this book is the law governing liability for accidents. By "liability" I mean the possible legal obligation of a party who causes harm to make a payment to the victim of the harm, and by "accidents" I mean harmful outcomes that neither injurers nor victims wished to occur—although either might have affected the likelihood or severity of the outcomes. The body of law determining liability for accidents is included in what is known to us in Anglo-American legal systems as tort law,[1] and I shall use this term and accident and liability law synonymously.

For clarification I should add two comments about the scope of the book and that of tort law. First, the book, like tort law, is concerned mainly with liability for accidents between parties who do not have a contractual relationship with each other. (However, liability of firms to customers, dealt with in Chapter 3, is a partial exception.) Second, tort law is concerned with intentional harmful outcomes as well as accidents, but intentional harm is treated only briefly here (in Chapter 6).

## Use of Models to Examine Two Types of Theoretical Questions

Two types of theoretical questions will be analyzed in the book: "predictive" questions, about the effects of employing legal rules, and "normative" questions, about the goodness of legal rules. The approach will be to use stylized models of parties' behavior and of the working of the legal system to examine the questions.

---

1. In France, tort law is known as *la responsabilité civile délictuelle* (delictual liability); in Germany, the counterpart to the tort is *unerlaubte Handlung* (unpermitted action) or *Delikt* (delict); and in the socialist countries, related terms are used. See Tunc 1974, pp. 9–12.

The predictive questions will have definite answers in the models because a complete set of assumptions about parties' situation, the nature and risk of accidents, and the legal system will always be specified. It will be stated, for instance, whether injurers have enough money to pay fully the judgments rendered against them, whether they own liability insurance, whether victims' losses are purely financial or include physical injury, whether liability rules are applied perfectly or are subject to error, and so forth. Given such assumptions, it will be possible to ascertain the effects of liability rules.

In particular, parties' behavior will be assumed to be determined by the theory of expected utility. According to the theory, if a party is to choose among different actions, each of which would result in some consequence with certainty, then he would simply select the action leading to the consequence having the greatest "utility" to him.[2] Typically, however, a party will face uncertainty over the consequences of his actions. In such cases a party will evaluate a potential action in terms of its "expected" utility. The expected utility of an action is obtained by multiplying the probability of each outcome that could follow from the action by the utility of the outcome and then adding these values over all the possible outcomes. Thus, if an action would result in an outcome producing a utility of 100 with probability 90 percent and in another outcome yielding a utility of 200 with probability 10 percent, the expected utility associated with the action would be 90% × 100 + 10% × 200 or 110. Parties will be assumed to take the action having the highest expected utility.[3]

---

2. As is conventional in economic theory, utilities are to be understood as numbers selected by the analyst to represent a party's underlying preferences in the following sense: one consequence is assigned a higher number—called a utility—than another consequence if and only if the party prefers the first consequence to the second. For example, if a party prefers consequence A to consequence B, the analyst might assign the utility 5 to A and the utility 3 to B; or, just as well, he might assign 50 to A and 30 to B. (The reader familiar with expected utility theory will realize, however, that different von Neumann–Morgenstern utility assignments must be positive linear transformations of each other.) The utilities, in other words, are not unique; the definition of utility used in this book is therefore to be contrasted with notions of "objective" utility. It should also be noticed that, given the definition of utility, parties make choices *as if* they were bent on maximizing some numerical magnitude, but *not* because they are in fact doing that. The party just mentioned will choose an action resulting in A over an action resulting in B simply because he prefers A to B; that this choice maximizes his utility is a statement only about an analyst's construct.

3. The theory of expected utility and decisionmaking under uncertainty described here is widely accepted among economists and statisticians, as it is an extremely versatile approach with an axiomatic basis that most consider to be intellectually compelling. See Savage 1972, chaps. 2–5; Arrow 1971, chaps. 1–2; and Raiffa 1968. Readers unfamiliar with the mathematical background should notice the qualitative properties of the expected utility of an

When answers to predictive questions are available in a model and a social welfare criterion is stipulated, normative questions can be answered. If, for example, the social goal is the minimization of the sum of accident losses and the costs of accident prevention, one legal rule would be said to be better than another if it resulted in a lower sum of accident losses plus prevention costs. Answers to normative questions obviously depend on the measure of social welfare under consideration. If the measure just mentioned were altered to take into account compensation of victims, say, the comparison of legal rules could well be different.

The advantage of studying models is that they allow predictive and normative questions to be answered in an unambiguous way. Practicality, however, requires that models be kept simple; although there is no conceptual bar to introducing in them all manner of complications, admitting even a few tends to make models difficult to solve or to interpret. Thus, the understanding of reality gained from models must be inexact, and rough judgments about the fit of models must be made.

**Organization of the Book**

Each of the chapters of the book (other than this one and the conclusion) contains several types of sections. Sections discussing the models comprise the core of the analysis and often include numerical examples, which are set off so that the flow of the text will not be interrupted. The reader should be careful to bear in mind that the predictive and normative statements made in these sections apply to the models only. Other sections attempt to go beyond the models and comment on their more general interpretation. Included throughout the book are summary descriptions of the actual law. These descriptions focus on Anglo-American law, but sometimes mention the French, German, and Soviet legal systems.[4] Notes on the relevant literature are provided as well. Citations refer mainly to literature with an economic orientation, or at least to works that view the liability system in a frankly instrumental way.

---

action: the expected utility rises with the likelihood of desired outcomes that might result from the action and with an index (the utility) of the importance placed on the outcomes. Presumably, these are properties that an analyst would demand of any ex ante evaluation of an action with an uncertain outcome.

4. The Soviet Union is of interest because of its importance among the socialist countries; and the other countries are of interest not only because of their importance in their own right but also because most legal systems in the modern nonsocialist world are patterned after theirs. See Tunc 1974, pp. 7–12, 54–62.

The claims made about the models in the chapters are demonstrated in mathematical appendixes that employ the standard methods of microeconomic theory. The appendixes are essentially self-contained.

The book begins with an analysis of deterrence, that is, of the effects of liability rules on parties' behavior and therefore on the occurrence of accidents. Here and throughout, the two major forms of liability are considered: negligence and strict liability. Under the negligence rule (to simplify) an injurer must compensate a victim only if he, the injurer, was at fault, which is to say, only if his behavior was subpar; whereas under strict liability an injurer must compensate a victim regardless of whether he was at fault.

Understanding deterrence under liability rules is aided by studying parties' behavior in the absence of insurance and by assuming that measures of social welfare depend on total accident losses and other aggregates, but not on the particular distribution of losses between victims and injurers. This assumption is made in Chapter 2 on the basic theory of deterrence, and it is maintained in Chapters 3 through 7, which extend the basic theory.

In Chapters 8 through 10 insurance is incorporated in the analysis and measures of social welfare are examined that do take into account the distribution of accident losses (or, more exactly, compensation of risk-averse parties and the allocation of risk). Both accident insurance covering victims directly against losses and liability insurance covering injurers against liability are considered. Insurance is of interest, it need hardly be emphasized, because its ownership is widespread. Insurance is an important determinant not only of the ultimate bearing of accident losses, but also of parties' financial reasons for avoiding doing or suffering harm.

The subject of Chapter 11 is the administrative costs of the liability system, namely, the legal and other costs borne by litigants and the public costs associated with operation of the courts. After administrative costs under different liability rules are discussed, a contrast is drawn between the private and the social incentives to make use of the liability system given its administrative costs.

In Chapter 12 liability is compared with other methods for controlling risk: safety regulation, the injunction, fines for harm done, corrective taxes based on anticipated harm, and imposition of criminal sanctions. This examination is intended to place liability in perspective and to enable us to appreciate its distinctive aspects.

Finally, in Chapter 13, concluding comments are offered on the analysis of the book. The value of the analysis for predictive and normative ends, the importance of omitted factors, and the purpose and future of tort law are briefly discussed.

# 2 | Liability and Deterrence: Basic Theory

Here and throughout I will be considering a model of accidents involving two types of parties, *injurers* and *victims*. We might think, for example, of injurers as drivers of automobiles and of victims as bicyclists, or of injurers as parties conducting blasting operations and of victims as passersby.[1] Injurers and victims will each have (at least potentially) two kinds of decisions to make: a decision whether, or how much, to engage in a particular *activity;* and a decision over the degree of *care* to exercise when engaging in an activity. The number of miles an individual drives, for instance, might be interpreted as his level of activity, and the precautions he takes when on the road (slowing for curves, paying attention to the presence of bicyclists) as his level of care. Similarly, how often a bicyclist rides where there is automobile traffic might be regarded as his level of activity, and his precautions when riding (staying close to the side of the road, use of a brightly colored vest) as his level of care.

Injurers may face liability for accidents they cause. They will be assumed, however, not to have made contractual or other agreements with victims to pay for accident losses or to reduce accident risk, for injurers and victims will be supposed to be strangers to one another.

In addition, injurers and victims will be assumed to make their decisions on the basis of evaluations of their expected utility, as described generally in the Introduction. The level of utility of an injurer or a victim will be taken to equal the amount he holds of a single, abstract good.[2] Hence, if a party faces, say, a

---

1. Accidents involving parties of only one type—like accidents involving just drivers of automobiles—are not in strict logic described by the model to be studied. But it will be clear to the reader that many of the conclusions that will be drawn would carry over to a model of "single-activity" accidents.

2. In the model, accident losses will be literal losses of the single good, the costs of exercising care will be literal reductions in the quantity of the good, and liability payments

10 percent chance of losing 100 units of the good, his expected utility will be lowered by 10% × 100 = 10. Notice that a party's expected utility would also be lowered by 10 if he faced instead a 1 percent chance of losing 1,000 units or a 0.1 percent chance of losing 10,000. This illustrates that under the present assumption, parties' decisions will not be influenced by the potential magnitude of their losses per se. Their decisions will be affected only by their *expected losses,* that is, by the potential magnitude of their losses multiplied by the probability of suffering the losses.[3] Parties will therefore be said to be *risk neutral.* Assuming risk neutrality will greatly simplify the analysis of liability and deterrence. Moreover, having studied the situation under this assumption will prove helpful later, in Chapters 8 through 10, when the often more realistic assumption is made that parties are risk averse and are concerned not only about their expected losses, but also about the possible size of their losses.

The effect of liability rules, given these assumptions, on the behavior of parties and on specified measures of social welfare will now be considered in several increasingly general versions of the model. The analysis of each version of the model will proceed in the same way. First the socially ideal situation will be discussed, and then the situation in the absence and in the presence of different liability rules will be examined.

## 2.1   Levels of Care the Only Determinant of Risk: Unilateral Accidents

In this version of the model it will be supposed that accidents are *unilateral* in nature: injurers' behavior will be assumed to affect accident risks, but victims' behavior will not. In other words, victims will have no role in the

---

will be transfers of the good from injurers to victims. The reader may wish to make different interpretations, however. He may wish to interpret care as effort, attention, or expenditures on safety devices. He may wish to interpret accident losses as the quantity or pecuniary value of destroyed property or as a measure of physical injury. (At later points in the analysis, the assumption that there is a single good will be relaxed and an explicit distinction will be drawn between pecuniary and nonpecuniary losses; see §§6.4, 10.1, and 10.2.) Also, the reader will undoubtedly wish to interpret liability payments as transfers of money.

3. More generally, expected losses are obtained by multiplying each possible loss by its probability and then by summing the products over all possible losses. (In the examples just mentioned in the text, there was only one possible magnitude of loss, but obviously that would not always be the case. If, for instance, losses would be 100 with probability 10 percent and 200 with probability 5 percent, expected losses would be 10% × 100 + 5% × 200 = 20.) It should be noted that expected losses are what an actuarially fair insurance premium would equal.

analysis. Where an airplane crashes into a building, for example, or where a break in a water main causes a flood in a basement, the victims presumably could not have done much to prevent harm. In these cases the accidents may be seen as unilateral—as might automobile-bicycle accidents where it is believed that bicyclists' actions are of minor importance in reducing risks.

It will also be supposed that the only way injurers affect accident risks is through their exercise of care; that is, their level of activity will be assumed fixed.

In addition, the social goal will be taken to be minimization of the sum of the costs of care and of expected accident losses. This sum will be called *total accident costs.*

*2.1.1    Social welfare optimum.* Before determining how injurers are led to act in different situations, we will find it of interest to identify the level of care that minimizes total accident costs. This socially optimal level of care will clearly reflect both the costs of exercising care and the reduction in accident risks that it would accomplish. Consider the following example.

EXAMPLE 2.1    The relationship between injurers' care and the probability of accidents that would cause losses of 100 is as in Table 2.1. To understand why exercising moderate care minimizes total accident costs, observe on the one hand that raising the level of care from none to moderate reduces expected accident losses by 5, but involves costs of only 3; it thus lowers total accident costs. On the other hand, observe that raising care beyond the moderate level would reduce expected accident losses by only 2, yet involve additional costs of 3; hence it would not be worthwhile.

Note that the example illustrates the obvious point that the optimal level of care may well not result in the lowest possible level of expected accident losses (for that would require the highest level of care). Let us now examine how much care injurers will be led to exercise in various situations.

*Table 2.1*

| Level of care | Cost of care | Accident probability | Expected accident losses | Total accident costs |
|---|---|---|---|---|
| None | 0 | 15% | 15 | 15 |
| Moderate | 3 | 10% | 10 | 13 |
| High | 6 | 8% | 8 | 14 |

*2.1.2   No liability.* In the absence of liability, injurers will not exercise any care. Total accident costs will therefore generally exceed their optimal level; in Example 2.1, for instance, they would be 15 rather than 13.

*2.1.3   Strict liability.* Under strict liability injurers must pay for all accident losses that they cause. Hence, injurers' total costs will equal total accident costs; and because they will seek to minimize their total costs, injurers' goal will be the social goal of minimizing total accident costs. Consequently, injurers will be induced to choose the socially optimal level of care. In Example 2.1 expected accident losses will become injurers' expected liability and total accident costs will become injurers' total costs. Accordingly, injurers will decide to exercise the optimal, moderate level of care.

*2.1.4   Negligence rule.* Under the negligence rule an injurer will be held liable for accident losses he causes only if he was negligent, that is, only if his level of care was less than a level specified by courts, called *due care*. If the injurer exercised a level of care that equaled or exceeded due care, he will not be held liable.

If due care is chosen by courts to equal the socially optimal level of care, then injurers will be led to exercise due care and the outcome will be socially optimal. To see why, first reconsider Example 2.1. If courts define due care to be the socially optimal, moderate level, the expected liability for an injurer would equal total accident costs when no care is taken and zero when moderate or high care is taken. When at least moderate care is taken, then, the injurer's total costs equal just the cost of care (see Table 2.2). Hence, injurers will indeed be best off exercising moderate care.

More generally, there are two reasons why injurers will necessarily be led to take due care if it is chosen to equal the optimal level. First, injurers plainly would not take *more* than due care, because they will escape liability by taking merely due care. Taking greater care would therefore be to no advantage yet would involve additional costs.[4] Second, injurers would not wish to take *less* than due care, provided that due care is the socially optimal level. If injurers took less than due care they would be exposed to the risk of liability, so that their expected costs would equal total accident costs. Thus, injurers would want to choose their level of care so as to minimize total accident costs. But this in turn means that they would wish to raise their level of care to the socially optimal point—which by hypothesis equals due care and therefore allows them to avoid liability entirely.

---

4. It is assumed here (and elsewhere in this chapter) that a court can determine a party's level of care with complete accuracy. Otherwise, it might well be worth a party's while to take more than due care to reduce the likelihood of a court mistakenly finding him negligent. This and related issues are analyzed in §4.3.

*Table 2.2*

| Level of care | Cost of care | Injurer liability | Expected liability | Injurer's total costs |
|---|---|---|---|---|
| None | 0 | Liable | 15 | 15 |
| Moderate | 3 | Not liable | 0 | 3 |
| High | 6 | Not liable | 0 | 6 |

*2.1.5 Liability rules compared.* Both forms of liability result in the same, socially optimal behavior, but they differ in what courts need to know to apply them.[5] Under strict liability, a court need only determine the size of the loss that occurred, whereas under the negligence rule a court must in addition determine the level of care actually taken (a driver's speed) and calculate the socially optimal level of due care (the appropriately safe speed). To do the latter, in turn, a court needs to know the cost and effectiveness of taking different levels of care in reducing accident risks.[6]

*2.1.6 Several dimensions of care.* Suppose, as would be usual, that there is more than one dimension of an injurer's behavior that affects accident risks (not only a driver's speed, but also the frequency with which he looks at the rear-view mirror). In this situation an injurer would be led to choose optimal levels of all dimensions of care under strict liability, because his goal would be to minimize his expected total costs. But under the negligence rule he would have a motive to choose optimal levels of only those dimensions of care that are incorporated in the due care standard. And in fact some dimensions of care will usually be excluded from the standard because of difficulties faced by courts in ascertaining certain elements of care (how would a court obtain information about the number of times per minute a driver usually looks at his rear-view mirror?) or in determining proper behavior in respect to these elements of care.

## 2.2 Levels of Care the Only Determinant of Risk: Bilateral Accidents

In the *bilateral* version of the model of accidents, it is assumed that victims as well as injurers can take care and thereby lower accident risks. The way in

5. The rules also differ in how they allocate risk, in their "distributional" effects, and in the administrative costs that they generate. As indicated in the Introduction, these issues will be discussed in later chapters.

6. The reader should be forewarned that these disadvantages of the negligence rule (as well as the disadvantage to be noted in the next section) may become attenuated or may be reversed in the bilateral version of the model; see §§2.2.10 and 2.2.11.

which injurers choose to behave may depend on the way victims behave, and conversely. For example, how watchful drivers are for bicyclists may depend on how cautious bicyclists generally are (drivers might be very watchful if bicyclists are not very cautious); and how cautious bicyclists generally are may depend on the usual attentiveness of drivers.

The possible interdependence of parties' behavior means that to show that injurers and victims will act in a particular way requires that two things be demonstrated: that injurers will choose to act in the asserted way, given that victims act in the asserted way; and that victims will choose to act in the asserted way, given that injurers act in the asserted way. A situation with these two characteristics will be called an *equilibrium*, since neither victims nor injurers will have a motive to alter their behavior.[7]

Injurers' and victims' behavior in equilibria will be determined in the analysis below under several different forms of strict liability and negligence rules. The social goal considered will continue to be minimization of total accident costs, which here will be the sum of injurers' and victims' costs of care plus expected accident losses.

*2.2.1   Social welfare optimum.* The optimum behaviors should reflect the parties' joint possibilities for reducing accident risks and their costs of care. Consider this example.

EXAMPLE 2.2   The probability of an accident that would cause losses of 100 is related to the different possible combinations of injurers' and of victims' levels of care as shown in Table 2.3, where it has been assumed for simplicity that there is only one positive level of care for parties of each type. From the last column of the table it is apparent that it is socially optimal for both injurers and victims to take care. To see why, observe, for instance, that if injurers alone take care, expected losses are 10, whereas if victims also take care, at a cost of 2, expected losses fall by 4; hence total accident costs are reduced by victims also taking care. Similar reasoning shows that the situation where victims alone take care can be improved by injurers also taking care.

Although in this example it is socially optimal for both injurers and victims to take care, other examples can be constructed in which it is optimal only for injurers or only for victims to take care (or for neither to do so). These possibilities are not the focus here (but see §2.2.12), because in most real

7. The reader will come to appreciate the meaning of the definition of equilibrium from its application and should probably not dwell over the definition at this point.

*Table 2.3*

| Levels of care | | Cost of care | | Accident probability | Expected accident losses | Total accident costs |
|---|---|---|---|---|---|---|
| Injurers | Victims | Injurers | Victims | | | |
| None | None | 0 | 0 | 15% | 15 | 15 |
| None | Care | 0 | 2 | 12% | 12 | 14 |
| Care | None | 3 | 0 | 10% | 10 | 13 |
| Care | Care | 3 | 2 | 6% | 6 | 11 |

situations one supposes that it would be best for both injurers and victims to take a positive degree of care, however small.

*2.2.2 No liability.* As before, injurers will not take care in the absence of liability, and the outcome will therefore generally depart from the optimal. However, because victims will bear their accident losses, they will have a reason to take care. In Example 2.2, though injurers will not take care, victims will, because for a cost of 2 they will lower their expected accident losses from 15 to 12.[8]

*2.2.3 Strict liability.* Since injurers will be liable for the accident losses they cause under strict liability, they will have a proper motive to take care, but because victims will be fully compensated by injurers for accident losses, victims will be indifferent to the occurrence of accidents. Therefore, victims will not take care,[9] and the outcome will not be optimal. In Example 2.2, injurers will take care because doing so will reduce their expected liability from 15 to 10 at a cost of only 3, but victims will not take care.

*2.2.4 Strict division of accident losses.* By "strict division of accident losses" I mean that injurers and victims each bear a positive fraction of any

8. Note that this outcome is an equilibrium. It is in victims' interest to take care, given that injurers do not take care; and it is in injurers' interest not to take care, given that victims take care (or, for that matter, given that they do not). The reader will be able to verify similarly that other outcomes below are equilibria, when this is not pointed out in the text.

9. However, victims would obviously have an incentive to take care if they would not or could not be fully compensated for their accident losses, as where the losses involve serious personal injury or death (which, as previously noted, will be considered in later chapters). Thus here (and often below) the reader may find it appealing to think about examples of accidents in which victims would suffer only property losses—such as in accidents in which victims' unoccupied, parked automobiles are damaged by drivers. Nevertheless, the example in which victims are bicyclists will continue to be used in the text for expositional convenience.

accident losses that occur. The fraction is assumed to be independent of their levels of care and, in particular, independent of whether someone was negligent (thus the division is called "strict").

Under this form of liability, injurers and victims may be led to exercise too little care and the outcome may not be socially optimal. Because parties of each type will bear only a portion of accident losses, what they will save by taking care is only a portion of the true reduction in expected accident losses that taking care accomplishes; hence their incentive to take care may be socially inadequate.

In Example 2.2, for instance, suppose that injurers and victims each bear half of any accident losses, that is, 50 rather than 100. In this case neither will take care. To verify that this is so, observe first that injurers will not wish to take care given that victims do not: injurers would reduce their expected liability from $15\% \times 50 = 7.5$ to $10\% \times 50 = 5$ by taking care if victims do not; but since taking care would cost 3, injurers will decide not to do so. Observe likewise that victims will not wish to take care given that injurers do not: victims would reduce their expected losses from $15\% \times 50 = 7.5$ to $12\% \times 50 = 6$ by taking care; but since that would cost 2, they too will not find taking care worthwhile.[10]

Altering the fraction of liability borne by injurers will not necessarily solve the problem. In the example, injurers would be induced to take care if their liability was raised substantially above 50, but that would dilute even further victims' incentives to take care. On the other hand, while victims would be led to take care if the portion of losses they had to bear was raised substantially above 50, that would further dilute injurers' incentives to take care. Thus, in the example and in general, there is no "magic" allocation of accident losses that would induce both injurers and victims to take appropriate care.

*2.2.5  Strict liability with the defense of contributory negligence.* Under this rule an injurer is liable for the accident losses he causes unless the

---

10. The reader will notice that this argument depends on the particular assumptions made about costs of care and accident risks. If, for instance, injurers' and victims' costs of care were 1, then each would be led to take care despite bearing only half of accident losses. This is why it was said in the previous paragraph that the parties "may," rather than "will," take too little care. But it should be emphasized that where in the text "may" appears, "will" usually appears in the mathematical appendixes. Thus in the appendix to this chapter, it is said that both injurers and victims *will* take too little care, whatever the division of accident losses. The reason "will" applies in the appendixes is that there levels of care (and other variables) are assumed to be continuously variable, which means that the effects described in the text always have a positive influence on care.

victim's level of care was less than his due care level. When that is the case, the victim is said to be *contributorily negligent* and must bear his losses.[11]

If the level of due care for victims is chosen by courts to equal the socially optimal level of care, then victims will be induced to exercise due care and injurers also will be induced to take their socially optimal level of care. Thus, the socially optimal outcome will be achieved. To establish that this is true, note, on the one hand, that injurers will exercise optimal care, given that victims take due care, because if victims take due care and therefore will not have to bear their accident losses, injurers will be liable for accident losses. Hence, injurers will have a socially appropriate motive to take care. (If bicyclists take due care, then drivers will be liable for accident losses and will decide to take optimal care.) Note, on the other hand, that victims will take due care. This is true because victims will wish to avoid being found contributorily negligent and thus having to bear their own losses. The specific reasoning is analogous to the explanation in §2.1.4 of why injurers will take due care under the negligence rule.[12]

To verify the claim in Example 2.2, assume that due care for victims equals "care," since their taking care is socially optimal. Presuming that victims take care, injurers will be liable for accident losses they cause. Therefore their expected liability will be reduced from 12 to 6 if they spend 3 to take care, and they will take care. Conversely, assuming that injurers take care, victims will be induced to take care; for if victims do not take care, they will bear their expected accident losses of 10, whereas if they take care at a cost of 2 they will not bear their losses.[13]

11. As many readers know, contributory negligence is called a "defense" because its successful assertion protects injurers who would otherwise be liable.

12. This paragraph has explained only why both injurers and victims taking care is *an* equilibrium. But the situation is in fact the *only* equilibrium that can exist. In other words, the only stable situation that can possibly exist under the rule of strict liability with the defense of contributory negligence (with due care for victims set at the optimal level) is the situation in which both injurers and victims take optimal care. This equilibrium will also be the only one that exists under the other liability rules to be considered in this part of the chapter, as is proved in the Appendix.

13. To see why the only equilibrium in this example is the situation where both injurers and victims take care, consider the other possibilities. Injurers taking care and victims not taking care cannot be an equilibrium, since victims will wish to take care if injurers take care (or, actually, if they do not). Similarly, injurers not taking care and victims taking care cannot be an equilibrium, since injurers will wish to take care given that victims take care. Finally, injurers and victims not taking care cannot be an equilibrium, since victims will wish to take care to avoid liability (for if they take care, their costs will be 2, whereas if they do not take care, they will bear expected losses of 15).

*2.2.6    Strict liability with the defense of relative negligence.* Under this rule, as under the last, an injurer is liable for the accident losses he causes if the victim took due care. If, however, the victim failed to take due care, the victim does not bear all his losses; rather, he bears only a fraction of them, the fraction depending on his actual level of care relative to due care.

It can be demonstrated that if this fraction is sufficiently large and if due care is chosen by courts to equal the socially optimal level of care, then victims will be induced to take due care and injurers will also be led to take the socially optimal level of care. This should be evident from the previous section (and details are therefore omitted), since if the fraction of losses that contributorily negligent victims would have to bear is high enough, then the rule here resembles the last one. In Example 2.2, for instance, if a victim who does not take care will have to bear more than 20 percent of his losses, he will be induced to take care if injurers do so, because the victim will then save more than 2 in expected losses by taking care.

*2.2.7    Negligence rule.* The description of this rule is virtually the same as in the unilateral case. If an injurer takes at least due care, he will not be liable for accident losses he causes; otherwise he will be liable, regardless of how the victim acted.

It is easy to see that if due care is chosen by courts to equal the socially optimal level, then injurers will be led to take due care and victims will also be induced to take the optimal level of care. Injurers will be motivated to take due care to avoid liability, by the argument of §2.1.4. And because victims will bear their losses if injurers take due care, victims will have a proper incentive to take care. (Drivers will be led to take due care; and bicyclists, knowing that they will bear their losses, will decide to take appropriate care.)

To illustrate this conclusion, assume in Example 2.2 that due care for injurers equals "care." If injurers do not take care, their expected liability will be 12, presuming that victims take care; thus injurers will choose to avoid liability by spending 3 on care. Also, because victims will bear their losses when injurers take due care, they will reduce their expected losses from 10 to 6 by taking care; since this will cost victims 2, they too will decide to take care.

*2.2.8    Negligence rule with the defense of contributory negligence.* According to this rule, an injurer will not be liable for accident losses he causes if he takes at least due care; and even if he does not, he will still escape liability if the victim too failed to take due care.

By an argument very close to that of the previous section, it can readily be seen that if injurers' and victims' levels of due care are chosen by courts to equal the socially optimal levels, then both injurers and victims will be led to take due care and the socially optimal result will be achieved. Injurers will wish to take due care to avoid liability, under the assumption that victims take due care and thus will not bear their losses on account of contributory negligence. Also, victims will wish to take due care, presuming that injurers take due care; for as victims will then bear their losses, they will be led to take the socially optimal level of care, which by assumption is due care. (This may be verified in Example 2.2 exactly as it was in the preceding section.)

Notice that the defense of contributory negligence is a superfluous addition to the negligence rule with respect to the objective of inducing victims to act optimally, for it was seen that victims take optimal care when the negligence rule is unaccompanied by the defense. The explanation should be clear on reflection. Under the negligence rule without the defense of contributory negligence, injurers take due care to avoid liability. Consequently, victims bear their losses, and this by itself supplies them an incentive to take appropriate care. Accordingly, there is no need to provide victims another incentive to take care.[14]

*2.2.9 Comparative negligence rule.* Under this rule, like under the last, an injurer will not be liable for accident losses he causes if he takes due care. But this rule differs from the previous rule in the situation where both an injurer and a victim fail to take due care. In that situation each party bears a fraction of the accident losses, where the fraction is determined by a comparison of the amounts by which the two parties' levels of care depart from the levels of due care. The fraction of losses a party bears will be higher the greater the difference between due care and his level of care.

If courts choose optimal levels of due care under the comparative negligence rule, then both injurers and victims will be led to take due care. The rationale for the result is precisely that of the last section. (Injurers will take due care to avoid liability if victims take due care, and so on.)

The reason there is no difference between the outcomes under the comparative negligence rule and under the negligence rule with (or without) the defense of contributory negligence is in essence this: under both rules, if parties of one type take due care, then parties of the other type will reason that they *alone* will be found negligent if they fail to take due care. The allocation of accident losses when *both* injurers and victims are negligent—

---

14. However, the defense of contributory negligence may set up beneficial incentives where some injurers act negligently. If some injurers act negligently and if there is no defense of contributory negligence, then a victim may decide not to take due care, since he may think he will be likely to obtain compensation for accident losses he suffers because they will be caused by a negligent injurer. See §4.4.4 for further discussion.

the distinguishing feature of the comparative negligence rule—therefore turns out to be irrelevant to the calculations of parties in equilibrium.[15]

*2.2.10   Liability rules compared.* We have seen that in the bilateral version of the model, strict liability does not lead to the socially optimal outcome for the obvious reason that it fails to supply victims a motive to take care. And although strict division of accident losses may provide victims some incentive to take care, it may leave injurers with an inadequate incentive to do so. A comparison of these two forms of strict liability with each other and with not having liability at all therefore depends on the importance of modifying injurers' as opposed to victims' behavior. The more important it is for injurers to take care, the greater the relative appeal of strict liability—or a division of losses in which injurers pay a high fraction—over no liability.

We have also seen that strict liability with the defense of contributory (or relative) negligence and all forms of the negligence rule result in the socially optimal outcome. Under these rules, parties have one of two sufficient reasons to take optimal care: either taking optimal care allows them to avoid entirely the bearing of accident losses (victims' situation under strict liability with the defense of contributory negligence, injurers' situation under the negligence rules); or else taking care reduces the expected losses that parties in fact bear (injurers' situation under strict liability with the defense of contributory negligence, victims' situation under the negligence rules).

To apply each of the rules leading to optimality, courts need to determine the magnitude of accident losses and the actual level of care and the optimal level of due care for injurers or victims. Moreover, to ascertain the optimal level of due care for one party, a court must generally determine (if only implicitly) the optimal level of care for the other, since the optimal level of care for one party will in principle depend on the other's costs of and possibilities for reducing risk.[16] This latter point makes the comparison of liability rules with respect to their ease of application different from what it might at first seem to be.

Consider, for instance, the rule of strict liability with the defense of contributory negligence and the negligence rule with the same defense. It may seem

---

15. But it is not irrelevant in situations where there are reasons why some injurers and victims act negligently. See §4.4.4.

16. That courts must consider the optimal level of care of both parties was evident from §2.2.1 and the remarks about bicyclists and drivers in §2.2, but it should be mentioned that in some situations the optimal level of care of parties of one type may be determinable without precise knowledge of the other's optimal level of care. Suppose, for instance, that the use of lights by bicyclists when riding at night will dramatically reduce accident risks whatever the level of care taken by drivers. Then it can be concluded that it is optimal for bicyclists to use lights at night without determining what particular level of care is optimal for drivers.

initially that strict liability with the defense of contributory negligence is the easier to apply, because courts are not directly concerned with injurers' behavior under the rule. But to apply the defense of contributory negligence, courts must determine optimal due care for victims, and, as just remarked, this ordinarily effectively requires courts to determine the optimal level of care for injurers. Therefore, the main difference affecting the ease of application of the two rules is only that under the strict liability rule courts do not need to determine the actual (as opposed to the optimal) level of care of injurers.

*2.2.11 Liability rules compared where care has several dimensions.* It was noted in §2.1.6 that there may be dimensions of injurers' care (such as the frequency with which drivers look at their rear-view mirrors) that would not be taken into account in the determination of negligence because of difficulties courts would encounter in assessing them. Injurers may therefore not take care in an optimal way in every dimension under the negligence rule, but they will be led to do so under strict liability. It is clear that a similar point applies where there are dimensions of victims' care (such as the frequency with which bicyclists look for traffic behind them) that could not be included in their standard of due care. Specifically, victims will not take optimal care in these dimensions under strict liability with the defense of contributory negligence, but they will do so under the negligence rule (because they will bear their losses under that rule). In consequence, to know how the presence of several dimensions of care affects the comparison of liability rules, one must make a judgment about the relative importance of the dimensions of injurers' and of victims' behavior that would be excluded from their respective standards of due care.

*2.2.12 The least-cost avoider.* The notion of the least-cost avoider applies in situations where the risk of accidents will be eliminated if *either* injurers or victims take care. In such situations it is clearly wasteful for *both* injurers and victims to take care; rather, it is optimal for the parties who can prevent accidents at least cost, the "least-cost avoiders," alone to take care.[17] Suppose, for example, that injurers can prevent accident losses of 100 by taking a precaution that costs 10 and that victims also can prevent the losses by taking a precaution that costs 20. In this case injurers alone ought to take precautions, because in that way the social goal of minimizing total accident costs is achieved.

---

17. Actually, it would also be optimal for the least-cost avoiders alone to take care in the following situations: where if either injurers or victims take care, the risk of accidents would be reduced by some amount—but not necessarily eliminated—and where the risk would not be further reduced if injurers and victims take care.

The model of the least-cost avoider may be misleading for thinking about the class of bilateral accidents examined in this book. In the situations examined here, there simply are no least-cost avoiders who alone ought to take care, since the assumption is that both injurers and victims generally ought to do something to avoid risk; the effect of liability rules is therefore different from that in the least-cost avoider model. If, say, injurers are the least-cost avoiders, an optimal outcome will be achieved under strict liability unaccompanied by the defense of contributory negligence. But in the bilateral model studied here the defense of contributory negligence must accompany strict liability in order to induce victims to take appropriate care.

Similarly, consideration of the least-cost avoider model may lead to the belief—though mistaken—that the liability rules shown here to result in optimal behavior can result in suboptimal behavior. For example, the following might be said about the situation noted above where the injurers who can prevent losses at a cost of 10 are the least-cost avoiders: "Since victims can also prevent the losses of 100 at a cost of 20 and 20 is less than 100, they could be found contributorily negligent for failure to take precautions. Thus, use of the defense of contributory negligence can lead to the undesirable result that victims rather than injurers take precautions." The error in this argument lies in the assumption that victims might be found contributorily negligent for failure to take precautions. If due care for victims is assumed to be optimally determined—which, recall, has always been the assumption in showing that rules of liability lead to optimal results—then the due care requirement for victims in the example should be vacuous: there should not be any duty for victims to take precautions.[18]

These remarks about the least-cost avoider model are not meant to suggest that the model cannot be helpful, but rather that the model is special and must be interpreted with caution.

*2.2.13   Liability rules in use.* The major rules of liability for accidents between strangers in the United States are the comparative negligence rule, the negligence rule with the defense of contributory negligence, and strict liability with that defense.[19] In England, France, Germany, and the Soviet Union, the usual forms of liability are the comparative negligence rule and strict liability with what was called here the relative negligence defense.[20]

---

18. Whether a court would in fact find a victim contributorily negligent for not spending 20 where an injurer could have prevented an accident at a lesser cost of 10 is another question. But the strong suspicion is that were these figures plain, a court would correctly decide not to hold a victim contributorily negligent.

19. See, for example, *Prosser and Keeton on Torts* (Keeton, Dobbs, et al. 1984), chaps. 5, 11, 13. The descriptions of actual law herein are necessarily brief.

20. See Tunc 1974, for a summary of and bibliography on tort law in the world today;

*2.2.14 The determination of due care and the "as if" interpretation.*
Negligence in American law as defined in the *Restatement (Second) of Torts*
is "conduct which falls below the standard [of due care] . . . for the protection of others against unreasonable risk of harm," and the concept is similar
in other legal systems. Deciding on the standard of due care often requires
some sort of weighing of the magnitude of risk against the disutility or cost of
more careful conduct.[21]

As the reader has seen in the analysis here, the level of due care that
minimizes total accident costs implicitly involves just such a weighing of risk
against the cost of care. This suggests that due care is in fact found by a
process that operates *as if* it were designed to identify behavior that minimizes total accident costs.[22]

I hasten to say that the words *as if* are stressed because the claim is hardly
made that individuals or courts think in terms of the mathematical goal of
minimizing a sum. They obviously do not do anything so unnatural. Rather,
they appear to gauge the appropriateness of behavior by a rough consideration of risk and the costs of reducing it, ordinarily on the basis of felt notions
of fairness.[23] Likewise, the *as if* interpretation carries with it no specific
implications about the degree to which individuals or courts concern themselves about goals of deterrence, although both sometimes appear to be concerned about deterrence.

With these caveats in mind, observe that the *as if* interpretation is borne

---

Fleming 1983, for a treatment of tort law focusing on England and Australia; Zweigert and
Kötz 1977, secs. 17–19, for a description of tort law in England, France, and Germany; Von
Mehren and Gordley 1977, chaps. 8–10, for materials on tort law in France and Germany;
Opoku 1972 for a survey article on tort law in Germany; and Barry 1979, Osakwe 1979, and,
especially, Rudden 1967 for descriptions of tort law in the Soviet Union. On comparative
and relative negligence defenses, see in addition to these references Honoré 1971, pp. 94–97.

21. See the *Restatement (Second) of Torts* 1965, secs. 282, 291–293. The *Restatement* is
a summary of and commentary on the doctrines of tort law produced by leading scholars
under the aegis of the American Law Institute. For discussion of the determination of
negligence in other legal systems see, for example, Limpens et al. 1979, secs. 23–27, and
Zweigert and Kötz 1977, pp. 266–269, 286.

22. It will be clear to the reader that the *as if* interpretation can also be made about many
other instances of consistency between actual law and the law that is theoretically optimal
(given the stated measure of social welfare). This topic will not, however, receive much
attention until it is addressed generally in Chapter 13.

23. An exception is Judge Learned Hand's algebraic formula for determining the due care
standard. In his opinion in *United States v. Carroll Towing Co.*, 159 F.2d 169 (2d Cir. 1947),
Hand said that a party is negligent if he failed to take a precaution when the precaution
would have reduced by $P$ the probability of a loss of magnitude $L$ and when the cost or
"burden" $B$ of the precaution was less than $PL$.

out not only by the mere fact that there is a weighing involved in the negligence determination, but also by a consideration of the character of the weighing. First, the elements that courts take into account in finding due care and the effect of the elements on the due care level are what we would expect were courts' aim to minimize total accident costs: the level of due care is generally higher the greater the likelihood of harm, the larger the probable size of harm, the greater the number of individuals at risk, and the easier it is for injurers to alleviate risk.[24] Second, the choice of due care levels probably reflects the possibilities for both injurers and victims to reduce accident risks, as is consistent with the bilateral model of accidents. Consider, for instance, accidents in which bicyclists run into car doors as the doors are opened. My surmise is that most of us would say that bicyclists should not have to proceed so slowly that were a car door to open suddenly, they could virtually always stop in time, and that before persons open car doors to leave, they should look around to see if anyone is approaching. I suggest too that in coming to this view most of us would have at the back of our minds—if not in our conscious thoughts—such ideas as that it would be a burden for bicyclists to have to go so slowly that they could stop immediately before running into car doors, that it is relatively easy for persons leaving cars to look for danger, and that it is not necessary for bicyclists to go very slowly if persons are properly cautious when leaving their cars. In other words, when deciding on the care that parties of one type ought to exercise, we quite naturally factor into our thinking the ability of parties of the other type to take care and what their taking care would accomplish.

*2.2.15  Note on the literature.* The first writer to study in an analytical way the theory of the effect of liability rules on parties' behavior was Calabresi (1961, 1965, 1970). He examined the desirability of different rules, emphasizing versions of strict liability and assuming for the most part the goal of minimization of total accident costs.[25] Posner (1972, 1973a,b) later made significant contributions, especially in his analysis of the various principles

24. See the *Restatement (Second) of Torts,* 1965, sec. 293; *Prosser and Keeton on Torts* (Keeton, Dobbs, et al. 1984), secs. 29, 31, 33; and sec. 2 of chap. 7 of Fleming 1983. Note too that these effects on due care are consistent with Judge Hand's formula.

25. See also Calabresi and Hirschoff 1972 and Calabresi 1975b. Many previous writers had, of course, recognized that liability rules would have some effect on behavior, but usually only in passing. Calabresi thus differed from his predecessors in that he made the effect of liability on behavior the focus of his work and carried it out in a self-conscious, sustained, and careful way. It should be mentioned, however, that at about the time of Calabresi's first paper, Coase published an article that also stimulated interest in analyzing the effects of liability rules. But the emphasis in Coase 1960 itself was on how parties would come to mutually beneficial agreements through bargaining rather than on how the various liability rules would alter parties' behavior.

and doctrines governing use of the negligence rule.[26] Although both these writers used suggestive numerical examples, neither recognized that liability rules would, as a general matter, lead calculating parties to choose levels of care such that total accident costs are minimized. Brown (1973) put forward the first clear statement and formal proofs of this result. He showed that the rules of strict liability with the defense of contributory negligence and the negligence rule (with or without the defense) induce injurers and victims to take optimal levels of care in equilibrium.[27]

## 2.3 Levels of Care and Levels of Activity the Determinants of Risk: Unilateral Accidents

Now that the effect of liability rules on parties' exercise of care has been studied, the influence of the rules on parties' levels of activity will also be considered. The analysis will begin with the unilateral case, where only injurers' actions affect risk, and will rely on two assumptions about injurers' level of activity. First, an increase in injurers' level of activity will result in a proportionate increase in expected accident losses, given their level of care. Thus, a doubling in the number of miles that individuals drive will result in a doubling in the number of accidents they cause, given the care with which they drive; or a doubling in the number of times individuals walk their dogs will result in a doubling in the risk that their dogs will bite strangers, given the care taken (leashing) to prevent attacks. Second, an increase in injurers' level of activity will result in an increase in their utility (at least up to some point); the more individuals drive or the more they walk their dogs, the greater will be their utility (until their need to drive is met or until walking their dogs turns into a chore).

The social goal will be taken to be maximization of the utility injurers derive from engaging in their activity less total accident costs, that is, less their costs of care and expected accident losses. It makes sense, of course, to introduce the utility injurers derive from their activity into the measure of social welfare, because the level of their activity is to be studied.[28]

26. See also Landes and Posner 1981b, pp. 892–903, discussing what is called here the *as if* interpretation of the negligence determination.

27. Soon afterward Diamond 1974a,b also showed in closely related models that the negligence rule with the defense of contributory negligence induces parties to take total accident cost minimizing levels of care.

28. The social goal considered in §§2.1 and 2.2, minimizing total accident costs, may be viewed as a special case of the present goal. If we imagine the level of activity to be held constant, as we assumed was the case above, then maximization of the utility derived from the activity less total accident costs is obviously equivalent to minimization of total accident costs.

*2.3.1   Social welfare optimum.* For social welfare to be optimized, an injurer must, as before, take care commensurate with the effect of care in reducing accident losses and with its costs. But now, also, the injurer should engage in his activity at the level that appropriately balances the utility he obtains against the additional risks he creates.

EXAMPLE 2.3   Assume that Example 2.1 describes the situation each time injurers engage in their activity. In this case injurers who behave optimally will take moderate care at a cost of 3 and will reduce expected accident losses to 10. Consequently, if an injurer engages in his activity twice, taking optimal care each time, his total costs of care will be 6, and the expected accident losses he causes will be 20; if he engages in his activity three times, the figures will be 9 and 30, respectively; and so forth. These figures are shown in the third and fourth columns of Table 2.4. The second column in the table shows the total utility injurers derive from engaging in the activity, from which the figures in the last column can be calculated.

The optimal activity level is 2 because social welfare is highest at that level. Each time an injurer engages in the activity, he will increase total accident costs by $3 + 10 = 13$. Therefore, social welfare will be enhanced by his engaging in the activity another time if and only if the marginal utility he would gain exceeds 13. Since the utility he obtains from engaging the first time is 40, the marginal utility he obtains from the second time is 20, time is 20, and that from the third time is only 9, it is best that he stop at the second time.[29]

The general point illustrated by this example is that the socially optimal behavior of injurers can be determined in two steps: first by finding (as in §2.1.1) the level of care that minimizes total accident costs incurred each time injurers engage in their activity; and then by raising the level of activity as long as the marginal utility injurers derive exceeds the increment to total accident costs.

*2.3.2   No liability.* In the absence of liability, not only will injurers fail to take care, they also will engage in their activity to too great an extent. Indeed, they will continue to engage in it as long as they obtain *any* additional utility (individuals will go for a drive or walk their dogs on a mere whim) rather than, as would be socially desirable, only as long as they obtain additional utility exceeding the costs of optimal care plus the expected accident losses they

---

29. Notice that utility actually falls beyond activity level 4. (The fifth time one walks his dog, it is more a chore than a pleasure.)

*Table 2.4*

| Activity level | Total utility from activity | Total costs of care | Total expected accident losses | Social welfare |
|---|---|---|---|---|
| 0 | 0 | 0 | 0 | 0 |
| 1 | 40 | 3 | 10 | 27 |
| 2 | 60 | 6 | 20 | 34 |
| 3 | 69 | 9 | 30 | 30 |
| 4 | 71 | 12 | 40 | 19 |
| 5 | 70 | 15 | 50 | 5 |

*Note*: Social welfare = total utility − total costs of care − expected accident losses.

cause. In Example 2.3 injurers will not take care and thus will choose activity level 4, the level at which they cease to gain utility from their activity, rather than the optimal activity level of 2.

*2.3.3  Strict liability.* Under strict liability an injurer's utility, net of his expected costs, will be equal to the measure of social welfare, since he will pay for the accident losses he causes and he will naturally enjoy the benefits of engaging in his activity and will bear the costs of care. Accordingly, injurers will behave so as to maximize social welfare; they will thus choose both the optimal level of care and the optimal level of activity.

More directly, injurers will choose the optimal level of care because doing so will minimize the expected costs they bear each time they engage in their activity. And they will choose the optimal level of activity because they will wish to engage in the activity only when the extra utility they derive exceeds their costs of care plus their added expected liability payments for accident losses caused. (People will walk their dogs only when their utility gain outweighs the disutility of having to leash the dogs and the added liability risk due to dog bites.) In Example 2.3, for instance, we know (from §2.1.3) that strictly liable injurers will take the moderate level of care. Hence, the last column in Table 2.4 will become injurers' utility, net of their expected costs, and they will therefore choose the optimal activity level of 2.

*2.3.4  Negligence rule.* As the reader recalls from previous analysis, injurers will be led to take optimal care under the negligence rule, assuming that the level of due care is chosen by courts to equal the optimal level of care. Because they will take due care, however, injurers will escape liability for any accident losses they cause. They will therefore not have a reason to consider the effect that engaging in their activity has on accident losses. Consequently,

*Table 2.5*

| Activity level | Total utility from activity | Total costs of care | Total utility, net of total costs of care |
|---|---|---|---|
| 0 | 0 | 0 | 0 |
| 1 | 40 | 3 | 37 |
| 2 | 60 | 6 | 54 |
| 3 | 69 | 9 | 60 |
| 4 | 71 | 12 | 59 |
| 5 | 70 | 15 | 55 |

injurers will be led to choose excessive activity levels. Specifically, they will engage in their activity whenever the utility they derive net of the cost of care is positive (whenever the pleasure from walking their dogs net of the disutility of leashing them is positive), rather than only when their net utility exceeds the additional expected accident losses they create.

This can be seen in Example 2.3, where we know (from §2.1.4) that if due care is the optimal, moderate level, injurers will take due care. Because injurers take due care under the negligence rule, they will not be liable for accident losses and their situation will be that described in Table 2.5. From the last column in the table it is evident that injurers will choose the activity level 3 rather than the optimal activity level 2: they will increase their activity level from 2 to 3 because this will raise their utility by 9 and their costs of care by only 3; they will not consider that increasing their activity level will also raise expected accident losses by 10 (as shown in Table 2.4), for they will not be liable for these losses.

*2.3.5 Liability rules compared.* Under both strict liability and the negligence rule injurers are led to take socially optimal levels of care, but under the negligence rule they engage in their activity to too great an extent because, unlike under strict liability, they do not pay for the accident losses they cause.[30] The importance of this defect of the negligence rule will clearly depend on the expected magnitude of the losses caused by an activity. If an activity is by its nature very dangerous even when carried out with appropriate precautions, then it may be significant that under the negligence rule the level of the activity would be excessive. For example, if the walking of dogs of a vicious breed or if blasting creates high risks of harm despite the use of all reasonable care, it may be of real consequence that under the negligence rule

---

30. The reader should be cautioned, however, that in the bilateral case, victims engage in their activity to too great an extent under strict liability. See §2.4.2.

people would walk their dogs excessively (rather than exercising them in a yard or rather than owning dogs of another breed) or that firms would blast excessively (rather than employing other methods of demolition). If, however, an activity creates only a low risk of accidents when due care is taken, then the importance of any excess in the level of activity under the negligence rule will be small. This is true, one suspects, of many and perhaps most of our everyday activities (mowing a lawn, playing catch, walking the friendly, domesticated dog).[31]

*2.3.6   The source of the defect of the negligence rule.* The failing of the negligence rule that is under discussion can be regarded as resulting from an implicit assumption that the standard of behavior used to determine negligence is defined only in terms of care.[32] Were the standard defined also in terms of the activity level, injurers would make sure not to engage in their activity to an excessive extent.

This consideration, however, immediately raises questions as to the reason it is assumed that courts do not include the activity level in the determination of negligence. A possible reason concerns the information that they would need to do so. To formulate a standard for the level of activity, courts would need to determine the character of the benefits parties derive from their activities. (Courts would have to inquire into the pleasure obtained from walking a dog or the need for and importance of driving somewhere.) Because these benefits often seem practically unknowable, attempts by courts to determine appropriate levels of activity would probably quickly land them in the most speculative of realms. Deciding on appropriate levels of care, although by no means an easy task, usually appears to be less problematic. (We can say with fair confidence that a dog that snaps at others should be leashed or that a person should not drive at 60 miles per hour along a residential street.)

Aside from the difficulties that courts would face in formulating appropriate standards for parties' levels of activity, courts would have to ascertain what parties' levels of activity actually were. This additional burden might be a substantial one in some situations, especially because determining a party's level of activity would require knowledge of what the party did in the past. (How many times did a person walk his dog before the last time, when it bit someone?) By contrast, assessing a party's level of care often requires knowledge of his behavior only at the time of an accident.

---

31. In this paragraph I have spoken only about the dangerousness of activities as a factor bearing on the appeal of strict liability over the negligence rule. But it is clear that a factor of importance that must be considered along with the dangerousness of activities is the degree to which use of strict liability would lead to a reduction in the levels of dangerous activities.

32. Notice therefore that the defect is similar to that discussed in §2.1.6 concerning dimensions of care omitted from the due care standard.

Nevertheless, there may be situations where a court would have sufficient information to incorporate the level of activity into the negligence determination. One notable example is a party engaging even once in an activity that is very dangerous despite the exercise of care and that obtains for the party an obviously small utility. In this case the party could be called negligent merely for having engaged in the activity.[33]

## 2.4    Levels of Care and Levels of Activity the Determinants of Risk: Bilateral Accidents

In this most general case, victims as well as injurers will be assumed to choose levels of activity and levels of care. As with injurers' levels of activity, increases in victims' levels of activity will be assumed to raise their utility, at least up to some point, and will result in proportionate increases in expected accident losses. Thus, a bicyclist riding an extra mile will enjoy extra utility and will increase his chances of being involved in an accident. The measure of social welfare will be taken to be the utility that victims and injurers derive from their activities less their costs of care and expected accident losses.

The analysis that follows will be brief because most conclusions can be explained by appeal to previous cases.

*2.4.1    Social welfare optimum.* Optimal behavior in the bilateral case will reflect not only the cost of care and its effect on accident risks, but also the utility that injurers and victims obtain from their activities.

EXAMPLE 2.4    Suppose for simplicity that victims either engage in their activity or they do not, and the same for injurers; in other words, for parties of each type, there is only one possible positive level of activity. Suppose also that if parties of one type engage in their activity and the others do not, no accidents can occur—it takes the presence of both injurers and victims for there to be accidents. Hence, if parties of only one type engage in their activity it would be pointless and socially wasteful for them to take care. Last, suppose that if both injurers and victims engage in their activities, the risk of accidents will be as described in Example 2.2. Thus in this case injurers ought to take care, which, recall, costs 3; victims also

---

33. In this regard, it is interesting to note the passage in the *Restatement (Second) of Torts* 1965, sec. 297, which reads in part, "A negligent act may be one which involves an unreasonable risk of harm . . . although it is done with all possible care." By way of example, the *Restatement* comments that "there are many mountain roads which may properly be regarded as dangerous no matter how careful . . . the driver may be . . . there is an inescapable risk in driving down a narrow and illkept mountain road . . . particularly if . . . snow or ice has rendered the road slippery . . . mere use of such a route . . . may be negligent unless the utility of the route is very great."

ought to take care, which costs 2; and expected accident losses will be 6. Therefore, total accident costs will be $3 + 2 + 6 = 11$ if both injurers and victims engage in their activities and take care.

Given these assumptions, it is easy to determine when it is optimal for injurers and for victims to engage in their activities, as a function of the utilities they would each derive from so doing. Were parties of only one type to engage in their activity, none of the accident costs of 11 would be borne (since no accidents could occur and no care would be taken). Therefore, it will maximize social welfare for both injurers and victims to engage in their activities only when each would obtain from their activity a utility exceeding 11. Otherwise, it will be best for the parties that would enjoy the greater utility to engage in their activity and for the other parties to refrain from engaging in their activity.

To verify this claim, suppose for instance that injurers would obtain utility of 35 and victims 25 from engaging in their activities. If both injurers and victims engage in their activities, social welfare will be $35 + 25 - 11 = 49$; if only injurers engage in their activity, social welfare will be 35; if only victims do so, social welfare will be 25; thus it will indeed be optimal for both injurers and victims to engage in their activities. On the other hand, suppose that injurers would obtain 35 from engaging in their activity and victims would obtain only 8. Then if both injurers and victims engage in their activities, social welfare will be $35 + 8 - 11 = 32$; if injurers alone do so, social welfare will be 35; if victims alone do so, social welfare will be 8; and it will be best for injurers alone to engage in their activity.[34] Similar calculations show that if injurers would obtain 8 and victims 25 from engaging in their activities, then it will be optimal for victims alone to engage in their activity.

The simplifying feature of this example, that parties either do not engage in their activity or engage in it at only one positive level, should not disturb the reader. The points to be illustrated below will carry over in obvious ways to the more realistic case where there are many different positive levels of activity.

*2.4.2 Strict liability with the defense of contributory negligence.* As the reader knows from previous analysis, if courts select the optimal level of due care, then under strict liability with the defense of contributory negligence both injurers and victims will be led to take optimal care when they engage in their activities. Furthermore, since victims will take due care, injurers will

---

34. It is not necessary that injurers enjoy utility greater than 11 for it to be optimal for them to engage in their activity. For instance, if injurers' utility were 10, it would still be optimal for them alone to engage in their activity, and social welfare would be 10.

pay for the accident losses they cause and thus, as noted in §2.3.3, will choose the correct level of their activity given victims' behavior.[35]

Yet because victims will be compensated for their losses, victims may engage in their activity too often. A victim's only cost of engaging in his activity will be his cost of taking due care. Therefore, he will engage in his activity whenever his utility from so doing would exceed the cost of taking due care. But what would be desirable is that he engage in his activity only when his utility would exceed the cost of taking due care plus the expected accident losses that would result from his engaging in his activity. (A bicyclist will go for a ride whenever the pleasure he would gain exceeds the disutility from having to exercise appropriate care, rather than only when the pleasure exceeds the disutility of exercising care plus the increment to expected accident losses.)

To illustrate this point, consider the case in Example 2.4 where injurers would obtain utility of 35 and victims utility of only 8 from their activities, and thus where it is not optimal for victims to engage in their activity. Under strict liability with the defense of contributory negligence, victims need only take due care, at a cost of 2, to be assured of compensation for accident losses suffered. Hence, when they compare the utility of 8 that they would obtain from engaging in their activity to the cost of care of 2, victims will, undesirably, decide to engage in their activity (along with the injurers, for they will compare their utility of 35 to their cost of care of 3 plus their expected liability of 6).

*2.4.3   Negligence rule with or without the defense of contributory negligence.* Again, the reader knows from before that under the negligence rule both injurers and victims will be induced to take optimal care when they engage in their activities if courts select optimal due care levels. And since injurers will escape liability by taking due care, it is evident from the argument of §2.3.4 that injurers may engage in too high a level of their activity.

Victims, however, will choose the correct level of their activity given injurers' behavior. Because victims will bear their own losses, they will engage in their activity another time only if the utility they would obtain net of the costs of taking care exceeds the addition to expected losses. Consider the situation in Example 2.4 where injurers would obtain utility of 8 and victims utility of 25 from engaging in their activities. In this case it is optimal for victims alone to engage in their activity; and while under the negligence rule they will do so (for they will compare 25 to 2 + 6), so will injurers engage in their activity (for they will compare 8 to 3).

---

35. The analysis under strict liability with the defense of relative negligence is virtually identical and is omitted.

*2.4.4 Other liability rules.* It follows from the last section and from the analysis in §2.2.9 that under the comparative negligence rule the outcome will be the same as under the negligence rule. It should be clear too that under strict liability without the defense of contributory negligence victims will not only fail to take care, but they will also engage in their activity too often, whereas injurers will choose socially appropriate levels of care and of their activity given victims' behavior.

*2.4.5 Liability rules compared.* It should be evident from §§2.4.2 and 2.4.3 that strict liability with the defense of contributory negligence will result in higher social welfare if its disadvantage—that victims engage too often in their activity—is not as important as the disadvantage of the negligence rules—that injurers engage too often in their activity. That is, strict liability will result in greater social welfare if it is more important to control injurers' level of activity than victims'.

Whether injurers' level of activity will be more important to control than victims' will depend on context. As discussed before, where an activity of injurers (walking dogs of a vicious breed) creates substantial risks despite the use of due care, the activity will be desirable to control. This point is not fundamentally altered if account is taken of the activities of victims that expose them to risk. Especially if these activities are just the activities of ordinary life (walking about, going to work), we would not want the activities constrained in favor of injurers'. Conversely, where an activity of injurers (playing baseball) is not very dangerous if appropriate care is taken, the importance of controlling the activity will not be great; and once victims' behavior is taken into account, we may see some advantage in their moderating engagement in certain activities that subject them to particular risks (such as pushing a baby in a carriage across a baseball field while a game is in progress).

*2.4.6 Nonexistence of a liability rule leading to optimal levels of activity.* Because no rule that has been examined induces both injurers and victims to choose optimal levels of their activities, one is led to ask whether there exists any conceivable liability rule that always results in optimal levels of activities. The answer is no. The reason, in essence, is that for injurers to choose the correct level of their activity they must bear accident losses, whereas for victims to choose the correct level of their activity they too must bear accident losses. Yet injurers and victims cannot each bear accident losses.

Three comments should be made about this conclusion. First, the explanation just given for it directly suggests methods that in principle would lead to optimal behavior. For example, let injurers pay fines to the state equal to harm done—or taxes equal to expected harm—and let victims bear their losses. Then the expected payments of injurers and of victims would each equal expected accident losses and they would each choose optimal levels of their activity.[36] Second, the conclusion depends on the assumption that courts cannot incorporate parties' levels of activity into the negligence or contributory negligence determination (an assumption that may be justified by what was said in §2.3.6). If negligence and contributory negligence could be defined in terms of levels of activity as well as levels of care, then the usual liability rules would lead injurers and victims to choose optimal levels of care and of their activity. Third, the conclusion should not be interpreted as an unduly negative one. As more factors are incorporated into a model, it naturally becomes less likely that a hypothetically ideal outcome can be achieved.

*2.4.7    The reciprocal nature of harm.* It is a truism that harm has a reciprocal aspect in that a victim must be present to suffer harm just as much as an injurer must be present to do harm. This observation has sometimes been said to imply that injurers should not necessarily pay for harm done, that harm should not necessarily be "internalized" to injurers. That conclusion is supported by the analysis here. As emphasized in §2.4.5, either strict liability or negligence rules could turn out to be best.

But the fact that harm has a reciprocal aspect has also occasionally been suggested to mean that it is conceptually impossible to decide whether strict liability or the negligence rule should be applied, and even that the very notion of harm is rendered ambiguous. There is, however, no difficulty in principle in deciding whether strict liability or the negligence rule will be better in a given situation in a well-defined model (there was no difficulty in deciding the question with regard to Example 2.4, for instance),[37] and there is nothing problematic about the notion of harm.

*2.4.8    Actual use of strict liability and negligence rules.* The choice between the two main forms of liability has been made in approximately the same way in different legal systems for accidents between strangers.[38]

---

36. Another scheme that would result in optimal behavior is to make injurers strictly liable and to levy taxes on victims equal to expected accident losses. Schemes like these may have disadvantages of their own, however. For instance, under the scheme in which injurers pay fines to the state, victims would not obtain a financial benefit from reporting the identity of injurers and injurers might often escape having to pay fines. See, more generally, the discussion of fines and taxes in Chapter 12.

37. But that there are no difficulties in principle does not mean that there will be no difficulties in application. Suppose that just as a woodsman cuts down a tree, a hiker happens to come along and is struck by the tree. Here we might feel that there is no appealing notion of who ought to have been present because it is hard to make a relative judgment about the benefits the hiker and the woodsman derived from their activities, and so forth.

38. Liability for accidents involving firms and their customers will be discussed in Chapter 3.

Namely, negligence is the usual basis of liability; strict liability is employed only in certain areas of accident. In Anglo-American law, liability for accident losses is "for most significant purposes governed by the concept of negligence"; use of strict liability is restricted to harms caused by wild animals, to certain types of harms due to fire, and to harms arising from "abnormally dangerous" or "ultrahazardous" activities (such as blasting, storage of flammable liquids, transport of nuclear materials).[39] Most of the provisions of the German civil code impose liability only if the injuring party was at fault; strict liability is adopted in connection with harms due to animals other than domestic animals and, according to special legislation, in connection with harms arising from rail, road, and air traffic and from use of electricity, gas, and atomic energy.[40] The situation in France is similar.[41] Two important articles of the French civil code specify fault or negligence as the general principle of liability; strict liability applies to harms due to animals or to certain dangerous inanimate objects (including automobiles and aircraft). Likewise, in the Soviet Union fault is the general basis of liability, with strict liability being reserved for harms due to "sources of increased danger."[42]

   *2.4.9 Strict liability and negligence rules in light of the theory concerning levels of activity.* As stressed in the analysis, use of strict liability rather than negligence rules in areas where activities create high risks despite the exercise of reasonable care has the advantage that it will tend to reduce in a desirable way participation in these activities.

   This theoretical advantage seems consistent with fact in the sense that the impression given by the foregoing section is that the areas of activity covered by strict liability are generally more dangerous than those covered by negligence rules (certainly the reverse is not true). The areas of strict liability do not appear uniformly more dangerous than those of negligence, however; the choices made between strict liability and negligence rules are not always easy to explain on the basis of differences in riskiness. (Is the chance of a wild animal escaping from the zoo and doing harm, for which strict liability would probably apply in the United States, greater than that of an automobile running down a pedestrian, for which the negligence rule would govern?) Moreover, differences among countries in the areas of strict liability and negligence

39. See Fleming 1983, chaps. 6, 14–17, quotation at p. 97; and see *Prosser and Keeton on Torts* (Keeton, Dobbs, et al. 1984), chaps. 5, 13.
   40. See Opoku 1972, pp. 230–243; Tunc 1974, secs. 13, 79–85; Von Mehren and Gordley 1977, pp. 557–566, 579–582; Zweigert and Kötz 1977, sec. 19; and Limpens et al. 1979, secs. 11–14.
   41. See Tunc 1974, secs. 12, 86–88; Von Mehren and Gordley 1977, pp. 555–557, 579–582; Zweigert and Kötz 1977, sec. 19; and Limpens et al. 1979, secs. 5, 23.
   42. See Osakwe 1979, pp. 9–22; Barry 1979, pp. 229–235; and Rudden 1967, pp. 597–608.

are sometimes difficult to explain in terms of differences in dangerousness. (Why should the negligence rule govern liability for automobile-pedestrian accidents in the United States while strict liability applies in Germany, the Soviet Union, and France?)[43] It seems that the conformity of the observed pattern of use of strict liability and negligence rules to what would be suggested by the theoretical considerations of this chapter is somewhat rough.

Putting aside questions concerning the *actual* dangerousness of the areas of strict liability versus those of negligence, I want to emphasize that one of the *aims* of the law is to impose strict liability on activities that are dangerous, or, more precisely, that are dangerous even if conducted with reasonable care.[44] A particularly direct expression of this aim is provided by the *Restatement (Second) of Torts,* which says that in deciding whether an activity should be subject to strict liability, one ought to take notice of possible "inability to eliminate the risk by the exercise of reasonable care." Further, the *Restatement* draws a contrast with most "ordinary activities" that can be made "safe by the taking of all reasonable precautions" and for which liability should be based on negligence.[45]

But it should be added that the deterrent effect of strict liability on the level of participation in activities is not mentioned in the *Restatement* and is only infrequently noted in other places. Evidently, the mere creation of an unusual risk is seen as a justification for imposition of strict liability.

*2.4.10   Note on the literature.* In Shavell (1980b) I introduced the issue of the choice of the level of activity as distinct from the level of care and developed the points discussed here.[46] The issue is elaborated upon in Landes and Posner (1981b).

# Mathematical Appendix

In this appendix the main elements of the theory concerning how liability affects behavior that influences accident risks will be presented formally. The assumptions will be much as they were described in the text. There is a single good, in terms of which all variables are defined. Parties are risk neutral; that is, a party's (von Neumann–Morgenstern) utility is taken to equal the amount

43. On Germany, see Opoku 1972, p. 240; on the Soviet Union, see Osakwe 1979, pp. 21–22; on France, see Tunc 1974, sec. 88.
44. This will be evident to any reader who consults, for example, the sources in nn. 39–42.
45. *Restatement (Second) of Torts* 1965, sec. 520.
46. But the issue is adumbrated in Posner 1973b, p. 208.

of the good he possesses, and his expected utility equals the expected amount of the good he will possess. The measure of social welfare is the sum of parties' expected utilities; equivalently, it is the sum of the expected amounts of the good that they will possess.[47]

Parties are of two types, injurers and victims, and are strangers to one another. Injurers are all identical, as are all victims, and only the victims suffer losses if accidents occur. The probability and severity of accidents may be influenced by parties' behavior. If an accident occurs, a rule of liability will apply. The rule will determine whether and how much the injurer involved shall pay the victim. The behavior of parties in equilibrium will be studied under various liability rules and will be compared with social-welfare-maximizing behavior. An equilibrium is a situation in which injurers have no motive to alter their behavior, taking as given victims' behavior and the liability rule, and, likewise, victims have no motive to alter their behavior, taking as given injurers' behavior and the liability rule.[48]

The analysis of equilibrium behavior under liability rules will be carried out first on the assumption that parties affect accident risks only through their choice of their levels of care, then on the assumption that they affect accident risks through their choice of their levels of activity as well. In each case, unilateral accidents—in which injurers' behavior alone affects risks—and bilateral accidents—in which victims' behavior too affects risks—will be separately considered.

## 2A.1  Levels of Care the Only Determinant of Risk

*2A.1.1  Unilateral accidents.* Let

$x$ = the level of care of an injurer, measured as the cost of taking care; $x \geqq 0$;

$l(x)$ = expected accident losses[49] caused by an injurer given $x$; $l(x) \geqq 0$; $l'(x) < 0$ and $l''(x) > 0$ where $l$ is positive.

47. See, for example, Varian 1978, p. 104, for definitions of risk neutrality and expected utility, and p. 152, for a discussion of social welfare functions.

48. This is, of course, the definition of a Nash equilibrium, the standard definition of equilibrium in a noncooperative setting; see Luce and Raiffa 1957, chap. 5. It is an appealing definition where there are large numbers of injurers and victims who are strangers, for then it is plausible that one party would assume that the other party's actions would not be affected by his own particular actions.

49. Because $l(x)$ is expected losses, that is, $p(x)\int lf(x,l)dl$, where $p(x)$ is the probability of an accident and $f(x,l)$ is the probability density of losses of $l$ given $x$ conditional on the occurrence of an accident, the model implicitly allows for accident losses to be of differing severity. In the examples of the text losses were of fixed severity. See for further discussion §6A.1.

Thus the exercise of care reduces expected accident losses, but at a decreasing rate.

The social goal will be to minimize total accident costs,[50]

$$(2.1) \qquad x + l(x).$$

Let $x^*$ denote the $x$ that minimizes Exp. (2.1). This socially optimal value, $x^*$, is unique, by our assumptions, and is illustrated in Figure 2.1. Assuming as we shall that $x^*$ is positive, it is determined by the first-order condition

$$1 = -l'(x);$$

that is, the marginal cost of care must equal the marginal benefit in terms of the reduction in expected accident losses.[51]

Consider now injurers' behavior under liability rules.[52] Because injurers will seek to maximize the expected amount of the good they hold, they will act to minimize their expected expenses, namely, the cost $x$ plus their expected liability. Hence under the "rule" of no liability, injurers will choose $x = 0$; total accident costs will thus be $l(0)$ and will not be minimized. Under strict liability, injurers will be liable for any accident losses they cause. Therefore, an injurer's expected liability will be $l(x)$ and so to minimize Exp. (2.1) he will choose $x^*$; this is shown in Figure 2.1. Under the negligence rule, injurers will be liable for accident losses they cause if and only if their level of care was less than a due care level, $\bar{x}$, specified by courts. If $\bar{x} = x^*$, then, as should be apparent from Figure 2.1, an injurer will choose $x^*$. Certainly an injurer will not choose $x > x^*$, for if $x$ merely equals $x^*$ he will avoid liability and his expenses will be $x^*$; choosing a higher $x$ would cost more but give no advantage. To show that an injurer will not choose $x < x^*$, observe that such a choice would make him liable for accident losses caused, so his expected

50. Under current assumptions, minimizing Exp. (2.1) is equivalent to maximizing the sum of injurers' and victims' expected utilities: since parties' levels of activity are taken as fixed, Exp. (2.1) measures the reduction from what the sum of their expected utilities would otherwise be.

51. The assumptions that $x^*$ is positive (and later, that $y^*$ is positive) and that $l$ is differentiable are not necessary to prove the main results below. Indeed, many of the arguments given will not rely on these assumptions. Nevertheless, the assumptions are made because they sometimes simplify the analysis and because examination of first-order conditions is sometimes helpful in comparing parties' behavior under different liability rules.

52. In the unilateral case the nature of equilibrium is trivial, for injurers' problem of expected utility maximization is, by assumption, uncomplicated by victims' behavior.

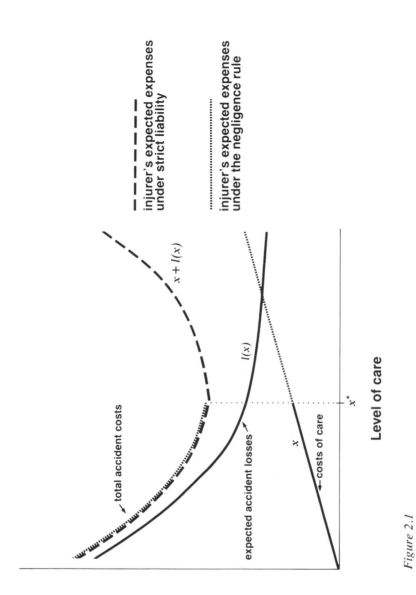

*Figure 2.1*

expenses would be $x + l(x)$. Moreover, since $x$ would be unequal to $x^*$ and since $x^*$ is unique,

$$x + l(x) > x^* + l(x^*)$$

would be true. And since $x^* + l(x^*) \geq x^*$,

$$x + l(x) > x^*$$

would hold. This reasoning shows that the injurer's expected expenses would be higher if he chose $x < x^*$ than if he chose $x^*$. We may summarize as follows.

PROPOSITION 2.1   In the absence of liability, injurers will take no care. Under strict liability they will choose the socially optimal level of care. Under the negligence rule, assuming that courts set due care to equal the socially optimal level, injurers again will choose the socially optimal level of care.

*Remarks.* (1) To employ strict liability, courts need only observe losses $l$. To employ the negligence rule, courts need to observe $l$ and $x$ and, in order to calculate $x^*$, to know the function $l$ $(\cdot)$.

(2) If care $x$ is a multidimensional variable, the proofs that strict liability and the negligence rule will lead to the socially optimal outcome $x^*$ still apply.[53] If, however, there are dimensions of $x$ that courts cannot observe and cannot include in the due care standard under the negligence rule, injurers will generally not choose optimal levels of these dimensions of $x$ under that rule.

*2A.1.2   Bilateral accidents.* Let

$y$ = the level of care of a victim, measured as the cost of taking care; $y \geq 0$;

and redefine $l$ as

$l(x,y)$ = expected accident losses given $x$ and $y$; $l(x, y) \geq 0$; $l_x(x, y) < 0$ and $l_y(x, y) < 0$ where $l$ is positive; $l$ is a strictly convex function of $x$ and $y$ where $l$ is positive.

---

53. Obvious analogues will be found in §§2A.1.2 and 2A.2.

Thus, the care of both injurers and victims now affects expected accident losses, and the care of each lowers expected losses, at a decreasing rate, given the care of the others.

The social goal will be to minimize total accident costs, which here[54] are

(2.2)    $x + y + l(x, y)$.

Let $x^*$ and $y^*$ denote the (unique) socially optimal values of $x$ and $y$, and assume that these are positive. Hence $x^*$ and $y^*$ satisfy

$$1 = -l_x(x, y^*) \quad \text{and} \quad 1 = -l_y(x^*, y).$$

Also, let $x^*(y)$ be the value of $x$ that minimizes Exp. (2.2) given $y$; equivalently, therefore, $x^*(y)$ minimizes $x + l(x, y)$; and let $y^*(x)$ be defined similarly. Observe from these definitions that $x^* = x^*(y^*)$ and $y^* = y^*(x^*)$.

Now consider the actual behavior of parties, assuming that injurers will minimize their expenses taking as given victims' level of care and that victims will minimize their expenses taking as given injurers' level of care. If there is no liability, injurers will choose $x = 0$ (whatever is $y$); thus, in particular, the outcome will not be socially optimal. Also, because $x = 0$, victims will select $y$ to minimize $y + l(0, y)$. Hence they will choose $y^*(0)$.

Under strict liability, victims will choose $y = 0$ (whatever is $x$) since they will be compensated for any losses they sustain; thus, again, the outcome will not be socially optimal. Because $y = 0$, injurers will choose $x$ to minimize $x + l(x, 0)$, so they will choose $x^*(0)$.

Under strict division of accident losses, injurers must pay a fraction $f$ of losses caused, where $0 < f < 1$. Hence, injurers will choose $x$ to minimize $x + fl(x, y)$. A positive value of $x$ will satisfy the first-order condition $1 + fl_x(x, y) = 0$; but since $x^*(y)$ satisfies $1 + l_x(x, y) = 0$ and $f < 1$, $l_x < 0$, and $l_{xx} > 0$, it follows that $x$ will be less than $x^*(y)$. Similarly, victims will choose $y$ to minimize $y + (1 - f)l(x, y)$, which means that $y$ will be less than $y^*(x)$. In particular, then, the outcome will not be socially optimal.

Under strict liability with the defense of contributory negligence, an injurer will be liable for accident losses he causes unless the victim's level of care $y$ was less than a due care level $\bar{y}$, in which case the victim must bear his losses. Let us establish that if $\bar{y} = y^*$, then both injurers and victims acting in a socially optimal way is an equilibrium and it is the only equilibrium. To show

---

54. Note that Exp. (2.2) is based on the implicit assumption that the number of injurers equals the number of victims. This assumption will be maintained for simplicity.

this, let us suppose first that $y = y^*$ and verify that injurers will choose $x = x^*$. Now since $y = y^* = \bar{y}$, victims will not bear their losses; an injurer's expected liability will therefore be $l(x, y^*)$, and he will choose $x$ to minimize $x + l(x, y^*)$; hence he will choose $x^*(y^*) = x^*$. Next, suppose that $x = x^*$. Then a victim will not choose $y > y^*$, for he will avoid having to bear his losses merely by choosing $y = y^*$; and he will not choose $y < y^*$ by the logic of the argument in the unilateral case demonstrating that under the negligence rule injurers would not take less than due care. Hence the victim will choose $y^*$.

It remains to be proved that there does not exist any other equilibrium (given that $\bar{y} = y^*$). To prove this, let us assume there is another equilibrium and demonstrate that that assumption leads to a contradiction. In another equilibrium it must be the case that $y \neq y^*$ (for if $y = y^*$, the argument in the preceding paragraph shows that $x = x^*$, which would contradict the assumption that the equilibrium is different). Now if $y > y^*$, victims would obviously be better off reducing $y$, for they can avoid liability so long as $y \geq y^*$. Hence it must be that $y < y^*$ in the equilibrium. But if this is true, victims will bear their losses and injurers will choose $x = 0$. Thus a victim's expected expenses must be $y + l(0, y) = 0 + y + l(0, y) > x^* + y^* + l(x^*, y^*) > y^*$, which means that victims would be better off if they chose $y^*$ (rather than $y < y^*$) and avoided bearing their losses, a contradiction.

The rule of strict liability with the defense of relative negligence differs from the rule just considered only in that if the victim's care $y$ was less than due care $\bar{y}$, then the victim will bear a fraction $f$ of his losses, where $0 < f < 1$ and $f = f(y)$ with $f'(y) < 0$. If the limit of $f$ as $y$ approaches $\bar{y}$ is sufficiently close to 1, then it can be verified, by the arguments of the last two paragraphs, that if $\bar{y} = y^*$ both injurers and victims acting in a socially optimal way is a unique equilibrium.

Next let us consider the negligence rule and show that if $\bar{x} = x^*$ both injurers and victims acting in a socially optimal way is a unique equilibrium. Suppose first that $y = y^*$. Then the argument concerning injurers' behavior under the negligence rule in the unilateral case can be applied to show that injurers will choose $x^*$. Now suppose that $x = x^*$. Because victims will bear their losses, they will choose $y$ to minimize $y + l(x^*, y)$, which means that they will choose $y^*(x^*) = y^*$.

To demonstrate that the equilibrium is unique (given that $\bar{x} = x^*$), essentially the same argument that was used under strict liability with the defense of contributory negligence can be employed. The argument is thus only sketched. If there is another equilibrium, it must be such that $x \neq x^*$ (since if $x = x^*$, then $y = y^*$); but $x > x^*$ cannot be, for an injurer could always do better by choosing a lower $x$ that exceeds $x^*$. Hence, $x < x^*$. If, however, this is true, victims will not bear their losses, so they will choose $y = 0$. This leads to a contradiction as before, but with a reversal of the roles of victims and injurers.

Under the negligence rule with the defense of contributory negligence, an injurer will be liable for accident losses he causes if and only if two conditions are met: his care was less than the due care level $\bar{x}$; and the victim's care was not less than the due care level $\bar{y}$. Otherwise the victim will bear his losses. We wish to show that if $\bar{x} = x^*$ and $\bar{y} = y^*$, then injurers and victims acting in a socially optimal way is a unique equilibrium. Assume that $y = y^*$. Then, since injurers will be liable if $x < x^*$, the argument used in the analysis of the negligence rule in the unilateral case may be applied to show that injurers will choose $x^*$. Now assume that $x = x^*$. Then, since victims will bear their losses, they will, as under the negligence rule, decide to choose $y^*$.

To show that the equilibrium is unique, assume otherwise. Hence $x \neq x^*$ (for $x = x^*$ implies $y = y^*$) and $y \neq y^*$ (for $y = y^*$ implies $x = x^*$). But $x > x^*$ cannot be, for injurers could then do better by lowering $x$ slightly. Therefore $x < x^*$. But then $y > y^*$ cannot be, for since $x < x^*$, victims can still avoid bearing losses if they lower $y$ slightly; thus $y < y^*$. This, however, means that victims will necessarily bear their losses, with the result that injurers will choose $x = 0$. Hence a victim's expected expenses must be $y + l(0, y) > y^*$ (as shown in the argument regarding strict liability with the defense of contributory negligence), implying that the victim would have been better off choosing $y^*$ and thereby shifting his losses to injurers.

Finally, under the comparative negligence rule, an injurer will be liable for a fraction $f$ of accident losses he causes if his care $x$ was less than $\bar{x}$ and the victim's care was less than $\bar{y}$, where $0 < f < 1$ and $f = f(x, y)$ (usually, with $f_x < 0$ and $f_y > 0$). On the other hand, if $x$ was less than $\bar{x}$ and $y$ was at least $\bar{y}$, the injurer will be liable for the entire losses; and if $x$ was at least $\bar{x}$, the victim will bear his own losses. Under this rule too, if $\bar{x} = x^*$ and $\bar{y} = y^*$, then both injurers and victims acting in a socially optimal way is a unique equilibrium. The proof that this is an equilibrium is identical to that under the negligence rule with the defense of contributory negligence, and verification is left to the reader. To show that the equilibrium is unique, suppose otherwise. Reasoning as in the case of the negligence rule with the defense of contributory negligence, we deduce that $x < x^*$ and $y < y^*$. But this means that $x + fl(x, y) < x^*$ (else $x < x^*$ would not have been chosen) and similarly that $y + (1 - f)l(x, y) < y^*$. Adding these two inequalities gives $x + y + l(x, y) < x^* + y^*$, which contradicts the social optimality of $x^*$ and $y^*$.

Proposition 2.2 summarizes the results of this section.

PROPOSITION 2.2    In the absence of liability or under strict liability, the outcome will generally not be socially optimal: injurers will take no care in the absence of liability and victims will take no care under strict liability; injurers, however, will choose the optimal level of care given the behavior of victims under strict liability, and victims will choose the optimal level of care given the behavior of injurers in the absence of liability. Under strict division of accident losses as well, the outcome will generally not be optimal; victims will take less care than is optimal given injurers' behavior, and vice versa.

But under each of the other rules—strict liability with the defense of contributory or relative negligence, the negligence rule with or without the defense of contributory negligence, and the comparative negligence rule— the outcome will be socially optimal. Specifically, if due care levels are socially optimal, then both injurers and victims taking socially optimal levels of care will be an equilibrium, and no other equilibrium exists.

*Remarks.* (1) To employ any of the rules leading to the socially optimal outcome, courts need to observe $l$ and to know the function $l(\cdot, \cdot)$ to be able to calculate either $x^*$ or $y^*$. The differences among the rules are thus that courts need to observe only $y$ under strict liability with the defense of contributory (or relative) negligence; only $x$ under the negligence rule; but both $x$ and $y$ under the negligence rule with the defense of contributory negligence. See the discussion in §2.2.10.

(2) If $x$ and $y$ are multidimensional variables, these liability rules will continue to lead to socially optimal behavior. If, however, there are dimensions of $x$ or $y$ not included in injurers' or victims' standards of due care, the situation changes. See the discussion in §2.2.11.

*2A.1.3    Note on the literature.* The results presented here were, except for several minor differences, first proved by Brown (1973);[55] but the result that use of the negligence rule with the defense of contributory negligence leads to socially optimal behavior was also shown shortly after by Diamond (1974a,b).

---

55. Brown did not consider the comparative negligence rule (he studied another rule that he called comparative negligence but is not in fact the comparative negligence rule) or strict liability with the defense of relative negligence. Also, he assumed that expected accident losses were of the form $p(x,y)A$ and that $p_{xy} < 0$, where $p$ is the probability of losses and $A$ is their magnitude, but, as seen here, such assumptions are unnecessary.

## 2A.2   Levels of Care and Levels of Activity the Determinants of Risk

*2A.2.1   Unilateral Accidents.* Let us now reconsider the unilateral case under the assumption that injurers may vary their level of activity as well as their level of care. Define

$s$ = level of activity of an injurer; $s \geq 0$;
$u(s)$ = gross utility to an injurer of engaging in his activity at level $s$; $u(s) >$
0, $u'(s) > 0$, $u''(s) < 0$ for $s < \hat{s}$; $u'(\hat{s}) = 0$.

Thus the gross utility increases with the level of activity, but at a decreasing rate, up to some point of satiation $\hat{s}$. The net utility to an injurer in the absence of liability will be assumed to equal the gross utility less his costs of care,

(2.3)     $u(s) - sx$;

here it is assumed that if an injurer engages in his activity $s$ times taking care $x$ each of these times, his total costs of care will be $sx$. The expected accident losses the injurer causes will similarly be assumed to equal $sl(x)$.

The social goal will be to maximize the net utility injurers obtain from their activities less expected accident losses,[56]

(2.4)     $u(s) - sx - sl(x) = u(s) - s[x + l(x)]$.

Denote the optimal values of $s$ and $x$ by $s^*$ and $x^*$ and assume that they and $l(x^*)$ are positive. From the right-hand side of Eq. (2.4), it is clear that $x^*$ is the $x$ that minimizes $x + l(x)$; hence $x^*$ is the optimal $x$ described in §2A.1.1. It also follows from the right-hand side of Eq. (2.4) that $s^*$ is determined by maximizing $u(s) - s[x^* + l(x^*)]$. Thus $s^*$ is determined by

(2.5)     $u'(s) = x^* + l(x^*)$,

the interpretation of which is that the marginal utility from an increase in the level of activity must equal the costs of taking optimal care plus the increase in expected accident losses.

Consider now injurers' behavior. If there is no liability, an injurer's utility will be $u(s) - sx$, so he will choose $x = 0$ and $s$ such that $u'(s) = 0$, that is,

---

56. Maximizing Eq. (2.4) is equivalent to maximizing the sum of injurers' and victims' expected utilities, for Eq. (2.4) differs from this sum by victims' utility from engaging in their activity, here taken to be fixed.

$s = \hat{s}$, the activity level of satiation. At $\hat{s}$ the level of activity will be excessive. This follows from the facts that $u'(\hat{s}) = 0$, that, from Eq. (2.5), $u'(s^*) > 0$, and that $u''(s) < 0$.

Under strict liability, since injurers will be liable for all accident losses that they cause, they will choose $s$ and $x$ to maximize $u(s) - s[x + l(x)]$, namely, Eq. (2.4). Hence they will choose $x^*$ and $s^*$.

Under the negligence rule, injurers will wish to take due care to avoid liability whatever $s$ they choose, assuming that the due care level $\bar{x}$ is $x^*$. (The proof of this conclusion is essentially the same as the proof of the result of §2A.1.1 that injurers will take due care and is omitted here.) Consequently, injurers will choose $s$ to maximize $u(s) - sx^*$, so that $s$ will be determined by

(2.6)    $u'(s) = x^*$.

Comparing Eqs. (2.6) and (2.5), we see that $s$ will exceed $s^*$. As was emphasized in the text, $s > s^*$ for the reason that, because injurers avoid liability by taking due care, the marginal cost to them of increasing their level of activity is only the cost of due care $x^*$; it does not include the increase in expected accident losses $l(x^*)$.

Let us demonstrate that social welfare under the negligence rule would be raised if a due care level $\bar{x}$ somewhat higher than $x^*$ were employed. In proving this, we restrict attention to the $\bar{x}$ to which injurers would be induced to adhere.[57] (If $\bar{x}$ is so high that injurers would not adhere to it, the negligence rule devolves into strict liability—which we know would result in a socially optimal outcome—and it does not seem natural to analyze this possibility under the heading of the negligence rule.) Thus injurers will choose $s$ to maximize $u(s) - s\bar{x}$, and $s$ will obey the first-order condition $u'(s) = \bar{x}$. Writing $s = s(\bar{x})$, differentiating Eq. (2.4) with respect to $\bar{x}$, and making use of Eq. (2.6), we obtain

(2.7)    $-s'(\bar{x})l(\bar{x}) - s(\bar{x})[1 + l'(\bar{x})]$.

This expression is positive for $\bar{x} \leq x^*$: because $s'(\bar{x})$ is negative (differentiate $u'(s(\bar{x})) = \bar{x}$ to obtain $s'(\bar{x}) = 1/u''(s(\bar{x})) < 0$), the first term is positive; the second term is nonnegative, since $x + l(x)$ is convex in $x$ and its derivative $1 + l'(x)$ is zero at $x^*$. Since Exp. (2.7) is positive for $\bar{x} \leq x^*$, it must be socially beneficial to choose an $\bar{x}$ exceeding $x^*$. The explanation is that raising $\bar{x}$ makes engaging in an activity more costly to an injurer and thus offers an

57. As is observed later (see §4A.3.4), the set of such $\bar{x}$ equals $[0, x^* + l(x^*)]$. Hence, the set of $\bar{x}$ we are considering properly includes $[0, x^*]$.

indirect means of reducing his excessive activity level; on the other hand, the first-order direct effect on social welfare of raising $\bar{x}$ above $x^*$ is zero, for $x^*$ is socially optimal.

The results are summarized as follows.

PROPOSITION 2.3   In the absence of liability, the outcome will not be socially optimal: injurers will not take care and will choose too high a level of activity.

Under strict liability, the outcome will be socially optimal: injurers will take optimal care and will choose the optimal level of activity.

Under the negligence rule, the outcome will not be socially optimal: if due care equals the socially optimal level of care, injurers will take optimal care but their level of activity will be excessive. Also, if due care is raised above socially optimal care, social welfare will be higher than if due care equals socially optimal care.

*Remark.* If under the negligence rule an injurer would be liable either if his care $x$ was less than $x^*$ or if his activity level $s$ exceeded $s^*$, then he would choose $x^*$ and $s^*$.[58] As suggested in the text, however, courts probably do not have sufficient information about $u(\cdot)$ to compute $s^*$ reasonably well.

*2A.2.2   Bilateral accidents.* Finally, let us consider the general case where both injurers and victims choose levels of care and levels of activity. Define

$t$ =  level of activity of a victim; $t \geq 0$;
$v(t)$ = gross utility to a victim of engaging in his activity at level $t$; $v(t) > 0$,
$\qquad v'(t) > 0$, and $v''(t) < 0$ for $t < \hat{t}$; $v'(\hat{t}) = 0$.

The interpretation of $t$, $\hat{t}$, and $v(t)$ is analogous to that of $s$, $\hat{s}$, and $u(s)$. Expected accident losses will be assumed to equal $stl(x, y)$ and the net utility to a victim of engaging in his activity to equal

(2.8)      $v(t) - ty - stl(x, y)$,

exclusive of any liability payments received.

The social goal will be to maximize the sum of injurers' and victims' net utilities,

---

58. Under this broader negligence rule, an injurer who decided to be nonnegligent would clearly choose $x^*$ and $s^*$, in which case his utility would be $u(s^*) - s^*x^*$; and an injurer would decide against being negligent since $u(s^*) - s^*x^* > u(s^*) - s^*[x^* + l(x^*)] > u(s) - s[x + l(x)]$ for all $(s,x) \neq (s^*,x^*)$, and in particular for any $(s,x)$ where $s > s^*$ or $x < x^*$.

(2.9)    $[u(s) - sx] + [v(t) - ty - stl(x, y)]$
            $= u(s) + v(t) - [sx + ty + stl(x, y)],$

that is, their gross utility from engaging in their activities less their costs of care and expected accident losses. It will be assumed that there is a unique optimum and that all variables are positive at the optimum; the optimal variables will be denoted by an asterisk. The first-order conditions determining $x^*$, $y^*$, $s^*$, and $t^*$ are

(2.10)    $1 + tl_x(x, y) = 0,$
            $1 + sl_y(x, y) = 0,$
            $u'(s) = x + tl(x, y),$
            $v'(t) = y + sl(x, y).$

The interpretation of the first two conditions is analogous to that made in §2A.1.2, and the interpretation of the latter two conditions is analogous to that made with respect to $s$ in Eq. (2.5).

Reconsidering each of the different liability rules of the previous section would be tedious. Let us discuss only strict liability with the defense of contributory negligence and the negligence rule and suggest why neither results in the socially optimal outcome. Then it shall be proved that in fact there does not exist any liability rule that would result in social optimality.

Suppose that under strict liability with the defense of contributory negligence the due care level $\bar{y}$ is $y^*$ and that victims would be led to adhere to it (otherwise the outcome would clearly be suboptimal). Then victims will choose $t$ to maximize $v(t) - t\bar{y}$, so $t$ will satisfy $v'(t) = \bar{y}$; thus victims will generally choose a socially excessive level of their activity given injurers' behavior, for, from Eqs. (2.10), social optimality requires $v'(t) = \bar{y} + sl(x, \bar{y})$. Injurers, however, will choose the socially optimal $x$ and $s$ given victims' behavior. This is because injurers, being liable for losses, will maximize $u(s) - [sx + stl(x, \bar{y})]$, which differs from Eq. (2.9) by a term that does not depend on $x$ or $s$.

Similar reasoning (essentially that of the last section) shows that under the negligence rule (with or without the defense of contributory negligence), while injurers may be induced to take due care, they will engage in too high a level of their activity. Victims, however, will take socially correct levels of care and of their activity given injurers' behavior.

Comparing the two rules, we see that either could result in a higher level of social welfare. Very roughly, strict liability with the defense of contributory negligence will be the better rule if the problem of controlling injurers' level of activity is more important than that of controlling victims' level of activity.

Otherwise the negligence rule (with or without the defense) will result in the higher level of welfare. (These statements could be made precise by introducing parameters describing the influence of activity levels on utility and on expected accident losses, but that does not seem worthwhile.)

Now let us prove that there does not exist any liability rule that will induce injurers and victims to act in a socially optimal way. The liability rules considered are assumed to be functions depending on the amount of losses and possibly on injurers' and victims' levels of care, but not on their levels of activity. Moreover, the expected payments of an injurer under a liability rule are assumed to be of the form $stq(x, y)$, where $q(x, y)$ is his expected liability given $x$ and $y$ if his and the victim's level of activity are each 1. (For instance, under strict liability with a defense of contributory negligence, $q(x, y)$ would equal $l(x, y)$ if $y \geq \bar{y}$ and 0 otherwise.) Supposing, then, that a liability rule that leads to optimal behavior exists, injurers in particular must behave optimally. Thus injurers must choose $x^*$, and they must also choose $s^*$. The latter implies that $s^*$ is the solution to the injurers' problem,

$$\max_s u(s) - sx^* - st^*q(x^*, y^*) = u(s) - s[x^* + t^*q(x^*, y^*)],$$

so that $u'(s^*) = x^* + t^*q(x^*, y^*)$. On the other hand, since $s^*$ is socially optimal, we know from Eqs. (2.10) that $u'(s^*) = x^* + t^*l(x^*, y^*)$. From this and the fact that $u''(s) < 0$, we obtain $x^* + t^*q(x^*, y^*) = x^* + t^*l(x^*, y^*)$; and from this and the fact that $t^*$ is positive, we conclude that $q(x^*, y^*) = l(x^*, y^*)$. (The expected liability of injurers must have been equal to expected losses for them to have chosen the correct level of activity.) Similarly, $t^*$ must be the solution to the victims' problem,

$$\max_t v(t) - ty^* - s^*tl(x^*, y^*) + s^*tq(x^*, y^*)$$
$$= v(t) - t[y^* + s^*l(x^*, y^*) - s^*q(x^*, y^*)],$$

so that $v'(t^*) = y^* + s^*[l(x^*, y^*) - q(x^*, y^*)]$. But, from Eqs. (2.10), $v'(t^*) = y^* + s^*l(x^*, y^*)$, which leads to the conclusion that $l(x^*, y^*) - q(x^*, y^*) = l(x^*, y^*)$, or that $q(x^*, y^*) = 0$. But this contradicts what we earlier showed, that $q(x^*, y^*) = l(x^*, y^*)$.

PROPOSITION 2.4    None of the usual liability rules will lead injurers and victims to act socially optimally. Strict liability with the defense of contributory negligence will result in victims engaging in too high a level of their activity, and negligence rules will result in injurers engaging in too high a level of their activity. In fact, there does not exist any liability rule that will lead both injurers and victims to engage in optimal levels of their activities.

*Remarks.* As should be clear from the remark following Proposition 2.3, the result that there does not exist any liability rule that leads to optimal levels of activities depends on the assumption that liability rules are not functions of levels of activity. Otherwise, it would be easy to design rules leading to optimality.[59] The result also depends on the characteristic of a liability rule that what the injurer pays, the victim receives. Were this not true, it would again be easy to induce parties to act optimally; for instance, if injurers were to pay fines to the state equal to harm done and victims were to bear their losses, both would be led to act optimally.

*2A.2.3   Note on the literature.* The analysis of the last two sections is taken from Shavell (1980b), where I introduced the issue of the choice of levels of activity as distinct from levels of care.

---

59. For example, were liability for negligence to depend on the injurer's level of activity as well as on his level of care, the negligence rule would result in injurers' acting optimally (by logic of n. 58) and in victims doing so as well.

# 3 | Liability of Firms

In this chapter I reconsider the analysis of liability and deterrence under the assumption that injurers are firms. The analysis consists of two parts. The first is concerned with accidents involving firms and strangers, such as where a trucking company's gasoline tanker crashes and explodes, harming other vehicles or homes near the roadside. The second part of the analysis deals with situations in which firms' products (or services) cause losses for the firms' customers, for example, where a water heater ruptures and damages a customer's property. The feature of chief interest about these situations is that the customers' willingness to purchase firms' products will be influenced by what they perceive to be the products' risks. As a consequence, firms will be motivated to reduce product risks not only to avoid liability, but also to sell products at a better price.

Firms will be presumed to maximize profits and to do business in a perfectly competitive environment. This means that the price of a product will equal the total unit costs associated with production, including liability costs.[1]

The measure of social welfare that will be studied is similar to that in §§2.3 and 2.4: the utility customers derive from products and, where relevant, the utility that strangers obtain from their activities, minus expected accident losses, the costs of care, and direct costs of production.[2]

---

1. Under perfect competition, a firm cannot maintain the price of a product at a level exceeding total unit costs because competitors could then attract its customers by offering them the product at a lower, yet still profitable price. (And, of course, a firm will not want to maintain the price at a lower level than total unit costs.) The assumption of perfect competition is made mainly for convenience—it means that the effect of changes in total unit costs on price is simple to calculate. See §3.2.11 for further discussion of this assumption.

2. This measure of social welfare should seem, on its face, a natural one to study, since it takes into account the obvious social benefits and costs associated with production of a risky

## 3.1   The Case Where Victims Are Strangers to Firms

Although the conclusions to be drawn about liability rules will be essentially the same in this case as in the last chapter, there are several differences in how the conclusions are demonstrated and how they are interpreted that merit attention. Let us therefore review what was said earlier.

*3.1.1   Levels of care.* The arguments given in Chapter 2 with respect to parties' levels of care apply directly in the present case. Victims are in an identical situation whether injurers are firms or other individuals; and, as before, injurers, in this case, firms, want to minimize their costs of care plus liability expenses (for by doing so they maximize profits). Hence, both firms and victims will be led to take optimal levels of care under strict liability with the defense of contributory negligence and under the various negligence rules.

The type of liability rule employed will, however, affect product price. In particular, the price will be higher under the strict liability approach than under the negligence rules. This is because under strict liability the price will include expected accident losses, whereas under the negligence rules it will not, since by taking due care firms will avoid liability for accident losses.[3]

> EXAMPLE 3.1   Firms' direct costs of production per unit are 10, and the risk of accidents that would cause losses of 100 depends on whether firms take care (for simplicity, I consider the case where accidents are unilateral). Because the exercise of care reduces expected accident losses by 6 and costs only 2, it is socially desirable for firms to take care (see Table 3.1). Thus, under the negligence rule, firms will have to take care to avoid liability. Firms therefore will take care, and their total costs per unit will be

---

product. Another motivation for considering the measure of social welfare, however, is that it is equivalent to the sum of the net utilities of customers, victims, and owners of firms. To verify this in the case where victims are strangers, observe that: net utility of customers = utility from product − price; net utility of strangers = utility from their activity − costs of care + expected liability payments; net utility of owners of firms, that is, firms' profits = price − direct production costs − costs of care − expected liability payments. Adding these equalities and canceling offsetting terms, one obtains: net utility of customers + net utility of strangers + profits of owners of firms = customers' utility from product + strangers' utility from their activity − strangers' costs of care − firms' cost of care − direct production costs, which is as claimed. (The verification of the equivalence in the case where victims are customers is almost the same.)

3. As in the last chapter, it is assumed here that the negligence rule works perfectly. If it does not and firms are sometimes found negligent, the price will include some component attributable to expected accident losses under the negligence rule (but a component less than expected accident losses). On this and related matters, see §§4.3 and 4.4.

*Table 3.1*

| Level of care | Cost of care | Accident probability | Expected accident losses |
|---|---|---|---|
| None | 0 | 9% | 9 |
| Care | 2 | 3% | 3 |

12—the direct production costs of 10 plus the costs of care. Accordingly, the product price will also be 12 (by assumption, competition will drive the price down to total unit costs). Firms will take care under strict liability too, in order to minimize their total unit costs. But these unit costs, and thus the price, will equal 15 because the unit costs will include expected liability expenses of 3.

*3.1.2   Levels of activity.* Assume, as is natural, that an increase in a firm's level of production will result in a proportional increase in expected accident losses, the firm's level of care held constant. The determination of the socially optimal level of production of firms will then be virtually the same as the determination of the socially optimal level of injurers' activity discussed in the previous chapter. This is illustrated by further examination of Example 3.1.

EXAMPLE 3.2   Since the total unit costs of production, including expected accident losses, are 15 in Example 3.1, social welfare will be maximized if production is carried out only when customers obtain utility exceeding 15 per unit. Suppose, for instance, that there are 5 customers who would derive the utilities shown in Table 3.2 from purchasing the product. (Or

*Table 3.2*

| Customer | Utility from one unit of product |
|---|---|
| A | 40 |
| B | 20 |
| C | 17 |
| D | 13 |
| E | 11 |

suppose that a single customer obtains increments to utility as shown in the table from purchasing successive units of the product.) Then only A, B, and C, who derive utility greater than 15, should purchase the product; the optimal level of production is 3.

The general point of this example is that it is socially optimal for production to proceed only as long as the utility customers derive from additional units exceeds direct production costs plus total accident costs.

With this in mind, the analogues to the results from Chapter 2 about levels of activity can easily be seen to hold. Specifically, under the negligence rule the level of production will be higher than optimal (and thus too many accidents will occur): since the price will not include expected accident losses, customers will make purchases when the utility they derive from the product is less than the true total unit cost of production. In Example 3.2, the price under the negligence rule will be 12. Therefore, not only A, B, and C, but also, undesirably, D will purchase the product. (Because the price of transporting gasoline by tanker truck will not incorporate expected accident losses under the negligence rule, too much gasoline will be shipped by truck rather than by safer, if somewhat slower, means, such as by rail or barge.) Under strict liability, however, the level of production will be optimal, because the price will equal the total unit costs of production. In Example 3.2, the price will be 15, so only customers A, B, and C will purchase the product. (Since under strict liability the price of transporting gasoline by truck will include expected accident losses, some gasoline that would be shipped by truck under the negligence rule will instead go by rail or barge.)

The conclusions about victims' levels of activity are also as before. Under the negligence rule victims will choose their levels of activity optimally, for they will bear their accident losses. And under strict liability with the defense of contributory negligence victims will engage in their activity to too great an extent, since they will be compensated for their accident losses as long as they take due care. Thus, again, the choice between strict liability and negligence rules will depend on whether it is more important to control injurers' level of activity—here firms' level of production—than victims' level of activity.

*3.1.3   Exclusion of the level of production from the determination of negligence.* It was implicitly assumed above that the level of production is not taken into account in the determination of negligence. This assumption describes actual practice—firms, of course, are never found liable for having produced too much—and is justified by the fact that were courts to decide on permitted levels of production, they would have to determine and balance costs of production against consumer valuations.[4] The courts' problem, in other words, would be tantamount to that of devising production responsibilities in a centrally planned economy.

*3.1.4   Actual liability of firms to strangers.* The liability of firms for harm done to strangers is determined as described generally in §§2.2.13 and 2.4.8. A distinction must be made, however, between accidents in which harm comes about in the course of productive activity (such as when gasoline explodes during transport) and accidents in which harm is caused by products after their sale (such as when a boiler is purchased and explodes during use). In accidents of the latter type, the finding of liability is complicated by certain doctrinal considerations and by the possibility that the purchasers of products may have played a contributory role.[5]

*3.1.5   Note on the literature.* Legal scholars and economists have virtually always mentioned that where strangers might be harmed by firms, imposing strict liability would raise prices and reduce purchases relative to the situation in which liability is not imposed. But comparison with the situation under the negligence rule has not usually been made. There are exceptions, however. See, for example, Stewart and Krier (1978, p. 227) and Posner (1973b, p. 208), who mention the comparison. The comparison is developed formally in Polinsky (1980b), where the number of firms in an industry is assumed to affect accident losses and plays the role of the activity level, and in Shavell (1980b), where, as here, I assume that the level of output of firms affects accident losses.

## 3.2   The Case Where Victims Are Customers of Firms

As was indicated at the outset, firms' behavior in this case will be influenced not only by their potential liability, but also by customers' perceptions of product risks, for the latter will affect customers' willingness to make purchases.[6] More precisely, a customer will buy a product only if the utility of

---

4. Note the similarity to the justification offered in §2.3.6 for why injurers' levels of activity are excluded from the negligence determination.

5. See *Prosser and Keeton on Torts* (Keeton, Dobbs, et al. 1984), secs. 93, 95–98; and see Stone 1972, secs. 260, 289–291, for a brief comparative discussion.

6. The analysis of liability where victims are the employees of firms would parallel the analysis of this part. In much the same way that customers, if informed, can decide not to purchase unsafe products or can insist on paying lower prices as compensation for bearing extra risk, employees, if informed, can decide not to work at firms with unsafe working conditions or can demand higher wages as compensation for bearing added risk. I do not examine the issue of firms' liability to employees in part because this would be repetitive with the present analysis and in part because, in fact, employers are not liable to employees. Employees are generally barred from suing employers by workers' compensation legisla-

the product to him exceeds its *perceived full price*—the price actually charged in the market plus the perceived expected accident losses that would not be covered by liability payments and thus that he would have to bear. The expected accident losses that a customer perceives that he would have to bear will depend on his information about product risks. Alternative assumptions about customers' information are considered in the following two sections.

*3.2.1   Customers' knowledge of risk is perfect.* Where customers' knowledge is perfect, firms will be led to take optimal care even in the absence of liability. To see exactly why, observe that in the absence of liability customers will bear their losses and the full price will equal the market price plus expected accident losses. (The full price of a water heater will be seen as its price in the market plus the expected losses due to the possibility that it will rupture.) If a firm were to take less than optimal care, its potential customers would recognize this and factor into the full price the relatively high expected accident losses. Consequently, the firm's customers would go elsewhere; they would prefer to make their purchases from competitor firms exercising optimal care and therefore offering the product at a lower full price, although at a higher market price. This potential loss of customers will lead firms to take optimal care even in the absence of liability. (A similar argument shows why a firm would lose customers if it took more than optimal care.)

EXAMPLE 3.3   Suppose the situation is as in Example 3.1, except that the victims are customers; and assume that firms do not face liability for accident losses. A firm that did not take care may be able to set the market price of its product at the direct production cost of 10, but the full price would be at least 19, for the firm's customers would add the expected accident losses of 9 that they would bear to the market price. The firm would thus lose its customers to firms that take care. The price charged by firms that take care would be 12 (because the price would have to include the cost of care of 2), yet the full price would be just 15, since expected accident losses would amount to only 3. Hence, a firm that did not take care would not survive in competition against firms that take care.

Firms will also be led to take optimal care under strict liability with the defense of contributory negligence and under the negligence rules. Similarly,

---

tion. (This legislation provides that employees may obtain compensation for any accidents arising at the workplace and that employers must pay insurance premiums to support the compensation program.) See, for example, Atiyah 1980, chaps. 14, 15, Fleming 1983, pp. 491–496, and Keeton et al. 1983, chap. 19, and references cited therein.

customers will be led to take optimal care in their use of products under these liability rules,[7] as well as in the absence of liability.

Moreover, customers will buy the socially optimal amount of the product regardless of the absence or presence of liability. This is true because the full price that customers will compare with their utility will not be affected by the absence or presence of liability. In particular, the market price both in the absence of liability and under the negligence rule will equal the cost of optimal care plus direct production costs, since firms will be led to take optimal care in either case; and customers will add to this market price the expected accident losses in calculating the full price. Under strict liability with the defense of contributory negligence, the market price will simply equal this same full price. In Example 3.3, the market price will be 12 in the absence of liability and under the negligence rule, and the full price will be 15; under strict liability the market price and the full price will be 15. Thus in all cases only those customers for whom the utility of the product exceeds 15 will buy it, the desirable outcome.[8]

*3.2.2   Customers' knowledge of risk is imperfect.* Suppose now that customers do not have enough information to determine product risks at the level of individual firms. (Customers cannot ascertain the risk of rupture of a particular firm's water heaters.) Then firms will not take care in the absence of liability. No firm will wish to incur added expenses to make its product safer if customers would not recognize this to be true and reward the firm with their willingness to pay a higher price. Liability will thus be needed to induce firms to take optimal care.

Furthermore, the level of care taken by customers will not be optimal in the absence of liability. Customers will take too little care if they underestimate risks and too much care if they overestimate them. In the presence of liability customers' behavior might be similar, but those who possess accurate knowledge of the level of due care used to determine contributory negligence may be led to take due care despite their misperception of risk.

In addition, the level of customers' purchases will not be optimal in the absence of liability or under the negligence rule. If customers overestimate risks, they will overestimate the full price and might decide not to buy prod-

7. Under strict liability without the defense of contributory negligence, however, firms might take excessive care and customers inadequate care. For example, users of water heaters might not drain them or watch for signs of leakage even though this would cost users little in time and effort. Manufacturers might therefore be led to produce heaters with safety features that are expensive relative to the cost of users' care.

8. Under strict liability without the defense of contributory negligence, however, customers might not make optimal purchases because, as explained in n. 7, the level of care of firms, and thus the market price, might exceed the optimal level.

ucts when the utility of the products exceeds the true full price. If customers underestimate risks, the opposite problem might occur; they might make purchases that are not in their interest. Under strict liability with the defense of contributory negligence, however, customers will make appropriate decisions whether to buy products regardless of their misperception of risk. It will not matter that customers incorrectly estimate risks since they will be fully compensated for their losses; the market price will reflect the true risk of accident losses and it will be the market price alone on which customers base their decisions to make purchases.[9]

*3.2.3   Actual customer knowledge of risk.* Before I comment on the analysis of the last two sections, I think it will be helpful to consider briefly the likely character of customers' knowledge of risks.

One point to emphasize is that customers' knowledge of risks will vary with the type of product or service. In particular, customers' knowledge of the risks attending use of a wide class of modern-day products (automobiles, drugs, power machines) is presumably limited in significant ways because of customers' quite natural inability to understand how the products function. And customers' knowledge of the quality of most professional services (medical, legal, architectural) is supposedly similarly limited. By contrast, customers' information about the risks of common items of fairly simple design (hammers, bicycles, can openers) is probably good on the whole, and the same is likely true of their knowledge of the risks of many of the services that they purchase in ordinary life (barbering, sports instruction).

Not only will customers' knowledge of risk vary with the type of product or service, it will vary also with the type of customer. Commercial customers will often have relatively accurate knowledge of risk because they tend to be repeat purchasers, buy in large quantity, and make decisions in a calculated way. On the other hand, the typical consumer may be in a quite different position; he buys many products (especially durables) only on an infrequent basis and may not have the ability or the motive to approach his decision in the manner the commercial customer would.

Where customers' knowledge of risk is imperfect, there does not seem to be an appealing general assumption to make about the direction of their errors. A customer's assessment of the risk of a particular product or service will be based on his estimate of the average risk for the class of products or

---

9. This conclusion might well be altered, however, if losses include nonpecuniary elements for which liability awards would not or could not fully compensate. Suppose, for example, that product-related accidents could result in death. Then a customer would base his purchases in part on his estimate of the risk of death in an accident; if he incorrectly estimated this risk, his decision whether to purchase the product might be inappropriate.

services that have the same outward appearance as the one in question. Since actual risks will deviate from average risks about as often from above as from below, the frequency with which customers underassess risks should approximate the frequency with which they overassess risks—assuming that they correctly perceive average risks. Of course, customers may not accurately perceive the average, but systematic mistakes in their assessment of risk for a class of products or services can be either positive or negative. Customers can readily be imagined to exaggerate certain kinds of risks, because, for instance, of their vivid aspect (dying in an airplane crash); and they can well be thought to underestimate other kinds of risk, because, say, of the innocuous appearance of the products creating the risks (could drinking hot liquids from styrofoam cups release a carcinogen resulting in stomach cancer?).[10]

That customers' information about risks sometimes may not be good seems inevitable. Customers' ability to ascertain risks directly is, as was suggested above, naturally limited by their incomplete knowledge of how products work and by their lay understanding of, certainly, professional services. Also, their ability to evaluate risks that are numerically small—as the risks of accidents often are—may be questioned. The problem that customers may be unable to learn directly about risks may be remedied if customers are apprised of risks by firms. But firms clearly lack appropriate incentives to provide information about the dangerousness of their products and services.[11] In addition, organizations specializing in the collection of information about risks may not be able to earn enough (through sale of publications like *Consumer Reports*) to finance their activities at a socially desirable scale, in part because individual buyers can pass on the information to others in various ways. Finally, the very capacity of customers to absorb and act on information about the risks they face seems restricted. Customers purchase a great variety of products and services, and the risks of even a single one may be complicated to describe because they depend on the manner and the circumstances in which the product is used or the service is performed. Customers could not realistically be expected to keep track of and to employ all this information if it were available to them.

With these observations in mind, but realizing that the importance of customers' lack of knowledge about risks will depend significantly on context, the reader should assume below that there will often be a potentially useful

10. Eisner and Strotz 1961 discuss the overestimation of the risk due to airplane crashes. For a general discussion of psychological factors affecting the assessment of risk, see Tversky and Kahneman 1974.

11. This is not to deny that firms may have a legal duty to provide information (liability for failure to warn of defects) or that they can secure marketing advantages or enhance their reputation by doing so. But such motives to provide information are arguably imperfect.

role for liability to play in reducing risks and in influencing the volume of purchases.

*3.2.4  Problems in applying the negligence rule.* Information about firms' conduct and about their products and services may be peculiarly difficult for courts to obtain or evaluate as they arrive at a determination of negligence.[12] Such information may be of a complicated, technical nature (dealing, for example, with industrial engineering, the practice of medicine), or it may be special in character (concerning idiosyncratic features of the production process, a particular patient's condition), or it may have to do with events that occurred relatively far in the past (the production of a machine or the treatment of a patient many years ago). Consider by contrast that information will be relatively easy to obtain or evaluate in the typical accident between strangers, as where a person fails to clear a sidewalk of ice and someone slips on it and breaks his leg.

Courts' difficulty in obtaining and evaluating information leads to two problems. First, courts may make errors in determining levels of due care. Where firms are able to predict courts' incorrectly calculated levels of due care, firms will often be led to take these levels of due care and thus to take excessive or insufficient levels of care, as the case may be. And where firms are unable to predict levels of due care, or where there are other uncertainties surrounding the determination of negligence, firms may be led to take excessive levels of care so as to avoid being found liable by mistake (a manufacturer may use an undesirably costly safety feature, a physician may practice "defensive medicine"; see §4.3). The second problem is that courts may fail altogether to consider certain dimensions of firms' behavior in ιne negligence determination, either for want of any evidence or because evidence is scant. With respect to such dimensions of behavior, firms may do little or nothing to reduce risk (see §§2.1.6 and 2.2.11).

These problems are avoided under the strict liability approach, because firms will be motivated to take all justified steps to reduce risk, and only those steps, independently of whether courts would be able to decide what steps could have been taken and what steps would have been justified.

*3.2.5  Problems in applying the negligence rule to research and development and product design decisions.* An important illustration of the problems with the negligence rule concerns research and development with regard to product safety and design. To make a determination of negligence in this area, courts are faced with a complex task: they must decide whether, at the time that a firm had an opportunity to engage in an investigation, the then relevant

---

12. Much of what is said in this and the following sections applies equally in the context of accidents involving firms and strangers.

probability and value of a success were sufficiently high to warrant the costs of the investigation. Because courts will be prone to make mistakes in determining the probability or value of success or the costs of investigation, firms may be led to make socially undesirable decisions. For instance, a firm that is highly uncertain whether a given degree of research or design effort will later be seen by courts as adequate may decide to engage in research to a socially excessive extent. Or a firm that believes that courts would never learn that it had a particular opportunity to reduce a risk (for example, that a pharmaceutical company had a chance to develop a substitute drug without an adverse side effect) may decide not to pursue the opportunity. Indeed, the likelihood of this outcome is increased by the perversity that the initial pursuit of an avenue of investigation could provide the very evidence that would allow courts to conclude that a research opportunity had existed.

*3.2.6 Problems in applying the defense of contributory negligence under strict liability.* Courts may experience difficulty in determining due care levels of customers and in incorporating various dimensions of their behavior into due care. It may be hard to determine what customers can and should do to reduce risk (whether users of lawn mowers should wear safety glasses in view of the danger that stones would be thrown up by the cutting blades), how customers actually use products (whether when mowing a person tries to steer clear of areas with stones), whether customers adequately maintain products, and the like. In addition, courts typically do not include the intensity of use of products (how often a lawn mower, a can opener, or a forklift truck is used) in determining negligence, because calculation of the appropriate intensity of use is a practical impossibility or because evidence on the actual intensity of use is difficult to obtain.

As with courts' difficulties in determining due care of firms, these difficulties in determining due care of customers can lead to two types of problem. With respect to dimensions of behavior that are included in the determination of contributory negligence, customers may be led to do too little or too much to reduce risk; and with respect to dimensions of behavior that are left out of the determination, customers will do too little to lower risk. In any event, the problems would be lessened if, as under the negligence rule, customers expect to bear their losses.

*3.2.7 Strict liability versus negligence reconsidered.* The discussion of the last several sections should help to organize thought about the factors determining the relative appeal of the approaches of strict liability versus negligence as means of providing incentives toward safety. To illustrate, suppose that individuals' knowledge of the health risks associated with use of microwave ovens is imperfect (there is a potential need for liability); that the harmful effects of microwave radiation might be of substantial importance (a liability-induced reduction in radiation might prevent significant injury); that the possibilities for changing the design of microwave ovens would be hard for courts to ascertain (a determination of negligence about oven design would be problematic); and that there is relatively little users of microwave ovens can do to reduce risk (there is no real issue of contributory negligence).[13] In this case employment of the strict liability approach rather than the negligence rule would be desirable on grounds of creation of incentives toward safety in product design.

The situation might be different, however, with respect to use of commercial freezers and the risk that they would break down and that frozen foods would thaw and spoil. Suppose that buyers of the freezers, being in business, know fairly well the risks that freezers would fail (the potential need for liability is small in the first place); that the scope for manufacturers of freezers to reduce risk of freezer failure is modest because the risk is already low (liability could not reduce risk substantially); that the adequacy of user maintenance of freezers—checking freon levels, keeping filters clean—could not easily be considered in a determination of contributory negligence and that the intensity of use of freezers—the amount and value of frozen food kept in each freezer—would be omitted from the determination (implying that users would not act to reduce risks properly unless they bear their losses). Here the negligence rule would be the better form of liability on grounds of creation of incentives.

Of course, in these two examples it was assumed that all the factors of relevance worked in the same direction, in favor either of strict liability or the negligence rule; in reality, this will rarely be the case.

*3.2.8   Strict liability for product defects.* In the next several sections I consider a number of additions to the model of the liability of firms. Suppose in this section that the model is extended so as to allow a distinction to be made between the quality of individual units of a product and the variable subject to firms' immediate control: the care exercised in the production process (selection of employees, choice of material inputs, methods of quality assurance). Thus, suppose that there may well be a probability that some low-quality or "defective" units of a product will be produced even where the level of care taken in the production process is high.[14]

In this extended model the meaning of strict liability for defective products is that firms must pay for losses arising from defects in units of their prod-

13. The doors of most microwave ovens today must be closed for them to operate, so users cannot "cook" themselves, but users could take care not to stand too close to ovens when they are in operation.

14. The case of an error in design making *all* units of a product defective was discussed in §3.2.5.

ucts.[15] For instance, a maker of water heaters will be liable for losses due to serious flaws in its heaters (such as for losses from an explosion caused by a faulty pressure relief valve). Because firms must pay for accidents caused by defects regardless of the adequacy of care taken in the production process, the defect rule resembles strict liability. Note, however, that the defect rule is different from strict liability in that under the defect rule firms do not pay for accidents that are not due to defects (such as where a heater cracks and ruptures because of metal fatigue). The defect rule is different from the negligence rule too, in that under the negligence rule firms are not liable in principle for losses caused by defects as long as their care in managing the production process is satisfactory.[16]

Several consequences follow from the fact that under the defect rule firms do not pay for the losses caused by nondefective units. First, product prices will not fully reflect accident losses (the price of water heaters will not reflect the losses due to ruptures caused by metal fatigue), and there may therefore be a tendency for purchases to be excessive. Second, firms may have inappropriate incentives to take care. For example, firms may do too little to reduce the riskiness of nondefective products (too little may be done to improve the durability of the metal used for water heaters if metal fatigue would not be considered a defect).[17]

Neither of these disadvantageous effects of the defect rule would occur under strict liability, since firms would pay for losses due to nondefective units as well as defective units. However, the potential significance of the undesirable effects of the defect rule depends on the size of losses caused by nondefective versus defective units. The greater the fraction of losses caused

---

15. As will be noted in §3.2.12, strict liability for defects is the chief form of product liability in the United States today. The reader may think of a defect as a condition in a unit of the product leading to a relatively large risk of failure or harm. For present purposes it is not necessary to discuss the precise definition of a defect.

16. Still, the defect rule has the flavor of negligence in that there has to be a "fault" in the product for there to be liability. This has led some to the conclusion that the defect rule is no different from the negligence rule. That conclusion fails to distinguish between negligence with regard to the production process and the poor quality of particular units of a product. For discussion of the meaning of the defect rule, see Schwartz 1979.

17. It is also possible that firms would spend a socially excessive amount to avoid producing defective units. To illustrate, suppose that defective units cause expected losses of 100 and nondefective units losses of only 30. The value to a firm of producing a nondefective rather than a defective unit is that it will avoid *entirely* the expected liability of 100. But the value to society of producing a nondefective unit is smaller; it equals only 70, the *reduction* in expected losses. Since the value to a firm of producing nondefective units is greater than the value to society of doing so, a firm might be led to spend too much to avoid production of defective units.

by defective units, the less important the effects, and the more the defect rule resembles strict liability.

In addition, the defect rule may have an advantage over strict liability with regard to customers' incentives to reduce risk. Under the defect rule customers bear their losses when products are not defective, which may be when customer behavior can most contribute to the avoidance of accidents. (Perhaps an owner of a water heater will notice signs of metal fatigue, such as discoloration, and replace or repair the heater before a rupture occurs; by contrast, he may have no way of knowing that, say, the opening to the pressure relief valve is too small.) Under strict liability customers' incentives to reduce risks associated with nondefective products will be inferior. This is obviously so in the absence of the defense of contributory negligence, and it is true too where the defense is employed if, as discussed in §3.2.6, there are difficulties in applying it.

Apparently, then, the defect rule is superior to strict liability in creating incentives for customers to take care, but inferior to strict liability in creating incentives for firms to take care and in its influence on the volume of purchases.[18]

How the defect rule compares with the negligence rule is similar to how strict liability compares with the negligence rule, as discussed above. A point worth reiterating, though, is that courts' ability to apply the negligence rule—which here means courts' ability to determine whether the organization of production is appropriate—is subject to doubt. To determine this, courts would have to judge the adequacy of the selection of workers, of material inputs, of technology, and so on. In other words, they would often have to acquire knowledge approaching that of firms themselves.

*3.2.9   Warnings.* Suppose in the present section that firms may be able to warn customers about dangers so that they can make more informed decisions about the purchase and use of products. Assume too that there are many types of warnings, rather than a unique and simply described one, for warnings in fact may take different forms (package inserts and brochures, decals, imprints on products themselves) and may vary in prominence and content. Furthermore, warnings of different kinds (direct mailings, notices in newspapers and trade journals) may be issued after the time of sale.

Against the costs of making the different possible warnings must be balanced the expected benefits they would provide to customers. These benefits depend on the ability of customers to employ the information contained in the warnings (physicians could make use of warnings about side effects of pre-

---

18. Also, the defect rule results in a lower volume of cases than does strict liability, a factor that is potentially important to administrative costs (see Chapter 11).

scription drugs in ways much different from laypersons); on the likelihood of the dangers about which warnings are made (separate warnings for remote dangers would be impractical and might not influence customer behavior); on the possibility that intermediaries (supervisors at work, physicians and other professionals overseeing the use of products) are in a better position than customers to monitor risks; and on the need for warnings in the first place (if the dangers are common knowledge, say, that knife blades can cut, warnings will not increase customers' information).

The determination of the optimal warning would take into account these various benefits and costs. In theory, firms will be led to issue optimal warnings under either strict liability or negligence approaches. But, as is now a familiar point, application of the negligence rule becomes problematic when it is difficult for courts to decide what constitutes negligence, in this case an inappropriate failure to warn.

*3.2.10 Product warranties.* Another addition to the model would allow firms to offer product warranties, which is to say, to choose their own liability rules.[19] The type of warranty that a firm would offer is the one that would minimize the full price of its product as perceived by customers. A firm not offering that warranty would lose its customers to competitors. From this observation it can be concluded that if customers do not misperceive risks, the warranty that is sold will be the one that results in the lowest true full price and therefore that is socially best. For example, if buyers of commercial freezers have good knowledge of the risks of breakdown, the character of the warranty on the freezers would reflect the optimal balancing of manufacturer and buyer incentives. A warranty that covered the freezer motor but not the coolant system might be regarded as an implicit inducement for manufacturers to improve the reliability of the motor and for buyers to maintain the coolant system properly. An arrangement like this would reduce the full price of freezers from what it would be were the warranty to cover the coolant system as well as the motor.

If, however, customers misperceive risks, the warranty that is sold in the market may be socially undesirable. Notably, customers who mistakenly think that a risk is lower than it is in fact will tend to buy warranties with terms limiting or disclaiming coverage of that risk. (In the opposite case, where customers overestimate risk, they will buy warranties that are too inclusive.) To illustrate, consider the case where customers erroneously believe that a risk is nonexistent. Imagine, for instance, that they believe there is no chance that automatic coffee makers will explode and cause serious injury when in fact there is such a chance. Customers will place no value on a

19. On warranties, see Spence 1977, Priest 1981, and Grossman 1981.

warranty term giving coverage against injury due to explosions, although offering the term would cost manufacturers a positive amount. Coffee makers will therefore be sold without a warranty term covering explosions. Consequently, manufacturers of coffee makers will not have an incentive to reduce optimally the risk of explosions. Moreover, because customers are unaware of the risk of explosions, they will buy too many coffee makers (as opposed to the safer coffee pot).

It follows that where customers misperceive risks, it could be socially beneficial for courts to override certain terms of warranties, especially by broadening firms' responsibilities for injury. For courts to know when to override terms in warranties, however, requires that they be able to distinguish between situations where customers misperceive risk and those situations where they do not. Courts would have to be able to determine whether customers misperceive the risk that coffee makers will explode, for if customers understand this risk they might still desire limitation of the warranty for losses due to explosions. The limitation, for example, might induce customers to prevent blockages of coffee grounds, thereby eliminating the risk of explosions and reducing the price of coffee makers.

*3.2.11 Imperfect competition and market power.* Finally, it should be noted how, if at all, the possibility that firms in a less than perfectly competitive market have the ability to set price above cost affects the conclusions of this chapter.[20] Firms that enjoy such "market power" will wish to minimize unit costs, as do firms in a perfectly competitive market, in order to maximize profits. Since the conclusions reached above about firms' exercise of care rested only on the assumption that firms seek to minimize unit costs, the statements made about liability and firms' levels of care will not be altered where firms possess market power.

The enjoyment of market power by firms will, however, make some difference with respect to the effect of liability on levels of production. Because firms with market power will set price higher than unit costs, customers will purchase less than they do in a perfectly competitive market setting. Under strict liability, for example, firms with market power will set price above their production cost plus the cost of care and accident costs per unit, and customers will tend to purchase too little, rather than the optimal amount, of the product. Under the negligence rule, because firms will set price above production cost plus the cost of care per unit, customers' tendency to purchase too much if they underestimate risks will be counteracted; and so forth.

*3.2.12 Actual liability of firms to customers.* In most jurisdictions in the

---

20. On market power and the effect of liability rules, see Epple and Raviv 1978 and Polinsky and Rogerson 1983.

United States today, firms are held strictly liable for accident losses caused by defects in their products.[21] Customers need not prove negligence in the production process; they need only show that their losses were due to defects. Firms may sometimes avoid or reduce their liability where accident losses were the result of product misuse or other contributory behavior of customers[22] or of dealers; and firms may challenge whether losses were in fact caused by their products. On the other hand, the tendency has been toward narrowing of the use of these defenses and thus toward expansion of firms' liability; moreover, firms are increasingly prevented from escaping liability by having disclaimed it in warranties.[23]

There are, however, two important areas—product design and warning of risk—in which the negligence rule is employed. Specifically, a firm will be held liable for harms resulting from a dangerous characteristic in all units of its product if an alternative, safer design could have been used at reasonable cost. And a firm will be held liable for failure to warn of a product risk if the firm is determined to have had a duty to do so.

In England, France, and Germany, the trend in product liability has been in the direction of strict responsibility for defects, with this result often being reached by other legal means (presumption of producer negligence where losses are caused by defects, contractual liability, implied warranties). But the scope of product liability does not appear as great in these countries as in the United States.[24]

*3.2.13 Note on the literature.* Oi (1973) and Hamada (1976) examine models of product liability where victims are customers and possess perfect

---

21. The description here is confined to liability of producing firms to customers; it does not include liability of dealers to customers. See generally *Prosser and Keeton on Torts* (Keeton, Dobbs, et al. 1984), chap. 17, and Epstein 1980 for a description of product liability in the United States. Historically, firms were liable only to those customers with whom a "privity" relationship existed—those customers to whom the firms had sold directly rather than through dealers—and to an important extent liability was based on contract principles. But the assumption that there were implicit contracts or warranties running with products was employed to find liability where express agreements were lacking, and the privity requirement was gradually weakened and ultimately discarded, allowing customers at the end of the chain of distribution of a product to sue the producing firm for the tort of negligence. Strict liability for product defects itself emerged primarily in the 1960s, led by several important California decisions and influenced by sec. 402a of the *Restatement (Second) of Torts,* 1965.

22. Although the defense of contributory negligence is often not permitted, use of comparative negligence and doctrines relating to product misuse and to assumption of risk may allow courts opportunity to take into account plaintiffs' behavior.

23. See generally Epstein 1980 on the trend toward expansion of firms' liability.

24. See Fleming 1983, chap. 22, for a discussion of product liability in England and Stone 1972, secs. 257–295, for a discussion of product liability in different countries.

information about risk. Spence (1977) analyzes strict liability in a unilateral model where victims are customers who misperceive risk and where firms offer warranties. In Shavell (1980b) I consider strict liability and negligence rules in a bilateral model along the lines presented here.

# Mathematical Appendix

In this appendix I will extend the theory of liability and deterrence to the case where injurers are firms. Here, as later, I will use the assumptions, notation, and, often, the proofs from previous appendixes. As in the text, the situation where victims are the customers of firms will be considered separately from that where the victims are strangers.

The assumptions about firms and customers will be as follows. Firms seek to maximize profits, are risk neutral, and face constant production costs per unit of the product (or service) that they sell equal to the sum of direct costs and of costs of care; let

$c$ = direct production cost per unit of the product; and
$x$ = cost of care per unit of the product.

As in the text, care will be interpreted either as precautions taken to prevent accidents from arising in the course of the production process (such as training of workers at a plant to prevent explosions that could harm people living nearby) or as safety features of products intended to prevent accidents from occurring during their use (such as guards on machines to prevent individuals from touching dangerous moving parts). The market for the firms' product is perfectly competitive, which means that the price of the product will equal total unit cost. Thus the price will equal $c + x +$ (expected liability costs per unit). Regarding customers, let

$s$ = quantity of the product purchased; and
$u(s)$ = gross utility derived from $s$ units of the product; $u'(s) > 0$ and $u''(s) < 0$.

The expected utility of customers depends on the gross utility they derive from the product, on the price of the product, and, in the situation where customers are victims, on the care they take to prevent losses and the expected losses they will bear for which they will not receive compensation from liable firms.

The measure of social welfare will continue to be the sum of parties' expected utilities. Equivalently, it will equal customers' gross utility plus, where victims are strangers, victims' utility from their activity, less costs of care, direct production costs, and expected accident losses.

## 3A.1   The Case Where Victims Are Strangers to Firms

When strangers rather than customers suffer losses, customers will ignore accident losses and will choose the quantity $s$ of the product to maximize their gross utility less $s$ times the price.

*3A.1.1   Unilateral accidents.* Social welfare equals

$$(3.1) \qquad u(s) - s[c + x + l(x)],$$

where, analogously to before, $l(x)$ are expected accident losses per unit of production, given $x$. It is clear from Exp. (3.1) that the optimal $x$ minimizes $x + l(x)$; thus $x^*$ is determined by the condition $1 = -l'(x)$, as in §2A.1.1. It follows that the optimal quantity $s^*$ of the product is obtained by maximizing Exp (3.1) over $s$ given that $x = x^*$. Hence $s^*$ is determined by

$$(3.2) \qquad u'(s) = c + x^* + l(x^*),$$

which has the familiar interpretation that marginal utility must equal the total cost of production per unit to society.

In the absence of liability, firms will not take care, so unit cost and the price will equal $c$, and customers will choose $s$ to maximize $u(s) - sc$. Hence, $s$ will satisfy $u'(s) = c$. Comparing this with Eq. (3.2), it follows that $s$ will exceed $s^*$ (the problem is that the price is too low). Under the negligence rule where the due care standard is $x^*$, firms, by the logic of §2A.1.1, will choose $x^*$ and will not be liable. Unit cost and the price will therefore be $c + x^*$. Customers will thus select $s$ satisfying $u'(s) = c + x^*$, so that $s$ will again exceed $s^*$ but will be less than it would be in the absence of liability (the problem is that the price is still too low). Under strict liability firms' expected unit cost will be $c + x + l(x)$, so they will choose $x^*$. The price will consequently be $c + x^* + l(x^*)$ and customers will select $s$ obeying Eq. (3.2) (because the price equals the total unit cost to society, customers will choose $s^*$).

PROPOSITION 3.1   In the absence of liability firms will not take care and customers will purchase a socially excessive amount of the product. Under the negligence rule firms will exercise optimal care, but customers will again purchase too much of the product (yet less than in the absence of liability). Under strict liability firms will take optimal care and customers will purchase the optimal amount of the product.

*3A.1.2   Bilateral accidents.* Social welfare in the bilateral case equals

$$(3.3)\qquad u(s) - s[c + x + tl(x, y)] + v(t) - ty,$$

where, recall, $y$ is victims' level of care, $t$ is their level of activity, and $v$ is their utility. Noting that Exp. (3.3) differs only by $sc$ from Eq. (2.9) and modifying the arguments in §2A.2.2 along the lines of the last section, we can show that the following proposition is true.

PROPOSITION 3.2   In the absence of liability or under the negligence rule (with or without the defense of contributory negligence), victims will choose optimal levels of care and of their activity (given firms' behavior); whereas under strict liability with the defense of contributory negligence, victims will choose optimal levels of care but they will select a socially excessive level of activity. Firms' and customers' behavior under the different rules will be as described in Proposition 3.1.

## 3A.2   The Case Where Victims Are Customers of Firms

As discussed in the text, customers' estimates of product risks may influence their willingness to make purchases (and to take care), because they may have to bear their accident losses. In particular, suppose that the *full price* of the product is defined as the price charged by firms plus the perceived expected accident losses that customers would bear (after taking into account liability payments they would receive). Customers will thus choose their purchases $s$ to maximize their utility from the product less $s$ times the full price.

The full price will depend on customers' knowledge of risk, and three assumptions about their knowledge will be examined. The first is that customers possess perfect knowledge of risk: they can determine the expected losses $l(x)$ associated with the product of each firm. The second assumption is that customers know only the average of the risks of products of different firms. Since, however, firms are assumed to be identical, the average risk will equal the actual risk. Thus customers will turn out to know the actual risk even though they cannot observe it directly. The third assumption is that customers misperceive the average risk: they believe that the expected losses are $z$ times the average expected losses, where $z$ may be less than or greater than 1.

*3A.2.1   Unilateral accidents.* Social welfare is still given by Exp. (3.1), and $x^*$ and $s^*$ are determined as described in §3A.1.1. Assume first that in the absence of liability customers have perfect knowledge and can observe $l(x)$. Then the optimal outcome will result. To see this, notice that a firm that chooses $x$ will have to charge (at least) $c + x$, and since customers will know $l(x)$ the full price will be $c + x + l(x)$. But because customers will make their purchases from firms offering the lowest full price, a firm that did not choose $x^*$ would lose its customers to a firm that did choose $x^*$ (for $x^*$ minimizes $x + l(x)$). Thus $x^*$ will be chosen in equilibrium, and the full price will be $c + x^* + l(x^*)$. Accordingly, customers will choose $s$ to maximize $u(s) - s[c + x^* + l(x^*)]$, so that $s$ will satisfy Eq. (3.2); that is, customers will choose $s^*$.

Now assume that customers cannot observe $l(x)$ directly but know it on average. Then firms will clearly select $x = 0$, for choosing a positive $x$ would be costly to a firm, yet not increase the price at which it could sell its product. Thus, in equilibrium, the price will be $c$. Since customers will know that the average expected losses are $l(0)$, the full price will be $c + l(0)$. Hence customers will choose $s$ to maximize $u(s) - s[c + l(0)]$, which is to say they will choose the optimal $s$ given that $x = 0$.

Next assume that customers misperceive average risk. Then, as in the last paragraph, firms will choose $x = 0$ and the equilibrium price will be $c$. But as the perceived full price will be $c + zl(0)$, customers will choose $s$ to maximize $u(s) - s[c + zl(0)]$, which means that they will choose a higher than optimal $s$ (given that $x = 0$) if $z < 1$, and a lower than optimal $s$ if $z > 1$.

Now consider the negligence rule and assume that customers can observe $l(x)$. As in the absence of liability, customers will buy from the firm offering the lowest full price. Firms will therefore choose $x^*$ in equilibrium, and the full price will equal $c + x^* + l(x^*)$.[25] Consequently, customers will choose $s^*$.

If customers know $l(x)$ only on average, then, assuming that $\bar{x} = x^*$, firms will choose $x^*$. While a firm's choice of $x$ will not affect its ability to sell its product (since customers cannot observe $l(x)$), its choice of $x$ will affect its costs plus expected liability; and by the argument of §2A.1.1, a firm will decide to choose $x^*$ to minimize its costs. Hence the price will be $c + x^*$, the full price will be $c + x^* + l(x^*)$, and customers will therefore choose $s^*$.

If customers misperceive average risk, then, as in the last paragraph, firms

---

25. Notice that this will be true whatever the level of due care $\bar{x}$. The due care level will affect only the price: if $\bar{x} > x^*$, the price will be $c + x^* + l(x^*)$, since firms will choose to be negligent; if $\bar{x} \leq x^*$, firms will not be negligent, and the price will be $c + x^*$.

*Table 3.3*   Firms' level of care and quantity of product purchased by customers

| Customers' knowledge of risk | No liability | Negligence | Strict liability |
|---|---|---|---|
| Perfect | Care and quantity optimal | Care and quantity optimal | Care and quantity optimal |
| Only average risk known | Care = 0; quantity optimal (given that care = 0) | Care and quantity optimal | Care and quantity optimal |
| Average risk misperceived | Care = 0; quantity not optimal | Care optimal; quantity not optimal | Care and quantity optimal |

will choose $x^*$, but the perceived full price will be $c + x^* + zl(x^*)$ and customers will choose $s > s^*$ if $z < 1$ and $s < s^*$ if $z > 1$.

Finally, consider strict liability. Under this rule customers' estimate of risk will not affect their willingness to make purchases, for they will be compensated for any losses they suffer. Customers will therefore buy from the firm offering the lowest price. Hence, firms will choose $x$ to minimize their production costs plus cost of care plus expected liability; they will thus choose $x^*$. The price will consequently be $c + x^* + l(x^*)$, and customers will choose $s^*$.

PROPOSITION 3.3   Table 3.3 summarizes firms' choice of care and the quantity of customers' purchases under the circumstances considered in this section.

*3A.2.2   Bilateral accidents.* Here social welfare equals

$$u(s) - s[c + x + y + l(x,y)],$$

where $sy$ is the total cost of customers' care if $y$ is their level of care per unit of the product.[26] In this case, following the logic of the previous section and of §§2A.1.2 and 2A.2.2, it is easy to show the next result.

---

26. In effect, the level of activity of firms and of customers is the same variable—the quantity of the product. In Shavell 1980b, however, I assumed customers were able to control an additional variable interpreted as their level of activity, namely, their intensity of use of products. The results obtained there were noted briefly in §3.2.6.

PROPOSITION 3.4 If customers do not misperceive risk, they will choose optimal levels of care given firms' levels of care; otherwise customers will choose inappropriate levels of care. Firms' levels of care and customers' purchases will be as described in Table 3.3.

*Remark.* If care is multidimensional and some components of care are not included in due care, then the situation changes, as discussed in §§3.2.4– 3.2.6. Among other things, the negligence rule might be superior to strict liability with the defense of contributory negligence, for under the former but not the latter rule victims would choose optimally dimensions of care that are not included in their standard of due care.

*3A.2.3 Extension of the model to include warranties.* For simplicity, consider again the unilateral model and suppose that firms make agreements with customers providing either for no liability, strict liability, or the negligence rule. Assume that these agreements or warranties determine firms' liability (but see Remark 2 below). Using the fact that the form of warranty-determined liability will be that which minimizes the full price of the product perceived by customers, let us examine the situation under each of the three assumptions about customers' knowledge studied in the last section.

For the case where customers can observe $l(x)$, it is known from §3A.2.1 that if the warranty specifies no liability, firms will choose $x^*$ and the full price will be $c + x^* + l(x^*)$; and it is also known that the same will be true if the warranty specifies negligence (with $\bar{x} = x^*$)[27] or strict liability. Hence, firms will be indifferent among warranties specifying no liability, negligence, or strict liability; under any of these, $x^*$ and $s^*$ will be chosen.

Where customers can observe $l(x)$ only on average, it is known from §3A.2.1 that if warranties specify no liability, firms will choose $x = 0$ and the full price will be $c + l(0)$. If warranties specify negligence or strict liability, firms will choose $x^*$ and the full price will be $c + x^* + l(x^*)$. Hence, warranties providing for negligence or strict liability will be sold; $x^*$ and $s^*$ will again be chosen.

Where customers misperceive average risk, it is known from §3A.2.1 that if warranties specify no liability, firms will choose $x = 0$ and the perceived full price will be $c + zl(0)$. It is known also that if warranties specify strict liability, firms will choose $x^*$, the full price will be $c + x^* + l(x^*)$, and $s^*$ will be chosen. If warranties specify that the negligence rule governs liability, firms will set $\bar{x} = x(z)$, where $x(z)$ minimizes $x + zl(x)$;[28] and the perceived full

---

27. Under the negligence rule $\bar{x}$ will be chosen so as to minimize the full price, so that $\bar{x}$ will equal $x^*$.

28. This is so because $x(z)$ minimizes the perceived full price under the negligence rule.

*Table 3.4*

| Customers' knowledge of risk | Warranty-determined form of liability | Firms' level of care | Quantity purchased |
|---|---|---|---|
| Perfect | Negligence, strict, or none (equally preferable to customers) | Optimal | Optimal |
| Only average risk known | Negligence or strict (equally preferable to customers) | Optimal | Optimal |
| Average risk misperceived | Negligence if risk is underestimated | Too low | Too high |
| | Strict if risk is overestimated | Optimal | Optimal |

price will equal $c + x(z) + zl(x(z))$. The latter is less than $c + zl(0)$ (assuming that $x(z) \neq 0$), indicating that warranties providing either for the negligence rule or for strict liability will be sold. Which of the two will be the form of warranty depends on whether $z$ is less than or greater than 1. Warranties will be based on the negligence rule if $z$ is less than 1, since then $c + x(z) + zl(x(z)) < c + x^* + zl(x^*) < c + x^* + l(x^*)$.[29] On the other hand, warranties will provide for strict liability if $z$ exceeds 1, since then $c + x(z) + zl(x(z)) > c + x(z) + l(x(z)) > c + x^* + l(x^*)$.[30]

PROPOSITION 3.5   Firms' and customers' behavior under different forms of liability governed by warranties are as shown in Table 3.4.

*Remarks.* (1) The form of warranty would generally be uniquely determined in a bilateral model involving elements of behavior that cannot easily be included in firms' or customers' due care standards.

(2) Social welfare might be raised if appropriate legally determined liability overrides warranties where customers misperceive risk. This, however, requires that courts know where customers misperceive risk (see §3.2.10).

---

29. Under the negligence rule customers believe that they will bear lower expected losses than they will in fact bear. Under strict liability, by contrast, they will pay in the price an amount based on the actual expected losses. The price under strict liability will therefore exceed the perceived full price under the negligence rule.

30. The explanation is the reverse of that in n. 29: under the negligence rule customers believe that they will bear higher expected losses than they will in fact bear, and so forth.

*3A.2.4 Extension of the model to include strict liability for product defects.* Consider again the unilateral model and suppose the model is extended to allow for units of the product to differ in quality.[31] Specifically, let there be two qualities of units of the product, "defective" and "nondefective," where $l_d(x)$ and $l_{nd}(x)$ are the expected accident losses due to defective and nondefective units, respectively, given the care $x$ taken in the production process. Also, let $h(x)$ be the probability of defective units;[32] and assume that $l_d(x) > l_{nd}(x)$ and that $h$, $l_d$, and $l_{nd}$ are all decreasing, convex functions of $x$. Expected losses per unit given $x$ are $l(x) = h(x)l_d(x) + [1 - h(x)]l_{nd}(x)$. The socially optimal level of care, $x^*$, is determined by minimizing this expression plus $x$, and thus by

$$(3.4) \qquad h'(x)l_d(x) + h(x)l'_d(x) - h'(x)l_{nd}(x) + [1 - h(x)]l'_{nd}(x) = -1.$$

Under strict liability for product defects, a firm's expected liability is only $h(x)l_d(x)$, so the firm will choose the $x$ satisfying

$$(3.5) \qquad h'(x)l_d(x) + h(x)l'_d(x) = -1.$$

The $x$ satisfying Eq. (3.5), say $\hat{x}$, could be less than or greater than $x^*$. For example, if $h'$ is sufficiently low, then the left-hand side of Eq. (3.5) will exceed the left-hand side of Eq. (3.4) at any $x$, implying that $\hat{x} < x^*$. (If the major effect of care is not to reduce the probability of defective units, but rather to reduce how risky both defective and nondefective units are, then firms will take too little care, since they do not pay for losses due to nondefective units.) On the other hand, if $l'_d$ and $l'_{nd}$ are sufficiently low, then the left-hand side of Eq. (3.4) will exceed the left-hand side of Eq. (3.5) at any $x$, implying that $\hat{x} > x^*$. (If the major effect of care is to reduce the probability of defective units, then firms will take too much care, since they escape liability entirely for nondefective units, yet society's gain from producing nondefective units is only the reduction in expected losses, $l_d(x) - l_{nd}(x)$. See note 17 above.)

The product price under strict liability for product defects will be $c + \hat{x} + h(\hat{x})l_d(\hat{x})$, which does not reflect the expected accident losses $[1 - h(\hat{x})]l_{nd}(\hat{x})$

---

31. Most of what is said here will apply as well to the case of accidents involving firms and strangers.

32. This model can be interpreted as deriving from a model with quality continuously variable. Let $l$ be losses (or expected losses) caused by a unit of the product of quality $l$, and let $f(l; x)$ be the probability density of $l$ given $x$. Call units of the product with $l \geq l^o$ defective. Then $h(x)$ can be interpreted as the integral of $f(l; x)$ over $l$ exceeding $l^o$, and $l_d(x)$ as the mean of $l$ conditional on $l$ exceeding $l^o$, given $x$, and so forth.

caused by nondefective units. Hence, customers who misperceive risk will tend to purchase too much, other things being equal.

*3A.2.5   Note on the literature.* Oi (1973) considered strict liability in a unilateral model of accidents where customers are victims and have perfect information about risk. Hamada (1976) studied strict liability and negligence in a bilateral model where customers are victims and have perfect information about risk. Spence (1977) studied warranty-determined strict liability in a unilateral model where customers are victims, allowing for misperception of risk; see also Grossman (1981) on warranties. Polinsky (1980b) examined strict liability and negligence in a unilateral model where strangers are victims and where the issue of concern is the number of firms in the industry. In Shavell (1980b) I considered, as here, strict liability and negligence rules in unilateral and bilateral models in which victims are strangers or customers, allowing for misperception of risk.

# 4 | Factors Bearing on the Determination of Negligence

Having analyzed the basic theory of liability and deterrence where accidents involve strangers and where they involve firms and strangers or customers, I begin here a more detailed consideration of the liability system, and take up three topics concerning the functioning of the negligence rule. The first is the question whether differences among parties should result in differences in standards of due care. The second deals with certain "prior" decisions of parties (such as whether to obtain information about risk) that affect their ability to exercise care later, at the time when accidents may occur. And the third involves uncertainty and error over the determination of negligence. The reader should keep in mind that the discussion of these topics below will apply also to victims and the determination of contributory negligence.

## 4.1 Differences among Parties

Parties may differ with respect to the costs they incur in exercising care and with respect to the effect that their exercise of care will have in reducing accident risks. For example, individuals presumably differ in their ability to clear ice from their sidewalks, and if they do so, will reduce accident risks by varying degrees (depending on the amount of foot traffic, and the like). In what follows, reference will be made, for simplicity, only to differences in parties' cost of taking care, although what will be said will plainly bear equally on differences in the effectiveness of their exercise of care. The relevance of individual differences in the cost of taking care to the determination of due care levels, to levels of care actually taken, and to levels of activity will now be examined.

*4.1.1 Levels of care.* First, it is apparent that the socially optimal level of care of a party will generally depend on his cost of taking care (see §2.1.1).

The socially optimal level of care of a party for whom the cost of taking care is low will usually exceed the optimal level of care of a party for whom the cost of taking care is high. Thus it may be desirable for a young, able-bodied person to clear a sidewalk of ice, but undesirable for an elderly individual to do so.

Because the socially optimal level of care will tend to vary among parties, levels of due care must vary among them if they are to be led to act optimally under the negligence rule. Accordingly, where it is simple for courts to determine differences in the cost of taking care among parties, levels of due care should be individualized. If courts can distinguish the young and able-bodied person who can readily clear a sidewalk of ice from the elderly person who cannot, the first but not the second should be found negligent for failing to clear ice.

On the other hand, where differences in the cost of taking care among parties in some class are hard (or impossible) for courts to assess, then it may be best for courts to employ (or there may be no choice but for them to employ) a uniform level of due care in determining negligence for the parties. For instance, courts would presumably experience problems were they to attempt to ascertain how difficult it was to clear ice on a given day for a particular young and able-bodied individual. (They would have to evaluate that particular individual's stamina, how well he happened to have been feeling on the given day, and so forth.) They may well find it best to determine negligence for the whole class of young and able-bodied individuals by reference to a single amount of ice that must have been cleared to avoid liability. For courts to choose this amount of ice optimally—that is, so as to minimize the sum, over the class of young and able-bodied individuals, of the costs of care and of expected accident losses—they might be imagined to do the following: to consider initially a low amount of ice as a standard and then to raise the contemplated standard as long as the advantage of doing so—that a greater number of individuals who ought to clear at least the contemplated standard amount of ice will be led to clear the ice—outweighs the disadvantage—that a greater number of individuals who ought not to clear the contemplated amount of ice will nevertheless be led to clear the ice. In other words, the optimal uniform level of due care involves an implicit balancing of advantages and disadvantages because of the varying cost of taking care among individuals.

It should be observed that the optimal uniform level of due care will actually correspond to the individually optimal level of care for some "representative" individual within the class of individuals under consideration (though the optimal uniform level of due care will be either too high or too low for all other individuals). Thus one can, if one wants, *phrase* the problem of determining the optimal uniform level of due care as the problem of determining the optimal individualized level of due care for an appropriately chosen representative individual.[1]

*4.1.2   Engagement in activities.* If the choice whether to engage in an activity is taken into account, we can identify a reason for courts to hold parties to some "moderate" level of due care—even where courts know that a particular party's ability to have exercised this level of care is slight or that he simply could not have done so, and thus that the optimal level of care for him was lower than the moderate level.

The reason is that insisting on a moderate level of care will discourage from engaging in an activity those parties who would create especially high risks of accidents because of their inability to meet that level of care. As was discussed in §2.3.1, it is socially undesirable for a party to engage in an activity when the expected accident losses he would cause exceed the utility he would derive less his costs of care. Hence, it would be undesirable for a party who would not take moderate care and thus would cause high expected losses to engage in an activity (unless he would derive unusually great utility from it). Such a party would refrain from engaging in the activity if courts hold parties liable for not taking moderate care. For example, a peculiarly inept person might be dissuaded from practicing archery (unless he were extremely enthusiastic about the idea) if he thought that he would probably be found negligent for failing to meet the standard of due care required for archery to be reasonably safe. Put a little differently, for the inept person archery may be regarded as an ultrahazardous activity; thus it makes sense, in effect, to impose strict liability on the inept person who engages in archery.

*4.1.3   Actual determination of due care in view of differences among parties.* Many differences among parties that affect the ability to take care, and that are relatively easy for courts to observe, influence the determination of due care.[2] Blindness, lameness, or infirmity, for instance, may lower the standard of care to which an individual would otherwise be held; strength, size, special knowledge, or professional skill may raise it.

But the consideration of individual characteristics in determining negligence is limited in a variety of ways. Small differences in physical attributes,

1. It is shown in the Appendix that the optimal uniform level of due care may equal the socially optimal level of care of the party for whom the cost of taking care is average.

2. The description in this section is based generally on the discussions of the reasonable man and of allied issues in Anglo-American law in *Prosser and Keeton on Torts* (Keeton, Dobbs, et al. 1984, sec. 32, and in sec. 1 of chap. 7 of Fleming 1983; see also *Restatement (Second) of Torts* 1965, secs. 283, 291. For a brief description and for references about essentially similar issues (involving what is sometimes called the "good family father") in other legal systems, see Tunc 1974, sec. 134.

difficult to observe, are not taken into account by courts and, normally, neither are differences in intelligence or in temperament; instead, due care is found by asking what would be appropriate for a "reasonable man" possessing "average" intellect and physical powers. Moreover, in some circumstances even an individual's easily ascertainable characteristics do not influence due care. A nearly blind person, a child, or a mental incompetent would probably be held responsible for causing an automobile accident, even if such a person drove with all the care of which he was capable; and it is doubtful whether a person's clumsiness, if established, would help to relieve him of liability. In addition, the fact that a person might weigh the costs of exercising care or the significance of the probable harm in a manner that departs from community norms would not affect the determination of due care.

*4.1.4  Justifications given by courts and commentators.* Several justifications are offered by courts and legal scholars for why certain characteristics of a party are not considered in determining negligence or, as it is sometimes expressed, for why negligence is often found by reference to "external" or "objective" standards rather than to individual or "subjective" standards.[3] One justification is the obvious difficulties of proof, for instance, of "drawing any satisfactory line[s] between . . . variations of temperament [and] intellect."[4] This agrees, of course, with §4.1.1. Further, courts' use of the fictitious reasonable man in finding due care agrees with §4.1.1; recall that the optimal uniform level of due care for the class of individuals among whom the law cannot distinguish may be interpreted as the optimal individualized level of due care for a representative individual in the class.

Another justification is the notion that an individual who acts in a highly dangerous way simply deserves to be held responsible for harm done. Thus the driver with very poor vision should be found liable for accidents caused by his failure to notice what a person with normal vision would have noticed, as should "a man . . . born hasty and awkward [who] is always having accidents and hurting himself or his neighbors . . . [for] his slips are no less troublesome to his neighbors than if they sprang from guilty neglect."[5] This notion is very close to that used generally to justify strict liability, and it comports with the discussion above in §4.1.2. A third justification for use of

3. Seavey 1927 draws out this distinction.

4. See *Restatement (Second) of Torts* 1965, sec. 283B. This reason is mentioned or implied in virtually all discussions (as are the other reasons to be noted below).

5. See Holmes 1963, p. 86. See also Seavey 1927, p. 22, who says "it is negligent for one to enter into a course of conduct when . . . because of his individual qualities he . . . should not enter into the undertaking at all."

objective standards of due care is unwillingness to credit idiosyncratic sensitivities in the comparison of the costs of care against the risks of harm.[6]

*4.1.5  Note on the literature.* Diamond (1974b) and Posner (1986, p. 151) make the argument of §4.1.1 that it is best for levels of due care to be individualized to the extent that courts can distinguish differences among parties. What is added here is the argument of §4.1.2 that insistence on at least a moderate level of due care discourages those who would create especially high risks from engaging in activities.

## 4.2  Prior Precautions

Many actions taken by parties influence their ability to take care at subsequent times. One important example of such a prior precaution is acquisition of information about risk (safety features of a power tool, likelihood of adverse reactions to a drug), since the possession of this information will enhance a party's ability to prevent accidents. Another example of a prior precaution concerns the amount of alcohol a person consumes: a person who is careful about indulging will be better able to avoid doing harm, notably when driving. A third example is maintenance of machinery, which may enable operators to avoid accidents.

*4.2.1  Optimal prior precautions.* Consider for simplicity the unilateral model of accidents, and suppose the social goal to be minimization of the costs of prior precautions plus the costs of care and expected accident losses. Then the socially optimal behavior of a party is easily determined, as is illustrated by Example 4.1.

EXAMPLE 4.1  Taking a prior precaution will enable a party to exercise care at a cost of 3, and taking care will lower the risk of a loss of 100 from 10 percent to 2 percent. On the other hand, not taking the prior precaution will mean the party will not be able to exercise care to reduce risk. (For exam-

---

6. This justification is offered, for example, in *Restatement (Second) of Torts* 1965, sec. 291, which says that a party "is not excused because he is peculiarly inconsiderate of others . . . nor is he negligent if his moral or social conscience is so sensitive that he regards as improper conduct which a reasonable man would regard as proper." Two additional justifications for not considering characteristics in determining negligence are also occasionally mentioned. One is that holding children, incompetents, and certain other parties liable for harms they could not have prevented exerts beneficial pressures on those who have charge over them; this shall be analyzed in §7.3 (on vicarious liability). The other justification is that holding individuals to at least a moderate level of care induces them to improve their ability to take care; this is discussed in §4.2.

ple, a party who does not obtain information about risk would not know of an opportunity to reduce risk; an intoxicated person may find it virtually impossible to exercise care.) Taking the prior precaution will allow the party to lower total accident costs by 5 (since the exercise of care will decrease expected accident losses by 8 at a cost of only 3). Hence, if the cost of the prior precaution is less than 5, it will be socially worthwhile.

More generally, a prior precaution will be socially worthwhile not only if its cost is sufficiently low, but also if its effect on the ability to take care results in a sufficiently high reduction in expected total accident costs.

*4.2.2   Negligence rule.*    Assume that the level of due care used to determine negligence is that which is socially optimal *provided* that parties have taken optimal prior precautions. Then parties will be led both to take optimal prior precautions and to exercise optimal care. The claim, in other words, is that if the level of due care is not relaxed for drunk drivers but is held to the level appropriate for sober drivers, then drivers will be induced both to be sober and to exercise the level of due care appropriate for sober drivers. Likewise, if individuals are held to the level of care that presumes they have made reasonable efforts to learn about risk, they will be led to make such efforts as well as to take the then called-for level of care.

The reason for these conclusions is as follows. If parties do not take optimal prior precautions, they will find it excessively costly or impossible to take due care. Hence they will be led to take optimal prior precautions. And just because they will do so, they will be induced, by familiar logic, to exercise due care. For instance, suppose that the cost of the prior precaution in Example 4.1 is 1 (hence taking the precaution is socially optimal) and, accordingly, that care must be taken to avoid being found negligent. Thus, if the party takes the prior precaution, he will find it in his interest to take care to avoid liability, so will spend only 1 + 3 or 4. If he does not take the prior precaution, his expected liability will be 10. Therefore he will take the prior precaution and exercise care. (By contrast, the party would clearly not take the prior precaution if the rule were that he could escape liability for failing to take care when he had not taken the prior precaution.)

It should be noticed that in applying the version of the negligence rule under consideration, courts do not (or have no need to) verify whether a party actually took optimal prior precautions. They verify only whether a party took due care. This is an advantage to the extent that it would be difficult for courts to ascertain a party's prior precautions (what knowledge he really possessed, how much alcohol he in fact consumed).

*4.2.3   Actual determination of negligence in view of prior precautions.* Courts normally determine negligence in the manner described above: they hold parties to the level of due care that would be required *if* their prior behavior had been appropriate. Courts generally hold individuals to the level of care that would be required of a sober individual.[7] Courts usually assume that parties have made reasonable efforts to apprise themselves of risk. They state that parties "know or should have known" easily obtained facts about risk, that parties ought to possess "common knowledge" about risk; that if parties are able to acquire knowledge about risk (as are physicians regarding the chance of adverse reactions to a drug), they are deemed to have that knowledge.[8] Similarly, in other contexts, courts usually presume that parties have taken appropriate prior precautions; in determining how quickly a driver should have been able to come to a halt, for example, courts will ordinarily assume that he had taken the prior precaution of keeping his brakes in good repair.

## 4.3  Uncertainty, Error, and Misperception

Factors leading to uncertainty over the finding of negligence, and the consequences of such uncertainty, will be considered in the initial sections of this part. Then the effect of systematic, anticipated error in the choice of due care levels will be analyzed. At the end the effect of misperception of due care levels will be discussed.

*4.3.1  Uncertainty over the finding of negligence.*  One factor leading to uncertainty over the finding of negligence is that courts may err in assessing a party's true level of care. For example, a court might not accept a physician's claim that he had performed a diagnostic test (that he listened carefully to a person's heartbeat after a series of exercises) when in fact he had. The possibility that a court would make an error of this type might lead a physician to administer redundant or uncalled-for tests (an electrocardiogram) that would reduce his chance of being found negligent by mistake. Of course, the possibility that a court would make an opposite type of error may also exist. A court might decide that a physician had taken proper care when in truth he had not. (A court might conclude from incomplete medical records that there

---

7. An exception occurs when an individual becomes intoxicated involuntarily, as when he does not know that his drink has been laced with whiskey, which is to say, when he could not have taken the prior precaution of remaining sober. Another interesting point confirming that the law applies the rule discussed in §4.2.2 is that an intoxicated individual who drives with all the care required of a sober individual would probably not be found negligent for an accident he caused. See, for brief discussions of intoxication, *Prosser and Keeton on Torts* (Keeton, Dobbs, et al. 1984), p. 178, and *Restatement (Second) of Torts* 1965, sec. 283C.

8. See *Prosser and Keeton on Torts* (Keeton, Dobbs, et al. 1984), pp. 182–185, Fleming 1983, p. 103, and *Restatement (Second) of Torts* 1965, sec. 290.

was no need for a physician to refer his patient to a specialist when the patient should have seen a specialist.)

The significance of the two types of error, however, is not likely to be the same. The disadvantage to a party of being found negligent by mistake is that he will have to pay the victim's losses. This disadvantage will often dominate in importance the savings in the cost of care that the party could obtain by reducing his level of care somewhat and hoping that he would erroneously escape liability if an accident occurred.

The reader should not be surprised, then, to learn that a general consequence of uncertainty over the assessment of true levels of care is that parties will tend to be led to take more than due care—and thus to take socially excessive levels of care (presuming that due care is set at socially optimal levels).[9] To illustrate, consider the following example.

EXAMPLE 4.2   The probability of an accident that would cause a loss of 100 is related to the level of care as shown in Table 4.1. The socially optimal level of care, which is assumed to be due care, is moderate care. If there were no chance of mistake in courts' assessment of care, parties could avoid liability for sure by taking moderate care at a cost of 3; they would not take high care, since that would involve a greater cost of 5.

Suppose, however, that there is a 33 percent chance that courts will misperceive care by one level and a 5 percent chance that courts will misperceive care by two levels. That is, there is a 33 percent chance that no care would be seen by courts as moderate care and a 5 percent chance that no care would be seen as high care. Further, there is a 33 percent chance that moderate care would be seen by courts as none and a 33 percent chance that moderate care would be seen as high care. And there is a 33 percent chance that high care would be seen by courts as moderate care and a 5 percent chance that high care would be seen as none.

In this situation parties will take high care. If they take no care, their expected expenses will be $62\% \times 15\% \times 100 = 9.3$ (since they will mistakenly escape liability $33\% + 5\% = 38\%$ of the time). If they take moderate care, their expected expenses will be $3 + 33\% \times 10\% \times 100 = 6.33$ (since they will mistakenly be found liable 33 percent of the time). Yet if they take

---

9. This is not to say that uncertainty over assessment of care will always lead to excessive care. Obviously, if there is a high enough chance of overassessment of care and a low enough chance of underassessment, parties will take less than due care. But in a wide class of situations (including ones in which the chance of overassessment of care exceeds by a not insignificant amount the chance of underassessment), parties will take more than due care. For a precise statement of the result, see Proposition 4.4 in the Appendix.

*Table 4.1*

| Level of care | Cost of care | Accident probability | Expected accident losses | Total accident costs |
|---|---|---|---|---|
| None | 0 | 15% | 15 | 15 |
| Moderate | 3 | 10% | 10 | 13 |
| High | 5 | 9% | 9 | 14 |

high care, their expected expenses will be only $5 + 5\% \times 9\% \times 100 = 5.45$ (since they will mistakenly be found liable only 5 percent of the time).

As this example shows, if raising the level of care reduces the chance of being found negligent by mistake, parties may decide to take more than due care, even where the chances of courts' overestimating care are as large as the chances of their underestimating care.[10] The example illustrates also the point that despite parties' increasing their level of care, they may still face a positive risk (5 percent in the example) of being found negligent if they cause accidents.

Much the same conclusions hold with respect to two other factors leading to uncertainty over the finding of negligence. One of these factors is that a party may be unable to control completely his *momentary* level of care. A driver may be unable to control completely his level of care at each instant (because of a lapse of attention, a sudden glare, a sneeze); or a physician may be unable to act with all the care he intends with each of his patients on each of their visits. But since it is the driver's care at the time of an accident and the physician's treatment of the particular patient that courts will ordinarily consider in determining negligence, the driver and the physician will generally bear some uncertainty over whether they will be found negligent. A little reflection should convince the reader that such uncertainty will lead parties to

10. Actually, in the example, as long as the chance of overestimating care by one level is less than 58.66 percent—a chance substantially exceeding the 33 percent chance of underestimating care—parties will still take high care. Assuming the chance of overestimating care is 58.66 percent, parties who take no care will escape liability $58.66\% + 5\% = 63.66\%$ of the time, so their expected expenses will be $36.34\% \times 15\% \times 100 = 5.45$; parties who take moderate or high care will expect to spend, as before, 6.33 and 5.45, respectively. Thus taking no care and taking high care will result in equally low expected expenses. If the chance of overestimating care is lower than 58.66 percent, taking no care will result in higher expected expenses.

try usually to take more than due care in order to reduce the likelihood that their momentary level of care will fall short of due care and thus cause them to be found negligent. (The logic behind this assertion is essentially that of the previous paragraphs, that the disadvantage of being found negligent will outweigh the advantage of conserving on the cost of taking care.)

The other factor leading to uncertainty over the determination of negligence is the level of due care applied by courts. It may be impossible to tell how courts will assess the cost of care or its effectiveness in reducing risk. There may be uncertainty, for instance, over how courts will evaluate the cost to a physician in time and effort of performing a diagnostic test or over how courts will assess the value of the test in providing information about a disease; in this case the physician will not know whether courts will see failure to perform the test as negligence. It should be clear to the reader that such uncertainty will tend to induce parties to take higher than desirable levels of care to guard against being found liable by mistake.

*4.3.2    Remarks on uncertainty.*   The relative importance of the three sources of uncertainty—courts' errors in assessing true levels of care, parties' inability to control their momentary level of care, and courts' errors in calculating levels of due care—will depend on context.[11] For example, where there are few witnesses to or where there is little evidence concerning a party's behavior, errors in assessing true levels of care may be important; where courts will not be able to obtain or to evaluate reliably information about the costs and benefits of care, errors in the calculation of the level of due care may be important (a problem that may be of general significance for physicians and other professionals, for firms using new technology); and so forth.

With respect to parties' inability to control their momentary levels of care, three comments seem worth making. First, an individual's momentary level of care can be regarded as an imperfect indicator of his true, and inherently unobservable, level of care, namely, the degree to which he adopts a *prudential mental attitude*. Hence, in strict logic, the cause of uncertainty over the finding of negligence due to an individual's inability to control his momentary level of care may be viewed as courts' inability to assess an individual's true prudential mental attitude. Second, one wonders whether courts might sometimes lower the level of due care in implicit recognition of parties' problems in controlling their momentary level of care. (Might not courts allow for some irregularity in driving behavior, knowing that individuals cannot maintain full concentration at all times?) Third, there are two types of situation that appear

---

11. See Tunc 1974, secs. 141, 143–146, for a discussion of the importance of uncertainty over the negligence determination in different legal systems.

to involve uncertainties similar to those over the momentary level of care: situations where parties are responsible for the negligence of subordinates whose behavior they cannot control completely; and situations where parties operate machines that occasionally function erratically.

Finally, it should be added that the more general interpretation of the fact that uncertainty over the level of due care may induce parties to take socially excessive care is that uncertainty over the law may lead parties to take socially undesirable steps to avoid liability.

*4.3.3  Anticipated errors in the choice of due care.*  Now suppose that parties know in advance that the level of due care will be different from the optimal level, and how so. (But, for simplicity, suppose that courts can correctly measure parties' true levels of care and that parties can control completely their levels of care.)

It might be that parties know the due care level will be less than the optimal level. This would be true, for instance, where parties know they will not be found negligent for failure to use a particular safety device despite its low cost and substantial effectiveness in reducing risk. In such a situation parties will obviously not purchase the safety device; they will not take more than due care.

The other possibility is that parties know due care will exceed the optimal level (that a safety device will be required despite its high cost and low effectiveness in reducing risk). In this situation parties will take due care unless its level is so high that they are better off acting negligently. In the latter case, parties will take optimal care since they will, in effect, be strictly liable.

*4.3.4  Misperception of the level of due care.*  Suppose last that parties misperceive the level of due care that courts will apply. Then parties will take the level of care that they believe constitutes due care, unless it exceeds optimal care by so much that they are better off acting in a way they think is negligent, in which case they will take optimal care. Hence, parties who overestimate due care will either take more than due care or take optimal care; those who underestimate due care will take less than due care.

*4.3.5  Note on the literature.*  Diamond (1974b) first studied how parties will respond to uncertainty over the finding of negligence, making many of the points discussed here; Calfee and Craswell (1984) further developed the subject.

## 4.4  Implications of Findings of Negligence

*4.4.1  There will be findings of negligence.*  The reader will recall that in the basic theory presented in Chapter 2 parties were never found negligent, because it was in parties' interests to act with due care and because the determination of negligence was perfect. It is evident from the analysis in this chapter, however, that there are a variety of reasons why parties may be found negligent: (1) limitations in courts' capacity to distinguish differences among parties may lead to findings of negligence against parties for whom taking due care is relatively difficult (see §4.1.1); (2) the undesirability of reducing the level of due care below a certain minimum, even if courts know some parties simply cannot meet it, may lead to findings of negligence against these parties (see §4.1.2); (3) uncertainty in the determination of negligence and parties' lapses of attention and inability to control their momentary level of care may result in parties being found negligent (see §4.3.1); (4) if courts set due care sufficiently above the optimal level, then parties will decide against taking due care (see §4.3.3); and (5) parties who underestimate the actual level of due care and thus take only what they believe to be due care may be found negligent (see §4.3.4). Two other reasons for findings of negligence, that parties will not find taking due care worthwhile because they do not have enough assets to pay a judgment or because they think they would escape suit, will be discussed in §§7.4 and 5.3.

*4.4.2    The significance of findings of negligence.*    The occurrence of findings of negligence implies that there is an element of strict liability—of having to pay for harm done—associated with use of the negligence rule. Hence, much of what was said in Chapters 2 and 3 about strict liability carries over to a degree to the negligence setting. For example, the fact that under strict liability injurers will take into account the losses their activity creates has relevance under the negligence rule; injurers will take some account of the losses their activity creates because they will face some risk of being found negligent.

In addition, the occurrence of findings of negligence will be called upon later, in Chapter 9, to explain why injurers should wish to purchase liability insurance against being found negligent.

*4.4.3    Strict liability and negligence compared.*    Because an injurer's goal will be the social goal under strict liability, injurers will act optimally under that rule in the situations studied in this chapter. Under strict liability each injurer will exercise his individually optimal level of care and will engage in an activity only when that is desirable; injurers will take appropriate prior precautions; and, of course, injurers will act without any concern over whether there would have been uncertainty surrounding a determination of negligence.

These points constitute an argument in favor of a strict liability approach over the negligence rule as far as injurers' behavior is concerned. But the problems with injurers' behavior under the negligence rule become problems with victims' behavior under strict liability with the defense of contributory negligence. Uncertainty over the determination of contributory negligence, for instance, may lead victims to take excessive care. Such problems complicate the comparison of strict liability and negligence rules.

*4.4.4 The different versions of the negligence rule reconsidered.* In Chapter 2 parties acted optimally under the negligence rule whether or not the rule was accompanied by the defense of contributory negligence, and parties also acted optimally under the comparative negligence rule. When, however, the factors studied in the present chapter are introduced into the bilateral model—so that findings of both negligence and contributory negligence will occur—parties will not necessarily act optimally under the different versions of the negligence rule and the different versions of the rule will have different effects.

As a general matter, to the extent that injurers will be found negligent, victims will have the greatest motive to take due care under the negligence rule with the defense of contributory negligence, a lesser motive to take due care under the comparative negligence rule, and the least motive under the negligence rule without the defense of contributory negligence. This is because, of course, under the negligence rule with the defense of contributory negligence a victim who does not take due care will receive no compensation from a negligent injurer, whereas under the comparative negligence rule he will receive partial compensation and under the negligence rule without the defense of contributory negligence he will receive complete compensation.

On the other hand, to the extent that victims will be found contributorily negligent, the situation is reversed. Injurers will have the greatest motive to take due care under the negligence rule without the defense of contributory negligence, a lesser motive to take due care under the comparative negligence rule, and the least motive under the negligence rule with the defense of contributory negligence.

This reasoning suggests that the comparison among the different versions of the negligence rule will depend importantly on the likelihood of victim negligence versus injurer negligence.[12]

---

12. See §4A.4.4 for an illustration of this conclusion. There findings of negligence arise because the standard of due care is uniform for parties of different types. It is shown that the negligence rule with the defense of contributory negligence is the best rule if the likelihood of victim negligence is low; otherwise, the comparative negligence rule is best; the negligence rule without the defense of contributory negligence is never best. But the explanation of these results appears somewhat special; it might not hold in situations in which the reason for findings of negligence is different (where, for example, negligence is found because of errors in courts' assessment of levels of care).

# Mathematical Appendix

The functioning of the negligence rule will be studied here in various extensions to the unilateral model of accidents. As noted in the text, however, the points to be made will have obvious analogues in the bilateral model with regard to victims' behavior and the determination of contributory negligence.

## 4A.1   Differences among Parties

Suppose that injurers differ in their cost of exercising care, and define

$k$ = per-unit cost of exercising care to an injurer of type $k$; and
$f(k)$ = probability density of $k$; $f$ is positive only on [a, b], where $0 < a < b$.

Hence, to an injurer of type $k$, the cost of exercising level of care $x$ is $kx$. Let us now analyze the negligence rule, assuming first that injurers engage in their activity (our concern then is with their choice of care) and next that injurers must choose whether to engage in their activity.

*4A.1.1   Levels of care the only determinant of risk.* Suppose here that the social goal is minimization of total accident costs, that is, minimization of the integral of $kx + l(x)$ over all injurers. Thus, the socially optimal level of care for an injurer of type $k$ is the $x$ that minimizes $kx + l(x)$. This level of care, denoted by $x^*(k)$, is determined by the first-order condition $k = -l(x)$. Implicitly differentiating the condition with respect to $k$, one obtains $x^{*\prime}(k) = -1/l''(x) < 0$. Therefore, as is illustrated in Figure 4.1, the higher the cost of care, the lower the socially optimal level of care.

If courts can determine an injurer's type, then under the negligence rule injurers can be induced to take socially optimal care. That is, if due care for injurers of type $k$ is set equal to $x^*(k)$, then by the proof in §2A.1.1 they will be led to take care of $x^*(k)$.

If, however, courts cannot determine an injurer's type (but do know the probability density $f$), courts' problem will be to choose a single due care level $\bar{x}$. Let us say that $\bar{x}$ must be in the interval[13] $[x^*(a), x^*(b)]$. Suppose first

---

13. We restrict attention to this interval principally because we do not want to allow $\bar{x}$ to be so high as to lead all injurers to choose to be negligent. Were we to allow such an $\bar{x}$, all injurers would act optimally—since then the negligence rule would in fact become the rule of strict liability. Yet it would be unnatural to analyze this situation under the heading of the negligence rule. (Recall that we had made a similar restriction about $\bar{x}$ in §2A.2.1.)

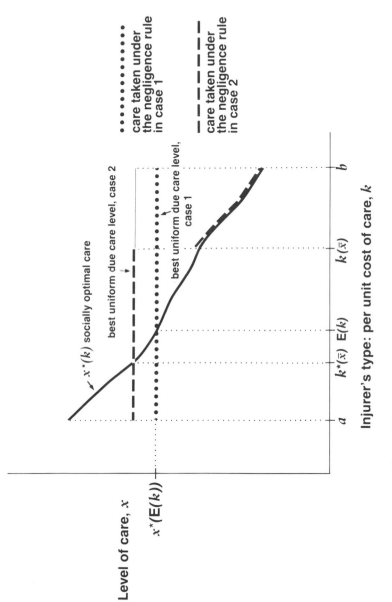

*Figure 4.1*

that for any such $\bar{x}$ all injurers will be induced to take care of level $\bar{x}$. Then the optimal $\bar{x}$ will minimize

$$\int_a^b [k\bar{x} + l(\bar{x})]f(k)dk = E(k)\bar{x} + l(\bar{x}),$$

where $E$ is the expectation operator. The best $\bar{x}$ will therefore equal $x^*(E(k))$, as is shown in case 1 of Figure 4.1. The other possibility is that for some or all $\bar{x}$, injurers' levels of care will be as is illustrated in case 2 of the figure. That is, if $k^*(\bar{x})$ denotes the $k$ such that $x^*(k) = \bar{x}$, then for all $k$ up to a point $k(\bar{x})$ exceeding $k^*(\bar{x})$, injurers will take care of level $\bar{x}$. To demonstrate this, use the argument of §2A.1.1 to prove that $\bar{x}$ will be chosen by injurers if $k \leq k^*(\bar{x})$; and the fact that at $k = k^*(\bar{x})$ it is still *strictly* better for injurers to choose $\bar{x}$ implies that $\bar{x}$ will be chosen in a neighborhood of $k$ greater than $k^*(\bar{x})$. Thus, if Figure 4.1 is to be justified, it remains to be shown that if $\bar{x}$ would not be chosen for some $k$, then $\bar{x}$ would not be chosen for any $k' > k$, and further that when $\bar{x}$ would not be chosen, $x^*(k)$ will be. The latter claim is obvious. The problem for an injurer who would not choose $\bar{x}$ would be

$$\min_{x < \bar{x}} kx + l(x).$$

Since $x^*(k) < \bar{x}$, he would choose $x^*(k)$. To show the former claim about $k$ and $k'$, we need to demonstrate that

(4.1)      $k\bar{x} > \min_{x < \bar{x}} kx + l(x)$

implies

(4.2)      $k'\bar{x} > \min_{x < \bar{x}} k'x + l(x)$.

But Ineq. (4.1) may be rewritten as $k\bar{x} > kx^*(k) + l(x^*(k))$, since $x^*(k)$ will be chosen if $\bar{x}$ is not; and clearly $(k' - k)\bar{x} > (k' - k)x^*(k)$. Adding these two inequalities gives $k'\bar{x} > k'x^*(k) + l(x^*(k))$. Moreover, $k'x^*(k) + l(x^*(k)) > k'x^*(k') + l(x^*(k'))$, which means that $k'\bar{x} > k'x^*(k') + l(x^*(k'))$, from which Ineq. (4.2) follows. Case 2 in Figure 4.1 is therefore explained. If at the optimal $\bar{x}$ the situation is as in case 2, social welfare will be

(4.3)      $\displaystyle\int_a^{k(\bar{x})} [k\bar{x} + l(\bar{x})]f(k)dk + \int_{k(\bar{x})}^b [kx^*(k) + l(x^*(k))]f(k)dk.$

Further, it can then be shown that the optimal $x$ will exceed $x^*(E(k))$.[14] This result implicitly reflects the fact that whereas in case 1 raising $\bar{x}$ above $x^*(E(k))$ had the undesirable effect that it increased care for all injurers with high $k$, raising $\bar{x}$ now does not alter care taken by parties with high $k$, for they choose to be negligent.

PROPOSITION 4.1    If courts can determine an injurer's type and thus set the due care level for each type equal to the socially optimal level, injurers of each type will be led to take socially optimal care. But if courts cannot determine an injurer's type and thus must set a uniform level of due care for all injurers, injurers generally will not take socially optimal care. The situation will then be either as in case 1 of Figure 4.1 (where the optimal uniform level of due care is that which is optimal for the average type of injurer) or as in case 2 (where the optimal uniform level of due care is higher).

*Remarks.* (1) It should be clear that were there other types of differences among parties (such as over the effectiveness of care in reducing expected losses), the main point of Proposition 4.1 would still hold (as would that of Proposition 4.2, below).

(2) Proposition 4.1 implies that it is socially desirable for courts to acquire information about an injurer's type if the cost of doing so is sufficiently low.

*4A.1.2    The choice whether to engage in the activity.* Suppose in this section that injurers either engage in their activity—and, if so, at one level—or they do not. (For present purposes, there is no need to consider a continuously variable level of activity.) Suppose also that if they do engage in their activity they will enjoy gross utility $u$, and that if they do not engage in it they will derive no utility (nor will they bear costs of care or cause accidents). Accordingly, assume the social goal is to maximize injurers' utility from engaging in their activity, less total accident costs; the goal is thus to maximize the integral of $u - kx - l(x)$ over all injurers who engage in the activity. Hence, socially optimal behavior will be as illustrated in Figure 4.2. Injurers with $k$ low enough that

(4.4)    $u > kx^*(k) + l(x^*(k))$

14. Using the fact that $k(\bar{x})$ decreases with $\bar{x}$, we can show the derivative of Exp. (4.3) to be negative for $\bar{x} \leqq x^*(E(k))$. Hence, for $\bar{x}$ to be a local minimum of Exp. (4.3), it must be that $\bar{x}$ exceeds $x^*(E(k))$.

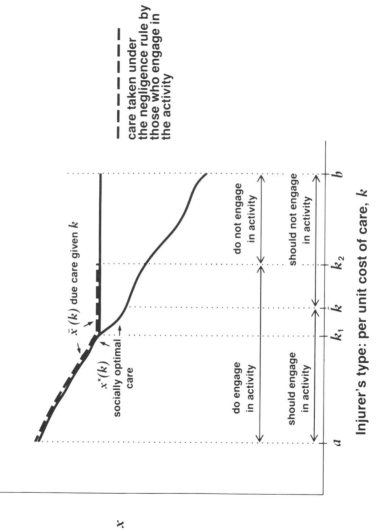

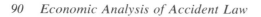

*Figure 4.2*

will engage in the activity and take optimal care; other injurers, those with $k$ exceeding $\hat{k}$, will not engage in the activity.[15]

Suppose that under the negligence rule courts can determine an injurer's type. Although courts could set $\bar{x}(k)$ equal to $x^*(k)$ and thereby induce all injurers who engage in the activity to take optimal care, injurers would engage in the activity too often; they would do so whenever $u > kx^*(k)$ rather than only when Ineq. (4.4) holds. (This is, of course, the defect of the negligence rule discussed in §2A.2.1.) Therefore social welfare might be raised by courts' setting due care equal to a constant $\bar{x}$ for all $k$ higher than some $k_1$. As illustrated in Figure 4.2, this might result in all injurers with $k$ higher than some $k_2 > k_1$ not engaging in the activity, which would be beneficial if $k_2 > \hat{k}$. (Figure 4.2 may be justified along the lines used to justify case 2 of Figure 4.1. The only point worth adding is that if a party with $k > \hat{k}$ decides not to take $\bar{x}$, he will decide not to engage in the activity since he will then be liable for losses and since Ineq. (4.4) will not hold.)

PROPOSITION 4.2   Even if courts can determine injurers' types, they may not wish to set due care equal to the socially optimal level for each type. Specifically, it may be socially beneficial for courts not to reduce due care for types of injurers for whom the socially optimal level of care would be low, because such types of injurers may thereby be induced not to engage in the activity (as illustrated in Figure 4.2).

*Remark.* The purpose of assuming that courts could determine an injurer's type was to abstract from the issues discussed in the previous section. But were it assumed that courts could not determine an injurer's type, the optimal uniform level of due care would be at least as high as that in §4A.1.1.

*4A.1.3   Note on the literature.* The points made in §4A.1.1 are essentially those illustrated in the analysis of the example in Diamond (1974b), sec. 12.

## 4A.2   Prior Precautions

Suppose that (now identical) injurers may reduce their cost of care by taking costly prior precautions—for example, acquiring information about risk, avoiding excessive consumption of alcohol, or maintaining equipment.

---

15. Inequality (4.4) holds if and only if $k$ is less than some $\hat{k}$ because $kx^*(k) + l(x^*(k))$ is increasing in $k$. It is assumed that $a < \hat{k} < b$; the case in which it is optimal for all injurers to engage in the activity or for none to do so is not interesting to consider and is omitted.

Define

z = level and cost of prior precautions; $z \geq 0$; and
$k(z)$ = per-unit cost of care to an injurer given $z$; $k(z) > 0$; $k'(z) < 0$.

If injurers choose prior precautions $z$ and, subsequently, level of care $x$, total accident costs will be

(4.5)      $z + k(z)x + l(x)$,

the minimization of which will be taken to be the social goal. The socially optimal $x$ and $z$, denoted $x^*$ and $z^*$, will be assumed to be positive and to be uniquely determined by the first-order conditions from Exp. (4.5), namely,

(4.6)      $k(z^*) = -l'(x)$

and

(4.7)      $1 = -k'(z)x^*$,

which have obvious interpretations.
    Under the negligence rule, if due care $\bar{x}$ equals $x^*$, injurers will choose both $z^*$ and $x^*$—even though courts do not base liability on whether $z^*$ is chosen. To prove this, observe that whatever his $z$, if an injurer chooses $x \geq \bar{x}$, he will clearly choose $\bar{x}$, since $\bar{x}$ is enough care to allow him to escape liability. Also, if he chooses $\bar{x} = x^*$, his costs will be $z + k(z)x^*$. The first-order condition for his choice of $z$ will thus be that in Eq. (4.7), so he will select $z^*$. On the other hand, the expected expenses for an injurer who chose $x < x^*$ would be $z + k(z)x + l(x)$, because he would be liable for losses. This amount must exceed $z^* + k(z^*)x^* + l(x^*)$ (since the social optimum is unique and $x$ is by assumption unequal to $x^*$), which equals or exceeds $z^* + k(z^*)x^*$, which is what his costs would be if he chose $\bar{x} = x^*$. Hence an injurer would not choose $x < \bar{x}$.

PROPOSITION 4.3   If due care equals the socially optimal level, then injurers will be led to choose both the socially optimal level of prior precautions and the socially optimal level of care.

*Remarks.* (1) The socially optimal level of care is, of course, the level which is socially optimal conditional on injurers having taken optimal prior precautions. Hence the level of due care in the model may be interpreted as that which is in fact employed by courts (see §4.2.3 of the text).

(2) Proposition 4.3 states that injurers are led to choose two variables, care and prior precautions, optimally under the negligence rule even though the determination of negligence is assumed to involve only one of them, care. The explanation for this result is that there is a special connection between the two variables. As was pointed out earlier, where there is no connection between variables, the determination of negligence generally would have to incorporate all the variables affecting risk for parties to be induced to choose each optimally (see Proposition 2.1, Remark 2).

(3) One interpretation of prior precautions, as mentioned in the text, is effort or expenditure to acquire information. This interpretation is appealing, but it is worthwhile sketching an explicit model of acquisition of information. Suppose that if a fixed amount $z$ is spent, the information (or "signal") $s_1$ will be received with likelihood $p_1$ and $s_2$ will be received with likelihood $p_2 (= 1 - p_1)$; that $l(x|s_i)$ is expected accident losses given $s_i$; that $x_i^*$ is the optimal $x$ given $s_i$; that $l(x) = p_1 l(x|s_1) + p_2 l(x|s_2)$ is expected losses if information is not acquired; and that $x^*$ is the optimal $x$ if information is not acquired. The expected value of information, $v$, is the expected reduction in total accident costs achieved by having the information: $v = [x^* + l(x^*)] - p_1[x_1^* + l(x_1^*|s_1)] - p_2[x_2^* + l(x_2^*|s_2)]$. Information will be socially desirable to acquire when $v$ exceeds its cost $z$. Suppose that if $v > z$, due care in state $i$ will be set equal to $x_i^*$; that is, if information ought to be acquired, the due care level will be set according to what is best given the information. The question then is whether injurers would be induced to acquire the information and to take due care. The answer is that they might, which seems to be the plausible case, but there is a possibility that they would not.[16]

## 4A.3  Uncertainty, Error, and Misperception

*4A.3.1  Uncertainty in courts' assessment of care.* Suppose that courts do not accurately assess injurers' levels of care; let

$e$ = error in courts' assessment of an injurer's level of care; and
$f(e)$ = probability density of $e$.

---

16. Injurers might not acquire information and take the appropriate level of care because, since they are not liable under the negligence rule when they take due care, they do not see changes in expected accident losses as part of the gain from acquiring information. In particular, if it is optimal for information to be acquired, injurers might choose not to acquire it and to take the higher $x^*$, say $x_2^*$, all the time: given that injurers do not acquire information, $x_2^*$ might be their best choice of care, as it allows them to escape liability whatever is $s_i$ (since $x_2^* > x_1^*$). Moreover, if $x_2^*$ is the best choice, the gain from acquiring information would be only $p_1(x_2^* - x_1^*)$, because information would enable them to save $x_2^* - x_1^*$ in costs of care whenever $s_1$ was true. The quantity $p_1(x_2^* - x_1^*)$ could be less than $z$ even though $v > z$.

Although $e$ will be assumed to be independent of $x$, it will be apparent that the points made below do not depend on this. Since the level of care observed by courts is $x + e$, an injurer will be found negligent if $x + e$ is less than due care $\bar{x}$, and his expected expenses will therefore be

(4.8)     $x + \Pr[e|x + e < \bar{x}]l(x)$,

where Pr stands for probability. The derivative of Exp. (4.8) with respect to $x$ is

(4.9)     $1 - f(\bar{x} - x)l(x) + \Pr[e|x + e < \bar{x}]l'(x)$.

Here 1 is the marginal cost of care, the second term is the marginal reduction in expected liability due to the decline in the likelihood of being found negligent when care is raised, and the third term is the marginal reduction in expected liability due to the decline in expected losses when care is raised. It was suggested in the text that one would expect this derivative to be negative at $\bar{x}$ on account of the second term and thus that the injurer would wish to raise care above $\bar{x}$.

In fact, we can prove—without, as it happens, referring to Exp. (4.9)—that if there is positive probability of underassessment of care and the distribution of error is not too dispersed, injurers will choose $x$ exceeding $\bar{x}$ whenever they would have chosen $\bar{x}$ in the absence of errors in assessing $x$.

Specifically, assume that $l(\bar{x})$ is positive[17] and consider any family of error distributions $f(e; \lambda)$, where $\lambda$ is a positive parameter with the following two properties: (1) the probability of underassessment of care is at least $\gamma > 0$ for all $\lambda$; (2) the probability that the absolute size of the error exceeds any given positive magnitude approaches zero as the parameter $\lambda$ approaches zero (that is, the error distribution becomes concentrated as $\lambda$ approaches zero). Now since by hypothesis an injurer would choose $\bar{x}$ in the absence of errors, it must be that[18]

(4.10)     $\bar{x} < \inf_{x < \bar{x}} x + l(x)$.

---

17. If $l(\bar{x}) = 0$, the result does not hold. Injurers will choose $\bar{x}$ despite the possibility of error for the simple reason that if $l(\bar{x}) = 0$ there is no chance of accidents if $x = \bar{x}$, and hence no opportunity for courts to find injurers negligent by mistake.

18. We know that $\inf_{x < \bar{x}} x + l(x) = \min_{x \leq \bar{x}} x + l(x)$. If this minimum is achieved at $\bar{x}$, then Ineq. (4.10) holds, for $\bar{x} + l(\bar{x}) > \bar{x}$; if the minimum is achieved at $x < \bar{x}$, Ineq. (4.10) again holds, by the hypothesis that $x + l(x) > \bar{x}$ for such $x$.

Hence, we can find a positive $\delta$ sufficiently small that

(4.11)    $\bar{x} + 2\delta < \inf_{x < \bar{x}} x + l(x).$

Further, since $\gamma l(\bar{x})$ is positive, we can always have chosen $\delta$ so that also

(4.12)    $2\delta < \gamma l(\bar{x}).$

Now suppose that an injurer chooses $\bar{x} + \delta$. Then it follows from property 2 above that for any positive $\varepsilon_1$ the probability of his being found negligent (given that there is an accident) must be less than $\varepsilon_1$ for all $\lambda$ less than some $\lambda_1$ (depending on $\varepsilon_1$). Hence his expected expenses must be less than $\bar{x} + \delta + \varepsilon_1 l(\bar{x} + \delta)$, which is less than

(4.13)    $\bar{x} + \delta + \varepsilon_1 l(\bar{x}).$

Next suppose that an injurer chooses an $x$ in the interval $[\bar{x} - .5\delta, \bar{x}]$. Then whatever is $\lambda$, the probability of his being found negligent is at least $\gamma$ (since he will certainly be found negligent whenever the error is negative). His expected expenses must thus be at least

(4.14)    $\bar{x} - .5\delta + \gamma l(\bar{x}).$

Last, suppose that an injurer chooses an $x$ that is less than $\bar{x} - .5\delta$. Then we know from property 2 that for any positive $\varepsilon_2$ the probability of his being found negligent must be at least $1 - \varepsilon_2$ for all $\lambda$ less than some $\lambda_2$. Hence his expected expenses are bounded from below by

(4.15)    $x + l(x) - \varepsilon_2 l(\bar{x}).$

It follows from Ineq. (4.12) that if $\varepsilon_1$ is sufficiently small, then Exp. (4.13) is less than Exp. (4.14); and it follows from Ineq. (4.11) that if $\varepsilon_1$ and $\varepsilon_2$ are sufficiently small, then Exp. (4.13) is less than Exp. (4.15). Hence if $\varepsilon_1$ and $\varepsilon_2$ are sufficiently small, an injurer will prefer $\bar{x} + \delta$ to $\bar{x}$ or to any lower $x$ for all error distributions with parameter $\lambda$ less than $\min(\lambda_1, \lambda_2)$; in particular, this means that an injurer's choice of $x$ must exceed $\bar{x}$ for all such distributions. We have therefore proved the following.

PROPOSITION 4.4   Suppose that injurers would take due care in the absence of errors in assessing their level of care. Then they will exercise more than due care in the presence of errors, so long as there is a positive probability of underassessment of their level of care and the distribution of errors is not too dispersed.

*Remarks.* (1) Many families of error distributions satisfy the two properties assumed above (for instance, uniform distributions over $[-\lambda,\lambda]$ or normal distributions with mean 0 and variance $\lambda$). Note that there is no need for the error distributions to be symmetric about 0; it is required only that there be some positive probability of a negative error.

(2) If at $\bar{x} = x^*$ (or at any other $\bar{x}$) injurers would choose $x > x^*$ because of courts' errors in assessing care, there must exist some lower due care level at which injurers would choose exactly $x^*$. That is, assuming that the chosen $x$ would be less than $x^*$ for some $\bar{x}$ (such as $\bar{x} = 0$) and that the chosen $x$ is a continuous function of the due care level, an $\bar{x}$ at which $x^*$ would be chosen must exist (by the intermediate value theorem).

(3) If the distribution of errors is very dispersed, then it is possible (but one would think unlikely) that injurers would choose $x < \bar{x}$. For example, suppose that the error is uniformly distributed over an extremely large interval and that $\bar{x} = x^*$. In this case injurers would be found negligent with a probability of about 0.5 over a wide range of $x$. Hence their situation would approximate that of parties who would be held strictly liable with probability 0.5, and they would thus choose $x < x^*$.

*4A.3.2   Parties' inability to control their momentary level of care with certainty.* Assume here that injurers control a variable $x$, but that this is not their *momentary level of care*. Rather, their momentary level of care equals $x + e$, where $e$ is an uncertain error term with probability density $f$. It is the momentary level of care that determines expected accident losses, $l(x + e)$. For example, $x$ might be interpreted as a driver's mental attitude toward safety and $x + e$ as his actual driving behavior at a particular moment, which could vary because of a sneeze or glare (see §4.3.1). Furthermore, assume that courts cannot observe the control variable $x$; they can observe only the momentary level of care $x + e$. Hence, injurers will be found negligent if $x + e$ is less than $\bar{x}$, in which case their expected liability will be $l(x + e)$. Given these assumptions, we can show that the analogue to Proposition 4.4 holds.[19] That is, if injurers would take due care in the absence of difficulty in controlling their momentary level of care, they will exercise more than due care in

---

19. The proof of Proposition 4.4 needs only slight modification: Ineqs. (4.10)–(4.12) still hold; the last term in Exp. (4.13) should be replaced with $\varepsilon_1 l(0)$; Exp. (4.14) still holds; and although Exp. (4.15) does not hold, it is clear that expected losses tend to $x + l(x)$ as $\lambda$ tends to zero. Hence, the argument following Exp. (4.15) still applies.

the presence of difficulty, so long as there is a positive probability of a negative error in controlling their momentary level of care and the distribution of errors is not too dispersed. Notice, therefore, that if what injurers control is the average level of momentary care (which would be so if the mean of $e$ is zero), then the interpretation of the analogue to Proposition 4.4 is that the mean of injurers' momentary level of care exceeds due care.

*4A.3.3  Uncertainty over the level of due care.* Assume now that although injurers can control perfectly their level of care, which is accurately observed by courts, there is uncertainty over the level of due care. Due care equals $\hat{x} + e$, where $e$ is a deviation with probability density $f$. Injurers will be found negligent if $x$ is less than $\hat{x} + e$ or, equivalently, if $x - e$ is less than $\hat{x}$. Their expected expenses will therefore be

$$x + \Pr[e|x - e < \hat{x}]l(x),$$

which is identical in form to Exp. (4.8); thus Exp. (4.9) applies (with $\hat{x}$ replacing $\bar{x}$ and $x - e$ replacing $x + e$). Hence, the analogue to Proposition 4.4 holds. That is, if injurers would take care of $\hat{x}$ were $\hat{x}$ known with certainty to be the level of due care, they will exercise more care than $\hat{x}$ so long as there is a positive probability that due care will exceed $\hat{x}$, and the distribution of the deviations is not too dispersed.

*4A.3.4  Anticipated error in the level of due care.* Suppose here that due care $\bar{x}$ is unequal to the optimal level $x^*$ and that injurers know $\bar{x}$ in advance. (Thus there are no uncertainties.) Then if $\bar{x} \leq x^*$, injurers will take care of $\bar{x}$: since $x^* < x + l(x)$ for $x < x^*$, certainly $x^* < x + l(x)$ for $x < \bar{x}$; therefore $\bar{x} < x + l(x)$ for $x < \bar{x}$. Also, if $x^* < \bar{x} \leq x^* + l(x^*)$, injurers will still take $\bar{x}$, but if $\bar{x} > x^* + l(x^*)$, they will take $x^*$. This follows because if $\bar{x} > x^*$, then

$$\min_{x < \bar{x}} x + l(x) = x^* + l(x^*).$$

We therefore have shown the following proposition, which is illustrated in Figure 4.3.

PROPOSITION 4.5  Suppose that injurers know what the level of due care will be. If due care will be less than the optimal level, then injurers will take only due care. If due care will be above the optimal level but will not exceed $x^* + l(x^*)$, then injurers will take due care; if, however, due care will exceed $x^* + l(x^*)$, injurers will not take due care and, in fact, will act optimally.

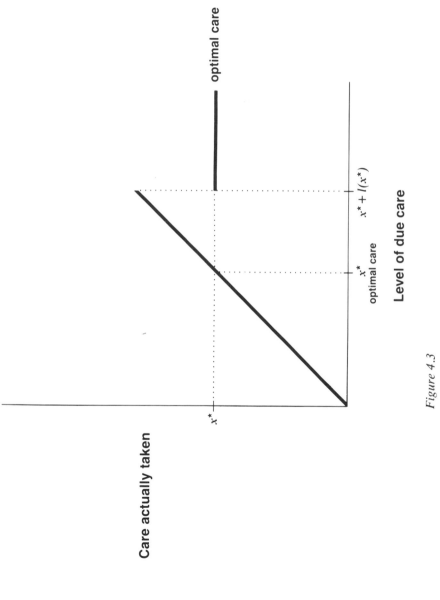

*Figure 4.3*

*4A.3.5   Misperception of the level of due care.* Suppose that injurers misperceive the level of due care; they believe it will equal a particular level with certainty, when in fact it will be different. In this case the following proposition is self-evident from the argument of the previous section.

PROPOSITION 4.6   Injurers will take the perceived level of due care if it is not too high—not above $x^* + l(x^*)$; otherwise, they will take optimal care.

*4A.3.6   Note on the literature.* Diamond (1974b) first studied uncertainty over the determination of negligence. Using examples involving uniformly and triangularly distributed random error terms, he examined uncertainty due to inability to control the momentary level of care and to errors in observing the true level of care and showed when parties would take more than due care and when less. Craswell and Calfee (1986) further analyzed uncertainty, exploiting the first-order condition from Exp. (4.9) and showing various comparative statics results. To this literature, §§4A.3.1–4A.3.3 adds a general proof that parties will take more than due care under the different sources of uncertainty if the distribution of the random term is not too dispersed.

## 4A.4   Implications of Findings of Negligence

*4A.4.1   Explanation for findings of negligence.* The above analysis has provided a variety of explanations for why injurers may be found negligent. In particular, in §4A.1.1 it was shown that when courts set a uniform level of due care for different types of injurers among whom they cannot distinguish, those injurers for whom the cost of care $k$ is greatest may take less than due care. (See case 2 of Proposition 4.1.) In §4A.1.2 it was shown that even if courts can distinguish an injurer's type, it may be best to set due care at a level that some injurers cannot or will not meet (so as to induce them not to engage in the activity). In §§4A.3.1–4A.3.3 three types of uncertainty were discussed that give rise to the possibility of findings of negligence despite injurers' attempts to avoid liability by their choice of $x$. (It is possible, however, to construct examples where there is no chance of finding negligence when $x$ is optimally chosen.) It was observed in §4A.3.4 that if injurers know the level of due care will exceed $x^* + l(x^*)$, then injurers will decide not to take due care. Last, it is clear from §4A.3.5 that if injurers take perceived due care that is less than actual due care, they will be found negligent if accidents occur; if they do not take perceived due care and the actual level of due care exceeds the optimal level, the same will be true.

*4A.4.2   Strict liability and negligence rules compared.* Injurers would act optimally under strict liability in the models studied in §§4A.1–4A.3, because injurers' objective function would in each case be the social one. In §4A.1.1 injurers of type $k$ would minimize $kx + l(x)$; in §4A.1.2 they would maximize $u - [kx + l(x)]$; in §4A.2 they would minimize $z + k(z)x + l(x)$. In §4A.3 they would minimize $x + l(x)$; uncertainty, error, and misperceptions about the negligence determination would be irrelevant.

Thus, in the extensions of the unilateral model of accidents above, strict liability is at least as good as the negligence rule (only in §4A.2 are they equivalent, where the negligence rule also results in optimality). However, were the same extensions considered in the bilateral model and were strict liability with the defense of contributory negligence compared with the negligence rule, it would not be clear which rule would be best. This is because under strict liability with the defense of contributory negligence victims might behave suboptimally, because of use of a uniform standard of due care or uncertainty over the contributory negligence determination, and the like.

*4A.4.3  The different versions of the negligence rule reconsidered.* It was shown in the bilateral model of Chapter 2 that parties will act optimally under the negligence rule whether or not the rule is accompanied by the defense of contributory negligence. They also will act optimally under the comparative negligence rule. But when the bilateral model is extended along the lines presented here, parties will not necessarily act optimally—and they generally will act differently—under the different versions of the negligence rule. In essence, this is because findings of negligence and of contributory negligence will occur.

The differences among the rules may be roughly described as follows. To the extent that *injurers* will be found negligent, victims will have less incentive to take care under the negligence rule without the defense of contributory negligence than under the comparative negligence rule, and less incentive to take care under the latter rule than under the negligence rule with the defense of contributory negligence. Conversely, to the extent that *victims* will be found contributorily negligent, injurers will have less incentive to take care under the negligence rule with the defense of contributory negligence than under the comparative negligence rule, and less incentive to take care under the latter rule than under the negligence rule without the defense of contributory negligence.

The precise nature of the comparison of behavior and of social welfare under the different rules appears subtle,[20] as is exemplified by the following section.

---

20. The comparison not only seems subtle, but it depends on the particular reason for findings of negligence and contributory negligence. In §4A.4.4 the reason for findings of negligence will be that parties differ in their ability to take care. If instead the reason for findings of negligence were that courts make errors in observing levels of care, the analysis, if not the conclusions, would be different.

*4A.4.4 Analysis of an illustrative situation.* Assume that there are two types of injurers and of victims: *atypical* injurers and victims, who are unable to take care (or whose costs of taking care are extremely high); and *typical* injurers and victims, for whom the cost of taking a unit of care is 1. Suppose too that courts cannot distinguish between the two types of injurers and of victims and will set a uniform level of due care for all injurers and for all victims.[21]

Let the proportion of atypical injurers among the population of injurers be $\alpha$ and that of atypical victims be $\beta$, where $\alpha$ and $\beta$ are each in $(0, 1)$. (The total population of injurers is normalized to 1, as is the population of victims.) Given the levels of care $x$ and $y$ exercised by typical injurers and typical victims, total accident losses will be

$$(4.16) \quad (1 - \alpha)x + (1 - \beta)y + \alpha\beta l(0,0) + \alpha(1 - \beta)l(0,y)$$
$$+ (1 - \alpha)\beta l(x,0) + (1 - \alpha)(1 - \beta)l(x,y).$$

Here, $(1 - \alpha)x$ are the costs of care taken by typical injurers, $(1-\beta)y$ the costs of care taken by typical victims, $\alpha\beta l(0,0)$ the expected losses due to accidents involving atypical injurers and atypical victims, and so on. (Assume for simplicity that the conditional probabilities of involvement in an accident follow the population proportions.) Denote as usual the socially optimal values of $x$ and $y$ by $x^*$ and $y^*$; denote the optimal values of $x$ given $y$, and of $y$ given $x$, by $x^*(y)$ and $y^*(x)$; assume that $x^*(y)$, $y^*(x)$, and $l(x,y)$ are positive; and assume that Exp. (4.16) is convex in $x$ and $y$. From Exp. (4.16) it is apparent that $x^*$ minimizes

$$(4.17) \quad x + \beta l(x,0) + (1 - \beta)l(x,y^*),$$

and that $y^*$ minimizes

$$(4.18) \quad y + \alpha l(0,y) + (1 - \alpha)l(x^*,y).$$

In other words, the optimal levels of care reflect the possibility that typical injurers might be involved in accidents with both atypical and typical victims and that typical victims might be involved with both types of injurers.

---

21. This model is studied in a section of my article, Shavell 1983, comparing the negligence rule with and without the defense of contributory negligence in a sequential context. The model is also studied in Rea 1986, who compares the comparative negligence rule and the two other versions of the negligence rule but arrives at results different from those shown here; see note 22 below. Other examinations of versions of the negligence rule in models where parties are not identical or where there is uncertainty surrounding the determination of negligence are in Diamond 1974a, sec. 9, and in Green 1976.

Consider now whether typical parties can be induced to act optimally under the different versions of the negligence rule and how the versions compare with each other.[22]

Under the negligence rule with the defense of contributory negligence, typical injurers and typical victims will be induced to act optimally if $\beta$ is sufficiently low. Specifically, suppose that $\bar{x} = x^*$ and $\bar{y} = y^*$. Then assuming that typical injurers choose $x^*$, typical victims will reason as follows. If they choose $y < y^*$, their expected expenses will be $y + \alpha l(0,y) + (1 - \alpha)l(x^*, y)$. Since we know from Exp. (4.18) that this expression will be minimized at $y^*$, typical victims will be strictly better off taking due care of $y^*$ and avoiding bearing their accident losses. Now assume that typical victims choose $y^*$. Then if typical injurers choose $x < x^*$, their expected expenses will be $x + (1 - \beta)l(x,y^*)$. But then, from Exp. (4.17), $x + \beta l(x,0) + (1 - \beta)l(x,y^*) > x^* + \beta l(x^*,0) + (1 - \beta)l(x^*,y^*) > x^*$. Hence if $\beta$ is sufficiently low, typical injurers will be better off taking $x^*$ and avoiding liability. Thus, typical injurers and typical victims will indeed act optimally in equilibrium for all $\beta$ sufficiently low.

Under the negligence rule without the defense of contributory negligence, typical injurers and typical victims will never act optimally in equilibrium. To show this, assume otherwise. In particular, typical injurers will take care of $x^*$, and due care must be $x^*$.[23] Thus typical victims' expected expenses will be $y + (1 - \alpha)l(x^*,y)$. Comparing this to Exp. (4.18), it is clear that typical victims will choose $y < y^*$, a contradiction.

It is possible, however, that use of the negligence rule without the defense of contributory negligence will be superior to use of the negligence rule with the defense. If $\beta$ is high and $\alpha$ is low, then under the negligence rule with the defense typical injurers will take very little care (since $\beta$ is high), while typical victims will take optimal care given injurers' care. Under the negligence rule without the defense, typical victims will take close to optimal care (since $\alpha$ is low), while typical injurers will take optimal care given victims' care. Hence, it is clear that it is possible for the rule without the defense to be superior. (Loosely, if it is more important to the reduction of total accident costs that

22. In Rea 1986, the main question addressed is different. Rea asks whether typical parties can be induced to take the levels of care that would be optimal were there no atypical parties; he shows that typical parties can be induced to do so under the comparative negligence rule.

23. If due care were unequal to $x^*$ and typical injurers took due care, then they would not take care of $x^*$, a contradiction. If due care were so high that typical injurers did not take due care and instead chose $x^*$, then typical victims would never bear their losses. Hence typical victims would take care of 0, a contradiction. We can therefore assume that due care is $x^*$.

typical victims take care than that typical injurers do, the rule without the defense will be preferred.)

The comparative negligence rule will always be superior to the negligence rule without the defense of contributory negligence. To demonstrate this, let $x^o$ and $y^o$ be the optimal values of care taken by typical parties if we assume that the rule is the negligence rule without the defense of contributory negligence. Then it must be that $x^o = \bar{x}$.[24] Assume first that typical injurers strictly prefer choosing $x^o = \bar{x}$. We know that typical victims will choose $y^o < y^*(x^o)$, because they choose $y$ to minimize $y + (1 - \alpha)l(x^o, y)$ rather than to minimize Exp. (4.18). Thus, because it has been assumed that Exp. (4.16) is convex, total accident costs will be lowered if typical victims marginally increase care and typical injurers continue to choose $x^o$. But that outcome can be accomplished through use of the comparative negligence rule. Let an injurer bear a large fraction of liability if both he and a victim are negligent; let $\bar{x} = x^o$; and let $\bar{y}$ be slightly greater than $y^o$. Then a typical injurer will continue to choose $x^o$, since he strictly preferred $x^o$ under the negligence rule without the defense of contributory negligence. Moreover, a typical victim will choose $\bar{y}$ for some appropriately chosen $\bar{y} > y^o$, since he now has a greater motive to take care than he had under the negligence rule without the defense of contributory negligence (he now bears a positive fraction of his losses if he takes care of $y^o$ and is injured by a negligent injurer).

The case where injurers are indifferent between choosing $x^o = \bar{x}$ and $x < \bar{x}$ remains to be considered. In this case it must be that $\bar{x} > x^*(y^o)$; for, from Exp. (4.17), it is clear that for $\bar{x} \leq x^*(y^o)$ injurers would strictly prefer $\bar{x}$ to a lesser $x$. It follows that total accident costs will be reduced if injurers marginally lower $x$ and victims continue to take $y^o$. But by an argument similar to that given in the other case, this outcome can be achieved under the comparative negligence rule.

Finally, an argument analogous to that given above can be constructed to establish that when the negligence rule with the defense of contributory negligence does not result in optimal behavior (that is, when $\beta$ is not low), the comparative negligence rule will be superior to the negligence rule with the defense.[25]

To summarize what has been said about the different versions of the negligence rule (assuming that each is used optimally): for $\beta$ sufficiently low, the

24. Otherwise typical injurers would be negligent, implying that typical victims would choose $y = 0$. This is an outcome that it is easy to show can be dominated under the negligence rule without the defense of contributory negligence by setting $\bar{x}$ slightly below $x^o$.
25. The argument, which is tedious, is available from me.

optimal outcome will be achieved under the negligence rule with the defense of contributory negligence; otherwise, comparative negligence will be superior to this rule; comparative negligence will always be superior to the negligence rule without the defense of contributory negligence; but the latter rule may be superior to the rule of negligence with the defense of contributory negligence.

# 5 | Causation and the Scope of Liability

To this point it has been assumed that any time an accident occurred one or another liability rule would automatically apply. In the present chapter, however, I examine the legal requirement that an accident must be of a certain type—that it must fall within the scope of liability—for a liability rule to apply. Specifically, in §5.1 I investigate restriction of the scope of liability to accidents that parties caused, and in §5.2 I consider a further restriction of the scope of liability concerning "coincidence."[1] In §5.3 I discuss the subject of uncertainty over causation.

## 5.1 Accidents Caused by Injurers

In this part "necessary causation" is defined and its relevance for the determination of the socially optimal level of care is described. Then the effect of restricting the scope of liability to accidents that were necessarily caused by injurers is analyzed, under both strict liability and the negligence rule.

*5.1.1 Definition of necessary causation.* In some accidents the victim would have suffered the harm he in fact suffered even if the injurer had acted differently. Suppose, for example, that a town does not erect a seawall to

---

1. As readers familiar with tort law know, these are two major ways in which most legal systems limit the scope of liability; see §§5.1.7 and 5.2.6. There are also other ways in which the scope of liability is restricted. Notably, in Anglo-American law a party is not liable unless he violates a "duty" of care to the victim; and in the German and some other legal systems he is not liable unless his behavior was "unlawful." Although these requirements may overlap to some degree with those that are examined here (especially in §5.2) and with the negligence determination itself, they do have distinctive aspects. In any case, they will not be discussed below.

*Table 5.1*   Consequences as a function of the action and the state of the world

| Actions | State A (moderate hurricane strikes town) | State B (severe hurricane strikes town) |
| --- | --- | --- |
| Town does not erect seawall | Water damage | Water damage |
| Town erects seawall | No water damage | Water damage |

protect beachfront property, that a severe hurricane strikes the town and ocean water damages the property, but that the wind-driven waves were so high that they would have breached a seawall, had one been erected, and resulted in losses identical to those which occurred. With regard to an accident like this, it is natural to say that the losses were not caused by the town's failure to take care, since the losses would have occurred anyway.

To be more precise, the consequences that will follow from an injurer taking a particular action will depend on the particular situation that obtains, that is, on the particular *state of the world* that obtains.[2] In the example concerning the seawall, consider for simplicity two states of the world and the consequences each state would have, given a particular action (see Table 5.1). We would say here that if state B obtains, the action "town does not erect seawall" would not be the cause—or, more exactly, the necessary cause—of the consequence "water damage." But we would say that if state A obtains, the action "town does not erect seawall" would be the necessary cause of the consequence "water damage," for if the action "town erects seawall" had been taken, the consequence "water damage" would not have occurred. In general, define one action to be the *necessary cause* of a consequence relative to another action if, given the state of the world, the consequence would have been different had the second action been taken. (For simplicity, though, I will often use the term "cause" instead of "necessary cause.")

*5.1.2   Necessary causation and socially optimal care.* Consider for convenience the unilateral model of accidents and the social goal of minimization of injurers' costs of care plus expected accident losses. Then, as the next example illustrates, the socially optimal level of care is determined only by the possibility of states of the world in which losses would be caused by injurers' failure to take greater care.

2. The notion of a state of the world (sometimes called a "state of nature") is discussed in any treatment of decision theory; see, for example, Savage 1972, chap. 2, or Raiffa's 1968 text.

*Table 5.2*

| Level of care | Cost of care | Losses in state A (where accidents would be caused by injurers' failure to take care) | Losses in state B (where accidents would occur regardless of care) |
| --- | --- | --- | --- |
| None | 0 | 100 | 100 |
| Care | 5 | 0 | 100 |

EXAMPLE 5.1   Suppose that the effect of taking care in each of two possible states of the world in which accidents can occur is as shown in Table 5.2 and that accidents do not occur in other states of the world. Whether it is socially optimal for care to be exercised is affected solely by the likelihood of state A. In particular, exercising care will be optimal if and only if the likelihood of state A exceeds 5 percent, for then and only then will the expected reduction in accident losses be greater than the cost of care. To verify this, and to see explicitly that the likelihood of state B is irrelevant, consider the situation if the likelihood of state A is, say, 7 percent. In this case taking care will reduce expected losses by 7 (and will be socially worthwhile), whatever is the probability of state B. When, for example, the probability of state B is 3 percent, expected losses if care is not taken will be 10 (since $7\% \times 100 + 3\% \times 100 = 10$) and expected losses if care is taken will be 3; so taking care will reduce expected losses by 7. Similarly, if the probability of state B is different, for instance, 10 percent, taking care will also reduce expected losses by 7, for expected losses if care is not taken will be 17 and expected losses if care is taken will be 10.

It is apparent from this example why the optimal level of care is determined only by the possibility of states of the world in which accidents would be caused by injurers' failure to take more care: by definition, care has no effect on losses in other states of the world. A seawall will have no effect on losses when hurricanes are so severe that the seawall will be breached; a seawall will be socially valuable only to the extent that hurricanes are not so severe that absence of a seawall would be the cause of losses.

*5.1.3   Necessary causation and restriction of the scope of strict liability.* Suppose that the liability rule is strict liability and that the scope of injurers' liability is restricted to accidents that they cause. Injurers will then be led to exercise socially optimal care because, as was just emphasized, it is only these accidents that determine optimal care. If injurers in Example 5.1 are liable only for accidents in state A, they will take care whenever the probability of state A exceeds 5 percent, which is the socially optimal behavior.

Observe, however, that if the scope of liability were unrestricted, injurers would also be led to take optimal care; they would not be motivated to take greater-than-optimal care since taking more care would not reduce their liability for accidents that would occur anyway. Injurers liable for accidents in both states A and B in Example 5.1 will, as before, take care only if the probability of state A exceeds 5 percent.

*5.1.4  Necessary causation and restriction of the scope of liability for negligence.* The conclusions under the negligence rule are essentially the same as those under strict liability. If the scope of injurers' liability for negligence is restricted to accidents that they cause, they will be led to take optimal care—assuming that the level of due care is optimal. Suppose in Example 5.1 that the probability of state A is 7 percent. In this case injurers will be led to take care if they would be found liable for failure to take care only in state A; for if they take care, their costs will be 5, whereas if they do not take care, their expected liability will be 7. The reason that this result is generally true is that, because the optimal level of care is determined by considering the effect of care only in circumstances where taking care would prevent harm, the threat of liability in those same circumstances is enough to induce optimal behavior.

Were liability for negligence unrestricted in scope optimal behavior would also result, since the threat of liability would be wielded more often.

*5.1.5  Affirmative reasons for restricting the scope of liability.* It has been shown that restricting the scope of liability to accidents caused by injurers does not disadvantageously affect incentives to take care, but affirmative reasons for restricting the scope of liability have not been offered. One such reason, applying primarily where liability is strict, is that without restriction of liability injurers could be discouraged from engaging in an activity that is socially worthwhile; they might find their potential liability "crushing." If injurers are to make correct decisions whether to engage in an activity, they must bear only the *increment* in expected losses occasioned by their activity. If injurers in Example 5.1 are to decide correctly whether to engage in their activity, they must bear only the losses in state A; the losses in state B are going to occur anyway. If a firm is to decide correctly whether to engage in an activity that creates a carcinogenic risk, the firm must be held responsible only for the increase in the incidence of the cancer it engenders, not for the background incidence that would have been observed in any case.

This point has some bearing under the negligence rule as well, for because of uncertainties and error in the negligence determination injurers might be found negligent even if they attempt to take due care (see §4.4.1).

Another affirmative reason for restricting the scope of liability concerns the possibility of a savings in the administrative costs of using the legal system. Restricting the scope of liability to accidents caused by injurers will lower the volume of cases that are brought and thus tend to reduce administrative costs. On the other hand, when cases are brought courts will have to decide on the issue of causation, which will tend to raise administrative costs. If this latter factor is less important than the former, the causal restriction of the scope of liability will decrease administrative costs.

*5.1.6  Remarks.* (1) The relevance of the analysis in the above sections will be greater the higher is the probability that an accident in which an injurer is involved was not caused by the injurer. This probability will sometimes be significant (as with cancers that could be caused by a variety of factors). But in many contexts the probability will be small; an injurer will be almost sure that an accident that occurs will have been caused by him. (If an individual is practicing archery, he will be almost certain that a person struck by one of his arrows would not otherwise have been harmed.)

(2) It will often be easy for courts to ascertain whether an injurer's act was the cause of an accident (as in a case where an arrow shot by a single archer strikes a person), but frequently it will be difficult. Sometimes problems will arise from courts' inability to tell which of several parties or factors was the one that caused harm (which of several archers shot the arrow that struck the person, which of several carcinogens led to the cancer); and other times problems will be due to courts' having to answer hypothetical questions (what would have happened during the hurricane had there in fact been a seawall?). In §5.3 I will, as noted earlier, discuss the determination of liability when there is uncertainty over causation.

*5.1.7  Actual restriction of the scope of liability and necessary causation.* A basic feature of all legal systems is that a party's behavior must have been what has here been called a necessary cause of an accident for liability to be found.[3] No liability would be found for failure to erect a seawall if a seawall would have been breached during a storm or for failure to maintain adequately an aircraft if it would have crashed in any case. The fact that the occurrence of an accident and an injurer's negligence, or his ostensible responsibility under strict liability, are not enough to make him liable is variously expressed: for a party to be held liable, his behavior must have been a

3. See *Prosser and Keeton on Torts* (Keeton, Dobbs, et al. 1984), sec. 41, Becht and Miller 1961, and Malone 1958 on Anglo-American law; and see Honoré 1971, secs. 15, 106–118, on other legal systems. There are, however, certain exceptions to the requirement of necessary causation. For example, where either of several injurers' acts alone would have been sufficient to cause harm, they will not all be free from responsibility even though had any one alone not acted, the harm would still have occurred.

"cause in fact" of harm, a condition sine qua non of harm, or a "but for" cause of harm (as in, "but for his negligence, the harm would never have occurred").

Courts and commentators usually offer little reason for the requirement of necessary causation. They seem to believe that there must be *some* connection between a party's act and harm done for liability to be imposed. And they appear to feel on intuitive grounds that the particular requirement of necessary causation is the only natural way to make the connection. (In what other conceivable way, they occasionally ask, could a connection be made?)

## 5.2  Coincidental Accidents

Some accidents that are caused by injurers are commonly described as involving an element of coincidence. Suppose, for instance, that lightning happens to strike a bus that was being driven at excessive speed. The excessive speed of the bus is the cause of the accident, since if the bus had been going more slowly it would not have reached the point of the road at just the "right" time to be struck by lightning. But we would probably say that the fact that the bus was speeding was unrelated to the accident, or had nothing to do with it, for the accident would have been avoided if the bus had been traveling faster as well as if it had been traveling at a lesser speed. Likewise, suppose that X invites Y to his home for dinner and that on the way Y slips on ice and breaks his leg. Here too we would be inclined to say that the accident was in some sense coincidental to, or was not closely related to, the injurer X's act, the dinner invitation, even though the invitation caused the accident.

In the next section I will show that there is a similar feature in these accidents and in most that we are likely to call coincidental. Then I will discuss the connection between the occurrence of coincidental accidents and socially optimal care and, finally, the effect of excluding coincidental accidents from the scope of liability.

*5.2.1  Characterization of coincidental accidents.* Accidents that are called coincidental can be demonstrated to be accidents of a type whose probability and severity are not altered by injurers' behavior. More precisely, they can be shown to be of a type for which expected losses are not altered by injurers' behavior. In the case of the bus struck by lightning, for example, the reader should find it plausible that the speed of the bus does not affect the probability or severity of its being struck by lightning. However, further discussion is merited. Suppose that the bus can be struck by lightning in either of two states of the world, as illustrated in Table 5.3.[4] Assume that the

4. It will be clear that if there were a continuum of states of the world—each corresponding to lightning striking one of the continuum of points along the road—there would be no real change in the following analysis.

*Table 5.3*  Consequences as a function of the action and the state of the world

| Actions | State A (lightning strikes near point along road) | State B (lightning strikes far point along road) |
|---|---|---|
| Bus speeds | Bus safe | Bus struck |
| Bus does not speed | Bus struck | Bus safe |

probability that lightning will strike the near point along the road equals the probability that it will strike the far point. Then the probability that lightning will strike the bus will not be altered by whether the bus speeds. Although it is true that if the bus speeds and state B occurs, the bus's speed will be the cause of the bus being struck by lightning, it is also true that if the bus speeds and state A occurs, the bus's speed will be the cause of the bus *not* being struck by lightning. This observation resolves the apparent paradox that the bus's speed may be a cause of the bus being struck by lightning, yet the bus's speed does not increase the probability of the type of accident in which the bus is struck by lightning.

An essentially identical analysis applies to the example concerning the dinner invitation. Suppose that the type of accident is "Y breaks his leg going somewhere"; that the two actions are "Y goes to X's for dinner" and "Y goes to the movies"; and that the two equally probable states of the world are "the sidewalk on the way to the movies is icy" and "the sidewalk on the way to X's home is icy." Then it is just as probable that Y will break his leg going to X's as it is that he will break his leg going to the movies; a dinner invitation will thus not increase the probability of the type of accident "Y breaks his leg going somewhere."

The reader can use the logic pertaining in the cases of the dinner invitation and the speeding bus to convince himself that, in general, accidents that have a coincidental aspect are of a type whose probability and magnitude are not affected by the injurer's level of care.

*5.2.2  Remark on the definition of the type of an accident.* The reader may note that there is no logical way of defining the type of an accident; a particular accident can be classified as being of many different types.[5] For instance, the accident where Y falls on the icy sidewalk on the way to X's home could be said to be of the type "Y breaks his leg on the way to X's home" rather than of the broader type "Y breaks his leg going somewhere." Furthermore, although we have seen that the probability of the type "Y breaks his leg going

---

5. Formally, a type of accident is defined to be the set of accidents involving a given harm occurring in any state among a specified set of states of the world. The larger the set, the broader the type of accident.

somewhere" is not raised by X's dinner invitation, the probability of the type "Y breaks his leg on the way to X's home" is presumably raised by X's invitation because the invitation increases the probability that Y goes to X's home. Thus the answer to the question "Did the injurer's action alter the probability of an accident of the type that occurred?" depends on the classification of the accident as to type.

This last point, however, does not make ambiguous the characterization of coincidental accidents given in §5.2.1. We are likely to call an accident coincidental as long as there exists *some* recognizable way of defining the type of the accident with the property that the injurer's act did not raise the probability of the defined type of accident. Moreover, the arguments to be made below depend only on the assumption that there exists some such definition of the type of an accident.

*5.2.3  Coincidence and socially optimal care.* Assume that there are two types of accident: coincidental accidents (buses being struck by lightning), whose probability and severity are unaffected by the level of care; and accidents that are not coincidental (buses colliding with other vehicles), whose probability or severity is affected by the level of care. The socially optimal level of care is determined only by the risk of accidents that are not coincidental, as is illustrated in the following example.

EXAMPLE 5.2    Table 5.4 shows expected losses given the occurrence of coincidental versus other types of accident. Whether it is socially optimal for care to be taken obviously depends only on the probability that a noncoincidental type of accident will occur. The reader can readily check that care will be worthwhile if the probability of the noncoincidental accident exceeds 10 percent, for then the expected reduction in losses will exceed $10\% \times 50 = 5$. The probability of coincidental accidents is irrelevant. Suppose, for instance, that the probability of noncoincidental accidents is 15 percent and that of coincidental accidents is 5 percent. If no care is taken expected losses will be $5\% \times 30 + 15\% \times 60 = 10.5$ and if care is taken expected losses will be $5\% \times 30 + 15\% \times 10 = 3$; so taking care will reduce expected losses by 7.5 (and will be socially worthwhile). Taking care will also reduce expected losses by 7.5 if the probability of coincidental accidents is other than 5 percent. If the probability of such situations is, say, 20 percent, then expected losses will be $20\% \times 30 + 15\% \times 60 = 15$ if no care is taken and $20\% \times 30 + 15\% \times 10 = 7.5$ if care is taken. That is, taking care will again reduce expected losses by 7.5.

The example shows that the socially optimal level of care is not influenced by the possibility of coincidental accidents since the exercise of care does not affect expected accident losses due to coincidental accidents.

*Table 5.4*

| Level of care | Cost of care | Expected losses in coincidental type of accident | Expected losses in noncoincidental type of accident |
|---|---|---|---|
| None | 0 | 30 | 60 |
| Care | 5 | 30 | 10 |

*5.2.4 Coincidence and restriction of the scope of liability.* It should be clear from the previous section that if the scope of strict liability is restricted to accidents that are not coincidental in nature, that is, to accidents of a type whose probability or magnitude is affected by the exercise of care, then injurers will be led to take socially optimal care. In Example 5.2, injurers who are strictly liable only for noncoincidental accidents will be led to take care if and only if the probability of that type of accident exceeds 10 percent, which is what is socially desirable.

Likewise, if the scope of liability under the negligence rule is similarly restricted, injurers will still be led to take optimal care, provided that due care equals optimal care. Suppose in Example 5.2 that the probability of noncoincidental accidents is over 10 percent and that injurers will be liable for failure to take care only if they cause noncoincidental accidents. Then if injurers do not take care their expected liability will exceed 6, whereas if they do take care their cost will be 5 and they will avoid liability. Consequently they will prefer to take care.

If, however, the scope of liability under either the negligence rule or strict liability includes coincidental as well as noncoincidental accidents, then injurers will still take optimal care, as the reader can easily verify.

*5.2.5 Affirmative reasons for restricting the scope of liability.* The affirmative reasons for restriction of the scope of liability here are as in §5.1.5. Namely, restriction of scope tends to prevent injurers from bearing more than the increment in expected accident losses that their activities create and thus forestalls the problem that injurers would be discouraged from engaging in socially worthwhile activities. Second, restriction of the scope of liability to noncoincidental accidents might reduce administrative costs by lowering the volume of cases brought.

Were these affirmative reasons for reducing the scope of liability introduced explicitly into the analysis of this part, it would become optimal to eliminate from the scope of liability not just coincidental accidents but also accidents of a type for which the exercise of care has a small, positive effect on expected losses.

*5.2.6   Actual restriction of the scope of liability and coincidence.* In Anglo-American law a variety of notions are employed to limit the scope of liability, after the requirement is met that the injurer's act must have been a necessary cause of the accident.[6] The accident involving the bus, for instance, would likely be said to be outside the scope of liability on the ground that the speed of the bus was not the "proximate cause" of its being struck by lightning, or that its being struck by lightning was not the "probable consequence" of speeding, or that lightning was not "within the normal risk" created by speeding. It appears from the cases that the use of such terms serves implicitly to accomplish the task of excluding from the scope of liability accidents of a type whose probability and severity could not have been much influenced by injurers' acts, that is, accidents that have here been called coincidental.[7]

In the German legal system, the scope of liability is restricted through application of a causal principle which by its definition looks immediately to the effect of injurers' behavior on the probability of the type of accident that occurred. This principle is that of "adequate cause," which says that injurers' behavior must have significantly or "adequately" raised the probability of the type of accident for it to be within the scope of liability. The adequacy theory and its variants have been influential in the legal systems of countries other than Germany as well.[8]

*5.2.7   Note on the literature.* Calabresi (1975a) first discussed the effect of restriction of the scope of liability on the behavior of parties. He suggested that use of the requirement of necessary causation would give parties proper incentives to reduce risk and that other causal requirements impose liability where the incentives thereby created to reduce risk are greatest.[9] In Shavell (1980a), I elaborated and formalized these ideas, along the lines presented in

6. See generally Fleming 1983, chap. 9, *Prosser and Keeton on Torts* (Keeton, Dobbs, et al. 1984), chap. 7, and *Restatement (Second) of Torts* 1965, secs. 430–462. Also, see the following books devoted to the topic: Green 1927, Hart and Honoré 1985, and Keeton 1963.

7. Consider the concept of the normal risk, which now tends to be important. According to this concept, only those accidents falling within the normal risk created by an act should be within the scope of liability. For example, since the normal risk created by a bus's speeding is that it will collide with other objects or go off the road, only these accidents should be within the scope of liability. Exclusion of harms falling outside the normal risk seems, on reflection, to be equivalent to exclusion of harms of a type whose probability and severity could not have been much affected by injurers' acts.

8. See generally Honoré 1971, especially secs. 20 and 80–90.

9. A key passage states that "the function of the . . . requirement . . . is to assure that the injury costs . . . include only those costs relevant to the choice between injury and safety" (p. 85). This and much of what Calabresi says makes the most sense if parties actually have to pay for the losses they cause, that is, if the form of liability is strict.

§§5.1 and 5.2 here. Landes and Posner (1983) and Grady (1984) further developed the subject.

## 5.3 Uncertainty over Causation

Two ways of treating cases in which there is uncertainty over whether an injurer was the cause of losses will be considered here. In what follows, the probability that an injurer was the cause of losses will be referred to as the *probability of causation.*

*5.3.1 Threshold probability criterion.* Under this criterion a liability rule will be applied only if the probability of causation exceeds a given threshold probability. Thus if the threshold probability is 50 percent, the relevant liability rule will be applied only if it is more likely than not that the injurer was the cause of the victim's losses.

Two types of problem can arise under a threshold probability criterion. First, the probability of causation might be systematically less than the threshold probability. In that situation an injurer will face too little liability and, consequently, will do too little to reduce risk. Suppose that 40 percent of all cases of lung cancer among individuals living near a factory are caused by a carcinogen released by the factory, but that courts cannot distinguish these cases from the 60 percent of cases due to other causes. Since the probability that the factory is the cause of lung cancer will be 40 percent in every case, the factory will always escape liability under the 50 percent threshold probability criterion. Hence the factory will have too little incentive to take care and too great an incentive to engage in its activity. (Examples like this one can obviously be constructed whatever the value of the threshold probability.)

On the other hand, the situation could be the reverse; the probability of causation might systematically exceed the threshold. In that situation an injurer will bear too much liability, creating opposite problems. If the probability that the factory is the cause of lung cancer is 60 percent, then the factory will always face liability according to the 50 percent threshold probability criterion. Thus, under strict liability, the factory will pay for all losses, and consequently for more losses than it truly causes. The result might be that the factory will take more than optimal care or decide not to operate when it is socially desirable that it continue to do so. Under a perfectly functioning negligence rule, however, this will not happen; the only consequence of the factory's being exposed to liability for all cases of lung cancer is that it will have an enhanced motive to take due care. But given the uncertainties surrounding the determination of negligence, disadvantages analogous to those under strict liability become relevant.

*5.3.2 Liability in proportion to the probability of causation.* Under this approach a liability rule will be applied no matter what the probability of causation is, but the amount a liable injurer will pay equals the victim's losses multiplied by the probability of causation. It follows that an injurer will face expected liability equal to the expected losses he causes. For example, where the probability that the factory causes lung cancer is 40 percent, the factory, if liable, will pay 40 percent of the losses in all cases of lung cancer. This amount is the same as what the factory would pay if it were liable for the entire losses in only the 40 percent of lung cancer cases it actually causes.[10] Since under the proportional approach injurers face expected liability equal to the expected losses they cause, injurers will behave as they would in the absence of uncertainty over causation. Thus injurers will be led to take optimal care under liability rules, to make desirable decisions about engaging in activities under strict liability, and so forth.

*5.3.3 Remarks.* (1) The above conclusions about the threshold probability criterion and the proportional approach are equally valid whether the uncertainty over causation concerns some "natural" factor—a radioactive gas escaping from the earth, say—or some other injurer. In regard to the latter, it should be noted that where courts do not know which of several sellers of an identical product sold the particular unit that caused harm, use of the proportional approach is equivalent to determining liability in proportion to market share (assuming that the probability that the unit was manufactured by a seller equals the seller's market share).

(2) Some writers employing an economic method of analysis have come to the conclusion that use of the 50 percent threshold probability is superior to use of the proportional approach. Their argument is based on the assumption that the social goal is minimization of "error costs," defined as the sum of dollars that injurers pay in cases where they were not truly the cause of losses and dollars that injurers do not have to pay in cases where they were in fact the cause of losses.[11]

10. Suppose, for instance, that the losses per case are $100,000, that there are 10 cases, and that the factory causes 4 of these. Then under the proportional approach, the factory faces liability of $40,000 × 10 or $400,000, which equals $100,000 × 4, the liability the factory would face in the absence of uncertainty over causation.

11. See, for example, Kaye 1982. The essence of the argument can be understood by considering the numerical example in n. 10 above, where under the 50 percent threshold probability criterion the factory will escape liability. Therefore, error costs will arise only from the 4 cases that the factory truly causes but does not pay for. Error costs will thus be $400,000. Under proportional liability, the factory will pay $40,000 in each case, and error costs will be as follows. In each of the 4 cases truly caused by the factory, error costs will be $60,000 (dollars not paid that should have been), or $240,000; and in each of the 6 cases not caused by the factory, error costs will be $40,000 (dollars paid that shouldn't have been), or

Apparently, minimization of these error costs is often taken as the social objective for two reasons: error costs are a mathematically workable criterion; and minimization of error costs seems to be a reasonable proxy for the true objective of minimization of the undesirable *consequences* flowing from legal errors (such as the number of cases of lung cancer). Because error costs are not a measure of accident losses, however, adherence to the goal of error-cost minimization can lead to anomalous implications. Notably, error-cost minimization leads to recommending use of the 50 percent threshold criterion even where that measure will result in injurers' never being liable for the losses they cause; it may thus provide grossly inadequate incentives to reduce risk (as in the example concerning the factory that causes 40 percent of the cases of lung cancer). In other words, error costs are a bad proxy for the undesirable consequences flowing from legal errors. Therefore, it may be a mistake for writers to adopt error-cost minimization as the social goal.[12]

(3) There are, nevertheless, reasons having to do with administrative costs to favor a threshold probability criterion over proportional liability. Specifically, a higher volume of cases would be expected under the proportional approach, because cases in which the probability of causation is less than the threshold could always be brought. Moreover, a greater number of defendants would be likely to be involved in the typical case under the proportional approach, for in principle any party for whom the probability of causation is positive could be named as a defendant. In addition, under the proportional approach the particular level of the probability of causation would be introduced as an issue of possible dispute among the parties, whereas under the threshold probability criterion all that matters is whether the probability of causation exceeds the threshold probability. Therefore the chance of settlement would be lower and the cost of trial higher than under a probability threshold criterion. Taken together, these disadvantages of the proportional approach suggest that its appeal may lie primarily in areas where there is substantial uncertainty over causation, which is to say, where use of the probability threshold criterion is likely to have substantial undesirable effects on incentives.

*5.3.4 Actual treatment of uncertainty over causation.* The general prac-

---

$240,000. Total error costs are consequently $480,000. Error costs are evidently higher under the proportional approach.

12. If making errors is felt to matter in itself, some measure of error costs would be appropriate to include as a component in the social calculus. But it would not be appropriate to adopt error-cost minimization as *the* social goal (unless of course all consequences flowing from errors were assumed to be unimportant—a supposition few analysts would wish to make).

tice is to hold a party fully liable if the probability that the party was the cause of losses is sufficiently high. What constitutes this threshold probability varies among the systems. In Anglo-American law the threshold is normally 50 percent; a "preponderance of probabilities" is required for liability to be found. In the German and several other legal systems the threshold is in theory near certainty. In the French system, it is said to be discretionary.[13] Use of the proportional approach is exceptional, although it has recently been employed (and vigorously debated) in the United States in cases involving uncertainty over which of multiple corporate defendants sold products that caused harm.[14]

   *5.3.5   Note on the literature.* Various of the points made here have been mentioned in a number of writings, such as Tribe (1971, p. 1350) and Posner (1986, p. 520). They have received the most emphasis in Rosenberg (1984); I extend and develop them formally in Shavell (1985b).


# Mathematical Appendix


Before proceeding to the issues concerning the scope of liability that were considered in the text, I will discuss the general meaning of the scope of liability. For convenience, I will restrict attention to the unilateral model of accidents and to injurers' choice of their level of care.

   Let *s* denote a *state of the world*, a complete description of the world; and let *S* denote the universe of possible *s*. Then given an injurer's level of care $x$, the losses, if any, arising in a state *s* are determined.[15] Specifically, suppose that

   $l(x,s)$ = losses given $x$ and a state of the world $s$; $l(x,s) \geqq 0$.

In previous chapters it was implicitly assumed that whenever an accident occurred, that is, whenever $(x,s)$ was such that $l(x,s) > 0$, a liability rule would apply. But here it is assumed that a liability rule will apply only if $l(x,s) > 0$ *and s* is in a set called the *scope of liability*. This set will be denoted

   13. See Honoré 1971, secs. 201–203.
   14. See the discussion of the DES cases in, for example, Robinson 1982.
   15. The general framework making use of states of the world, actions (which here are levels of care), and consequences (which here are losses) is, of course, that of decision theory. See Savage 1972 or Arrow 1971, chaps. 1 and 2.

by $S_c$; $S_c$ may in principle depend on $x$ and $l$. In other words, if payment under a liability rule is a function $f(x,l)$, an injurer will pay $f(x,l)$ when $l$ is positive only if $s$ is contained in $S_c$. It should be observed that use of the most general form of the scope of liability together with liability rules $f(x,l)$ would result in a less general form of liability than would liability rules $g(s,x,l)$. Under such rules $g$, liability can vary arbitrarily with $s$ for fixed $x$ and $l$. But under the general form of the scope of liability and rules $f$, liability cannot vary arbitrarily with $s$ for fixed $x$ and $l$; liability equals either $f(x,l)$ or 0.

## 5A.1 Necessary Causation

*5A.1.1 Definition of necessary cause.* Given the state of the world $s$, taking level of care $x_1$ is a *necessary cause* of losses of $l(x_1,s)$ relative to taking level of care $x_2$ if $l(x_1,s) \neq l(x_2,s)$. This definition must be stated as relative to a particular level of care $x_2$ since whether taking a level of care different from $x_1$ would change losses may depend on what the level of care alternative to $x_1$ is.

For simplicity, assume that given $s$ there are four types of loss functions $l$: (1) losses are strictly decreasing in $x$ wherever they are positive (corresponding to a situation where an accident's severity can be reduced by taking more care or where an accident can be entirely avoided by doing so); (2) losses are positive for one and only one level of $x$ and zero otherwise (corresponding to a situation such as that in the example in the text, where a bus would arrive at the right point along the road to be struck by lightning if and only if it went at one precise speed); (3) losses are positive and unaffected by $x$ (corresponding to a situation where there is another cause of losses); (4) losses are zero for all $x$ (corresponding to a situation where there can be no accident).

Let $C$ (for cause) be the set of states of the world with loss functions of types 1 or 2. Notice that if an accident occurs in any state in $C$, then the $x$ chosen by the injurer will be the necessary cause of the losses relative to any other $x$; in this case we shall say that the injurer was the cause of losses. Let $\sim$ stand for set subtraction, so that $S \sim C$ is the complement of $C$; if an accident occurs in any state in $S \sim C$, then, the chosen $x$ will not be the necessary cause of losses relative to any other $x$ (for if an accident occurs, the loss function must be of type 3). Observe also that $l(x|S \sim C)$, expected losses conditional on $S \sim C$, do not depend on $x$; and let

$$(5.1) \qquad l_{S \sim C} = l(x|S \sim C).$$

*5A.1.2 Necessary causation and socially optimal care.* It follows from the definitions above that the socially optimal level of care $x^*$ depends only on the loss function $l$ over the set $C$ of states such that injurers would be the necessary causes of any losses that occur. To show this, note that $l(x)$, expected losses given $x$, obey the identity

(5.2)     $l(x) = l(x|C)\Pr[C] + l(x|S \sim C)\Pr[S \sim C]$,

where $l(x|C)$ are expected losses given $C$ and Pr stands for probability. But, using Eq. (5.1), we may rewrite Eq. (5.2) as

$$l(x) = l(x|C)\Pr[C] + l_{S\sim C}\Pr[S \sim C].$$

It is therefore evident that the socially optimal level of care $x^*$ that minimizes $x + l(x)$ also minimizes

(5.3)     $x + l(x|C)\Pr[C]$,

which is to say that $x^*$ depends on $l$ only over $C$.

   *5A.1.3   Necessary causation and the scope of liability.* Suppose first that liability is strict. If the scope of liability $S_c$ equals $C$, then injurers will choose $x$ to minimize Exp. (5.3), so they will choose $x^*$. If the scope of liability is unrestricted (that is, $S_c = S$ and injurers will be liable for all accidents), injurers will minimize $x + l(x)$ and again choose $x^*$.

   Now consider the negligence rule and suppose that the scope of liability is restricted to $C$. Then assuming that due care $\bar{x} = x^*$, injurers will be led to take $x^*$ by the usual logic. If injurers choose $x \geq x^*$, they will clearly choose $x^*$ and their expenses will be $x^*$. If injurers choose $x < x^*$, their expected liability will be given by Exp. (5.3). But since $x^*$ minimizes Exp. (5.3) and is unique, it follows that

(5.4)     $x + l(x|C)\Pr[C] > x^* + l(x^*|C)\Pr[C] \geq x^*$,

which means that injurers will be best off choosing $x^*$. Last, suppose that the scope of liability for negligence is not restricted to $C$ and that $\bar{x} = x^*$. In this case injurers will certainly be led to take $x^*$, since if $x < x^*$ injurers' expected liability will be at least as great as the left-hand side of Ineq. (5.4).

   PROPOSITION 5.1   Suppose that the scope of liability is restricted to accidents for which injurers are the necessary causes of losses. Then under both strict liability and the negligence rule (with due care optimally determined) injurers will be led to take optimal care. If the scope of liability is unrestricted, then under both rules injurers will also be led to take optimal care.

*Remarks.* (1) Consider injurers' decisions whether to engage in their activity, and assume that injurers can engage in their activity at only one level, which will yield gross utility of $u$. Assume also that if injurers do not engage in their activity, victims' expected losses will be $l(x|S \sim C)$. Then it will be socially optimal for injurers to engage in their activity when $u > x^* + l(x^*|C)\Pr[C]$, or when $u - x^* > l(x^*|C)\Pr[C]$. That is, it will be optimal for injurers to engage in their activity when their utility, net of the cost of care, exceeds the *increment* in expected losses caused by their engaging in their activity. Hence under strict liability restricting the scope of liability to $C$ will induce injurers to engage in their activity exactly when they ought to; if liability is not restricted to accidents that injurers cause, injurers might be discouraged from engaging in their activity even though it would be optimal for them to engage in it.

It is clear that whether the scope of liability is restricted to $C$ will not influence injurers' decision to engage in their activity under the negligence rule, for whether or not the scope of liability is larger than $C$, injurers will engage in their activity whenever $u > x^*$ (which is too often, as explained earlier in §2A.2). (But whether the scope of liability is restricted to $C$ might be of significance if the factors noted in §4A.4.1 lead to findings of negligence.)

(2) Achievement of a savings in administrative costs is an affirmative reason for restricting the scope of liability to accidents that injurers cause.

(3) In practice, courts usually exclude an accident from the scope of liability if, given the state $s$, the injurer could not have lowered losses by taking more care. Under this principle courts would limit the scope of liability to $C$, for the injurer could have lowered losses if and only if the loss function given $s$ was of type 1 or 2. If, however, the loss functions given $s$ are allowed to be of arbitrary form, it is possible to construct examples in which injurers will not be led to exercise optimal care if courts use the principle under consideration.

## 5A.2   Coincidence

*5A.2.1   Definition of coincidental accidents.* It was argued in the text that accidents that are called coincidental are of a type whose probability and severity are not affected by the level of care. This motivates the following definition: An accident occurring in state $s$ is a *coincidence* if there exists a set $T$ of states containing $s$ with the property that expected losses given $T$, $l(x|T)$, do not depend on $x$. Notice that by this definition an accident occurring in any state $s$ in such a set $T$ is a coincidence, so $T$ may be referred to as a coincidental set. (The reader should recall from the example of the speeding bus discussed in the text that states $s$ with loss functions of type 2 might comprise a coincidental set.)[16] In general, there may be many coincidental sets.[17]

*5A.2.2  Coincidence and socially optimal care.* For any set, and thus for any coincidental set $T$, the identity below holds:

$$l(x) = l(x|T)\Pr[T] + l(x|S \sim T)\Pr[S \sim T].$$

Since $l(x|T)$ does not depend on $x$, we know that $x^*$ must minimize $x + l(x|S \sim T)\Pr[S \sim T]$. In other words, the socially optimal level of care does not depend on the loss function over the coincidental set. Moreover, making the assumptions of §5A.1.1 about the types of loss functions given $s$ and assuming there is a coincidental subset $T$ of $C$, we have the identity

$$l(x) = l(x|C \sim T)\Pr[C \sim T] + l(x|T)\Pr[T] + l_{S \sim C}\Pr[S \sim C],$$

and we thus know that $x^*$ minimizes

(5.5)    $x + l(x|C \sim T)\Pr[C \sim T].$

The socially optimal level of care is determined by the loss function only over $C \sim T$, that is, only by the possibility of accidents that injurers cause and that are not coincidental.

*5A.2.3  Coincidence and restriction of the scope of liability.* For any given coincidental subset $T$ of $C$, the next proposition follows by the logic of §5A.1.3, with $C \sim T$ in place of $C$ and Exp. (5.5) in place of Exp. (5.3).

PROPOSITION 5.2   Suppose that the scope of liability is restricted to accidents that injurers cause and that are not coincidental. Then under both strict liability and the negligence rule (with due care optimally determined), injurers will be led to take optimal care.

16.  Suppose that for every $x$ (speed of bus) there exists a unique state $s(x)$ (point on road that lightning will strike) such that $l(x, s(x))$ equals $l > 0$; for all other states $l(x, s)$ is 0; and the states $s(x)$ are equally likely.

17.  There may easily be more than one coincidental set containing a given state. Consider the following example supplied to me by Marcel Kahan. There are three equally likely states $s_1$, $s_2$ and $s_3$. If an injurer takes care and $s_1$ or $s_2$ occurs, no losses will result, but if $s_3$ occurs, losses of $l$ will result. If the injurer does not take care and $s_1$ or $s_2$ occurs, losses of $l$ will result, but if $s_3$ occurs, no losses will result. Then both $\{s_1, s_3\}$ and $\{s_2, s_3\}$ are coincidental sets and contain a common state ($s_3$).

*Remarks.* (1) Consider injurers' decisions whether to engage in their activity, as in Proposition 5.1, Remark 1, and assume that even when injurers do not engage in their activity the expected losses $l(x|T)$ will be borne by victims.[18] Then the conclusions parallel those from before. Namely, it will be socially optimal for injurers to engage in their activity when $u > x^* + l(x^*|C \sim T)\Pr[C \sim T]$. Thus both coincidental accidents and accidents where injurers are not the necessary causes must be excluded from the scope of strict liability for injurers to make optimal decisions whether to engage in their activity.

Suppose, however, that $l(x|T)$ will not be borne by victims if injurers do not engage in their activity.[19] Then it will be socially optimal for injurers to engage in their activity only when $u > x^* + l(x|C)\Pr[C]$; if coincidental accidents are excluded from the scope of strict liability, injurers might engage in their activity when they ought not.

(2) Achievement of a savings in administrative costs is, as before, an affirmative reason for excluding from the scope of liability accidents that are coincidental. Also, it should be clear that these savings will make it optimal to exclude sets for which the effect of care on expected losses is sufficiently small.

*5A.2.4   Note on the literature.* In Shavell (1980a) I first analyzed a model of causation and the scope of liability; §§5A.1 and 5A.2 largely follow that model.

## 5A.3   Uncertainty over Causation

*5A.3.1   The probability of causation.* Consider the following version of the model analyzed in §5A.1. The injurer's care affects the probability $p(x)$ that he will cause an accident involving losses of $l$ (where $p'(x) < 0$ and $p''(x) > 0$). There is also a fixed probability $q$ that a "natural" source will cause an accident involving losses of $l$. In every accident, either the injurer or the natural source will in fact be the cause, but courts will be uncertain which is the cause.

Under these assumptions total accident costs are $x + p(x)l + ql$, and the optimal level of care $x^*$ is the $x$ that minimizes $x + p(x)l$. Also, if an accident

---

18. This would be natural to assume if, for instance, riders on buses that could be struck by lightning by coincidence would in the absence of buses ride in streetcars—and thus could equally well be struck by lightning.

19. This would be appropriate to assume if riders on buses would in the absence of buses ride in subways and thus not bear the risk of being struck by lightning.

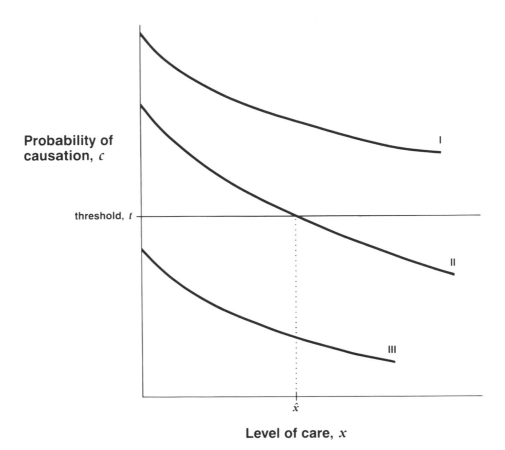

*Figure 5.1*

occurs, the conditional probability that an injurer caused the accident will be

$$c = \frac{p(x)}{p(x) + q};$$

$c$ shall be called the *probability of causation*. Note that since $p$ is decreasing in $x$, so is $c$. Consider now the two ways of treating uncertainty over causation that were discussed in the text.

*5A.3.2  Probability threshold criterion.* Under this criterion a liability rule will be applied when and only when the probability of causation exceeds a threshold probability $t$, where $0 < t < 1$. The relationship among $x$, $c$, and $t$ can be of three types, as shown in Figure 5.1.

In case I a liability rule will be applied regardless of $x$, and thus with probability $p(x) + q$. Accordingly, it is apparent by the usual logic that under the negligence rule injurers will take due care of $x^*$. In addition, under strict liability injurers will choose $x$ to minimize $x + [p(x) + q]l$, so they will also choose $x^*$.

Whether a liability rule will be applied in case II depends on $x$, and injurers' behavior will depend on the location of $x^*$ in relation to $\hat{x}$, defined as the $x$ at which $p(x)/[p(x) + q] = t$. Suppose first that $x^* < \hat{x}$. Then under the negligence rule an injurer will choose $x^*$: he will obviously not take more care; and if he takes less care, he will be found negligent and pay $l$ with probability $p(x) + q$ and thus by the usual logic be worse off than if he chose $x^*$. Under strict liability there are two possibilities. The injurer might choose $x < \hat{x}$, in which case, because his expected liability will be $[p(x) + q]l$, he will in fact choose $x^*$. However, if $\hat{x} < x^* + [p(x^*) + q]l$, he will choose $\hat{x}$ and escape liability. Now suppose that $x^* \geq \hat{x}$. Then under both liability rules an injurer will choose only $\hat{x}$, for this level of care will be sufficient to allow him to escape liability; whereas if he chooses a smaller $x$ his costs of care plus expected liability will be larger than $x^*$, which by assumption is at least $\hat{x}$.

In case III a liability rule will never be applied, hence under either rule an injurer will choose $x = 0$.

PROPOSITION 5.3   Suppose that a liability rule will be applied only if an injurer's probability of causation exceeds a threshold probability. Then under the negligence rule injurers might take too little care, and under strict liability they might take too little or too much care.

*Remark.*   An injurer's decision whether to engage in an activity under strict liability might be inappropriate. In case I he might choose not to engage in an activity when he ought to, for his expected liability will exceed the losses he causes by $ql$; and in cases II and III it is obvious that he might engage in an activity when he ought not to. (He might engage in an activity when he ought not to under the negligence rule also, but only for the reason discussed in §2A.2.)

*5A.3.3   Proportional liability.* Under this approach a liability rule will always be applied and a liable injurer will pay the victim's losses $l$ multiplied by the probability of causation. A liable injurer's expected liability will thus be

$$[p(x) + q]cl = p(x)l,$$

which means that, by the proofs in §2A, injurers will take optimal care under the liability rules.

PROPOSITION 5.4    Suppose that a liability rule will be applied whatever the level of the probability of causation, but that the amount a liable injurer will pay is the victim's losses multiplied by the probability of causation. Then injurers will take optimal care under strict liability or the negligence rule.

*Remark.*    An injurer's decision whether to engage in an activity under strict liability will also be optimal.

*5A.3.4    Note on the literature.* In Shavell (1985b) I analyze uncertainty over causation along the lines presented here, but there I consider uncertainty that concerns not only whether an injurer or a natural source was the cause of losses but also which of several injurers was the cause of losses.

# 6 | The Magnitude of Liability: Damages

Once it has been established that an injurer is liable, the amount he is to pay the victim must be determined. The term "damages" is usually understood to refer to this amount. I shall generally speak of the magnitude of liability (or simply of liability), however, because the word "damages" is suggestive of the victim's losses whereas I shall want to discuss the possibility that the amount the injurer pays differs from the victim's losses. I examine in this chapter the relationship between the magnitude of liability and the level, probability, and type of victims' losses (pecuniary, nonpecuniary, and economic). I consider also courts' difficulties in evaluating losses, certain particularistic elements of losses, victims' opportunities to mitigate losses, and imposition of liability in excess of losses (so-called punitive damages).[1]

## 6.1 The Level of Losses

*6.1.1 Liability equal to the level of losses.* It has been implicit all along that if liable parties pay for the actual level of losses they cause, they will be led to act optimally under liability rules. For if a liable party must pay for the actual losses he causes, whatever the level of losses happens to be, a party's expected liability will equal the expected losses he causes. And that expected liability equals expected losses is the assumption on which the arguments about optimality of parties' behavior under liability rules has been based.

---

1. Several other topics bearing on the magnitude of liability are discussed elsewhere in the book: in Chapter 2, strict division of liability and the comparative negligence rule (under which the injurer's liability is reduced in accord with the degree of the victim's fault); in Chapter 5, liability in proportion to the probability of causation; in Chapter 7, apportionment of liability among multiple injurers.

Consider the following illustration, in which there are two possible levels of losses.

> EXAMPLE 6.1    If injurers do not take care, there will be a 9 percent chance of an accident involving a loss of 100 and a 1 percent chance of an accident involving a loss of 1,000. Expected losses if care is not taken will therefore be $9\% \times 100 + 1\% \times 1{,}000 = 9 + 10 = 19$. Hence, the exercise of care that will eliminate the possibility of an accident and cost less than 19 will be socially desirable.
>
> Suppose that liable injurers must pay for the losses that occur, whether these are 100 or 1,000. Under strict liability injurers will bear expected liability of 19 if they do not take care, and thus will be led to take care when they ought to. Injurers will behave in the same way under the negligence rule because they will be liable if they fail to take care and if the cost of taking care is less than 19.

This example illustrates why, in the general setting where an accident can result in more than one level of losses, injurers will act optimally if liability equals actual losses. (Later in this chapter, however, assumptions will be examined under which it might be desirable for liability to be different from losses.)

*6.1.2    Actual magnitude of liability.* The beginning principle in most legal systems is that a liable party should pay for the actual level of losses caused, whether they be high or low. It is said, for instance, that an injurer "takes his victim as he finds him," that the injurer should pay for losses caused if the victim turns out to be affected by a latent aggravating condition (a thin skull, hemophilia), and that the injurer should pay similarly if the property he damaged had some structural weakness or was unusually valuable. At the same time, a liable injurer is responsible only for small losses if only a small harm resulted from his act.[2]

## 6.2    The Probability of Losses

The conclusion of §6.1.1 that behavior will be optimal if the magnitude of liability equals the actual level of losses suggests that behavior will not be optimal if liability is adjusted on the basis of other factors—in particular, if

---

2. See sec. 5 of chap. 9 of Fleming 1983 on the Anglo-American situation, and Stoll 1972, secs. 26–28, for a comparative discussion. As is evident from these sources and as I shall discuss subsequently, however, the principle that liability should be equal to actual losses is subject to limitation and exception.

liability is made to depend on the probability of losses. This point will now be considered both when the probability of losses is low and when it is high.

*6.2.1 Limitation of liability for unusual losses.* Suppose that liability is limited to an average or typical level when losses happen to be unusually high. Then expected liability will be less than expected losses and the incentive to take care may be inadequate. In Example 6.1, if liability for the relatively unlikely losses of 1,000 is limited to 100, then an injurer's expected liability if he does not take care will be only 10% × 100 = 10, which is less than the expected losses of 19. An injurer will therefore take care only if the cost of doing so is less than 10, rather than whenever the cost is less than 19. If drivers would not be fully liable for unusual harms (as where an automobile strikes a pole while being backed into a parking space and the pole falls through a shopfront window, breaking a valuable antique vase), then their incentives to exercise caution will be inadequate.

To better appreciate the conclusion that, under present assumptions, liability for unusual accidents should not be limited, observe that the contrary conclusion would lead to a reductio ad absurdum. Any accident, after all, can be seen as extremely unlikely if it is described in sufficient detail. For example, the initially likely-sounding accident in which a person drives his automobile into his neighbor's picket fence becomes a very unlikely one when it is mentioned that the accident occurred on a Tuesday at 4:23 P.M., that the left side of the automobile's fender struck the fence, and that the eighteenth through twenty-seventh pickets were broken. Were one to contend that liability for unlikely accidents should be limited, one would thus be led to say that liability for any accident whatever should be limited.

Another way to understand this point is to recognize that the magnitude of expected losses reflects all manner of possible accidents (striking the neighbor's fence with the right side or the middle part of the fender if not with the left side, breaking the nineteenth through twenty-eighth pickets if not the eighteenth through twenty-seventh). Expected losses are a probability-weighted *aggregation* of losses that can arise in many individually unlikely ways. Were liability reduced owing to the improbability of the particular accident, expected liability could not equal expected losses.

*6.2.2 A qualification.* Nevertheless, it might not be undesirable to limit liability for certain accidents: if the possibility of some type of accident is overlooked, then there would clearly be no decrease in injurers' incentives caused by reducing liability for that type of accident. (Note that this argument is not an affirmative reason for reducing the magnitude of liability; it says only that reducing liability may not have a detrimental effect on incentives.)

To decide what types of accident may be overlooked, consider that individuals cannot practically contemplate each and every one of the multitude of possible accidents that could follow from their actions. People must amalgamate potential accidents into a relatively small number of categories, assign probabilities to the categories, and make decisions with reference to them. In the process, the possibility of some accidents will not be taken into account because they do not fit into the list of categories used in decisionmaking. Such accidents are likely to be what one might describe as "freak."[3]

There are, however, several problematic aspects of a policy limiting liability for accidents whose possibility is overlooked. First, this policy invites parties to deceive courts about accidents that they had in fact contemplated; second, the policy reduces parties' incentives to consider the full range of consequences that could result from their actions; and third, it may increase the costs of adjudication.[4]

*6.2.3   Actual liability for unlikely losses.* As stated in §6.1.2, the beginning principle in most legal systems is that liability equals losses caused, and this is true even if the losses were unlikely. But there are exceptions to the principle in Anglo-American law that come under the rubric of "unforeseeability."[5] According to this notion, liability should not extend to harms that the injurer could not reasonably foresee. It appears from examination of cases and of legal commentary that the accidents that are held not to be reasonably foreseeable generally have a far-fetched, extraordinary character.

*6.2.4   Liability for highly likely losses.* If liability for accidents that are very likely to occur exceeds the level of actual losses, then parties may have too great an incentive to reduce risk.[6] Suppose, to take the extreme case of losses that are certain to occur, that an injurer will definitely cause losses of 100 if he does not exercise care and that he will definitely not cause any losses if he exercises care. In this case it will be best for him to exercise care only if the cost of doing so is less than 100. But if the injurer must pay more than 100, say 150, for causing harm because harm is so likely, then he will be led to take

---

3. As in the celebrated American case of *Palsgraf v. Long Island R.R.*, where a package containing fireworks was dislodged from the arms of a man boarding a train and fell under the train's wheels, causing an explosion, the concussive force of which allegedly knocked a scale into and injured a woman who was standing on another platform some distance away.

4. Limiting the magnitude of liability will have two effects on administrative costs associated with use of the legal system: it will increase the cost per case brought, but it may reduce the number of cases that are brought.

5. On unforeseeability, see generally sec. 6 of chap. 9 of Fleming 1983, *Prosser and Keeton on Torts* (Keeton, Dobbs, et al. 1984), sec. 43, and the *Restatement (Second) of Torts* 1965, sec. 435. In other legal systems there are some parallels with unforeseeability (chiefly in the interpretation of the adequacy theory), but there does not seem to be an exactly corresponding notion; see the discussion in Honoré 1971, secs. 91–93.

6. Although the reader may feel uncomfortable about this conclusion, his hesitancy is probably attributable to factors not yet considered; see §6.8.

care whenever the cost is less than 150, rather than only when it is less than 100. Or suppose that a construction firm that blasts to excavate a large area will be virtually sure to cause some property losses. If the firm would have to pay for more than these losses because of their high likelihood, the firm might be led to take excessive precautions in blasting, or it might decide to use alternative, more expensive means of excavation even where blasting is socially best.

*6.2.5   Actual liability for highly likely losses.* Again, because the beginning principle is that liability should equal actual losses, the fact that the probability of losses might have been high does not ordinarily result in liability greater than the losses.[7]

## 6.3   Courts' Uncertainty about the Level of Losses

*6.3.1   Liability equal to estimated losses.* Suppose that courts are not able to assess accurately the level of losses that occur in accidents, but use estimates of losses that are correct on average. Then liable parties' expected liability will still equal the expected losses they cause, so they will still be led to act optimally under liability rules.

EXAMPLE 6.2   If an injurer causes an accident, losses will in fact be 100, but injurers know that courts' estimates of losses may be incorrect: a court's estimate of losses will be too low—equal to 50—25 percent of the time, correct half the time, and too high—equal to 150—the other 25 percent of the time. The expected value of courts' estimates will thus be correct—$25\% \times 50 + 50\% \times 100 + 25\% \times 150 = 100$—so the expected amount a liable injurer will pay will equal the losses he causes and he will be induced to act optimally under liability rules. If, for instance, he is strictly liable and can reduce the risk of an accident from 5 percent to zero by taking care, he will take care if the cost of doing so is less than 5, the optimal outcome. Specifically, if the injurer does not take care, his expected liability will be $5\% \times (25\% \times 50 + 50\% \times 100 + 25\% \times 150) = 5\% \times 100 = 5$, so he will indeed take care if the cost of care is less than 5.

On the other hand, if courts employ estimates of losses that are systematically low, parties' incentives to reduce risk may be inadequate, and the opposite will be true if courts use estimates that are systematically high.

---

7. A partial exception occurs where the injurer intended harm or was reckless; see §6.8.11.

*6.3.2   Remarks on courts' uncertainty.* (1) Courts may be uncertain about the level of losses when the harm has already occurred, as where a house burns and the value of its contents are not easy to determine. Similarly, uncertainty may arise when some of the harm will occur in the future. A primary example of the latter is where an individual's subsequent earnings will be reduced due to an injury.[8] The interpretation of the point of §6.3.1 in this type of situation is that if courts' estimates of future losses are correct on average, injurers will have appropriate motives to reduce risk. There will be no need for courts to determine what victims' losses turn out to be in fact.

(2) Estimating uncertain elements of losses may be a difficult and much disputed process, raising the administrative costs of use of the legal system. Therefore, it may be socially desirable for courts to exclude uncertain components of losses from the computation of liability if the probable magnitude of these losses, and the consequent dilution of incentives to reduce risk, is not too large.

*6.3.3   Actual determination of liability in the face of uncertainty over the level of losses.* When losses involve harm to property, courts ordinarily attempt to estimate uncertain components that are not too speculative; they follow the same course when property losses are associated with forgone profits, but their approach is conservative.[9]

With respect to accidents resulting in injuries to persons, courts can usually ascertain medical expenses borne and income lost up to the time of trial fairly reliably, but subsequent medical expenses and the diminution in earning capacity may be highly uncertain. In many countries courts estimate these amounts as best they can, often using actuarial and statistical data, and award a lump sum to injured parties or, in the case of fatal accidents, to their dependents for loss of support. However, in the Soviet Union and, as a rule, in Germany, lump-sum awards are not made; instead, awards for reduced earnings are paid on a periodic basis only as long as injured parties actually suffer them.[10]

---

8. In computing the reduction in earnings, care must be taken not to count expected future losses that would occur due to future risks. It is, of course, only the expected increment in future losses due to an injury that should properly determine the magnitude of liability.

9. The description here is based mainly on secs. 8 and 10 of chap. 9 of Fleming 1983, and on Stoll 1972, secs. 12–48, a general comparative treatment of damages and other remedies. On the treatment of forgone profits, see §6.5.4.

10. Awards to dependents for fatal accidents are also made on a periodic basis. See McGregor 1972, secs. 49–52.

## 6.4 Pecuniary versus Nonpecuniary Losses

*6.4.1 Definition of the two types of losses.* Consider a model where in addition to the single good from before there are two other goods: a *produced good,* which can be made from the single good; and an *irreplaceable good,* which cannot.[11] For present purposes, the single good might be interpreted as wealth; the produced good might be, for instance, refrigerators or automobiles; and the irreplaceable good might be identified with family portraits and other unique objects, or, importantly, with health, physical integrity, or emotional well-being.[12] Assume that the utility of an individual equals the number of units of the single good that he holds, plus the utility to him of the produced good if he possesses this good, plus the utility to him of the irreplaceable good if he possesses that. Also, assume that the measure of social welfare is the sum of individuals' utilities.

In this model a *pecuniary* loss will be said to occur either when there is a loss of the single good or when there is a loss of the produced good. If there is a loss of the produced good, the amount of the pecuniary loss is defined as the number of units of the single good required to make the produced good. Thus, if a produced good whose production cost is 3 is destroyed, the amount of the pecuniary loss will be 3. The motivation for this definition is that the reduction in social welfare due to loss of a produced good is only the production cost. The social loss is not the often higher utility the individual attached to the produced good, since the good can be replaced at the production cost. If the produced good (a refrigerator) whose production cost is 3 is lost and the utility of the good to its owner was 15 (the refrigerator was very useful), the loss in social welfare is not 15 but the cost 3 of a replacement.

On the other hand, a *nonpecuniary* loss will be said to occur when there is a loss of the irreplaceable good. The amount of such a loss will be taken to be the utility of the good to the individual. As the good cannot be replaced, the utility of the good is the reduction in social welfare due to loss of the good.

*6.4.2 Liability equal to the sum of pecuniary and nonpecuniary losses.* Because pecuniary and nonpecuniary losses are defined so that they correspond to losses in social welfare, it is clear that parties will be led to act appropriately under liability rules if the magnitude of liability equals the sum

11. This model will be further considered when nonpecuniary losses and insurance are studied in §§10.1 and 10.2.

12. What is interpreted as irreplaceable depends to some extent on technology and the state of medical knowledge. For example, certain types of injury that at one time might have resulted in permanent loss of health or in disfigurement might today be largely remediable and thus involve mainly pecuniary losses (costs of medical care and forgone income).

of pecuniary and nonpecuniary losses. In particular, if liability does not fully reflect nonpecuniary losses, parties' incentives to reduce risks may be inadequate.

*6.4.3   Courts' ability to assess pecuniary and nonpecuniary losses.* Since pecuniary losses are equal either to actual losses in wealth or to the cost of replacing goods, such losses are often easy for courts to determine.[13]

By contrast, because nonpecuniary losses cannot be observed directly, they are difficult for courts to estimate. Hence, it may be best for courts not to attempt to estimate nonpecuniary losses if they are probably small. In this way administrative costs will be avoided, while incentives to reduce risk will be little affected, as was generally suggested in the case of courts' uncertainty about the level of losses (see §6.3.2). If, however, nonpecuniary losses are likely to be large, it will be important for courts to attempt to estimate them, and especially where pecuniary losses are at the same time small. Otherwise, incentives to reduce risk may be seriously compromised. This may be the situation, for example, with respect to the death of young children.[14]

*6.4.4   Actual liability for nonpecuniary losses.* The categories of losses typically described as nonpecuniary include pain and suffering, emotional distress, and the like. Losses of money and of goods for which substitutes can be bought are regarded as pecuniary, with the prices of the substitutes measuring the losses.

The willingness to increase awards on account of nonpecuniary losses varies considerably among legal systems.[15] French law is apparently the most liberal in the types of nonpecuniary losses recognized. Anglo-American law is less liberal (though the size of awards, when given, seems highest in the United States). German law is more restrictive than French or Anglo-Ameri-

13. To be sure, courts would find it difficult to determine the maximum amount an individual would have been willing to pay for a refrigerator (and perhaps just as difficult to determine as the maximum amount he would be willing to pay for his family portrait). But this presents no problems because, as was argued, the socially appropriate measure of the losses due to loss of a refrigerator is the pecuniary loss, its replacement cost.

14. As will be suggested below, the nonpecuniary component of awards for the death of children is low or nonexistent. The pecuniary awards are usually small as well, because they are based on the future loss of support—often zero—that parents will suffer in their later years. (For these reasons, one might wonder about the adequacy of the incentives of, say, manufacturers of children's play equipment to reduce the risk of fatal accidents.) See McGregor 1972, secs. 253–255, 273.

15. See Fleming 1983, pp. 211–213, 225, for a description of Anglo-American law; Stoll 1972, secs. 35–48, for a general comparative survey; and McGregor 1972, secs. 35–47, 146–172, 212–217, 264–273, for a comparative treatment of liability for personal injury and death.

can, and Soviet law altogether refuses to take into account nonpecuniary losses in determining awards.[16]

Moreover, treatment of nonpecuniary losses within legal systems may depend on the type of accident and other factors. Nonpecuniary losses are not usually compensated unless there is accompanying physical injury (but if the injury results in death, nonpecuniary losses suffered by the victim's family are not ordinarily compensated, at least in Anglo-American law). Additionally, nonpecuniary losses associated with losses of unique objects of property are rarely compensated.

## 6.5   Economic Losses

The term *economic losses* usually refers to forgone profits or earnings rather than to the value of property losses or the costs of physical injury.

Two questions will be asked about accidents causing economic losses. First, what are the social losses associated with such accidents? And second, what is the relation between social losses and economic losses? If liability is based on economic losses, and economic losses do not correspond to social losses, incentives to reduce risk will not be appropriate.

*6.5.1   Economic versus social losses due to a firm's inability to sell.* Economic losses often arise where an accident halts a firm's production of a good or provision of a service (because, for instance, the supply of electricity or of some material input is interrupted) or where an accident prevents the actual making of sales (for example, because access to a store is blocked).

Several factors bear on social losses in such situations.[17] First, some of the sales that a firm would have made may never be made. In this case the benefits that customers would have obtained from their purchases are forgone and economic losses provide a measure—in fact an underestimate—of social losses. Consider the following example.

EXAMPLE 6.3   An accident stops production of a good. The cost of production would have been 10 per unit and the utility customers would have derived is 15 per unit. Therefore, the loss in social welfare per unit not produced is 15 − 10 = 5. The economic loss per unit (the loss in profits) is

16. Although Hungary and Rumania follow the Soviets in refusing to acknowledge nonpecuniary losses, most other socialist countries allow such awards; see Stoll 1972, sec. 36.

17. The definition of social welfare in this section is that used in Chapter 3: the utility customers obtain from goods less production costs, costs of care, and expected accident losses. Social losses are diminutions in social welfare.

the price less the production cost of 10. Thus, if the price[18] of the good were, say, 13, the economic loss per unit would be 3, which is less than the social loss of 5. The price cannot be higher than 15, since that is the maximum that customers would pay. Therefore, the economic loss per unit cannot exceed the social loss.

A second factor that needs to be taken into account is that some of the sales a firm does not make may be alternatively made—either by rival firms or by the "victim" firm at a later date. If sales are alternatively made, social losses will clearly be lower than if sales are truly forgone. In the extreme case, social losses will be nonexistent. If perfect substitutes are produced at the same cost and sold by other firms, no social losses will result even though the victim firm suffers economic losses; if in Example 6.3 a rival firm produces the same good at a cost of 10 and sells the same quantity, social welfare will be unaffected even though the victim firm suffers economic losses of 3 per unit.

But, of course, when sales are alternatively made, there may well be some losses in social welfare. One reason is that the cost of production by other firms may be higher than that of the victim firm, especially when other firms must increase their output above normal levels. Or the cost to the victim firm of later making up lost production may be higher than the cost of uninterrupted production would have been. In these cases social losses will be measured by the increase in production costs, which, note, is different from the victim firm's economic losses. If in Example 6.3 another firm produces and sells additional units of the good at a cost of 11, then the social loss per unit will be 1 (since the victim firm's production cost would have been 10), which is lower than the victim firm's economic loss of 3 per unit. In fact, social losses will generally be bounded from above by the victim firm's economic losses if the price of the good does not change.[19]

An additional reason for social losses when alternative sales are made is that the alternative sales may be of substitutes that are less than perfect. In

---

18. I assume here that the firm is not in a perfectly competitive market. The price the firm charges is thus determined, among other factors, by its market power. (If the firm were in a perfectly competitive market, the case under consideration could not arise because competitors would make the sales that the firm in question could not.)

19. The explanation for the upper bound can be understood from Example 6.3. If the price remains at 13, one can infer from the fact that the other firm is willing to sell that its production cost must be less than 13. Hence the difference between the other firm's production cost and the victim firm's production cost must be less than $13 - 10 = 3$, the victim firm's economic losses. Under perfect competition, one can infer that other firms' increased production costs will equal the victim firm's economic losses, for, to a first approximation, competitor firms will replace the victim firm's production at marginal cost equal to price; see §6A.3.2.

this case social losses will reflect the decline in utility that customers derive from the imperfect substitutes. Suppose in Example 6.3 that another firm can produce (for simplicity, at the same cost) and sell a similar but inferior good, yielding customers a utility of 14. Then losses in social welfare per unit will be 1. In this instance, therefore, social losses are less than economic losses, a result that would be expected but is not necessary.[20]

To summarize, it has been seen that when sales are not alternatively made, economic losses are less than social losses. Accordingly, in this case it will certainly be socially desirable for liability to include economic losses. When, however, sales are alternatively made, economic losses are likely to be (but are not always) greater than social losses. Social losses here depend on the extent to which the alternative sales involve higher production costs or are of lesser utility to customers. If liability is based on economic losses and these losses exceed social losses, two types of undesirable consequences will result: parties that might cause economic losses will engage in their activities too little and will tend to take socially excessive levels of care when they do engage in their activities.[21]

*6.5.2   Conditions for and effects of alternative sales when a firm is unable to sell.* Whether sales will be alternatively made, and the extent to which they will be made, depend on at least the following considerations. (1) Proximity of other firms to the victim firm. If two nearby movie theaters are exhibiting the same film and one theater's electricity is shut off, the second theater might gain the customers of the first; but if the single restaurant in a small town loses its electricity, its customers will have nowhere else to go. (2) Price-setting behavior of other firms. If the inability of the victim firm to sell leads other firms to increase price temporarily, alternative sales will be lower than otherwise. This outcome will be more likely in markets having a smaller number of firms. (3) Character of what is sold: a durable good, a perishable good, or a service. It is relatively likely that a potential purchaser of a durable good can defer purchases until he finds another seller or until the victim firm

20. Suppose in Example 6.3 that the utility to customers of the victim firm's good had been 20 rather than 15. Then the decline in social welfare per unit would be $20 - 14 = 6$, exceeding the economic losses of 3.

21. The reader may wonder if such problems would be avoided by using as a measure of losses the change in profits of *all* affected firms, not just the victim firm. It may appear that setting off the increase in profits of firms that make additional sales against the losses of the victim firm would better reflect social losses than just the victim firm's losses. That this is not necessarily true should be evident on reflection, however. Consider, for instance, a case in which alternative sales result in the same addition to profits for other firms as the victim firm's losses, so that total profits are unaltered. But if the customers are not as well off with the alternative good or service, there will have been social losses even though there is no change in total profits.

is again in a position to make sales; if an automobile dealership loses its electricity, customers may well come back the next day. With perishables or services (restaurant meals, movies), deferral is less often feasible.

When sales are alternatively made, whether production costs are higher, and how much so, depends on factors including these. (1) Existence of inventory. If other firms (or the victim firm later) can sell from inventory, then production costs should not be much raised, if they are raised at all (restoring inventory to desired levels can be done over time). It should be noted, though, that inventory is, by its nature, something that can exist only for goods; services cannot be held in inventory. (2) Existence of excess capacity. In some cases other firms will have excess productive capacity (for reasons having to do with peak loads or the ability to accommodate random changes in demand). For instance, the movie theater whose electricity did not fail may have extra seats and be able, virtually costlessly, to seat additional customers. (3) Ability to obtain additional factor inputs at the same cost. Some inputs to production can readily be purchased at no increased cost (perhaps food for restaurant meals), whereas others may be in short supply (experienced workers may be hard to locate; current workers may have to be paid overtime to boost output).

The degree to which an alternative purchase is or is not a substitute in the eyes of customers depends not only on differences in quality of the good or service. It also depends on the time and cost to customers of traveling to and buying from the other firms.

*6.5.3   Caution is recommended in making awards for inability to sell.* A conservative approach to the award of damages for economic losses due to inability to sell appears best, in view of the considerations discussed above— namely, the complexity and the variable nature of the connection between economic losses and social losses, together with the likelihood that economic losses will exceed social losses. A regular practice of making awards for economic losses might have an undesirable chilling effect on activities that are relatively likely to lead to economic losses (construction work that could cause power losses or block roads) and to the exercise of excessive care.

Moreover, economic losses may often be difficult to measure because of uncertainties in answering the hypothetical question concerning what profits would have been had there been no accident. (How many individuals would have gone to see the movie at the theater had its electricity not failed?) Finally, the routine award of economic losses could also raise administrative costs by adding to the volume of litigation, since the number of parties who could claim such losses is presumably large.

The foregoing is not meant to imply, however, that liability for economic losses will only rarely be desirable. The discussion of the last two sections suggests there may well be a not insignificant number of situations in which it will be beneficial for economic losses to be awarded, most notably, when sales would be unlikely to be alternatively made (as in the example of the loss of sales by the single restaurant in a town).

*6.5.4 Economic losses due to other reasons.* There are, in addition to a firm's inability to sell, various other reasons why economic losses may be suffered. Two reasons are mentioned here to illustrate again the general utility of considering explicitly social losses in evaluating the desirability of liability for economic losses.

First, a buyer may be prevented from making a purchase. For instance, a person who would have purchased redecorating services does not because his home burns, in which case the decorator loses profits. Or ranchers who would have hired an auctioneer to sell their cattle do not do so because the cattle became diseased through someone's negligence, where the auctioneer loses profits. Here, the social loss might include the utility the buyer would have enjoyed had he made his purchase—the utility to the person of having his house redecorated, the value of having the auctioneer sell the cattle. But utility forgone by a buyer will represent a social loss only if the seller does not sell to an alternative buyer. If the seller does sell to another buyer (if the decorator provides services to another homeowner), the social loss will be less; it will be only the difference in valuations between the two buyers. Thus the situation is analogous to that discussed above, where a firm is prevented from making sales yet alternative firms can make sales.

Second, a firm may lose profits because of actions taken by a competing firm. That in the normal course of business such economic losses do not justify liability (and that a suggestion to the contrary would be considered an absurdity) makes sense from the vantage point of the present analysis, for the economic losses in this case do not correspond to social losses but rather to social gains. If firm A develops a cost-saving innovation that enables it to lower price and attract firm B's customers, B's losses in profits do not represent a social loss. Instead, they reflect a social gain, because A now produces for B's customers at a lower cost than had A. Were A to be liable to B for B's losses, A's incentives to devise cost-saving innovations and to lower price would be undesirably reduced.

On the other hand, liability might be justified for economic losses caused by a competitor's behavior that creates social losses rather than gains. If firm A attracts B's customers by disparaging B's product or misrepresenting its own, A creates social losses by inducing customers to purchase products on the basis of incorrect information. Hence holding A liable for B's losses might be warranted.

*6.5.5 Actual treatment of economic losses caused by accidents.* In Anglo-

American law there are important doctrines against making awards for economic losses caused by accidents—particularly when the economic losses are not accompanied by property losses or physical injury—although exceptions in certain circumstances are made. In German law the approach appears similar. There are no special doctrines restricting liability for economic losses in French law, yet such liability is in fact limited by, among other factors, the standards used for proof of causation and for the certainty of losses.[22]

*6.5.6   Note on the literature.* Bishop (1982) presents the first economically oriented analysis of the general subject of economic losses caused by accidents, stressing the possibility that such losses may be larger than social losses. Rizzo (1982) offers another economic treatment of the subject.

## 6.6   Particularistic Elements in the Computation of Liability

For each of the issues affecting the computation of liability discussed here, the magnitude of the social losses due to an accident will be identified, because liability must be calculated so as to equal the social losses for incentives to reduce risk to be optimal.

*6.6.1   Setoffs.* A victim who suffers a loss will often bear expenses that he would have borne in any event. For instance, a person who must stay in a hospital because of an injury will pay for meals, but he would have had to spend on meals had he not been injured, and similarly with regard to an individual's purchase of gasoline for a rental automobile while his own is in the shop because of a collision. Such expenses that would have been incurred anyway are not part of the social loss due to an accident. Thus they should be subtracted or "set off" from the total in determining the magnitude of liability.

*6.6.2   Repair versus replacement.* When a victim's property is damaged, he often can repair or replace it. If repair is cheaper than replacement, then the social loss is clearly the cost of repair; otherwise it is the cost of replacement. Hence the magnitude of liability should be the minimum of either the costs of repair or of replacement.

Suppose, however, that although the damaged property can be repaired, only an imperfect substitute for it exists; the property, in other words, has a unique or irreplaceable character (see §6.4). Then if the property is sufficiently valuable to the individual, the social loss and the desirable magnitude

---

22. On the Anglo-American situation see Atiyah 1967 and sec. 6 of chap. 8 of Fleming 1983, and see also Rabin 1985; on German law see the remarks in Zweigert and Kötz 1977, pp. 270–273, 292–293; and on French law see Marshall 1975. It should be noted that these references and the present paragraph summarize liability for economic losses caused by accidents, as opposed to economic losses caused by intentional, unfair business practices.

of liability will correspond to the cost of repair, even if the imperfect substitute is cheaper. Thus the appropriate award for damage to a family portrait may be the cost of restoration even if a painting with similar market value costs less.

*6.6.3 Actual setoffs and repair versus replacement costs.* Computation of liability is in fact as described in the last two sections. Expenses that would have been borne anyway are generally set off in determining what a liable party must pay. And the minimum of repair or replacement cost is normally employed in determining awards for property damage, but when the property is special, the cost of repair may be used in calculating awards although the cost of imperfect substitutes is lower.[23]

*6.6.4 Interest on past losses and discounting of future losses.* A victim may have suffered losses prior to the time he establishes an injurer's liability. This and the fact that money earns interest—reflecting the productivity of resources—must obviously be taken into account in determining the magnitude of liability if injurers' incentives to reduce risk are to be appropriate. Unless an injurer pays the amount of the losses plus interest, his incentives to reduce risk may be inadequate. Suppose that an injurer might cause losses of 100 in an accident today; that if he causes an accident, he will not have to pay the victim for a year; and that interest over the period will be 3 percent. If the injurer's liability will be only 100 a year from now, he will, inappropriately, treat the possibility of an accident today as one that will cost him only 97.09, for he can set aside that amount today and, after obtaining 3 percent interest, be able to pay an award of 100 in a year. For the injurer to treat the possibility of an accident today as one that will cost 100, his liability in a year must be 103, for then he will have to set aside 100 if an accident occurs today.

Conversely, where a victim will suffer losses (such as wage losses) after an injurer is found liable, the injurer should pay only the discounted or "present value" of the losses. That is, he should pay only the amount which, if invested at the interest rate, will accumulate to the losses at the time they will occur. It is this present value that represents the present social cost of the future losses. Thus if a victim will suffer losses of 103 a year after an injurer is found liable and the interest rate is 3 percent, the injurer should pay the victim only 100.

*6.6.5 Adjustments for inflation.* Suppose here that there is inflation in the

---

23. See generally secs. 8 and 10 of chap. 9 of Fleming 1983 on Anglo-American law. See also Stoll 1972, a comparative work in which occasional references are made to setoffs and repair versus replacement. Observe as well that the conclusions described follow in any event from the general principle, noted in secs. 22 and 26 of Stoll 1972, that an injured party must be restored to the financial position he would have occupied in the absence of an accident.

price level and that the rate of interest—the so-called nominal rate of interest—equals the rate of inflation plus the "real" rate of interest—that is, the rate of interest that would obtain in the absence of inflation. For instance, the nominal rate of interest will be 7 percent if the rate of inflation is 4 percent and the real rate of interest is 3 percent.

Now consider again the situation where victims suffer losses today and injurers pay them awards later. For injurers' incentives to be correct, awards must be such that injurers will have to set aside today an amount equal to the losses they cause today. Therefore, the awards they pay in the future must equal the losses they cause today, measured at today's price level, plus nominal interest. If an injurer causes losses of 100 today and the nominal rate of interest is 7 percent, the injurer should pay an award of 107 a year from now. It should be noted that there is a mathematically equivalent way to arrive at the figure of 107 a year from now: measure today's losses a year from now in terms of the price level of a year from now (in the example, therefore, the losses will be 104 rather than 100) and then apply to this number the real rate of interest (apply the 3 percent real rate to 104 to obtain 107).[24]

Similarly, in the case where a victim will suffer losses after an injurer is found liable, the injurer should pay the future losses at the future price level, but discounted to the present at the nominal rate of interest. Equivalently, he should pay the future losses measured at the current price level, but discounted at the real rate of interest.[25]

*6.6.6  Actual treatment of interest, discounting, and inflation.* Interest is often paid on losses sustained before the time of judgment if the losses are pecuniary and sufficiently definite; interest is not permitted on nonpecuniary losses and, in any case, compound interest is usually not allowed. Losses that will occur after the time of judgment are ordinarily discounted to present value if, again, they are pecuniary and not too uncertain. Inflation may be taken into account, but this is largely discretionary.[26]

*6.6.7  Collateral benefits and gifts.* Victims of accidents often obtain compensation from *collateral* sources (so named because they are sources other

24. This procedure may seem only approximately equivalent to the last, since 1.03 × 104 = 107.12, not 107. But if interest is compounded continuously, the two procedures are identical.

25. If losses next year at next year's prices will be 107 and the nominal rate of interest is 7 percent, then an injurer should pay today the present value of 100. Alternatively, as next year's losses will equal 103 in terms of today's prices, one can discount them at the real rate of interest of 3 percent to obtain the figure of 100.

26. The present paragraph describes the situation in the United States; see, for example, the *Restatement (Second) of Torts* 1965, sec. 913, and, though somewhat dated, McCormick 1935, secs. 51–57.

than the injurer), including private accident insurance or social insurance and gifts from friends or relatives. (See also §10.3.) The question arises whether the magnitude of injurers' liability should be reduced on this account. If the goal is to provide incentives to reduce risk, the answer is plainly negative, since the receipt of collateral benefits by a victim hardly alters the fact that an injurer has caused a social loss. (If an accident results in a loss, *some* party or parties will of necessity bear the loss—if not the victim, then the individuals who pay premiums to the victim's insurer or the person who makes a gift to the victim.)

*6.6.8   Actual adjustment of liability in light of collateral benefits and gifts.* Liable parties must usually pay an amount equal to the losses they have caused regardless of victims' receipt of gifts or collateral benefits. The payment may not, however, be made to the victim directly. A liable party often pays some or all of a victim's losses to the victim's insurer if the insurer has a right to sue in place of the victim.

Nevertheless, there are situations where liable parties pay less on account of victims' receipts of collateral benefits. The main such situation arises where liability is reduced by the amount of the victim's collateral insurance benefits and yet where the insurer does not have the right to collect from injurers. For example, in England liability is reduced by the (adjusted) social insurance benefits that victims receive, but the social insurance fund has no right of recoupment against liable parties.[27]

*6.6.9   Taxes on wages.* When a victim is unable to work for a period or his future ability to work is diminished because of an accident, the injurer's liability should be based on the victim's pretax losses in earnings rather than on his after-tax losses. This is clearly the case if it is assumed that an individual's pretax wages equal the amount he produces, for then his loss in wages measures the social loss.[28] Basing liability on the posttax wage losses would result in inadequate incentives to reduce risk because it would allow injurers to pay only a portion of the social losses they cause. For example, if the tax rate were 40 percent and liability were based on the 60 percent posttax wage losses, injurers would be allowed to escape having to pay for 40 percent of the losses they cause.

27. On collateral benefits and gifts, see sec. 9 of chap. 9 of Fleming 1983, discussing the Anglo-American situation, and Fleming 1971, for a comparative treatment. See also §§10.3.5 and 10.3.9.

28. The nonpecuniary elements associated with injuries resulting in inability to work have been ignored here. These may include on the one hand the avoidance of the disutility of work and, on the other, pain and suffering resulting from the injury and perhaps a loss of self-esteem. If these are on net hurtful, as one would suppose, then in principle liability should be greater than even the pretax wage losses for incentives to be appropriate.

If individuals' pretax wages are assumed to be less than what they produce, this argument is only strengthened, for then incentives will be inadequate even if liability is based on pretax losses; use of posttax losses would only exacerbate the problem.

*6.6.10   Actual treatment of taxes on wages.* In England and several Commonwealth countries liability is generally set equal to after-tax wage losses, while in the United States, Germany, and the Soviet Union it is ordinarily based on pretax earnings. It should be mentioned too that victims do not usually pay taxes on awards in England and the United States, whereas they do in Germany and the Soviet Union; thus only in the United States do victims in principle receive pretax earnings.[29]

*6.6.11   Remark on a possible divergence between the optimal magnitude of liability and victims' need for compensation.* In the cases of collateral benefits and wage losses, one is presented with instances in which the magnitude of liability that is best for providing incentives to reduce risk is different from (and exceeds) that necessary to compensate victims. (Victims do not need to be compensated to the extent they receive collateral benefits, and they lose only their posttax earnings.) Such a divergence between the magnitudes of liability that are desirable for the two different purposes is not an infrequent phenomenon. It will be discussed generally later, in §10.2, where it will be suggested that it would be optimal for victims to receive an amount different from what injurers pay.[30]

## 6.7   Victims' Opportunities to Mitigate Losses

In the event of an accident, the victim may be able to limit the harm by taking various actions. For instance, if a tree falls on the roof of a man's home because of his neighbor's negligence, the man may be able to keep losses to a minimum by the timely removal from his attic of articles that could be damaged by rain or snow before the roof is repaired. Such actions that victims can take to mitigate losses after accidents occur will now be discussed. These are, of course, to be distinguished from precautions victims can exercise before accidents occur to reduce the likelihood or severity of harm.

*6.7.1   Social welfare optimum.* Given the goal of minimizing total accident costs, including here the costs of mitigation of losses, it will be socially

29. See Fleming 1983, pp. 209–210, on Anglo-American law, and McGregor 1972, secs. 135–139, for a comparative discussion.

30. This can be accomplished by requiring injurers to pay a fine to the state in addition to an award to victims. In the case of forgone wages, there is another possibility: as in Germany and the Soviet Union, make injurers pay forgone pretax wages, but make victims pay taxes on these awards.

desirable for a victim to act to mitigate losses if the cost of so doing is less than the reduction in losses thereby accomplished.

EXAMPLE 6.4   If a victim takes an action to mitigate losses due to an accident, the losses will equal 100; otherwise losses will equal 150. It will therefore be socially desirable for him to take the action if its cost is less than 50.

Thus, the man whose roof is damaged should immediately remove articles from his attic, if this can easily be done, and have his roof repaired promptly if a roofer is available. If, however, access to the attic is blocked or repair is hard to arrange (suppose the home is in a remote vacation area), the conclusion might be different.

Note also that in determining the optimal level of care for injurers to exercise, the level of losses due to an accident should be regarded as the optimally mitigated level of losses plus the costs of mitigation. In Example 6.4 the level of losses should be regarded as 120 if the cost of mitigation is 20.

*6.7.2   Level of liability.* It will be argued that if the level of liability equals optimally mitigated losses plus mitigation costs, then victims will be led to mitigate losses optimally and injurers will be led to take optimal levels of care. A victim will know that he will not receive a higher award from a liable injurer if he allows his losses to become large through failure to mitigate them optimally. Victims will therefore have an incentive to mitigate their losses optimally. (Since the victim whose roof is damaged will receive only the losses he would suffer if he repairs the roof in reasonable time, he will be motivated to have this done.) Suppose that the cost of mitigation in Example 6.4 would be 20, in which case mitigation of losses will be optimal. Then a victim's award in the event of an accident will be 120 even if his actual losses are 150 because of his failure to mitigate them. Hence a victim will choose to mitigate his losses: if he does so, he will be fully compensated; but if he does not, he will suffer losses of 150, receive 120, losing 30 on net.[31]

The usual arguments show that injurers will take optimal levels of care under strict liability or the negligence rule if the level of liability equals optimally mitigated losses plus mitigation costs, for this sum measures the full social losses resulting from an accident.

*6.7.3   Actual law regarding mitigation.* In the Anglo-American and French legal systems the size of awards is held to losses that an injured party

---

31. It should be pointed out that there is another way that victims could be induced to behave optimally, namely, through denying victims *any* recovery for failure to mitigate optimally their losses. This would in effect treat mitigation behavior in the same way that the victims' care before accidents occur is treated under the defense of contributory negligence.

could not reasonably have avoided plus expenses reasonably incurred in so limiting losses. Thus awards are based on the assumption that any reasonable repairs to damaged property have been made; that injured parties have obtained proper medical treatment to alleviate their condition (but not that they have submitted to dangerous procedures); and so forth. In the German legal system, as well as some others, the problem of mitigation of losses is viewed as an aspect of the injured party's contributory fault. Since liability is normally reduced on account of contributory fault, the end result is presumably similar to that under Anglo-American and French law.[32]

*6.7.4   Note on the literature.* Wittman (1981) first suggested that both victims and injurers will act desirably if liability equals optimally mitigated losses plus mitigation costs.[33]

## 6.8   Liability in Excess of Losses

In this part I will examine several versions of the unilateral model of accidents in which it will turn out to be desirable for the magnitude of liability to exceed the level of a victim's losses. (See also §10.2.)

*6.8.1   Injurers experience disutility from exercising care that is not recognized as socially valid.* Suppose that along with the usual costs of care, injurers may experience disutility that is not credited in the calculation of social welfare. For example, we might say that a driver who goes 80 miles per hour in a residential area because he wants to reach a movie theater in time for the performance attaches an impermissibly high utility to not being late or, equivalently, that the disutility incurred by a driver speeding for this reason is not considered socially valid. As the socially optimal level of care will reflect only the socially valid costs of care, it is clear that for injurers who incur socially unrecognized utility costs to be led to take optimal care, the magnitude of liability must exceed the losses they cause. For the individual on the way to the movies to be induced to drive slowly, he must face potential liability greater than the losses he might cause.[34]

*6.8.2   Courts' ability to determine the character of the disutility of care.*

32. See sec. 11 of chap. 9 of Fleming 1983 on Anglo-American law, and also McCormick 1935, chap. 5. And see Stoll 1972, sec. 155, for brief comparative observations.

33. But legal scholars occasionally mention that desirable incentives are created by limiting awards to what reasonably mitigated losses would be; see, for instance, the beginning of chap. 5 of McCormick 1935.

34. The Appendix shows that the formula for the magnitude of liability is $l + lw$, where $l$ is the level of losses and $w$ is the socially invalid utility cost per unit of care. In particular, then, and in contrast to what will be the situation in the next section, the excess of liability over losses depends on the level of losses.

Courts may be able to ascertain whether an injurer experienced socially un-recognized disutility from exercising care not only from evidence about the character or purpose of his act (testimony that the individual was speeding in order to get to the movie theater), but also from the extent to which his level of care deviated from the optimal level (80 miles per hour is far from appropriate). It is unlikely that a party who took markedly little care incurred only those utility costs from exercising care that are recognized as being socially valid.

*6.8.3  Injurers obtain possibly socially illicit utility from the occurrence of losses.* Suppose here that injurers will cause losses by making an effort of some type;[35] that they will obtain utility from the losses; and that this utility may be either socially valid or socially illicit (that is, it either will or will not augment social welfare). Where, for instance, a man kicks his neighbor's dog because he positively enjoys the unhappiness his neighbor will feel over it, we may not want to count the man's utility as an addition to social welfare. But where an individual throws a stone at a dog to ward him off for fear of being attacked, or where a person breaks into an unoccupied cabin in the woods to shelter himself during a storm, we undoubtedly would wish to count the utility he obtains in social welfare.

It is clearly socially best that injurers not act to cause losses if injurers will obtain only socially illicit utility from the losses. Injurers should act to cause losses only if they will obtain socially valid utility that exceeds the losses plus the cost of their effort.

EXAMPLE 6.5   An injurer can act, at a cost of 10, to cause losses of 100. It is therefore undesirable for the injurer to act unless he will derive valid utility exceeding 110.

It follows that for injurers to be induced to behave optimally, the magnitude of liability should equal the sum of losses caused and of illicit utility gained. This will mean that, net of their liability payments, the only utility injurers will be able to obtain from the losses is socially valid utility. Consequently injurers will be led to make socially appropriate calculations. If an injurer in Example 6.5 will obtain illicit utility only, liability will equal 100 plus this illicit utility and the injurer will therefore decide against causing losses. If the injurer will obtain only valid utility, his liability will equal 100 and he will spend 10 to cause losses whenever his utility exceeds 110.

*6.8.4  Remarks on the identification of socially illicit utility.*   (1) The situ-

---

35. It will be supposed that injurers cause losses with probability 1, but it will be obvious that what is said does not depend on that assumption.

ations in which many seem to regard the utility an injurer derives as socially illicit often have the following characteristic: the injurer derives utility only if the victim suffers disutility, as is true of the man who kicks at his neighbor's dog and obtains enjoyment only if he harms the dog and his neighbor experiences displeasure. Utility that is customarily viewed as socially valid does not usually have this feature, as in the case of the man who throws a stone at his neighbor's dog and obtains utility from scaring the dog away; if the stone does not actually hit the dog or if the neighbor does not know about the event, the man's utility will be just the same (if not greater).

(2) Courts may be able to make rough judgments from the circumstances of cases whether injurers obtained illicit utility. They may have evidence, for example, that the man kicked the dog in front of his neighbor and said, "How do you like that?"

*6.8.5   Injurers might escape suit.* Suppose truly liable injurers will sometimes not be sued for losses they cause (because, for instance, victims are unable to identify them). Then injurers may not have adequate incentives to take care unless the amount they pay when they are sued exceeds the losses they cause in the particular case. Injurers' liability when sued must be high enough to cover the losses for which they escape having to pay. Liability must therefore equal the level of losses multiplied by the inverse of the probability of suit. If, for instance, the probability of suit is only 50 percent, liability must equal twice the level of losses for injurers' expected liability to equal the losses they cause.[36]

*6.8.6   Courts' ability to estimate the probability of escape from suit.* Although courts may be able to recognize well enough when the probability of escape from suit is significant (as when a driver strikes down a pedestrian and immediately leaves the scene), they may find it difficult to estimate the exact level of the probability (as is the case with regard to the level of socially illicit utility or of socially unrecognized utility costs of care).

*6.8.7   Injurers can be induced to bargain with potential victims; reaching a bargain would be best.* Assume that an injurer can bargain with and pay a potential victim to be allowed to engage in an activity that would cause the victim losses. An individual might, for example, bargain with the owner of a boat to rent it for the day (here the harm to the victim owner would be not having the use of his boat). Suppose also that the outcome of bargaining will be socially optimal, that is, there will be an agreement under which an injurer

36. More precisely, only if injurers are risk neutral does liability need to be twice the level of losses to give injurers adequate incentives to reduce risk. If injurers are risk averse (see Chapter 8), then the level of liability necessary to provide appropriate incentives is less than twice the level of losses (or, more generally, less than the inverse of the probability multiplied by the level of losses).

engages in an activity if and only if the benefit to him is larger than the victim's losses. In addition, suppose that it is possible for an injurer to engage in an activity without bargaining (to take the boat for the day without paying for it) and that courts cannot evaluate losses accurately (it is hard to determine the loss to the boat owner of being denied use of his boat for the day).

Under these assumptions, it will be socially advantageous for courts to set the magnitude of liability at a level that is known to be higher than whatever are true losses. This will result in the optimal outcome because an injurer will prefer to bargain with the victim than to pay the high level of liability. Were courts to set liability equal to their best estimate of losses, by contrast, the outcome might not be optimal. An injurer might then engage in his activity when his benefit exceeds a court's estimate of losses rather than, as under bargaining, when his benefit exceeds true losses.

*6.8.8  Relevance of the possibility of inducing parties to bargain.* In assessing the importance of the above reason for liability to exceed losses, several limiting factors should be kept in mind. First, where parties cannot readily bargain—notably, where accidents involve strangers—the reason obviously does not apply.[37] Second, where parties are able to bargain, the process will not be costless and may not succeed (because, perhaps, of bluffing and other strategic behaviors). In such cases inducing injurers to bargain by threat of imposition of excessive liability may be undesirable. Instead, it may be best for injurers to face liability equal to courts' estimates of losses and thus to engage in their activities if their benefits exceed this amount. (Factories whose operations cause pollution may not be able to come to mutually satisfactory agreements with harmed parties. It may therefore be best to allow the factories to operate and to make them liable for estimated harms.) Third, in many situations where parties can bargain, there often seem to be other factors of substantial significance in justifying liability exceeding victims' losses. (The possibility that a person who takes a boat for the day will escape detection provides a reason for use of liability exceeding losses.)

*6.8.9  Injurers are highly likely to cause losses and the usual level of liability is less than losses.* Suppose that the level of liability is less than the true level of losses because of difficulty in estimating nonpecuniary (or other) components of losses, but that in the ordinary run this causes incentive problems of only small importance (see §§6.3.2 and 6.4.3). In the subset of situations where the probability of losses is high, however, incentive problems may be substantial. In these situations it may be desirable to employ a level of

---

37. Nor does it probably apply where an injurer causes harm in order to enjoy the victim's disutility (as where the man kicks his neighbor's dog because he enjoys the neighbor's displeasure). In such a situation it is hard to contemplate parties engaging in bargaining.

liability better approximating true losses. Where parties might take much too little care, or where they might act to cause losses in order to obtain socially illicit utility, the usual, low level of liability will not be expected to work adequately. Where, for example, a newspaper might knowingly misrepresent a person's statement to increase its circulation, use of only the usual magnitude of liability may not provide an acceptably good deterrent because it does not properly account for nonpecuniary losses (in, say, damage to reputation). By contrast, such liability may well provide a reasonably satisfactory deterrent where the newspaper might through negligence, and with fairly low probability, misquote a person.

*6.8.10    The relation between high probability of losses and the desirability of liability exceeding losses.* The preceding section discusses the only apparent reason that a high probability of losses should itself lead to liability exceeding the norm. Nevertheless, the previous sections suggest why there may be a *correlation* between the use of liability exceeding losses and a high probability of losses. The probability of losses is likely to be high where parties act to cause losses to gain illicit utility or where they take very little care owing to socially illicit utility costs or owing to a belief that they will not be sued.

*6.8.11    Actual liability in excess of losses.* In the United States, the use of liability exceeding victims' losses, that is, of "punitive" or "exemplary" damages, is limited primarily to cases where parties acted with ill will, malice, or conscious disregard for others, or where their behavior was outrageous or provoked indignation for some other reason. Award of punitive damages occurs most frequently in cases involving wanton and reckless behavior (such as drunken driving), assault and battery, and defamation; it is not very common in cases where harm has been done to property alone. Although in England "aggravated" damages may be awarded where courts in the United States award punitive damages, the use of higher punitive damages has been sharply curtailed. Similarly, in Germany awards may be higher than usual in approximately the same types of case, but in theory the higher awards are made to give the victims "satisfaction" and to compensate them for nonpecuniary losses rather than to give them an amount that exceeds their losses.[38]

*6.8.12    Note on the literature.* Landes and Posner (1981a) discuss escape from suit and inducing injurers to bargain as reasons for use of punitive

---

38. See generally Stoll 1972, secs. 103–125, for a comparative discussion, and *Prosser and Keeton on Torts* (Keeton, Dobbs, et al. 1984), sec. 2, Fleming 1983, pp. 2, 23, 27, 562–564, and McCormick 1935, chap. 10, on Anglo-American law. The reader should note that I did not mention here the occasional use of liability equal to fixed multiples of losses, as specified by special-purpose statutes, such as the treble-damage provisions of American antitrust law.

damages. Cooter (1982) emphasizes that if injurers obtain socially illicit utility, or bear socially illicit costs of taking care, punitive damages must be employed to induce them to act appropriately under the negligence rule.


# Mathematical Appendix


In this appendix examining the amount that liable injurers pay victims, it will be convenient to restrict attention to versions of the unilateral model of accidents in which injurers' levels of care alone are variable. (For simplicity, issues of causation and the scope of liability are set aside.)


## 6A.1   The Level and Probability of Losses and Courts' Uncertainty about the Level of Losses

*6A.1.1   Level of losses.* Let us consider here the usual unilateral model and let us be explicit about the distribution of possible losses. Suppose that

$p(x)$ = probability of an accident (that is, of positive losses) given care of $x$; and

$f(l;x)$ = probability density of losses of $l$ given $x$, conditional on the occurrence of an accident; $f$ is positive only on $[a,b]$; $0 < a < b$.

Expected losses are therefore

$$l(x) = p(x)\int_a^b lf(l;x)dl.$$

Thus if liable injurers have to pay $l$, their expected liability will be $l(x)$. Hence, as we know from §2A, injurers will act optimally under liability rules. That is,

PROPOSITION 6.1a   If the magnitude of liability equals actual losses, liable injurers will face expected liability of $l(x)$ and will thus be led to act optimally under both strict liability and the negligence rule.

It should also be mentioned that to induce optimal behavior it is not necessary that liability equal actual losses:

PROPOSITION 6.1b   If, regardless of actual losses, the magnitude of liability for an accident equals $\int_a^b lf(l;x)dl$—expected losses *conditional* on the occurrence of an accident—then liable injurers will face expected liability of $l(x)$ and will thus also be led to act optimally under liability rules.

*Remark.*   It would be desirable to set the magnitude of liability equal to $\int_a^b lf(l;x)dl$ if courts are able to determine this amount but are not able to observe $l$ (as when a lake is accidentally polluted and the number of dead fish can be estimated but not actually counted).

*6A.1.2   Probability of losses.* It follows from Proposition 6.1a that, other things equal, *the probability of losses should not affect liability*; if liability depends on the probability of losses, then injurers will generally have inappropriate incentives to reduce risk. If liability is greater than $l$ when $l$ is very likely, expected liability and incentives to reduce risk will tend to be excessive; and if liability is less than $l$ when $l$ is very unlikely, incentives to reduce risk will tend to be too low.

With respect to the latter point, however, note that if injurers incorrectly believe that the probability density of losses over some set of $l$ is zero (the situation corresponding, it was suggested in the text, to what is called an "unforeseeable" accident), then their behavior will not depend on their liability over the set. Therefore, if liability is less than actual losses (or is zero) over the set, injurers' behavior will be unaffected.

*6A.1.3   Courts' uncertainty about the level of losses.* Suppose now that courts are uncertain about the true level of losses. Specifically, let

$e$ = error in courts' assessment of losses, meaning that $l + e$ are losses as observed by courts, and let

$g(e)$ = probability density of $e$; $g$ is positive only on $[-\underline{e}, \bar{e}]$, where $\underline{e}$ and $\bar{e}$ are nonnegative.

If liable injurers must pay $l + e$, expected liability will be

$$(6.1) \qquad p(x) \int_a^b \left[ \int_{\underline{e}}^{\bar{e}} (l + e)g(e)de \right] f(l;x)dl.$$

Consequently, if the expected value of $e$ is zero, expected liability as given in Exp. (6.1) will be $l(x)$.[39]

PROPOSITION 6.2   Suppose that the magnitude of liability equals courts' assessment of losses, that the assessment is subject to error, but that the

39. The same will clearly be true if the distribution of $e$ is allowed to depend on $x$ or $l$.

expected error is zero. Then liable injurers' expected liability will be $l(x)$, so they will be led to act optimally under liability rules.

*Remarks.* (1) As noted in the text, courts may make errors in assessing losses not only where losses have already occurred, but also where a portion of losses (such as forgone earnings) will be incurred in the future. In this latter situation, courts' expected error will be zero if they employ an actuarial, unbiased estimate of future losses.

(2) If the expected value of courts' assessment of losses is less than actual losses, injurers will have too little incentive to reduce risk. This could occur if losses equal the sum of an observable component, $l_1$, and an unobservable component, $l_2$, and if courts limit liability to $l_1$ on the grounds that $l_2$ is speculative. (Here the error would equal $-l_2$.) Such a policy might be socially justifiable, however, if the administrative costs saved by not considering $l_2$ outweigh the increase in accident losses due to the dilution of injurers' incentives; this will be one of the points in §6A.6.5.

## 6A.2  Pecuniary versus Nonpecuniary Losses

To analyze this issue, consider the unilateral model of accidents modified so as to include three types of good: a good that is both consumed and used in production, called *wealth*; a good that can be made with $c$ units of wealth and that is consumed, called the *produced good*; and a good that is also consumed but that cannot be produced, called the *irreplaceable good* (such as land or physical integrity).

Assume that the utility of a party is the sum of the utility he obtains from the three types of good. Specifically, assume that the utility he derives from each unit of wealth is 1. Assume also that the utility he derives from the first unit of the produced good equals $u$, that he derives no utility from further units of the good (his demand is for exactly one unit), and that $u > c$ (his utility is greater than production cost). In addition, assume that the utility he derives from the first unit of the irreplaceable good is $z$ and that he derives no utility from further units of it.

Suppose that accidents may involve the loss to victims of any of the three types of good and that injurers' care involves use of wealth. Last, assume as usual that the measure of social welfare is the sum of parties' utilities.

Consider the reduction in social welfare associated with losses of each type of good. If a unit of wealth is lost, the reduction in social welfare is 1. If a unit of the produced good is lost, the reduction in social welfare is the production cost $c$; since use of $c$ units of wealth lowers social welfare by $c$ and, because $u > c$, it is socially worthwhile using $c$ units of wealth to produce another unit of the produced good to give to the individual who lost the unit. If a unit of the irreplaceable good is lost, the reduction in social welfare is $z$.

Call the loss of a unit of wealth a *pecuniary* loss of 1, a loss of the produced good a pecuniary loss of $c$, and a loss of the irreplaceable good a *nonpecuniary* loss of $z$. Then it is clear that the following proposition holds.

PROPOSITION 6.3   The conclusions reached in this and earlier appendixes about liability rules apply to the present model provided that losses are measured by the sum of pecuniary and nonpecuniary losses.

*Remarks.* (1) If liability does not include the entire nonpecuniary component of losses, then injurers will have an inadequate incentive to reduce risk.

(2) Since the socially correct amount that liable injurers should pay for loss of the produced good is the production cost $c$, courts do not need to observe the utility $u$ of the good to victims. And, of course, courts can observe $c$, at least in an economy with competitive markets, since $c$ will equal the price of the good. By contrast, as the socially appropriate amount that liable injurers should pay for loss of the irreplaceable good is its utility $z$, courts need to observe $z$ (that is, the number of units of wealth a victim would exchange for the irreplaceable good). It is reasonable to assume that courts would find that difficult.

## 6A.3   Economic Losses

In this section I compare losses in social welfare and losses in profits—so-called economic losses—arising from accidents that prevent victim firms from producing and selling goods. The comparison is made under the assumption, as in §6A.2, that goods are produced at constant marginal cost using the single good, wealth, as an input; that customers (who are identical) each demand (derive utility from) only one unit of the produced good; and so forth. Following the text, I will consider situations where other firms do not make sales to a victim firm's customers and situations where they do.

*6A.3.1   Victim firm's sales are not replaced by other firms.* Suppose here that a victim firm's production and sales will not be made up by other firms. Then if $u$ is the utility of the firm's good to customers and $c$ is again the production cost of the good, the loss in social welfare due to an accident preventing the firm from selling the good will be $u - c$. The economic loss will be $p - c$, where $p$ is the price of the good. (These are per-customer losses, as will be the case with most of the statements in this section.) Since $p \leq u$ (otherwise customers wouldn't have been willing to purchase the good), $p - c \leq u - c$; economic losses are bounded by social losses. Since this is the case, imposing liability equal to economic losses is socially superior to not imposing liability.

The degree to which economic losses understate social losses depends on the deviation between the price $p$ and the utility $u$ of the product. What the price is depends on further assumptions. For instance, if the firm is a monopolist and has perfect knowledge of $u$, it will set $p = u$, so economic losses will equal social losses. If the firm is a monopolist and has imperfect knowledge of $u$, it might set $p$ lower, as it might if it cannot practice price discrimination and customers differ, and so forth.

*6A.3.2  Victim firm's sales are alternatively made; perfect substitutes are sold by another firm.* Assume now that a good identical to a victim firm's good is sold by a second firm. Let $c'$ be the cost of production of the good for the second firm. The loss in social welfare due to an accident preventing the victim firm from selling will be the difference between the two firms' production costs, $c' - c$ (since customers of the victim firm are assumed to buy from the second firm). The economic loss of the victim firm will be $p - c$. Since $c' \leqq p$ (otherwise the second firm wouldn't have been willing to sell the good before the accident at the price $p$), $c' - c \leqq p - c$; again, social losses are bounded by economic losses.[40]

Whether imposing liability equal to economic losses is superior to not imposing liability is not clear, however. It depends on how close social losses $c' - c$ are to $p - c$. If the second firm's production costs are sufficiently close to the first's and thus $c' - c$ is low, then not imposing liability will be superior to imposing liability equal to economic losses.

The exact relationship between economic losses and social losses depends on what the price is, which in turn depends on assumptions about market structure and other factors. The two firms, for instance, might act jointly and set the monopoly price, or they might set price lower, as explained by a duopoly model. A more general model would allow for more than two firms, for marginal cost of production for each firm to vary with quantity produced, and so forth. Under certain assumptions, special results may hold. For example, under perfect competition the first-order loss in social welfare will equal the victim firm's economic losses. This is because the victim firm's sales will be replaced by the other firms in the industry, each of which will be producing at marginal cost equal to price.

*6A.3.3  Victim firm's sales are alternatively made; imperfect substitutes are sold by another firm.* Assume here that an imperfect substitute having utility $u' < u$ is sold by a second firm and, for simplicity, that its production

---

40. This result might not hold in a model in which marginal cost rises, for then the cost of the second firm's added production could exceed $p$.

cost is the same as the victim firm's. Then the change in social welfare associated with an accident preventing the first from selling will be $u - u'$. The economic loss of the victim firm $p - c$ could be higher or lower than $u - u'$. Clearly, $u - u'$ could be less than $p - c$, for $u'$ could be only slightly less than $u$. To see that $u - u' > p - c$ is possible, suppose, for instance, that $p = c + d$, $u' = c + 2d$, and $u = c + 4d$. Then $u - u' = 2d > d = p - c$. (Note that at $p$, customers would purchase the inferior good (since $u' > p$) and the second firm would sell it (since $p > c$), which justifies the assumption that they purchase the inferior good.)

Again, whether imposing liability equal to economic losses is superior to not imposing liability is not clear. It depends on how close social losses $u - u'$ are to economic losses $p - c$, and for reasons analogous to those given in §6A.3.2, the relation between economic losses and social losses depends on assumptions about market structure, among other elements.

*6A.3.4 Extensions and complications.* As suggested in the text, there are a variety of complicating factors that could be taken into account in assessing the connection between economic losses and social losses (victim firms making up lost sales later, existence of inventory or of excess capacity at other firms, time spent by customers traveling to other firms, price changes made by other firms during absence of victim firms from the market). Moreover, economic losses arise for reasons other than a victim firm being unable to sell (for example, a buyer may be prevented from buying). In situations such as these a different analysis is required. As also indicated in the text, the complexity of the relationship between economic losses and social losses, together with considerations of administrative costs, point toward the desirability of a cautious approach in the award of judgments for economic losses.

*6A.3.5 Note on the literature.* Bishop (1982) presents a highly suggestive informal treatment of economic losses; Rizzo (1982) contains graphical analysis of economic losses in perfectly competitive markets.

## 6A.4  Particularistic Elements in the Computation of Liability

In each of the modifications of the unilateral model considered here, I determine the reduction in social welfare due to an accident and observe that the magnitude of liability must equal this amount for injurers to act optimally under liability rules. As what is to be said will be by and large obvious, I will omit details.

*6A.4.1 Setoffs.* Suppose that if an accident occurs, a victim's loss will be $l$, but he would have borne an expense $k$ if the accident had not occurred. (For instance, suppose as in the text that the victim in an automobile accident will have to send his automobile to the shop, rent another, and purchase gasoline for it, but that he would have purchased gasoline for his own automobile had there not been an accident.) Then the diminution in social welfare due to an accident is not $l$ but $l - k$, and it is thus optimal to set off from liability the expense that would have been borne in any event.

6A.4.2 *Repair versus replacement.* Suppose first that an accident will involve damage to a produced good that, undamaged, yields utility $u$ to a victim (see §6A.2); that the good will have no value to a victim if not repaired; that the cost of repair is $r$; that the good can be replaced with a perfect substitute at a cost $c$; and that the repaired good is equivalent to a replacement. Then it is clear that choosing whichever costs the least, repair or replacement, will minimize the loss due to an accident (assuming here and below that repair or replacement is better than doing nothing). Thus, the loss in social welfare is $\min(c, r)$, and setting the magnitude of liability at this amount will result in optimal incentives for injurers.[41]

Now suppose that although a victim can repair a good, he can obtain only an imperfect substitute for it at cost $c$. In particular, suppose that he would derive utility $s < u$ from the substitute. It is evident that repairing the good will minimize the loss in social welfare if $r < u - s + c$. (Notice that repair may be better than replacement even if $r > c$.) Therefore, the decline in social welfare due to an accident is $r$ if repair is called for and $u - s + c$ if replacement is called for; and the level of liability should thus be $r$ and $u - s + c$, respectively, in these two cases. However, because $u - s$ is unobservable, the comments following Proposition 6.3 about nonpecuniary losses apply in the second case.

6A.4.3 *Interest, discounting, and inflation.* Suppose here that the real rate of interest is constant and equals $r$; that $q$ is the rate of inflation; and that the nominal rate of interest is $s$. (In this section compounding and discounting are assumed to be continuous.) The payment made by an injurer who causes real losses of $l$ at some time but will not be found liable until $t$ periods later should be $e^{st}l$, for if this is so the present value of the liability at the time of the loss is $e^{-st}e^{st}l = l$. On the other hand, if real losses of $l$ will not occur until $t$ periods after liability is found, then the injurer's payment when liability is found should be only $e^{-rt}l$, for this is the real present value of the losses that will occur. Equivalently, the injurer's payment should be $e^{-(q+r)t}$ multiplied by the nominal losses at time $t$, namely, $e^{qt}l$; and if $s = q + r$, his payment should be $e^{-st}$ multiplied by the nominal losses at time $t$.

6A.4.4 *Collateral benefits and gifts.* Because victims' receipts of payment

---

41. Also, it will follow from the logic of the discussion below, in §6A.5, that the victim will elect the cheaper of the two, repair or replacement, if what he receives is, as here, not his actual loss but his minimal loss.

from collateral sources or elsewhere obviously do not alter the fact that a loss *l* has been suffered, injurers' liability must still equal *l* for their incentives to be appropriate.

*6A.4.5   Taxes on wages.* Assume that victims work and earn wages *w* equal to the amount of the good they produce, but that they pay a tax at rate *t* (to finance some public project). If because of an accident a victim cannot work and loses *w* in pretax wages, the amount *w* is the loss in the good produced and in social welfare. Hence liability should equal pretax wages *w* rather than posttax wages $(1 - t)w$ for injurers' incentives to be appropriate. (As mentioned in the text, however, this ignores nonpecuniary losses associated with injury and not working, and also the value of leisure.)

## 6A.5   Victims' Opportunities to Mitigate Losses

Assume in this section that victims are able to lower the level of losses or to prevent further losses once an accident has occurred by making *mitigation expenditures*. More precisely, assume that $p(x)$ is the probability of an accident given level of care of *x*, that

$z$ = victims' expenditures to mitigate losses if an accident occurs; and
$l(z)$ = losses given $z$; $l'(z) < 0$; $l''(z) > 0$.

Hence expected total accident costs are

$$(6.2) \qquad x + p(x)(z + l(z)).$$

From Exp. (6.2) it is clear that socially optimal mitigation expenditures, $z^*$, are those that minimize

$$(6.3) \qquad z + l(z)$$

and thus that the optimal level of care, $x^*$, minimizes

$$(6.4) \qquad x + p(x)(z^* + l(z^*)).$$

Suppose that if injurers are liable they must pay $z^* + l(z^*)$. Under strict liability, then, injurers will minimize Exp. (6.4), so they will choose $x^*$. Moreover, if an accident occurs, victims will choose $z^*$, for since they will receive $z^* + l(z^*)$ whatever their actual $z$, they will maximize $z^* + l(z^*) - [z + l(z)]$, meaning they will minimize Exp. (6.3). The usual proof shows that under the negligence rule injurers will be led to choose $x^*$, in which case victims will bear their own losses and therefore naturally minimize Exp. (6.3) and so choose $z^*$.[42]

PROPOSITION 6.4   Suppose that the magnitude of liability equals the losses victims would sustain if they made optimal mitigation expenditures plus these expenditures. Then under strict liability or the negligence rule injurers will take optimal care and victims will make optimal mitigation expenditures when accidents occur.

*Remark.* This result easily carries over to the general situation where (as in §6A.1.1) there are multiple levels of loss possible (each calling for a different level of mitigation expenditures), where victims can take care ex ante to reduce risks, and so forth.

## 6A.6   Liability in Excess of Losses

Several modifications of the unilateral model are considered here in which it may be optimal for liability to exceed the level of the victim's losses. (As mentioned in the text, the excess of liability over losses is often called punitive or exemplary damages.)

*6A.6.1   Injurers incur costs of care that are not recognized as socially licit.* Suppose that an injurer's cost of care includes a component that does not enter into social welfare (such as, perhaps, where a person says it was "just too much trouble" to drive more slowly than 80 miles per hour on his way to the movie theater). In particular, suppose that

$w$ = socially illicit cost per unit of care;

the cost of taking level of care $x$ to the injurer, then, is $(1 + w)x$, whereas the social cost is only $x$. Hence $x^*$, the socially optimal $x$, minimizes

$$x + p(x)l,$$

where $l$ (for simplicity) is the single level of losses occurring if there is an accident.

Assume that injurers' liability for losses equals $l(1 + w)$. Then under strict liability injurers will choose $x^*$, for they will minimize

$$(1 + w)x + p(x)l(1 + w) = (1 + w)[x + p(x)l].$$

42. The result of this section is suggested in the discussion of a numerical example in Wittman 1981, sec. III.

Similarly, under the negligence rule injurers will take due care of $x^*$, by essentially the usual proof: if they take due care their costs will be $(1 + w)x^*$, whereas if $x < x^*$ then their expected costs will be $(1 + w)[x + p(x)l]$; but as $x^*$ minimizes $[x + p(x)l]$, it also minimizes $(1 + w)[x + p(x)l]$; so injurers must be better off taking care of $x^*$. We therefore have the following proposition.

> PROPOSITION 6.5a   If liability equals losses caused plus $wl$, reflecting socially illicit costs of care incurred by the injurer, then injurers will be led to take socially optimal care under strict liability and under the negligence rule.

*Remark.* As noted in the text, to determine whether an injurer's choice over the level of care has been motivated by socially unrecognized costs of care, the courts may rely, among other things, on the degree by which his level of care deviated from $x^*$. In particular, a very low level of care would itself signal that the injurer incurred socially unrecognized costs under some assumptions that could give rise to the observation of the choice of $x$ different from $x^*$. If, for instance, the likelihood that an injurer would be sued is low (see §6A.6.3 below), then under the negligence rule he might choose to act in a negligent way; and it is obvious that the level of care he would choose will be lower the greater are his socially unrecognized costs of care. Hence, in this case, it seems that it would be socially optimal for liability to be higher if $x$ is very low than it would be otherwise.[43]

*6A.6.2   Injurers obtain possibly socially illicit utility from the occurrence of losses.* Suppose here that injurers will obtain utility from the occurrence of losses and that they can increase the probability of losses by making costly efforts. Specifically, assume as in the text that there are two types of utility injurers may obtain from the occurrence of losses:

$u$ = licit utility enjoyed if losses occur; and
$w$ = illicit utility enjoyed if losses occur.

Licit utility (such as would arise when a person breaks into an empty cabin in a forest to gain shelter during a storm) enters into social welfare, but illicit

---

43. However, one must be cautious about this point. Depending on why injurers would behave suboptimally, there might not be a reason to raise liability on the basis of how low is the level of care. Suppose, for instance, negligent behavior is explained by the possibility that injurers will be unable to pay for losses (see §7A.2). In this case raising liability would be ineffective by assumption.

utility (such as would arise when a person batters another for pleasure) does not. Assume also that

$x$ = effort to increase probability of losses;
$p(x)$ = probability of losses; $p'(x) > 0$; $p''(x) < 0$.

Social welfare is therefore

(6.5)    $p(x)(u - l) - x$.

Hence, if $u \leq l$, socially optimal effort $x^*$ is 0. But if $u > l$, then $x^*$ is determined by

$p'(x)(u - l) = 1$

if there is an interior solution (if there is no such solution and $x^*$ is positive, then $x^*$ is the minimum $x$ such that $p(x) = 1$).

Now assume that liability for losses equals $l + w$. Then under strict liability injurers will act optimally, for because they will obtain net utility of $u + w - (l + w) = u - l$ if losses occur, they will choose $x$ to maximize Exp. (6.5). Similarly, they will act optimally under the negligence rule. (The present interpretation of this rule, note, is that injurers are liable if they make effort exceeding $x^*$.) Specifically, if injurers choose $x > x^*$, their expected utility will be $p(x)(u - l) - x$, which is less than $p(x^*)(u - l) - x^*$ and thus less than $p(x^*)(u + w) - x^*$, their expected utility if they choose $x^*$. Moreover, they will not choose $x < x^*$, for then their expected utility would be $p(x)(u + w) - x$, the derivative of which is greater than that of Exp. (6.5) and which thus does not achieve a maximum below $x^*$. Injurers will therefore choose $x^*$, as claimed.

PROPOSITION 6.5b    If liability equals losses caused plus $w$, reflecting illicit utility enjoyed by the injurer from the occurrence of losses, then injurers will act socially optimally under liability rules. In other words, they will not try to cause losses when they would obtain only illicit utility, but they will do so when expected licit utility is greater than expected losses plus the cost of effort.

*6A.6.3  Injurers might escape suit.* Suppose, in the usual unilateral model, that there is a positive probability $q$ that injurers will escape suit when they cause losses for which they would be liable if sued. Then if the magnitude of liability equals only losses caused, injurers' expected liability will be only

$(1 - q)l(x)$, so they will have too little incentive to reduce risk. For injurers' incentives to be correct, expected liability must equal $l(x)$, expected losses; and this will clearly be true if injurers who are sued pay $l/(1 - q)$.[44]

PROPOSITION 6.5c    If liability equals losses caused multiplied by $1/(1 - q)$, the inverse of the probability of suit, injurers will act optimally under liability rules despite the chance that they will escape suit.

*6A.6.4    Injurers can be induced to bargain with potential victims; reaching a bargain would be best.* Assume the following. First, injurers can choose to engage in an activity that will give them a benefit $u$ and will cause losses $l$. (For simplicity, assume there is no variable "care.") Thus it will be optimal for injurers to engage in the activity when $u > l$. Second, injurers who engage in the activity will be liable for losses unless the injurers bargain with and pay victims for permission to engage in the activity. (Bargaining is possible because injurers and victims know each other's identity.) Third, if injurers bargain with victims, then if and only if $u > l$ there will be an agreement allowing injurers to engage in the activity; under an agreement injurers will pay victims an amount $z$ between $l$ and $u$. Fourth, courts cannot observe $l$; rather, they observe $l + \varepsilon$, where $\varepsilon$ is a random-error term distributed in $[-a, a]$. Given these assumptions we have the following result.

PROPOSITION 6.5d    If courts set liability equal to an amount $l'$ that they are certain is greater than true losses, an optimal outcome will result.

Note that courts can determine such an amount $l'$; for instance, the observed losses plus $2a$ would exceed true losses. To see why the proposition holds, consider that if $u > l$, injurers will engage in the activity: for if $z < l'$, injurers will bargain, pay $z$, and obtain a net benefit of $u - z$; and if $z \geq l'$ (which can only happen if $u > l'$), they will engage in the activity, pay $l'$, and obtain a net benefit of $u - l'$. On the other hand, if $u \leq l$, then injurers will not be willing to engage in the activity and pay $l'$ since $l' > l$ (and by assumption injurers will not bargain with victims in this case). Hence an optimal outcome will always result.[45]

*6A.6.5    Injurers cause losses with high probability and the usual level of liability is less than losses.* Suppose for convenience here that there is only

44. If injurers are risk averse, then liability need not be raised so much to induce optimal behavior.

45. One would want to show that, by contrast, if courts set liability equal to observed losses, an optimal outcome might not result. To show this would require a more detailed consideration of bargaining than can be undertaken here.

one level of care, $x$, and that taking care will reduce the probability $p$ of loss $l$ to 0. Then it will be optimal for care to be taken if and only if $p \geq x/l$.

If liability equals $l$, then injurers under strict liability will, of course, always act optimally. (The situation under the negligence rule is omitted for simplicity.) If, however, the level of liability is $l_1 < l$, injurers might not act optimally because they will take care only if $p \geq x/l_1$. Assume that setting liability equal to $l_1$ is administratively costless, because $l_1$ can easily be verified; whereas verifying that $l$ has occurred will involve administrative costs (borne, let us say, by courts) of $a > 0$, where $a < l$. Then it will be socially desirable for liability to equal only $l_1$ for all $p$ not too high; but for $p$ above some critical level, liability equal to $l$ may be desirable, because if liability equals $l_1$ and $p$ is in $(x/l, x/l_1)$, injurers will not take care even though they ought to. In that case the addition to total accident costs relative to such costs if care is taken will be $pl - x$. Since this increment to costs equals 0 at $p = x/l$, is increasing in $p$, and can be avoided by imposing liability of $l$, at an expected administrative cost of $pa$, the claimed result follows.

PROPOSITION 6.5e   It may be socially desirable, in order to avoid administrative costs of estimating losses, to impose liability of $l_1$ less than losses $l$ when the probability $p$ of losses is sufficiently low, but for larger $p$ to impose liability equal to losses.

*6A.6.6   Note on the literature.* Landes and Posner (1981a) examine a model in which injurers can raise the probability of losses by making a costly effort and discuss escape from suit and inducing injurers to bargain as reasons for liability to exceed losses. Cooter (1982) studies a model similar to that in §6A.6.1 and concludes, essentially, that because some part of injurers' utility or costs of care may not enter into social welfare, liability in excess of losses may be desirable.

# 7 | Other Topics in Liability

## 7.1 Multiple Injurers

Suppose here that more than one injurer may contribute to the occurrence of an accident, as where chemicals in the smoke discharged by two factories happen to react and cause pollution damage, or where a building collapses because of the architect's faulty design and the contractor's improper method of construction. In such cases optimal levels of care for the different injurers are determined along familiar lines, as illustrated in the following example.

EXAMPLE 7.1 Two injurers, A and B, may cause an accident that will result in losses of 1,000. The probabilities of an accident as a function of their levels of care, together with their costs of care and total expected accident costs, are as shown in Table 7.1. In this case total accident costs are minimized when both injurers exercise care.

Now consider whether multiple injurers will be led to take optimal levels of care under strict liability and under the negligence rule.

*7.1.1 Strict liability.* Assume that under strict liability each injurer is liable for a fraction (possibly zero) of losses[1] and that the fraction does not depend on his level of care. (This is the natural interpretation of strict liability in the present context.) Then the expected liability of each injurer will fall by only a fraction of the reduction in expected losses in which his exercise of care will result. Therefore, injurers may not be led to take adequate care if they act independently. In Example 7.1 if A and B each bear half of accident losses,

---

1. Note that in effect an injurer's liability will equal a fraction of losses where he initially bears the entire losses but then sues others for "contribution"; see §7.1.4.

*Table 7.1*

| Levels of care of injurers | | Costs of care of injurers | | Accident probability | Expected accident losses | Total accident costs |
|---|---|---|---|---|---|---|
| A | B | A | B | | | |
| None | None | 0 | 0 | 8% | 80 | 80 |
| Care | None | 6 | 0 | 7% | 70 | 76 |
| None | Care | 0 | 8 | 7% | 70 | 78 |
| Care | Care | 6 | 8 | 6% | 60 | 74 |

then neither will take care, because for each the reduction in expected liability from taking care will be 5 whereas the cost of taking care is greater than 5. Moreover, if the fraction of A's liability is increased by enough to make him take care, B certainly will not take care. Thus there is no division of liability that will induce injurers to behave optimally in the example.[2]

If, however, injurers act in concert, that is, so as to minimize their joint expenses, they will all choose to exercise optimal care, regardless of the particular assignment of liability among them. Where injurers act together to minimize their joint expenses, the situation will be equivalent to one where a single injurer minimizes his expenses under strict liability, and in that situation we know behavior will be optimal.

*7.1.2 Negligence rule.* Under the negligence rule if only one injurer fails to take due care he will be liable for the victim's entire losses, and if several injurers fail to take due care they must share the losses in some way.[3] Under this rule independently acting injurers will each be led to take optimal care in equilibrium, since each will bear the full brunt of liability if he alone does not take due care (which is assumed here, as usual, to equal optimal care). Also, that is the only equilibrium possible; a situation in which more than one injurer fails to take care cannot be an equilibrium. To verify these facts in Example 7.1, observe that both A and B taking care is an equilibrium, as each will reason that if he fails to take care, his expected liability will be 70 (rather than 0). Further, neither party taking care is not an equilibrium, for if neither takes care either A or B must bear expected liability of at least 40 (since

2. Although in general no division of strict liability will guarantee optimal behavior, the best division will be such that an injurer will bear more liability the lower his cost of exercising care and the greater its effectiveness in reducing risk.

3. Again, division of liability might come about through some of the negligent injurers suing others for contribution; an equivalent assumption is that some or each of the negligent injurers will be fully liable with a probability.

together they bear expected liability of 80). Hence that party, if not both, would have been better off taking due care and avoiding liability.

If injurers act in concert, they will, of course, also all be led to take optimal care.

*7.1.3   Remarks.* (1) Injurers who are strangers (the two factories might be considered such if they are not in contact) presumably act independently, whereas injurers who have some type of relationship with one another (the architect and the contractor) may act in concert.

(2) The importance of the problem of inadequate incentives under strict liability could be substantial where the number of injurers is large. The more injurers among whom losses are shared, the greater the dilution in incentives for each. If twenty rather than two factories share liability for pollution dam- age, each particular factory will enjoy only 5 percent rather than 50 percent of the savings in expected liability accomplished by a precaution. Consequently, few precautions will be taken. In addition, organizing an effort to minimize joint costs will be difficult when the number of injurers is large.

(3) That injurers will each take due care under the negligence rule means, in strict logic, that it is irrelevant how liability would be shared were several injurers to act negligently. But, obviously, the sharing of liability among several negligent injurers will not be irrelevant in a model in which error and other factors may lead to instances of negligence (see §4.4.1). In this case sharing of liability will matter: it will tend to dilute incentives. Nevertheless, the importance of sharing of liability will be limited by the probability that multiple parties would simultaneously be found negligent. If this probability is small, the way in which liability is shared might best be decided on grounds of administrative simplicity.

*7.1.4   Actual liability of multiple injurers.* The determination of liability for one among multiple injurers is made on the same general basis as is the determination of liability for a single injurer, although there can be significant differences regarding procedure and proof.[4]

Once found liable, an injurer must as a rule pay to the victim whatever proportion of his losses the victim chooses to collect from that injurer (includ- ing the entire losses). Whether a liable injurer who pays the victim is then able to recover an amount from other liable injurers is a complicated matter that varies considerably in its details among countries and by area of law. Some- times a party who pays the victim is able to obtain complete recoupment from other liable parties. This recoupment is known as *indemnity* and may apply, for instance, when there is a contractual arrangement to that effect among the

---

4. See, for instance, the discussion in Fleming 1983, chap. 10, of the consequences in Anglo-American law of whether injurers were acting jointly or independently (''severally'').

liable parties. Other times, a party who pays the victim is not able to obtain any recoupment or only partial recoupment. Partial recoupment is known as *contribution* and may be based on notions of responsibility and fault or, occasionally, on a mechanical formula. Historically, contribution was not allowed in Anglo-American law, but today in England and other Common-wealth countries statutes allow contribution quite broadly. In the United States there is a trend in this direction, with legislation permitting it to a greater or lesser extent having been passed in many jurisdictions.[5]

*7.1.5   Note on the literature.* Landes and Posner (1980) first studied the incentives to take care on the part of multiple injurers, assuming that the injurers act independently and restricting attention to the negligence rule. They showed that all injurers will be led to take due care regardless of how liability would be shared among several negligent injurers.

## 7.2   Injurers' Inability to Pay for Losses

*7.2.1   Effect of inability to pay.* Assume in this section that injurers may not be able to pay fully for the losses they cause. Their incentives to take care may therefore be inadequate, since they will treat losses that they cause and that exceed their assets as imposing liabilities only equal to their assets. The importance of this point clearly depends on the size of losses that injurers may cause in relation to their assets. It also depends on the form of liability, as the next example illustrates.

EXAMPLE 7.2   The probability of an accident that will result in losses of 100 will be reduced from 25 percent to 15 percent if injurers take care, at a cost of 5. Because the exercise of care will lower expected losses by 10% × 100 = 10 and costs 5, it will be socially desirable. Under strict liability an injurer who has less than 50 in assets will not be led to take care, for if he does so his savings in expected liability payments—10 percent multiplied by his assets—will be less than 5. Under the negligence rule, on the other hand, only an injurer who has less than 20 in assets will fail to take care. Only if assets are less than 20 will expected payments for negligence—25 percent times assets—be less than the cost of taking care.

The reason that assets must be lower under the negligence rule than under strict liability for injurers to find it advantageous not to exercise adequate care

5. See generally Fleming 1983, chap. 10, and *Prosser and Keeton on Torts* (Keeton, Dobbs, et al. 1984), chap. 8; for a comparative treatment see Weir 1976, secs. 105–141.

is that the motive to take adequate care is sharp under the negligence rule: under that rule an injurer escapes liability entirely by taking due care, whereas under strict liability he merely reduces the chance of liability.

*7.2.2   Remarks on the significance of dilution of incentives.* (1) Despite the presence of the foregoing mitigating effect of the negligence rule, there are many contexts where inability to pay for losses plausibly may lead to dulling of incentives to reduce risk. This is so not only for parties with low or moderate assets, but also for parties with substantial assets whose activities pose special risks. (Consider, for instance, even large corporate enterprises and the chance of fires or explosions causing mass injury, or the possibility that a widely distributed product has toxic or other dangerous properties.) Incentives are particularly likely to be diluted with respect to those actions that would serve primarily to lower the severity or likelihood of extremely large losses exceeding parties' assets but not of small or moderate losses. (Consider the motive of the owner of a nuclear power plant to spend on a safety device that would limit harm only in a catastrophic accident involving rupture of the reactor core and causing losses far greater than the owner's net worth.)

(2) Incentive problems are exacerbated if parties have the opportunity to shield assets, as where an individual puts his property in a relative's name or where a firm sets up wholly owned subsidiaries, the holdings of each of which are only a fraction of the holdings of the parent.

(3) The possibility that parties will not find taking due care worthwhile because of inability to pay for losses supplies a reason (in addition to those mentioned in §4.4.1) for the occurrence of negligent behavior.

(4) The problem of dilution of incentives is, of course, quite different from the problem that scholars and practitioners often identify with injurers' inability to pay fully for losses, namely, victims' inability to obtain complete compensation. This and related issues (concerning, chiefly, insurance) will be addressed in §10.4.

(5) A problem of dilution of incentives similar in character to that due to injurers' inability to pay arises where liable injurers might escape suit (because, for instance, of victims' inability to identify them or to prove causation).[6]

*7.2.3   Solutions to the problem of inadequate incentives.* Several types of social responses to the problem of inadequate incentives to reduce risk are possible, depending on circumstances. First, if there is another party who has some control over the behavior of the party whose assets are limited, then the

---

6. Recall §6.8.5, and see also Chapter 12.

former party can be held vicariously liable for the losses caused by the latter. This will be discussed in §7.3, below.

Second, parties with assets less than some specified amount could in some contexts be prevented from engaging in an activity. This approach would ensure that parties who do engage in an activity have enough at stake to be led to take adequate care. However, the approach suffers from the defect that it establishes an otherwise inappropriate criterion for deciding which parties shall participate in an activity. Recall from §2.2 that it is socially desirable for a party to participate in an activity if the benefits the party will obtain will outweigh the *expected* losses the party will cause. Imposing an asset requirement is a different criterion because it asks that a party be able to pay for the *actual* losses the party causes (or for a large portion of them). Suppose, for example, that by engaging in an activity a firm can cause losses ranging up to $1,000,000, but that expected losses will be in the neighborhood of only $20,000 (because the likelihood of losses will be low). A firm therefore ought to be able to engage in the activity whenever it would be willing to pay about $20,000. To insist that firms have assets sufficient to pay liability awards as high as $1,000,000 will exclude from the activity some firms that will be willing to pay the $20,000 expected harm—and that may be induced to take tolerably good care, despite having assets considerably less than $1,000,000. Although potentially helpful, then, asset requirements are a somewhat undiscriminating device for alleviating the incentive problems under consideration.

A third response to inadequate incentives, one closely related to asset requirements, is regulation concerning liability insurance. One form of regulation would require the purchase of (perhaps full) coverage. This approach does not suffer from the drawback of asset requirements just mentioned, since liability insurance premiums will approximate expected losses. (Thus, in the example above, firms will engage in the activity whenever they are willing to pay a premium of about $20,000, even if their assets are substantially below $1,000,000.) But ownership of liability insurance may affect incentives to take care; a fuller discussion of requirements to purchase liability insurance is deferred to §10.4. A second form of regulation, also discussed in §10.4, is prohibition of the purchase of liability insurance. This might improve incentives to take care because without the insurance parties' entire assets would be put at risk by their engaging in an activity.

Still another way of correcting for dilution of incentives is for the state to regulate parties' behavior. Thus, for example, the procedures employed to pasteurize milk or the routes followed by trucks carrying explosives may be determined by a regulatory authority rather than left to the choices of dairies and trucking companies. On the other hand, a regulatory authority's ability to devise appropriate regulations is limited by its knowledge. This and other difficulties with regulation as an alternative to liability will be discussed generally in Chapter 12.

A final way of mitigating dilution of incentives is resort to criminal liability. A party who would not take care if only his assets were at stake might be induced to do so for fear of a criminal sanction. This subject too will be taken up in Chapter 12.

*7.2.4   Note on the literature.* Summers (1983) first formally analyzed the problem discussed here, and I extend his work in Shavell (1986).

## 7.3   Vicarious Liability

The concern here is with the imposition of liability on one party for some or all of the losses caused by a second party. The second party shall be called the *actor* because it will be assumed that his actions alone directly affect risk, and the first party shall be called the *principal*. It will also be assumed that the principal has a relationship with the actor that may allow him to observe the actor's level of care and, if so, to control it or come to an agreement about it. Finally, it will be assumed that the actor's assets are less than the losses he might cause, but that the principal's assets are sufficient to pay for the losses.[7] The reader may wish to think of the principal and the actor as employer and employee or as contractor and subcontractor, but other examples will be mentioned (including, in the section below, that of shareholders and the corporation). The areas where the model is relevant will be seen to be quite general.

*7.3.1   Effect of vicarious liability on the exercise of care.* If the actor alone is liable, his incentive to take care may be inadequate owing, as discussed in §7.2, to his inability to pay fully for losses. If, however, the principal can observe and control the actor's level of care, then imposition of vicarious liability will induce the principal to compel the actor to exercise optimal care.

EXAMPLE 7.3   An actor with assets of 30 can reduce the probability of an accident that will result in losses of 100 from 20 percent to 10 percent by taking care at a cost of 8. Liability is strict (the case under the negligence rule is similar). Suppose first that the actor alone is liable. Then, because his expected savings from taking care will be only $10\% \times 30 = 3$ (30 is all he can pay) while the cost of taking care is greater than that, he will not take care.

---

7. Note that the situation here differs in two respects from that in §7.1 where multiple injurers act in concert: here it is assumed that one party does not have assets sufficient to pay for losses and that one party does not directly affect the risk of losses.

Suppose next that a principal who can observe whether the actor takes care will be vicariously liable for the entire losses due to an accident. In this case the principal will save $10\% \times 100 = 10$ if the actor takes care. Consequently, the principal will certainly want the actor to take care. Even if the principal has to bear the cost of care of 8 himself (as where an employer pays his employee overtime to proceed with caution on a dangerous task), he will have the actor exercise care.

Suppose instead that the principal will be vicariously liable for only the 70 of the losses that the actor will be unable to pay. Then, again, the principal will be led to have the actor take care, but for a more complicated reason. The principal will not be willing to bear the entire cost of care himself, because taking care at cost 8 will lower his expected liability by only 7. Yet because taking care will reduce the actor's expected liability by 3, the actor and the principal should together be willing to bear the cost of care. The exercise of care should make both the actor and the principal better off (as where a subcontractor agrees to absorb some of the costs of precautions when on a job under the direction of a vicariously liable contractor). If, for example, the actor contributes 2 toward care he will be better off because he will save, net of his contribution, $3 - 2 = 1$. The principal will also be better off because he will save $7 - 6 = 1$ (for his share of the cost of care will be 6).

This example illustrates the general conclusion that where the principal can observe and control the actor's level of care, the actor will take optimal care whether the principal is vicariously liable for full losses or only for the balance not paid by the actor and whether the principal or the actor initially bears the cost of care. Whenever two parties' joint liability equals the whole of losses and they can jointly pay for these losses, it will be in their mutual interests to take optimal care (just as it was in the mutual interests of multiple injurers acting in concert to take optimal care).

If vicarious liability is imposed when the principal cannot observe and directly control the actor's level of care, the principal can and will attempt to induce the actor to take care by the threat of suit against the actor when he causes losses or by the threat of other penalties, such as demotion or discharge. But since the actor's assets are less than the losses he might cause, the principal will not generally be able to induce the actor to choose the optimal level of care.[8]

*7.3.2 Effect of vicarious liability on engagement in risky activity.* While

8. The principal will, however, be able to induce the actor to choose at least as much care as he does in the absence of vicarious liability; see §7A.3.

only if the principal can observe and control the actor's level of care will imposition of vicarious liability guarantee that the actor will exercise optimal care, imposition of vicarious liability will always lead the principal to consider the full liability cost of the actor's activity in deciding whether to have the actor engage in the activity.

*7.3.3   Remarks on factors bearing on the appeal of vicarious liability.* (1) The advantage of vicarious liability on grounds of desirably affecting incentives to reduce risk will be greater the lower the actor's assets are and the higher the principal's assets are relative to the probable magnitude of harm the actor can cause. It will also be greater the better able the principal is to control the actor's behavior.

To illustrate the relevance of these factors, consider the important example of the large firm and its employees.[9] It is apparent that the assets of employees are likely to be much lower than the losses they could cause, for the scope of a firm's activities is frequently such that a single employee's behavior may result in harm to many parties or otherwise lead to significant losses. Thus, were employees only individually liable, one suspects that their incentives to take care would often be seriously inadequate. One also supposes that imposition of vicarious liability on the firm helps to cure this problem because the firm's assets are usually much greater than those of any of its employees and because the firm may have the ability to exert significant control over its employees' behavior.

Outside the area of the large firm and its employees, and especially where a principal engages an actor on a one-time or sporadic basis, the situation is different. There is no natural presumption that can be made about the actor's assets relative to the principal's. Contrast, for instance, these two examples. (a) A homeowner (the principal) of average means pays a national pest-control firm (the actor) to carry out extermination services; here the principal's assets are much smaller than the actor's. (b) A large construction firm (the principal) subcontracts with a small, family-owned plumbing company (the actor) to help on the job; here the principal's assets are much greater than the actor's. These examples serve also to illustrate that the principal's ability to control effectively the actor's behavior may be adequate in one situation but poor in the next—whereas the construction firm should be able to watch over the subcontractor quite well, the likelihood that the homeowner can judge the performance of the exterminator is presumably not great. Evidently, then, the

---

9. The reader should be reminded that I am considering in this part of the book only issues of incentives. In particular, I am not considering any advantages (or disadvantages) vicariously liable parties may have as risk bearers.

attractiveness of vicarious liability will depend significantly on the features of the situation at hand.

(2) The desirability of vicarious liability is enhanced by three factors that were not considered in the analysis of §7.3.1. First, principals may have better knowledge than actors about the nature of risk or be able themselves to take actions that can lower it. Where this is so, imposition of vicarious liability will obviously lead principals not only to have actors take appropriate care, but also to take additional actions of their own to reduce risk. Given vicarious liability, firms will be led to issue instructions, organize the conditions of the workplace, schedule operations, select employees, and so forth, in ways that better reduce risk.[10] Or, say, if parents are subject to vicarious liability, they will be led to consider more carefully whether to let children use potentially dangerous devices (power tools, snowmobiles, guns) or do other things that increase risk.

The second advantage is that principals may have more information than courts about the appropriateness of actors' behavior. If that is the case and if under vicarious liability principals frequently replace courts as the discipliners of actors, fewer mistakes will be made and better conduct promoted. Were employees of the large firm only personally liable and courts to make errors in the determination of negligence (see §4.3.1), some employees would be led to take excessive care (for example, those whose actions would naturally be noticed by courts and who are uncertain about the standard of care courts would apply), and others would take too little (those whose role would not so easily be discerned). Such consequences are less likely when the firm, with its superior knowledge, is motivated by its vicarious liability to discipline its employees.

The third additional advantage of vicarious liability is relevant primarily in regard to firms and their employees: victims do not need to show which employees were responsible for their losses, but only that some employees must have been responsible. This advantage can be important since the particular employee that caused harm may be hard to identify (as where all that is known is that a truck with the sign of company X on its side hit the victim's parked car) or because the exact roles of different employees may be difficult to evaluate (the engineers who designed the oil storage tank that exploded

---

10. To the extent that a firm's actions (that is, management's actions) directly affect risk, however, the firm could in principle be found liable as a joint tortfeasor (what I called a multiple injurer). But it may be difficult for courts to obtain information about many such actions of a firm (selection of employees, other aspects of the organization of production). Hence, in part, vicarious liability may be seen as an indirect way of solving the problem of courts' inability to determine in which respects a firm's actions were inappropriate.

versus the production unit that made the tank versus the workers who maintained and used it). Were victims constrained to prove employees individually liable, employees might anticipate that they would escape suit with significant probability, and their incentives to take care might thereby be diluted.[11]

These three advantages, together with the interpretation made in Remark 1 above, appear to constitute a strong case in favor of imposition of vicarious liability on large firms.

(3) There are, however, disadvantages of vicarious liability that should be kept in mind. Specifically, imposition of vicarious liability will increase the administrative cost of using the legal system, since it will raise the number of defendants named in actions brought by victims, complicate proceedings, and engender claims (or extralegal sanctions) by principals against actors. The administrative costs associated with imposition of vicarious liability may outweigh the beneficial effects on incentives. For example, the administrative costs associated with suits against homeowners, were they held vicariously liable for harms done by pest-control firms they had hired, arguably would not be justified by any enhancement in the pest-control firms' incentives to reduce risk. The same could similarly be argued, perhaps, with regard to the costs (including strains on family relations) were uncles held vicariously liable for harms done by their nieces and nephews while temporarily under their charge.

*7.3.4   Actual use of vicarious liability.* Vicarious liability is a significant feature of legal systems today.[12] Most important, firms are held responsible for the losses caused by their employees. How this comes about, though, and the position of employees differ somewhat among systems.[13] In the Anglo-American and French legal systems a firm's liability is based on a showing that its employee would be liable as an individual; essentially the same is true with regard to an employee of a state enterprise or a cooperative in the Soviet

11. A closely related advantage of vicarious liability concerns the chance that an employee responsible for a victim's harm will be dead by the time the harm comes to pass. Given that many harms may occur only after the lapse of many years, this is a very real possibility. (Consider the collapse of bridges and other accidents due to design defects or faulty construction, or environmental and health-related harms due to substances and organisms with long latency periods.) Under vicarious liability the victim does not face difficulties on account of the death of responsible employees; he may still sue the firm.

12. See generally Fleming 1983, chap. 18, and *Prosser and Keeton on Torts* (Keeton, Dobbs, et al. 1984), chap. 12, on Anglo-American law; and Le Gall 1976 and, especially, Eörsi 1975 for comparative treatments.

13. What is said here about firms and employees is summarized in the following parts of Eörsi 1975: secs. 22 and 93–96 on Anglo-American and French systems; secs. 23 and 103–104 on the German system; secs. 27 and 128 on the Soviet system. Section 17 provides a comparison.

Union. According to German law, by contrast, a firm itself has to be shown negligent (except of course in areas of strict liability), notably in its supervision of employees or in their selection.[14] Under all three of the Western legal systems, a victim has a right to sue an employee, although the victim usually chooses to collect from the firm. Also, a firm ordinarily has the right to sue an employee, although this too is not often done; the firm may, however, discipline the employee or discharge him. In the Soviet Union a victim does not have a right of legal action against an employee, but only against a state enterprise. An employee may nevertheless be sued by the enterprise or he may be sanctioned in other ways.

Vicarious liability is in addition sometimes imposed on principals for losses caused by their agents, on automobile owners for accidents caused by those whom they allow to drive, on parents for harms resulting from their children's acts, on teachers for their students' negligence, and so forth.[15]

Although the pattern of use of vicarious liability is complicated and varies among legal systems, the general principles that are applied seem to be such that the greater the degree of a party's control and authority over an actor, and the more knowledge he has about the actor's behavior, the more likely the party is to be held responsible for the losses caused by the actor.[16]

*7.3.5 Note on the literature.* Sykes (1984) contains an analysis of vicarious liability stressing, in addition to some of the issues of incentives discussed here, the allocation of risk between actors and principals. See also Kornhauser (1982) and Sykes (1981).

## 7.4 Limited Liability of Shareholders for Losses Caused by Corporations

*7.4.1 Effects of limited liability on incentives, and where it will and will not have appeal.* Limiting the liability of a corporation to its assets rather than extending liability to its shareholders ("piercing the corporate veil") is none other than deciding against imposing vicarious liability on shareholders. It

14. It may not be entirely appropriate to call this vicarious liability. Yet as Eörsi 1975 discusses, the situation under German law is particularly complex and may result in vicarious liability in the end. For example, if a person slips on the floor in a store because of an employee's negligence, the person may be able to circumvent the requirement that he show the store was at fault in its supervision or selection of the employee. If the person can maintain that an implicit contractual relationship between him and the store was established the moment he entered the store, then by appeal to contract principles the store might be held vicariously liable for the negligence of its employee.

15. See Eörsi 1975, secs. 61–74.

16. See Eörsi 1975, secs. 52–54.

therefore follows from §7.3 that limited liability will tend not to have disadvantageous effects on incentives where shareholders are not well able to observe or to control the risk-creating behavior of the corporation and where the probability of losses exceeding corporate assets (and thus the dilution of the corporation's incentives) is small.[17]

Both these conditions are apparently relatively likely to be met for the large, publicly held corporation. Were its shareholders personally liable, they would probably not find it worthwhile to devote much effort on an individual basis to monitoring the corporation and, in any event, they would be unlikely to have the expertise to do so. Moreover, the torts of the large corporation would not normally be expected to result in bankruptcy. Still, it should be kept in mind that in some settings today, the chance of bankruptcy (especially arising from environmental and health-related harms) is becoming increasingly important. Nor should it be overlooked that were shareholders personally liable, agents acting on their collective behalf (such as their liability insurers) might well monitor the corporation's activities.

The situation with respect to small, closely held corporations is different. Their shareholders are more likely to have the requisite knowledge and, if personally liable, the desire to watch over the corporation's activities. In addition, the probability of bankruptcy due to tort liability might be greater for such corporations.

Similarly, the appeal of limited liability is lessened where the corporation in question is a subsidiary of a parent corporation. Here the knowledge of the parent—the shareholder—about its subsidiary, and the parent's power over the subsidiary, should often give the parent the ability and the motive, if vicariously liable, to reduce risks created by the subsidiary.

Curiously, there is a potential advantage in holding a parent corporation liable for losses caused by a purchased subsidiary *before* the time of purchase—and thus before the parent could possibly have directly influenced its behavior. The advantage is that the owners of the future subsidiary will realize before it is purchased that any future liability arising from its actions will reduce its value to a purchaser and will therefore reduce the price the purchaser will pay. To the extent that they anticipate a purchase, they will have an incentive to reduce risks even if the risks exceed the level of their company's own assets.

17. The principal affirmative advantage of limited liability may be avoidance of the administrative costs associated with suits against shareholders. Although limited liability also protects risk-averse shareholders against risk, shareholders would presumably purchase liability insurance in the absence of limited liability (as will be discussed generally in Chapter 9). Thus it is not clear that protection of risk-averse shareholders against risk should be considered an affirmative advantage of limited liability.

*7.4.2 Actual use of limited liability.* The tort liability of a corporation is usually limited to its assets. The relatively few exceptions to this principle have been made mainly for closely held corporations and for subsidiary corporations.[18]

*7.4.3 Note on the literature.* A number of writers have recently discussed the connection between limited liability and corporations' incentives to reduce risk. See, for example, Stone (1980) and Easterbrook and Fischel (1985).

# Mathematical Appendix

## 7A.1 Multiple Injurers

In the situation to be considered here, the actions of more than one injurer will affect the probability of losses. For simplicity, the unilateral model of accidents will be examined, where $x_i$ is the level of care of the $i$th injurer, $i = 1, \ldots, n$, and where $p(x_1, \ldots, x_n)$ is the probability of an accident causing (the single level of) losses $l$. The optimal $x_i$ minimize

$$(7.1) \qquad x_1 + \cdots + x_n + p(x_1, \ldots, x_n)l.$$

Denote the optimal $x_i$ by $x_i^*$ and assume that they are unique. Note that $x_i^*$ must minimize

$$(7.2) \qquad x_i + p(x_1^*, \ldots, x_{i-1}^*, x_i, x_{i+1}^*, \ldots, x_n^*)l$$

over $x_i$.

The levels of care of injurers under strict liability and under the negligence rule will now be determined under two alternative assumptions: that injurers act independently of one another, and that they act in concert (that is, so as to minimize joint expenses).

*7A.1.1 Strict liability.* Suppose that if there is an accident injurer $i$ will be liable for a fraction $f_i$ of losses (or, equivalently, will have to pay the entire losses with probability $f_i$), where the $f_i$ do not depend on the $x_i$; suppose also that the $f_i$ sum to 1. (This is the natural analogue to strict liability in the single-injurer context.)

---

18. This, at least, is the situation in the United States. See Easterbrook and Fischel 1985.

If injurers act independently, they will not all act optimally in equilibrium. To show why, assume otherwise. Now because $n > 1$, there must be some injurer for whom $f_i < 1$. This injurer will select $x_i$ to minimize $x_i + p(x_1^*, \ldots, x_{i-1}^*, x_i, x_{i+1}^*, \ldots, x_n^*)f_i l$, so that $x_i$ will not minimize Exp. (7.2), a contradiction.

If, on the other hand, injurers act in concert, then injurers' joint expenses are as given in Exp. (7.1), because the sum of the $f_i$ is 1, so they will act optimally (assuming they can observe one another's $x_i$).

PROPOSITION 7.1   Under strict liability, injurers who act independently will not act optimally in equilibrium; but injurers who act in concert will act optimally.

*7A.1.2   Negligence rule.* Suppose that if an accident occurs and injurer $i$ took at least due care, $\bar{x}_i$, he will not be liable. He will be liable, however, if he did not take due care, and losses will be divided among him and all other injurers who also failed to take due care, with the fractions $f_i$ paid by them adding to 1 and possibly depending on their number and their levels of care. Note that these assumptions imply that if there is only one injurer who failed to take due care, he will pay all the victim's losses. Note also that the assumptions implicitly allow for any scheme of ''contribution'' or ''indemnity'' (see §7.1.4).

Assuming that $\bar{x}_i = x_i^*$, let us show that for injurers acting independently, each taking due care is the unique equilibrium. That this is *an* equilibrium is obvious: if injurer $i$ assumes that all other injurers take due care, then he will pay $l$ if an accident occurs and he failed to take due care; the argument from §2A.1.1 may therefore be applied to demonstrate that the injurer will be best off choosing $x_i^*$.

To prove that all injurers' exercising due care is the only equilibrium given that $\bar{x}_i = x_i^*$, assume that there is another equilibrium. Clearly, no injurer will take more than due care in the alternative equilibrium. Consequently, some injurers must take less than due care. Let $S$ be the index set of such injurers. Since for $i \in S$, injurers will be liable and prefer taking $x_i$ to taking due care, we must have

$$x_i + pf_i l < x_i^* \qquad \text{for } i \in S.$$

(Here $p$ is $p(x_1, \ldots, x_n)$ where $x_i = x_i^*$ for $i \notin S$.) Adding, and remembering that the $f_i$ sum to 1 over $S$, we obtain

$$\sum_{i \in S} x_i + pl < \sum_{i \in S} x_i^*.$$

Adding this to the equalities $x_i^* = x_i^*$ *for* $i \notin S$, we obtain

$$\sum_{i \in S} x_i + \sum_{i \notin S} x_i^* + pl < \sum_{i=1}^{n} x_i^*.$$

But

$$\sum_{i=1}^{n} x_i^* \leq \sum_{i=1}^{n} x_i^* + p(x_1^*, \ldots, x_n^*)l,$$

implying that

$$\sum_{i \in S} x_i + \sum_{i \notin S} x_i^* + pl < \sum_{i=1}^{n} x_i^* + p(x_1^*, \ldots, x_n^*)l.$$

This, however, is a contradiction, since the $x_i^*$ minimize Exp. (7.1).

Next, observe that if the injurers act in concert, they will all take due care. Because they will wish to minimize their joint costs of care plus their joint expected liability, the argument of §2A.1.1 shows that they will all take due care.

PROPOSITION 7.2   Under the negligence rule, if due care levels are optimally determined, all injurers' taking due care will be the unique equilibrium both if they act independently and if they act in concert.

*7A.1.3   Note on the literature.* Landes and Posner (1980) showed that multiple injurers' taking due care is the unique equilibrium under the negligence rule.

## 7A.2   Injurers' Inability to Pay for Losses

Suppose in this part that injurers' assets are less than the losses that they might cause. Specifically, if

$a$ = assets of an injurer,

suppose that $a < l$; $l$ is the single level of losses that injurers will cause with probability $p(x)$.

*7A.2.1   Strict liability and the negligence rule.* Because injurers will pay $a$ rather than $l$ if liable, under strict liability they will choose $x$ to minimize

(7.3)      $x + p(x)a$

rather than total accident costs $x + p(x)l$.[19] Noting that the derivative of Exp. (7.3) is $1 + p'(x)a$, we observe that if $a$ is sufficiently low (less than or equal to $-1/p'(0)$, a positive amount) injurers will choose $x = 0$. Otherwise they will choose a positive $x$, but since $x$ will then be determined by the condition

(7.4)      $1 + p'(x)a = 0$

instead of by the social-optimality condition $1 + p'(x)l = 0$, $x$ will be less than $x^*$. It also follows from Eq. (7.4) that $x$ will be higher the higher is $a$.[20]

Under the negligence rule with due care equal to $x^*$, injurers will choose $x^*$ if

$$x^* \leqq x + p(x)a \qquad \text{for } x < x^*.$$

Injurers will decide to be negligent otherwise, in which case they will choose $x$ to minimize $x + p(x)a$ over $x < x^*$. Thus injurers will decide to be negligent if $a$ is sufficiently low. (Certainly this will be so if $a < x^*/p(0)$, for then choosing $x = 0$ will be less costly than choosing $x^*$.) Also, since we know from the last paragraph that the $x$ that minimizes Exp. (7.3) over all $x$ is less than $x^*$, it must be that if injurers decide to be negligent they will select the same $x$ as they would under strict liability. In addition, it follows from this fact that if injurers will choose to be negligent for $a$, they will choose to be negligent for any $a' < a$, since the minimized value of Exp. (7.3) decreases as $a$ decreases. On the other hand,

$$x^* < x^* + p(x^*)l = \inf_{x<x^*} x + p(x)l,$$

assuming $p(x^*) > 0$. Hence, by continuity,

$$x^* < \inf_{x<x^*} x + p(x)a$$

must hold for all $a$ sufficiently close to $l$. Thus, injurers will choose $x^*$ for such $a$. We have therefore shown the following proposition, which is illustrated in Figure 7.1.

19. Observe that an implicit assumption of Exp. (7.3) is that care is nonpecuniary. If care were pecuniary Exp. (7.3) would be written $x + p(x)(a - x)$, since spending $x$ on care would itself reduce the assets available to be paid to a victim by $x$. Considering this effect of care on assets that can be paid would complicate the analysis without changing its main point: that lack of assets dilutes incentives to take care.

20. Differentiating Eq. (7.4) with respect to $a$, one obtains $p''(x)x'(a)a + p'(x) = 0$, so that $x'(a) = -p'(x)/[p''(x)a] > 0$.

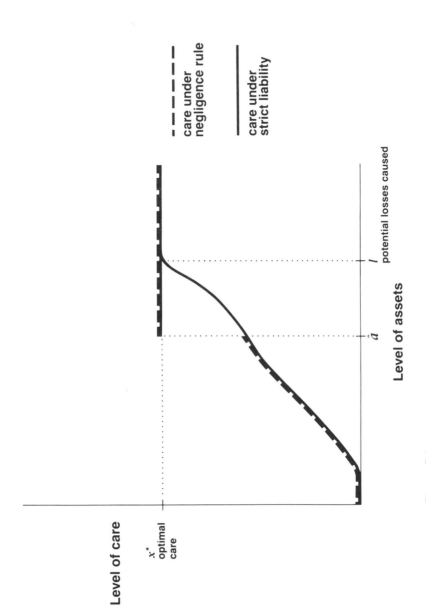

*Figure 7.1*

PROPOSITION 7.3    Under strict liability, injurers will take no care if their assets are sufficiently low. They will take a positive and increasing level of care as their assets rise, but their level of care will be suboptimal as long as their assets are less than the losses they might cause.

Under the negligence rule (with due care equal to the optimal level), injurers will act negligently—and thus as they would under strict liability— if their assets are less than a critical level $\hat{a}$ that is strictly lower than the losses they might cause. Beyond this critical level, injurers will take optimal care.

*Remarks.* (1) The proposition is easily shown to carry over to the more general setting where there is a probability distribution of losses of different sizes. In that setting the assumption made here that the single level of losses exceeds an injurer's assets would be replaced by the assumption that there is a positive probability that losses will exceed an injurer's assets.

(2) If, rather than the level of an injurer's assets being less than $l$, the probability of an injurer being sued is less than 1, an analogue to Proposition 7.3 (with level of probability replacing level of assets) holds.

*7A.2.2    Note on the literature.* The results here are proved in Summers (1983) and extended by me in Shavell (1986).


## 7A.3    Vicarious Liability

The concern in this section will be with two parties, an *actor* and a *principal*, about whom the following assumptions are made. The actor is like the injurer of the last part in that he can take care to reduce the probability of causing losses $l$ and in that his assets $a$ plus any wages he might receive from the principal are less than $l$.[21] The principal has assets of at least $l$ and is unable to affect the probability of losses by his own actions;[22] he may or may not be able to observe the actor's level of care.

The principal and the actor make a contract for the performance of some service. The contract specifies a wage $w_n$ to be paid if there is no loss caused, a wage $w_l$ to be paid if there is a loss, and possibly the level of care $x$ if the principal can observe it. Note that the assumption in the previous paragraph about assets and wages means that $a + w_n < l$ and $a + w_l < l$. The contract is assumed to be *Pareto optimal*—such that no alternative contract would be

---

21. The possibility that his assets plus wages received exceed $l$ could be allowed, but this is not an interesting case since then the actor would take optimal care under liability rules.

22. The weaker assumption that the principal's assets combined with the actor's are at least $l$ could also be made.

preferred by both parties or be preferred by one and found equivalent by the other. A contract is thus Pareto optimal if and only if the contract maximizes the expected utility of the principal subject to the constraint that the actor's expected utility equals a constant, say $\bar{w}$. (More precisely, the constraint is that the actor's expected utility is greater than or equal to $\bar{w}$, but it is assumed here that the constraint is binding.)

The behavior of the actor given that the contract is Pareto optimal will be determined in the discussion that follows both when the actor alone is liable and when the principal is vicariously liable. Under vicarious liability the victim may recover his losses from the principal. Liability (whether or not vicarious) will be assumed to be strict, although the analysis under the negligence rule would be similar and the conclusions virtually the same.

Assume first that the actor alone is liable and that the principal can observe the actor's level of care $x$. Since the principal can observe $x$, he can in effect control $x$ by not paying the actor unless the actor chooses the agreed-upon $x$. Hence, the Pareto optimal contract is found by minimizing the expected wage payments of the principal subject to the constraint that the actor's expected utility is $\bar{w}$; that is, the contract solves

(7.5) $$\min_{x,w_n,w_l} [1 - p(x)]w_n + p(x)w_l$$

subject to

(7.6) $$[1 - p(x)](a + w_n) - x = \bar{w}.$$

The constraint expressed by Eq. (7.6) reflects the assumption that $a + w_l < l$, so that the actor will be left without any wealth if there is an accident.[23] Substituting Eq. (7.6) into Exp. (7.5), the problem reduces to

(7.7) $$\min_{x,w_l} \bar{w} - [1 - p(x)]a + x + p(x)w_l.$$

It is clear that according to the solution, $w_l$ must be as low as possible. If $w_l$ is assumed to be nonnegative, then $w_l$ will equal 0 (the interpretation is that paying the actor a positive wage when he causes a loss would be a waste for him and the principal, since the wage payment would only go to the victim). If $w_l$ is allowed to be negative, $w_l$ will equal $-a$ (the actor will avoid having to

---

23. Note also from Eq. (7.6) that it is assumed, as in the previous section, that $x$ is nonpecuniary; see n. 19, above. The results would be similar were $x$ pecuniary, and whether borne initially by the actor or by the principal.

pay the victim anything by surrendering his assets to the principal).[24] It also
follows from Exp. (7.7) that if, according to the solution, $w_l = 0$, then $x$ must
minimize $x - [1 - p(x)]a$, which is to say, $x$ must minimize $x + p(x)a$, so
$x < x^*$. If, on the other hand, $w_l = -a$, then $x$ must minimize $x$, so $x = 0$.

Now assume that the actor alone is liable and that the principal cannot
observe $x$. Then the Pareto optimal contract is found by minimizing Exp. (7.5)
subject to Eq. (7.6) and to

(7.8)    $-p'(x)(a + w_n) = 1.$

Equation (7.8) determines the actor's choice of $x$ (assuming $x > 0$); it and the
assumption that $a + w_n < l$ imply that $x < x^*$. In addition, because Eqs. (7.6)
and (7.8) alone determine $w_n$ and $x$, Exp. (7.5) implies that $w_l$ is as low as
possible, so again $w_l = 0$ or $-a$.

Next assume that the principal is vicariously liable and will pay the entire
losses to the victim of an accident. Consider first the case where the principal
can observe $x$. Then the problem of choosing the Pareto optimal contract is

(7.9)    $\min_{x,w_n,w_l} [1 - p(x)]w_n + p(x)(w_l + l)$

subject to

(7.10)    $a + [1 - p(x)]w_n + p(x)w_l - x = \bar{w}.$

Substituting Eq. (7.10) in Exp. (7.9), the problem reduces to

(7.11)    $\min_x \bar{w} - a + x + p(x)l$    or    $\min_x x + p(x)l.$

Hence, under the Pareto optimal contract the socially optimal level of care $x^*$
will be taken (and $w_n$ and $w_l$ will satisfy Eq. (7.10)).

Last, consider the case where the principal is vicariously liable and cannot
observe $x$. Then the problem is to minimize Exp. (7.9) subject to Eq. (7.10)
and to the following condition determining the actor's choice of $x$,

(7.12)    $-p'(x)(w_n - w_l) = 1.$

---

24. The wage cannot be less than $-a$, for $a$ is all the actor can pay, but because it would
be illegal for an actor to transfer his assets after an accident occurred to a principal who
would not be vicariously liable—so as to avoid having to pay the victim—the assumption
that $w_l \geqq 0$ is the more reasonable one to make here.

If there exist $w_n$ and $w_l$ (greater than or equal to $-a$, of course) obeying Eq. (7.10) and such that $w_n - w_l = l$, then they will be a solution to the problem, for then Eq. (7.12) implies that $x$ will equal $x^*$. If all $w_n$ and $w_l$ obeying Eq. (7.10) are such that $w_n - w_l < l$, then Eq. (7.12) implies that $x < x^*$ and it can be shown that the actor will take as much or more care than he does when he alone is liable.

PROPOSITION 7.4   Assume that the actor does not have assets sufficient to pay for the losses he might cause, but that the principal does have assets sufficient to pay for the losses. Then if the actor only is liable, he will take suboptimal care, whether or not the principal can observe his level of care. If the principal is vicariously liable, however, he will have the actor take optimal care if he can observe the actor's level of care; otherwise the actor may take suboptimal care, but at least as much care as he does when he alone is liable.

*Remarks.* (1) The analysis and conclusions about vicarious liability would be essentially unchanged if it were assumed that the victim would collect a positive amount (such as $a$) from the actor rather than collect all from the principal.

(2) If the principal can directly affect the risk by a control variable of his own, say $z$, then, as discussed in the text, the use of vicarious liability will have the advantage that it will lead the principal to choose an appropriate $z$ (given $x$).[25]

25. Points related to the ones made in this section have been discussed in a context emphasizing the allocation of risk; see Sykes 1981 and Kornhauser 1982.

# 8 | The Allocation of Risk and the Theory of Insurance

Having completed the analysis of liability and incentives assuming that parties are risk neutral, I introduce here the concept of risk aversion and discuss the allocation of risk and the theory of insurance. With this additional background I will then return to the analysis of liability in the next chapter.

## 8.1 Risk Aversion and the Allocation of Risk

*8.1.1 Assumption of risk aversion.* In contrast to risk-neutral parties, *risk-averse* parties care not only about the expected value of losses, but also about the possible magnitude of losses. Thus, for instance, risk-averse parties will find a situation involving a 5 percent chance of losing 20,000 worse than a situation involving a 10 percent chance of losing 10,000, and this situation, in turn, they will find worse than a situation involving a sure loss of 1,000—even though each of the situations involves the same expected loss of 1,000. (Risk-neutral parties would not find any one of the situations worse than any other.) Risk-averse parties, in other words, dislike uncertainty about the size of losses per se.

The assumption that a party is risk averse turns out to be equivalent to a simple assumption concerning the utility the party attaches to his wealth. In particular, suppose that while the party's utility increases with the level of his wealth, it does so at a decreasing rate (the interpretation being that the value to him of having more wealth falls as he fulfills his more important needs).[1]

---

1. Interpretations like this one are made here because they seem to have strong intuitive appeal to readers who think of utility as objective and measurable. Those readers who have studied the axiomatic foundations of expected-utility theory will consider such interpretations problematic, however, because for them the utility-of-wealth function is wholly notional; it is constructed by the analyst to reflect preferences over uncertain prospects. See n. 2 in Chapter 1; and see in particular Savage 1972, sec. 5.6.

That is, suppose the graph relating the party's utility to his wealth has the concave shape drawn in Figure 8.1. It should seem plausible that a party for whom the graph of the utility of wealth has this shape will especially dislike bearing the risk of large losses, for such losses will evidently matter to him disproportionately in terms of utility. To be precise, recall from the Introduction that a party is assumed to evaluate a risky prospect by measuring its effect on his expected utility. Expected utility is obtained by multiplying the utility of each possible consequence—here the utility of each possible level of wealth—by its probability. Calculations will show that for a party whose graph of utility is as drawn in Figure 8.1, expected utility will be lower if he faces the 5 percent chance of a 20,000 loss than if he faces the 10 percent chance of a 10,000 loss, because a loss of 20,000 will result in more than twice the diminution in utility than will follow from a loss of 10,000. This conclusion can be verified in the following example.

EXAMPLE 8.1   Consider a party for whom the graph of the utility of wealth is as in Figure 8.1 and assume that the party has wealth of 30,000 and faces the 5 percent risk of losing 20,000. Then his level of wealth will be 30,000 with probability 95 percent and 10,000 with probability 5 percent. His expected utility will therefore be 95% × (utility of 30,000) + 5% × (utility of 10,000), or—see Table 8.1—95% × 1,000 + 5% × 665.24 = 950 + 33.26 = 983.26. On the other hand, if the party faces the 10 percent risk of losing 10,000, his expected utility will, by similar logic, be 90% × 1,000 + 10% × 909.97 = 900 + 91 = 991, which is higher. (The party's expected utility will be higher still if he loses 1,000 for certain, for then his expected utility will just be the utility of having 29,000, or 994.49.)

This illustrates that a party for whom the graph of the utility of wealth is concave is indeed risk averse.

There are different degrees of risk aversion corresponding to different degrees to which suffering large losses would matter to parties. Formally, the degree of risk aversion depends on the concavity of the graph of utility of wealth: the greater the concavity, the greater the degree of risk aversion (because the greater the rate at which utility losses grow with losses of wealth).[2]

2. The degree of risk aversion is defined for each level of wealth; thus (and as is about to be suggested in the text) it may change with the level of wealth. To predict a party's behavior, one must know his degree of risk aversion at every level of wealth or, equivalently, the graph of his utility of wealth. For a discussion of this and of how actually to ascertain the graph, see Raiffa 1968, chap. 4.

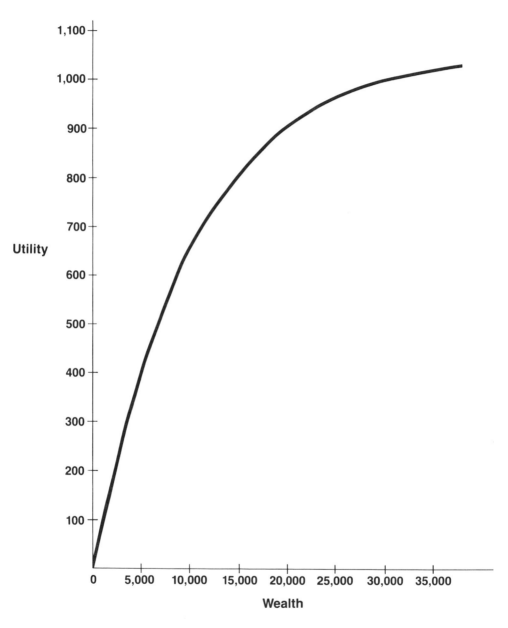

*Figure 8.1*

*Table 8.1* Selected values from the
utility-of-wealth curve shown in
Figure 8.1

| Wealth | Utility | Wealth | Utility |
|--------|---------|--------|---------|
| 1,000 | 100.15 | 27,500 | 985.12 |
| 2,000 | 190.77 | 27,600 | 985.79 |
| 5,000 | 414.09 | 28,500 | 991.52 |
| 9,000 | 624.52 | 28,900 | 993.91 |
| 10,000 | 665.24 | 29,000 | 994.49 |
| 15,000 | 817.57 | 29,500 | 997.31 |
| 19,000 | 894.99 | 29,600 | 997.86 |
| 20,000 | 909.97 | 30,000 | 1,000.00 |
| 24,500 | 961.58 | 33,500 | 1,015.47 |
| 25,000 | 966.01 | | |

*Note*: The equation of the graph is given
by $u = 1,052.396[1 - \exp(-w)]$, where $w$ is
wealth in ten thousands. This equation was
chosen so that the utility of 30,000 would
be the round number 1,000.00.

*8.1.2 Importance of risk aversion with regard to individuals and firms.*
The importance of risk aversion will ordinarily depend on the size of risk in
relation to an individual's assets and to his needs. Thus it may make sense to
think of a person with assets of $10,000 as quite averse to a risk of a $5,000
loss, especially if he will soon want to use (say, for medical or educational
purposes) the greater part of his $10,000. But where a person with assets of
$300,000 faces a $5,000 risk, risk aversion will likely be an unimportant factor, and it will usually do no harm to consider the person as risk neutral
(although risk aversion would probably become relevant if the magnitude of
the risk he faced was $200,000).

The attitude toward risk of firms will reflect the attitudes towards risk of
their managers, employees, and shareholders. To the extent that the managers and employees of a firm are risk averse and that their rewards (or
positions) are tied to the firm's performance, they will want the firm to behave
in a risk-averse way. One would therefore expect there to be some tendency
for firms to avoid risks jeopardizing their profitability or their assets. However, to the extent that shareholders hold well-diversified portfolios, they will
not be much concerned about the risks borne by a firm (since the risks of
different firms in a portfolio will tend to cancel one another). Consequently,
shareholders will often wish firms to be operated in an approximately risk-

neutral manner, and firms will be operated in that way insofar as shareholders exercise control over managers and employees.

*8.1.3   Risk aversion, the allocation of risk, and social welfare.* The presence of risk-averse parties means that the distribution or allocation of risk will itself affect social welfare. Specifically, and assuming for convenience that social welfare is the sum of parties' expected utilities,[3] the shifting of risks from the risk averse to the risk neutral, or, generally, from the more to the less risk averse will raise social welfare. This is because the bearing of risk by the more risk averse would result in a greater reduction in their expected utility than will the bearing of risk by the less risk averse or by the risk neutral. Indeed, for this reason, it is always possible for the more risk averse to pay the less risk averse or the risk neutral to assume risk, so as to leave both better off in terms of expected utility.[4]

> EXAMPLE 8.2    Assume that the risk-averse party of the preceding example initially bears, say, the 10 percent risk of losing 10,000, and consider the situation if he pays 1,000 to a risk-neutral party for him to bear the risk. The risk-averse party will be better off, for it was shown before that his expected utility will be 991 if he bears the risk, yet 994.49 if he pays 1,000 and does not bear it. And the risk-neutral party will be just as well off, since he will be indifferent between not bearing any risk and being paid 1,000 to bear the 10 percent risk of losing 10,000. It is therefore clear that if the risk-averse party pays a little more than 1,000 (say, 1,100), he will still be better off having shifted the risk (his wealth will be 28,900, so his utility will be 993.91, which is still greater than 991), but now the risk-neutral party will also be better off (by 100) rather than just as well off.

Social welfare is raised not only by the complete shifting of risks from the more to the less risk averse or to the risk neutral, but also by the sharing of risks among risk-averse parties. Sharing risks reduces the magnitude of the potential loss that any one of them might suffer, as is illustrated in the following example.

> EXAMPLE 8.3    Suppose that the risk-averse party of Example 8.1 initially bears the 5 percent risk of losing 20,000 and that another, otherwise identi-

---

3. Most of the conclusions drawn in this discussion will be true as long as the measure of social welfare rises when any individual's expected utility rises. This, in effect, is all that is assumed in the appendix.

4. This of course means that the sum of their expected utilities rises; but, obviously, the sum may also rise without the expected utilities of parties of each type rising.

cal, risk-averse party bears no risk. Then since the expected utility of the first party will be (as was shown) 983.26 and that of the second 1,000, the sum of their expected utilities will be 1,983.26. If, however, losses are divided equally between the parties, so that each bears a 5 percent risk of losing only 10,000, then the expected utility of each will be 95% × 1,000 + 5% × 909.97 = 995.50. The sum of their expected utilities will thus be 1,991, and social welfare will be higher.[5]

Whereas in this example the parties were equally risk averse and an equal sharing of losses was shown to be socially beneficial, some unequal sharing of losses can always be shown to be beneficial where the parties are not equally risk averse.[6] Also, although in this example losses were shared by two parties, social welfare can in theory always be enhanced by bringing additional parties into a risk-sharing agreement (here we ignore the ''transaction'' costs of so doing), because this further reduces the size of the losses each might face. (Insurance, the subject of the next section, is an important example of beneficial sharing of risk among many parties.)

*8.1.4   Remarks on the allocation of risk and social welfare.* (1) The proper allocation of risk raises social welfare not only directly, by reducing the risk borne by the risk averse, but also indirectly, by making the risk averse willing to engage in socially desirable, risky activities. Thus, for example, an individual may decide to undertake a promising business venture only because he has partners with whom he can share the risk.

(2) Protection of the risk averse against risk is socially beneficial for reasons quite distinct from those appealing to the desirability of equity in the distribution of wealth. This is apparent, for instance, from the point that two risk-averse parties with equal levels of wealth (and therefore about whom there can be no questions concerning lack of distributional equity) may each be made better off, ex ante, by arranging to share a risk. That there should be a tendency to conflate the issue of distributional equity with that of the allocation of risk is no doubt engendered by the fact that *after* a party has suffered a

5. It can also be demonstrated along the lines of the last example that the first party can pay an amount to the second to assume the 5 percent risk of losing 10,000, such that both parties are made better off by the transaction.

6. The Appendix to this chapter demonstrates that the socially optimal allocation of a risk between two risk-averse parties necessarily involves each bearing a positive fraction of the losses. Hence it is never *optimal* for the entire losses to be shifted from one risk-averse party to a second, although this may be *better* than leaving the entire losses on the first party if he is the more risk averse. (Shifting the entire losses is optimal only if the party who would assume them is risk neutral.)

loss he will be in a disadvantageous position relative to others in the absence of any risk-bearing agreement.[7]

(3) It should also be emphasized that the allocation of risk is in principle just as important a determinant of social welfare as the production of goods and services or the reduction of accident losses. The impression some may have that the conventional normative economic calculus is concerned only with the latter, "real" elements is incorrect.

## 8.2   The Theory of Insurance

*8.2.1   Assumptions of the theory.* Under the arrangement known as *insurance,* parties referred to as *insureds* pay *premiums* to an *insurer* in exchange for protection against possible future losses. The insurer is obligated to pay insureds an amount specified by an insurance policy if the insureds make claims for losses they suffer.[8]

In the analysis of insurance here it will be assumed that there are many risk-averse insureds facing identical, independent risks of loss and that there are essentially no administrative expenses associated with the insurer's operations.[9] This assumption implies that the insurer can be virtually sure of covering its costs by collecting from each insured the expected value of the amount it will have to pay him. If, for instance, each insured faces a 5 percent risk of losing 10,000 and will be paid that amount in the event of a loss under the insurance policy, the insurer can cover its costs by collecting premiums of 500.[10]

---

7. Another cause of confusion is that the language of marginal utility is used in explanations of both the advantage of protecting risk-averse individuals against risk and of distributional equity. But the marginal utilities to which reference is made in these two contexts are different. In the context of risk aversion, reference is made to the marginal utilities of a *single individual* at different possible levels of wealth, and the utility is his (von Neumann–Morgenstern–Savage) utility as used in expected utility theory. In the context of distributional equity, the marginal utilities are those of *different individuals* at possibly different levels of wealth, and their utilities are the utilities in a (Bergsonian) social welfare function.

8. For articles on the theory of insurance accessible to those unfamiliar with the topic, see Arrow 1971, chaps. 5, 8, 9; but see also the references in the Appendix to this chapter.

9. The remarks in §8.2.4 address the situation where these assumptions are relaxed.

10. The premium of 500—and, in general, the expected value of the amount the insurer has to pay the insured—is sometimes called the *actuarially fair* premium. If the premium equals the actuarially fair amount plus any small additional amount (even, say, .0001), then the probability that the insurer will cover its costs approaches 100 percent as the number of insureds grows large. Thus, for simplicity (and as is customary in the analysis of insurance), I will speak as if the insurer can definitely cover its costs by charging the actuarially fair premium.

In the following sections the theory of insurance will be examined in two situations: where insureds cannot affect risks and where they can.

*8.2.2   Expected utility maximizing insurance policies where insureds cannot influence risks.* There are many types of loss the probability or severity of which insureds can do relatively little to alter. Consider, for instance, property damage suffered by insureds caused by objects dropped from airplanes or injuries sustained while insured are under general anesthesia. Keeping such examples in mind, assume here that insureds have no influence over risks, so that their ownership of insurance policies cannot itself lead to a change in risks.

Although in principle insureds may own any type of policy—such as a policy covering only a percentage of losses, one imposing a low ceiling on payments, or one supplying greater than full coverage[11]—the policy offering exactly full coverage against loss is optimal for an insured: the full-coverage policy will yield an insured higher expected utility than any other type of policy. The explanation for this result is twofold. First, obviously, a policy offering less than complete coverage will not protect an insured against risk, which, being risk averse, he will wish to avoid. Second, and perhaps not obviously, a policy offering more than complete coverage[12] will require, in effect, that an insured make an added expenditure (in the form of a higher premium) to engage in a gamble (where "winning" will occur if he suffers a loss), and being risk averse, the insured will not wish to engage in such a gamble.[13] These points are illustrated in the following example.

EXAMPLE 8.4   Suppose that the risk-averse party described in Example 8.1 faces a 10 percent risk of losing 10,000. He will be better off with full insurance coverage than with none or with partial coverage, say with 5,000. If he has full coverage, he will pay a premium of 1,000. His wealth will thus be 29,000 for certain (as he will be completely compensated for a loss), so his expected utility will be the utility of 29,000, or 994.49. If he has no coverage, his wealth will be 30,000 with probability 90 percent and 20,000

---

11. This last type of policy is not fanciful to consider; one situation where payments to insureds will exceed their losses is discussed in §10.3.

12. See also the beginning of the next section on another disadvantage of policies offering more than complete coverage.

13. This is not meant to imply that a risk-averse person would never wish to gamble in the usual sense. There clearly are reasons for a risk-averse person sometimes to gamble, for example, enjoyment of the activity accompanying the gamble—going to the horse race—or belief that the odds are truly favorable, but such reasons are not of immediate relevance here.

with probability 10 percent, so his expected utility will be 90% × 1,000 + 10% × 909.97 = 991. This is less than 994.49, so he will be worse off than he would be with full coverage. And if he has 5,000 coverage, his premium will be 500, his wealth will be 29,500 with probability 90 percent and 24,500 with probability 10 percent (since he will have to absorb 5,000 of his loss), so his expected utility will be 90% × 997.31 + 10% × 961.58 = 993.74. Hence he will still be worse off than with full coverage (though better off than with none).

The party will also be better off with full coverage than with more than full coverage. For instance, with 15,000 coverage, his premium will be 1,500, his wealth will thus be 28,500 with probability 90 percent and 33,500 with probability 10 percent, so his expected utility will be 90% × 991.52 + 10% × 1015.47 = 993.92—less, again, than his expected utility with full coverage.

*8.2.3    Expected utility maximizing insurance policies where insureds can influence risks.* Insured parties may be able to *cause* losses, and for this reason, in addition to the element of gambling mentioned above, it will be disadvantageous to insureds for insurance coverage to exceed losses. Were coverage to exceed losses, there would be an incentive for insureds to create losses (and an enhanced incentive to falsify claims), as where an owner of a building worth 20,000 arranges to burn it down to collect against a fire damage policy in the amount of 25,000. (A similar incentive would operate were someone who is *not* the owner of a building—someone who does not have an "insurable interest" in the building—able to insure it.) This behavior will raise insureds' premiums undesirably.[14]

On the other hand, insured parties are, of course, also often able to *lower* the probability or the magnitude of the losses they might suffer. They may be able to reduce the risk of fire by purchasing safety devices or by exercising various precautions; they may be able to limit the losses arising from an accident by taking remedial actions; and so forth. The question therefore arises whether insureds will in fact act in these ways, and in particular whether their ownership of insurance might not dull their incentives to do so.

---

14. That is, owners of property will not wish to pay the premiums necessary to obtain a policy under which they might be led to cause losses. This is easiest to see in the extreme case where they will necessarily be led to cause losses, for then the premium will have to *equal* the face amount of the policy. Therefore, through payment of the premium, the party will suffer the very loss against which the insurance was designed to protect him. The party in the example will pay a premium of 25,000, he will be induced to burn his building worth 20,000, and he will then collect 25,000. Accordingly, he will be left having suffered a certain loss of 20,000.

(Such dulling of incentives is called the *moral hazard* in the insurance litera-ture.)

To answer this question, suppose first that insurers can obtain perfect information at no cost about insureds' risk-reducing actions (whether an in-sured installed fire extinguishers). In this case there will be no problem of adverse incentives created by insureds' ownership of coverage because insur-ers will be able to link the terms of policies to insureds' actions: insurers may make premiums depend on insureds' risk-reducing actions (as where premi-ums are lowered for those who install extinguishers); and insurers may limit or deny coverage in the event of a loss if insurers determine that insureds' actions did not conform to policy requirements (as where coverage is not paid to those who failed to install extinguishers or who did not prevent greater losses by moving valuable property away from a fire).

EXAMPLE 8.5   Assume that the party described in Example 8.1 can lower the probability of a 10,000 loss from 10 percent to 5 percent by taking a risk-reducing action that will involve a cost of 100. Suppose also that the party has an insurance policy giving complete coverage and that the premium charged will be 1,000 if he does not take the action and 500 if he does.[15] Then the party's total costs will be 500 + 100 = 600 if he takes the action and 1,000 if not. Consequently, he will take the action—as indeed he will as long as the cost of the action is less than 500, the difference between the premiums where care is not taken and where care is taken. Notice too that the party's utility under the policy will be higher than it would be under a policy not offering a premium reduction for taking the risk-reducing action. Under a policy not offering a premium reduction, the party will not be led to take the action and the risk will therefore be 10 percent and the premium will have to be 1,000.

This example illustrates that insureds will be induced by the terms of insur-ance policies that maximize expected utility to take risk-reducing actions when the cost of the actions is less than the decrease in expected losses due to the actions.

Assume now that insurers are not able to obtain information about in-sureds' risk-reducing actions (that insurers cannot tell whether insureds dis-card oily rags and take other precautions to prevent fire). In this case insurers plainly cannot make premiums or other policy terms depend directly on in-

---

15. An argument similar to the one about to be discussed can be made if the policy involves a premium of 500 and promises coverage against loss only if, at the time of a loss, the insurer determines that the action had been taken.

sureds' actions, and insureds therefore cannot be rewarded with premium reductions for reducing risk nor be punished by denial of their claims for failing to do so. Hence insureds' ownership of insurance will affect their incentives to reduce risk. If insureds possess complete coverage, the problem will be most serious, for they will then have no reason to avoid losses (here we ignore nonpecuniary losses).[16] Thus premiums for coverage will be high and insureds' utility low. This problem may often be ameliorated if insureds have only partial coverage, for because insureds will bear a fraction of their losses and have some motive to avoid losses, insurers' costs and premiums charged will be lower.[17]

EXAMPLE 8.6   Suppose that parties like the one described in the previous example own insurance policies giving them complete coverage and that the insurer cannot tell whether they take the risk-reducing action. Because the parties will be charged the same premium whether or not they take the action, they will not take it, the probability of loss will be 10 percent, and the premium they will have to be charged will be 1,000. Hence their expected utility will be the utility of 29,000, or 994.49.

But if the parties own policies giving them coverage of only, say, 8,000—so that they will not be compensated for 2,000 of the 10,000 loss they might suffer—they will be led to take the risk-reducing action and will be better off. Assuming the premium will be 5% × 8,000 = 400,[18] a party's wealth if he takes the action will be 29,500 (that is, 30,000 − 400 − 100) with probability 95 percent and 27,500 with probability 5 percent. His expected utility will therefore be 95% × 997.31 + 5% × 985.12 = 996.70. By contrast, a party's wealth if he does not take the action will be 29,600 with probability 90 percent and 27,600 with probability 10 percent (because the risk of loss will be 10 percent). Hence his expected utility will be 90% × 997.86 + 10% × 985.79 = 996.65, which is lower than 996.70. Thus parties will indeed decide to take the risk-reducing action and will be better off than they would be if they had no coverage (996.70 being greater than 994.49).

In general, the level of coverage provided in policies that maximize expected utility under present assumptions are those that strike the best balance between the advantage and the disadvantage of lowering coverage from full coverage, namely, those that balance the creation of incentives to reduce risk

16. On the issue of nonpecuniary losses and insurance see §10.1.

17. Insureds will have a similar motive to avoid losses if their policies specify that their future premiums or insurability depend on loss history.

18. The assumption here that the premium rate is 5 percent will be justified by the demonstration that parties will be led to take the risk-reducing action.

on the one hand and the increased exposure to risk on the other. In Example 8.6 the expected utility maximizing level of coverage will be the greatest level that will still leave the insured bearing enough risk to induce him to take the risk-reducing action. This level of coverage can be shown to be a little higher than 8,000.

*8.2.4 Further remarks on expected utility maximizing policies.* (1) It should be emphasized that expected utility maximizing insurance policies are the policies that will be sold in a competitive insurance market, since parties will prefer to purchase these policies over any alternatives. In addition, they are the policies that will be sold by a self-financed social insurer that desires to maximize the welfare of insureds.

(2) It is clear from the analysis in §8.2.3 that the expected utility of insureds will be higher where insurers have information about their actions than where insurers do not, for in the former but not the latter case full coverage can be provided while at the same time insureds can be supplied incentives to reduce risk. Thus insureds will want insurers to obtain information (by means of inspections and the like) about their risk-reducing activity and should be willing to pay (directly or in the form of a higher premium) for that to be done if the cost is not too high. The cost, however, will vary. One suspects that as a general matter it will often be relatively easy for insurers to learn about safety features and other "fixed" physical characteristics that affect risk, but it will frequently be difficult for them to monitor effectively insureds' precautionary behavior (such as drivers' attention to the road) since this is so readily modified.

A more complete analysis of the foregoing would recognize that information about insureds' behavior may be inaccurate. (Despite appearances, was the fire really due to the insured's failure to put out his cigarette?) Such analysis would conclude that under the expected utility maximizing policy, use of imperfect information will be limited (evidence pointing to the cigarette will result in only a moderate reduction in payment to the insured), because if a policy were to depend on possibly erroneous information in a substantial way (notably, so as to lead to complete denial of payment) insureds would be subjected to too great a risk due to the chance that their true behavior would be mistakenly assessed. Similarly, an insured's loss history may be a faulty indicator of the care he has taken (he can have suffered his losses through bad luck). If so, the use of loss history in the expected utility maximizing policy will be restricted.

Another point related to the analysis in §8.2.3 is that insureds as a group should be willing to pay insurers to develop information about risk (as where fire insurers determine the flammability of different types of furnishings and building materials and provide advice to insureds). This will allow insureds to benefit through premium reductions and, if they are not fully insured, through a reduction in their expected out-of-pocket losses. Of course, insureds could develop the information on an individual basis (each insured could ascertain for himself the flammability of various furnishings), but it will generally be more efficient for insurers to carry out this function for the whole group of insureds.

(3) If it is supposed, realistically, that there are positive administrative costs associated with the supply of insurance, then the premium must include a component to cover these costs and the nature of expected utility maximizing insurance policies will change. Specifically, the policies will involve less coverage than will otherwise be desirable and, often, will include a *deductible* feature (according to which the insured receives only the excess of his loss over the deductible amount). Policies with a deductible have the virtue that they reduce insurers' administrative costs because losses falling below the deductible do not lead to claims. At the same time, the policies protect insureds against the major portion of large losses, which is what insureds care about most, being risk averse.

(4) If it is supposed, contrary to what was true in the analysis, that the risks facing different insureds are correlated with each other or large (as with earthquakes, nuclear war, design defects affecting most units of a widely distributed product, or major changes in liability law), then insurers cannot be confident of meeting their costs by charging premiums equal to the expected value of the payments they have to make. Insurers will therefore wish to charge higher premiums, presuming some degree of risk aversion on their part, and insureds' expected utility will be maximized if they obtain less coverage than otherwise.

(5) Where the correlation or size of risks, administrative costs, or problems with incentives are sufficiently important, the expected utility maximizing amount of coverage may be none at all. That is, it may turn out that parties do not have any insurance against certain types of loss. For example, they do not generally have insurance against business losses, because of the problems with incentives that would arise were they to own such insurance.

(6) If insureds or insurers misperceive risks, the amount of insurance coverage purchased may be inappropriate. Insureds who overestimate risks will tend to buy too much coverage (because premiums will appear low to them), and those who underestimate risks will buy too little. Similarly, insurers who underestimate risks will charge too little for coverage so insureds will tend to buy too much, and those who overestimate risks will charge too much so insureds will buy too little. The latter possibility may help to explain (along with the correlation of risks and the risk aversion of insurers) why insurance is sometimes not sold where the risks are hard for insurers to estimate.

*8.2.5  Actual insurance in view of the theory.* The character of insurance policies and of insurance practice seems to comport with the theory presented in this part. When parties have no real influence over risks (as, for instance, with the possible loss of goods during transport by others), insurance policies are relatively simple and parties frequently purchase complete coverage. When parties can influence risks, insurers often supply advice about risk reduction and include in policies a great variety of features that serve to induce insured parties to lower risk. Moreover, as the discussion in §8.2.4 should have suggested, a detailed examination of these policy features (where premiums and conditions of payment are based on information about insureds; where coverage is partial or is excluded; and so forth) would further confirm the theory.

# Mathematical Appendix

In this appendix on the allocation of risk and the theory of insurance I will consider a model with one good, referred to as wealth. Parties will be assumed either to be risk neutral or risk averse. A risk-neutral party, recall, is a party whose utility of wealth equals his wealth (or is linear in his wealth), so his marginal utility of wealth is constant. A *risk-averse* party is a party whose utility of wealth is increasing and strictly concave in his wealth, that is, his marginal utility of wealth is positive but decreases with the level of his wealth.[19]

## 8A.1  The Optimal Allocation of Risk

To study the allocation of wealth between parties where there is a risk of loss, suppose for simplicity that there are only two parties, U and V, and a fixed risk of only one level of loss, *l*. The possible allocations of wealth are allocations between U and V contingent on the occurrence of the loss. Let

$u_n$ = wealth of U if there is no loss; $u_n \geq 0$;
$u_l$ = wealth of U if there is a loss; $u_l \geq 0$;
$U$ = utility function of U;
$v_n$ = wealth of V if there is no loss; $v_n \geq 0$;

19. See Arrow 1971, chap. 3, or Pratt 1964.

$v_l$ = wealth of V if there is a loss; $v_l \geq 0$;
V = utility function of V;
w = total wealth to be allocated if there is no loss;
$w - l$ = wealth to be allocated if there is a loss; $w - l > 0$.

A feasible allocation corresponds to a choice of $u_n$, $u_l$, $v_n$, and $v_l$ such that

(8.1)     $u_n + v_n = w,$

and

(8.2)     $u_l + v_l = w - l;$

in other words, exactly the available wealth is allocated in each contingency. If

$p$ = probability of the loss, $0 < p < 1,$

then the parties' expected utilities will be

$$EU = (1 - p)U(u_n) + pU(u_l)$$

and

$$EV = (1 - p)V(v_n) + pV(v_l).$$

We are interested in Pareto optimal feasible allocations[20]—feasible allocations such that there are no alternative feasible allocations under which one party would be better off and the other at least as well off. Of course, one reason for interest in Pareto optimal (feasible) allocations is that, no matter what the social welfare function is, the social welfare maximizing allocation must be Pareto optimal.[21] A Pareto optimal allocation is found by solving the problem

(8.3)     $\max_{u_n, u_l, v_n, v_l} EV$

20. On Pareto optimal risk-sharing see Borch 1962.
21. If an allocation is not Pareto optimal, then, by definition, the expected utility of U, say, would be raised and V not lowered under some alternative allocation. Hence social welfare could be increased (assuming that it depends positively on the expected utilities of U and of V).

subject to

(8.4)    $EU = k$

(where $k$ is a constant) and to Eqs. (8.1) and (8.2).[22] If Eqs. (8.1) and (8.2) are solved for $v_n$ and $v_l$, a Pareto optimal allocation is found by maximizing Exp. (8.3) over $v_n$ and $v_l$ subject only to Eq. (8.4); the solution is determined by setting the partial derivatives of $EV - \lambda[EU - k]$ with respect to $v_n$ and $v_l$ equal to zero. Here $\lambda$ is the Kuhn Tucker multiplier.[23] From setting the derivatives equal to zero we obtain

(8.5)    $(1 - p)V'(v_n) + \lambda(1 - p)U'(w - v_n) = 0$

and

(8.6)    $pV'(v_l) + \lambda pU'(w - l - v_l) = 0,$

from which it follows, after dividing Eq. (8.5) by $1 - p$, dividing Eq. (8.6) by $p$, and solving each for $\lambda$, that

(8.7)    $\dfrac{V'(v_n)}{V'(v_l)} = \dfrac{U'(w - v_n)}{U'(w - l - v_l)} = \dfrac{U'(u_n)}{U'(u_l)}.$

Using Eq. (8.7) we will show the following proposition.

PROPOSITION 8.1    In a Pareto optimal allocation, (a) if one party is risk averse and the other is risk neutral, the risk-neutral party will bear all the risk of loss, whereas (b) if both parties are risk averse, each will bear a positive part of the loss. (c) If both parties are risk neutral, then any allocation is Pareto optimal.

To prove (a), suppose that, say, U is the risk-neutral party. Then since the right-hand side of Eq. (8.7) will equal 1, so must the left. But since V is risk averse, $V'' < 0$, implying that $v_n = v_l$. Hence, from Eqs. (8.1) and (8.2), it follows that $u_l = u_n - l$; that is, U bears all the risk of loss.

To show (b), observe from Eqs. (8.1) and (8.2) that if $v_n - l \geq v_l$, then $u_n \leq u_l$. Therefore, if $v_n - l \geq v_l$ and U is risk averse, the right-hand side of Eq.

---

22. As is well known and as should be clear on reflection, if this problem is solved, the allocation must be Pareto optimal; and if an allocation is Pareto optimal, it must be the solution to this problem.

23. On Kuhn Tucker theory, see, for instance, Mangasarian 1969.

(8.7) will be greater than or equal to 1. This, however, is a contradiction, since the left-hand side of Eq. (8.7) will be less than 1 if V is risk averse. Hence it must be that $v_n - l < v_l$. On the other hand, if $v_l \geq v_n$, then it follows from Eqs. (8.1) and (8.2) that $u_l < u_n$. Thus, the right-hand side of Eq. (8.7) will be less than 1, whereas the left-hand side will be greater than or equal to 1. We conclude that $v_n - l < v_l < v_n$; this and Eqs. (8.1) and (8.2) imply also that $u_n - l < u_l < u_n$; in other words, U and V each bear some but not all the risk of the loss of $l$.

Finally, note that in case (c), the right- and left-hand sides of Eq. (8.7) equal 1 for any $v_n$, $v_l$, $u_n$, and $u_l$.

## 8A.2   The Theory of Insurance

*8A.2.1   Assumptions of the theory.* The main elements of the theory of insurance that we will need to call upon later will be presented here.[24] *Insurance* is an arrangement whereby parties called *insureds* pay *premiums* to an *insurer* and, in return, will be paid an amount specified by an insurance *policy* if they suffer a loss.

It will be assumed, as is conventional, that the risks facing insured parties are independent and that there are no administrative costs involved in the supply of insurance. That is, it will be assumed that the insurer can cover its costs by charging premiums equal to the expected payments it will make to insureds under their insurance policies.

The problem of interest is to determine the type of insurance policy that will maximize the expected utility of insureds subject to the constraint that they pay premiums equal to the insurer's expected payments. (This is the type of policy that would be sold in a competitive insurance market or by an expected utility maximizing self-financed social insurer.) It will be assumed, again for simplicity, that there is only a single level of loss $l$ occurring with probability $0 < p < 1$. The insureds will be assumed to be identical and to be risk averse. Let

> $W$ = utility function of insureds;
> $w$ = initial wealth of insureds; $w > 0$;
> $\pi$ = premium for insurance; $\pi \geq 0$; and
> $q$ = level of coverage; $q \geq 0$.

In the next section it will be assumed that $p$ is fixed, and in the succeeding section, that $p$ can be influenced by insureds.

24. See Arrow 1971, chaps. 5, 8, 9, Becker and Ehrlich 1972, Holmström 1979, and Shavell 1979. Note that I leave the discussion of insurance where losses may be nonpecuniary to §10A.1.

*8A.2.2   Situation in which insureds cannot influence risk.* If an insured purchases coverage $q$, his wealth will be $w - \pi$ if he does not suffer a loss and $w - \pi + q - l$ if he does. His expected utility will be

$$(8.8) \qquad (1 - p)W(w - \pi) + pW(w - \pi + q - l).$$

Thus, to maximize his expected utility subject to the constraint that the premium equals the insurer's expected payments, an insured will choose $q$ to maximize Exp. (8.8) subject to $\pi = pq$. Substituting $pq$ for $\pi$ in the expression and differentiating with respect to $q$, we obtain (after some cancellation) the first-order condition $W'(w - pq) = W'(w - pq + q - l)$. Because $W'' < 0$, this implies that $w - pq = w - pq + q - l$, or that $q = l$. That is, we have shown the following proposition.

PROPOSITION 8.2   Under the expected utility maximizing insurance policy, the level of coverage will be full.

*Remark.* This result holds true also in the general case in which there is a probability distribution of losses. In that case, $q$ is a function $q(l)$ and under the best policy $q(l) = l$.

*8A.2.3   Situation in which insureds can influence risk.* Assume here that the probability of loss is $p(x)$, where $x$ is an insured's level of care.[25] Thus if an insured purchases coverage $q$, his expected utility will be

$$(8.9) \qquad [1 - p(x)]W(w - \pi - x) + p(x)W(w - \pi - x + q - l).$$

Suppose initially that the insurer can observe $x$. It is therefore possible for the insurer to base the premium on $x$; assuming that this is done, the premium will be

$$(8.10) \qquad \pi = p(x)q.$$

To maximize his expected utility, an insured will then choose $q$ and $x$ to maximize Exp. (8.9), using Eq. (8.10) to substitute for $\pi$. Differentiating Exp. (8.9) with respect to $q$ yields, as in §8A.2.2, a first-order condition implying that insureds will choose $q = l$. Therefore, Exp. (8.9) reduces to

---

25. I assume, as usual, that $p'(x) < 0$. In particular, I do not consider here the possibility that insureds may be able to cause losses. As noted in the text, however, this would supply a reason why coverage exceeding losses would not maximize insureds' expected utility. Indeed, since insureds would be led to cause losses (presuming their actions could not be observed) if $q > l$, their premiums would be $q$ and their wealth would be $w - q + q - l = w - l$. That is, the situation would be exactly as if they were certain to lose $l$.

$W(w - p(x)l - x)$, and since insureds will maximize that function over $x$ they will select $x$ to minimize $p(x)l + x$.

PROPOSITION 8.3    Assume that the insurer can observe the level of care taken by insureds. Then under the expected utility maximizing insurance policy, the level of coverage will be full and the level of care will minimize the sum of expected losses and the cost of care.[26]

*Remarks*. (1) As indicated in the text, the reason that full coverage does not create disadvantageous incentives is that care $x$ affects the premium $\pi$.

(2) The result holds true in the general setting in which there is a probability distribution of losses that $x$ influences.

(3) A policy in which the amount of coverage $q$ depends on $x$ is also possible. Under the expected utility maximizing policy of this type, coverage will also be full and $x$ will also minimize $p(x)l + x$.[27]

Now assume that the insurer cannot observe $x$, so that the premium cannot be made to depend on $x$. In this case, since an insured who purchases coverage $q$ will not obtain any reduction in his premium if he increases $x$, he will choose $x$ to maximize Exp. (8.9), treating $\pi$ as a constant. But $\pi$ must nevertheless obey Eq. (8.10) since the insurer must cover its costs. (The interpretation is that, although an insured knows his premium will be essentially independent of his particular behavior, it will be influenced by the behavior of insureds generally.) Formally, then, the expected utility maximizing insurance policy is found by maximizing Exp. (8.9) over $\pi$, $q$, and $x$ subject to the constraint that Exp. (8.9) is maximized over $x$ alone and subject also to Eq. (8.10).

The fact that insureds will maximize Exp. (8.9) over $x$ implies that

---

26. Actually, this proposition has not been quite proved. It was shown that $q = l$ and that $x$ minimizes $p(x)l + x$ *if* the policy is such that $\pi$ is the explicit function $p(x)q$, but the logical possibility exists that some other type of policy (say with $\pi$ not a function of $x$ but with $q$ a function of $x$—see n. 27 below) might yield insureds greater expected utility. But this possibility can be ruled out on reflection, for no policy could yield insureds higher expected utility than a policy in which a dictator chooses optimally both $q$ and $x$ subject to Eq. (8.10); yet the problem of the dictator is identical to the one in which $\pi$ is the explicit function $p(x)q$.

27. Consider policies in which $q = \pi/p(x)$, which means that $\pi = p(x)q$, and that maximize expected utility, $[1 - p(x)]W(w - \pi - x) + p(x)W(w - \pi - x + \pi/p(x) - l)$, over $\pi$ and $x$. Differentiating this with respect to $\pi$, one obtains a first-order condition implying that $\pi = p(x)l$, so that $q = l$. Thus expected utility reduces to $W(w - p(x)l - x)$ and $x$ must consequently minimize $p(x)l + x$.

(8.11)    $p'(x)[W(w - \pi - x + q - l) - W(w - \pi - x)]$
$$= [1 - p(x)]W'(w - \pi - x) + p(x)W'(w - \pi - x + q - l).$$

The left-hand side of Eq. (8.11) is the marginal benefit to an insured of taking care, which, note, will be positive only if coverage is incomplete. The right-hand side is the marginal cost of taking care. Eq. (8.11) determines $x$ as a function of $\pi$ and $q$, so $x$ may be written $x(\pi,q)$. Hence, Eq. (8.10) becomes $\pi = p(x(\pi,q))q$. This determines $\pi$ as a function of $q$, which may be written $\pi(q)$. Given this function, $x$ may be written $x(q) = x(\pi(q),q)$. Therefore, the problem of maximizing Exp. (8.9) over $\pi$, $q$, and $x$ subject to the constraint that Exp. (8.9) is maximized over $x$ and subject also to Eq. (8.10) reduces to the unconstrained problem of maximizing over $q$ alone

$$[1 - p(x(q))]W(w - \pi(q) - x(q))$$
$$+ p(x(q))W(w - \pi(q) - x(q) + q - l).$$

Setting the derivative of this expression with respect to $q$ equal to zero and using facts about $x(q)$ and $\pi(q)$, we can show that $q$ will be strictly less than $l$ under quite general conditions and that $x$ will not minimize $p(x)l + x$.[28]

PROPOSITION 8.4    Assume that the insurer cannot observe the level of care taken by insureds. Then under the expected utility maximizing insurance policy the level of coverage will generally be less than full and the level of care will generally not minimize expected losses plus the cost of care.

*Remarks.* (1) As suggested in the text, the reason that less than full coverage is usually desirable is that this arrangement gives insureds an incentive to choose a positive $x$ and thus lowers the premium rate. Were coverage full, insureds would choose $x = 0$ and their premiums would be $p(0)l$.
(2) The expected utility of insureds here is lower than before, when the insurer could observe $x$. (Insureds' expected utilities here and before are determined by maximizing the same function, Exp. (8.9), but here under an additional constraint and with a different solution.) Hence insureds will be willing to pay a positive amount to the insurer to enable the insurer to observe $x$ and thus to link the policy terms to $x$. It is also the case that insureds will be willing to pay a positive (but lesser) amount for the insurer to obtain even imperfect information about $x$.

---

28. I have only sketched the proof here. For details see Shavell 1979.

# 9 | Liability, Risk-bearing, and Insurance: Basic Theory

The discussion of the last chapter will allow me to recognize in the analysis here that the accident problem involves not only the goal of reducing appropriately the risks of accident losses, but also the objective of properly allocating those accident losses that do occur. I will begin this chapter by reconsidering the socially ideal solution to the accident problem and will then examine the problem in the absence and in the presence of liability and of insurance.

For simplicity, I will study the unilateral model of accidents in which all losses are pecuniary; the main points will carry over in obvious ways to the bilateral model, and I will investigate the case of nonpecuniary losses in the next chapter. Where insurance is available, I will suppose that the policies sold are as described in Chapter 8. That is, the policies maximize insureds' expected utility given that premiums must equal insurers' costs. Such policies, recall, are those that will be purchased by well-informed insureds from insurers in a competitive market or from a self-financed social insurer that wishes to maximize insureds' expected utility.

## 9.1 Risk Aversion and the Socially Ideal Solution to the Accident Problem

Social welfare here, as in Chapter 8, may be assumed to equal the sum of parties' expected utilities. However, what is said here, as before, will be true for any measure of social welfare that rises when the expected utility of an individual rises (see §9A.1 and note 15).

Under the socially ideal solution to the accident problem, parties will make decisions about engaging in activities and about their exercise of care in the way that was first described in Chapter 2 as optimal. In addition, risk-averse parties—be they victims or injurers—will not bear risks, which is to say, their risks will be perfectly spread through insurance arrangements or will be shifted to risk-neutral parties.

EXAMPLE 9.1   If injurers engage in an activity and spend 60 on care, they will reduce the risk of causing an accident loss of 10,000 from 8 percent to 6 percent; and if they spend an additional 90 on care, they will further reduce the risk to 5 percent. Hence it will be optimal for injurers who engage in the activity to spend 60 + 90 = 150 on care; they should therefore engage in the activity if the benefits they would obtain from it exceed 650 (the cost of care plus expected accident losses).

With regard to the allocation of the 5 percent risk of losses that will exist whenever it is optimal for injurers to engage in the activity, suppose first that both victims and injurers are risk averse. In this case it will be optimal that neither bear risk. Victims will therefore be compensated through an insurance arrangement when they would otherwise suffer losses, and injurers will be compensated through an insurance arrangement when they would otherwise pay for victims' losses. In the case where victims are risk averse and injurers are risk neutral, it will be optimal that victims be compensated through an insurance arrangement when they would otherwise bear losses, but it will also be optimal for injurers to bear the risk of victims' losses. Conversely, in the case where injurers are risk averse and victims are risk neutral, it will be optimal that victims bear their losses or, if injurers do, that they be compensated through an insurance arrangement.

As the last case in the example illustrates, and as should be stressed, protection of risk-averse injurers against risk is just as important a determinant of social welfare as is protection of risk-averse victims, other things being equal.

In thinking about the attitudes toward risk of injurers and of victims, the reader should keep in mind the following types of situation: (1) where large firms may do harm to individuals (here the injurers would often be regarded as risk neutral and the victims as risk averse); (2) where individuals may cause losses for large firms, as where a person's improperly doused fire spreads and burns a firm's property (here the injurers would often be regarded as risk averse and the victims as risk neutral); (3) where individuals may do harm to other individuals (here both the victims and the injurers would often be regarded as risk averse); and (4) where large firms may cause losses for other large firms (here both the victims and the injurers would often be regarded as risk neutral).

Furthermore, in making judgments about the importance of risk aversion, the reader should consider the size of losses in relation to parties' assets (see §§8.1.1 and 8.1.2). He should also note that while firms may usually be fairly seen as less risk averse than individuals, there are two important reasons why they should not always be. First, not all firms are large (stores and restaurants are often owned by small numbers of persons; professional services are often provided by single or only a few individuals), and many individuals are well-to-do. Second, even large firms may cause losses that are high relative to their assets yet that are the aggregation of only relatively modest losses for each victim. This possibility may arise, for example, where design errors affect a high percentage of the units of a firm's product. In such cases a firm's risk aversion could be a more important consideration than victims'.

## 9.2   The Accident Problem in the Absence of Liability

If injurers will not be liable for accident losses, they generally will not reduce risk appropriately. They may engage in risky activities to an excessive extent and will have no motive to take care. In Example 9.1, for instance, injurers not liable for losses will engage in their activity as long as it provides them any benefits, and when doing so they will take no care and thus will cause expected losses of 800. On the other hand, injurers will bear no risk; this aspect of the outcome is socially desirable if injurers are risk averse.

Since victims will not be able to obtain judgments from injurers, they will be left bearing risk if accident insurance is not available. This is socially undesirable if victims are risk averse. But if accident insurance is available, risk-averse victims will purchase full coverage,[1] and the only difference in the outcome from the ideal will be that injurers do not act to reduce risk appropriately.

A restatement of the preceding point, notice, is that where victims can secure accident insurance coverage (or can be supplied with social insurance), the main advantage of the liability system is that it provides injurers incentives to reduce risk.

## 9.3   The Accident Problem Given Liability Alone

Assume here that injurers are subject to liability but that neither they nor victims are insured. This case is of interest because, for a variety of reasons, risk-averse parties may in fact not be insured,[2] and because study of the case will enable the reader to appreciate better the next case, in which risk-averse parties are insured.

1. Because unilateral accidents are being considered, victims' behavior does not affect accident risks, so we know that they will purchase full coverage; see §8.2.2. Were bilateral accidents under study (or were other assumptions relaxed), victims might not purchase full coverage; see §§8.2.3 and 8.2.4, and see especially §10.5.
2. See §§8.2.4, 9.4.4, 10.1.2, and 10.4.1. See also §10.4.3, discussing prohibition of liability insurance.

*9.3.1   Strict liability*. Under strict liability victims will, by definition, be compensated for any losses they sustain; it is injurers who will bear risk, and it is their attitude toward risk that is of possible concern. If injurers are risk neutral, however, their bearing of risk will not matter to the optimal allocation of risk. Also, as is known from Chapter 2, such injurers will take optimal care if they engage in an activity and will decide to do that when appropriate. Thus the outcome will be socially optimal.

If injurers are risk averse, on the other hand, the outcome will not be socially optimal. Social welfare will be lowered relative to the ideal if injurers engage in an activity not only because injurers will bear risk, but also because they may be led to exercise excessive care to avoid liability (consider how cautiously risk-averse and uninsured individuals would drive if subject to strict liability). In addition, for these reasons injurers may be discouraged from engaging in an activity in the first place (individuals might decide against owning and driving automobiles) even though doing so would be socially optimal.

EXAMPLE 9.2   Suppose that the injurers in Example 9.1 are risk averse, have initial wealth of 30,000 and the utility-of-wealth graph depicted in Figure 8.1, and are subject to strict liability. Then if injurers engage in the activity, their bearing of the risk of losing 10,000 means that the outcome will not be socially optimal. In addition, they may exercise too much care. For instance, if they can reduce the risk from 5 percent to 4 percent by spending an additional 110, they will do so even though that will not be socially worthwhile.[3] Also, they may decide against engaging in the activity when they would engage in it in the socially optimal situation. That will be the case, for example, if the benefits injurers would obtain from the activity are 700.[4]

---

3. If they do not spend the additional 110, their wealth will be 29,850 with probability 95 percent and 19,850 with probability 5 percent and their expected utility will be 95% × 999.21 + 5% × 907.82 = 994.64. But if they do spend the additional 110, their wealth will be 29,740 with probability 96% and 19,740 with probability 4 percent, so their expected utility will be 96% × 998.62 + 4% × 906.22 = 994.92, which is higher than 994.64. So they will spend the 110 even though it is not socially worthwhile for them to do so. (It is not socially worthwhile because the increment in the cost of care exceeds the decrease in expected losses.)

4. If these injurers do not engage in the activity they will have their wealth of 30,000 and therefore their utility will be 1,000. If the injurers do engage in the activity and spend 150 on care (for simplicity, I do not consider the possibility of spending the additional 110), their wealth will be 30,550 (that is, 30,000 + 700 − 150) with probability 95 percent and 20,550 with probability 5 percent; their expected utility will thus be 95% × 1,002.80 + 5% × 917.59 = 998.54, which is lower than 1,000. The injurers therefore will choose not to engage in the activity.

One way of alleviating such problems is to reduce the magnitude of liability; indeed, it can be shown always to be beneficial to do that to some degree. In other words, if injurers are risk averse, it is not socially desirable to "internalize" fully the harm they do.[5]

*9.3.2  Negligence rule.* The situation is quite different under the negligence rule, since, at least in the absence of uncertainty over the negligence determination,[6] injurers will not bear risk provided that they take due care, which they will decide to do. Hence there will be no particular problems where injurers are risk averse, and they will not be led to take excessive care nor be undesirably discouraged from engaging in an activity (although, of course, there will be the usual problem of their deciding to engage in an activity when it is undesirable for them to do so).

Victims, on the other hand, will bear their losses, presuming that injurers are not mistakenly found negligent. As a consequence, social welfare will be lower than optimal if victims are risk averse and are not insured.

*9.3.3  Comparison of rules.* Under strict liability risk will be borne by injurers, whereas under the negligence rule it will be borne largely by victims. In the absence of insurance, therefore, the relative appeal of strict liability will be enhanced where injurers are risk neutral or, more generally, where they are less risk averse than victims; and the relative appeal of the negligence rule will be enhanced where the reverse is true.

It should be observed also that the appeal of liability rules that have the effect of dividing losses between injurers and victims (the comparative negligence rule and strict division of liability) will be increased where both types of party are risk averse.[7]

## 9.4   The Accident Problem Given Liability and Insurance

Now reconsider the accident problem under liability rules assuming that both accident insurance for victims and liability insurance for injurers are available.

*9.4.1  Strict liability.* Suppose initially that liability insurers can determine

5. See Proposition 9.3 of the Appendix. But note that this is true only under the present assumption that liability insurance is unavailable.

6. See §§4.3 and 4.4.

7. With regard to comparative negligence, however, the degree of sharing of risk is not as great as might at first appear. Recall from §2.2.9 that under this rule injurers will in principle be led to take due care and will avoid liability, leaving victims bearing the entire risk. Thus only to the extent that uncertainty over the negligence determination or some other factor results in a finding of negligence on the part of both an injurer and a victim will the comparative negligence rule result in a sharing of risk.

injurers' levels of care. The outcome will then be socially optimal. Victims will be protected against risk by definition of strict liability and injurers, if risk averse, will purchase liability insurance. Moreover, since insurers can determine injurers' levels of care, their liability insurance policies will supply them with full coverage and will have provisions inducing them to take optimal care (see §8.2.3). Also, since insured injurers will pay premiums equal to the expected losses they cause, they will decide to engage in an activity only when they should (risk-neutral injurers we know will do so). Thus, the outcome will indeed be optimal, as the following example illustrates.

EXAMPLE 9.3    In the situation of Example 9.1, injurers who are risk averse and who decide to engage in their activity will obtain full liability insurance coverage and will spend 150 on care, for spending only 60 on care will reduce their premium from 800 to 600 and spending another 90 will reduce it to 500. (For simplicity it is assumed that the premium, rather than the condition under which coverage is paid, depends on the exercise of care.) Because their cost of engaging in the activity will also include the 150 cost of care, injurers will choose to engage in the activity if and only if the benefit they will obtain exceeds 650. Thus they will behave optimally. Also, as injurers will be insured if they engage in the activity (and victims will be paid for any losses), no risk-averse parties will bear risk.

It should be noticed here that the ability to purchase liability insurance is socially beneficial because it leads to the socially ideal outcome. Where liability insurance is unavailable, as discussed in §9.2, injurers are exposed to risk and there are accompanying problems of their exercising excessive care and possibly of being undesirably discouraged from engaging in their activity.

Next suppose that liability insurers cannot determine injurers' levels of care and thus cannot link the terms of policies to their care. In this case the outcome will be more complicated and it will depart from the socially optimal one. Specifically, although risk-averse injurers will purchase insurance policies, the policies will usually involve less than complete coverage. Policies with less than complete coverage will tend to be favored by injurers because these policies will leave them with some motive to reduce the risk of liability. This will mean that the premium rate will be lower than the rate for full coverage (recall again the argument of §8.2.3). Of course, the fact that injurers are risk averse and will bear part of the risk of losses means immediately that the outcome will not be ideal.[8] In addition, the fact that injurers will be

---

8. The outcome will not be ideal even if injurers happen to purchase a policy with full coverage and bear no risk, for in that event they will have no incentive to take care.

protected from part of the risk of losses suggests that they will generally not take optimal care. In the situation of Example 9.3 for instance, if injurers have coverage of, say, 7,000 against their possible 10,000 liability, they will be led to spend only 60, rather than the optimal 150 amount, on care.

Yet despite the possibility that the purchase of liability insurance will result in a level of care that differs from the optimal, it should be emphasized that the availability of liability insurance will still be socially desirable. The reasoning is as follows. The availability of liability insurance cannot affect the welfare of victims under present assumptions. Victims will be compensated for accident losses whether or not injurers have liability insurance. For that reason, it will not matter to victims what the risk of accidents is or what influence injurers' ownership of liability insurance may have on the risk.[9] Hence the only way the availability of liability insurance can affect social welfare is by changing the welfare of injurers. But since injurers choose to buy liability insurance, it must be that the insurance makes them better off.[10]

*9.4.2.  Negligence rule.* Assume first that under the negligence rule there is no uncertainty over the determination of negligence. Then injurers' levels of care will be optimal, as will the bearing of risk by them and by victims. This will clearly be the case *if* injurers take due care, since injurers will then bear no risk and victims will purchase full accident insurance coverage against losses. What needs to be shown, then, is that injurers will take due care. The usual argument establishing that it is rational for injurers to take due care will apply if injurers do not possess liability insurance protecting them against their negligence. And, as it turns out, we can see on reflection why injurers will not purchase such insurance: the premium for the insurance would be too high to make it worth purchasing. Because all injurers who owned the insurance would act negligently, insurers' costs and the premium charged would equal the level of expected accident losses produced by negligent behavior. Injurers would therefore be better off not buying the insurance and taking due care. In Example 9.3, for instance, the premium for policies covering negligence would be 800, whereas the cost of exercising due care is only 150.

Now assume that there is uncertainty over the determination of negligence. In this case the main difference to note is that injurers might be found negligent even if they try to take due care. Thus risk-averse injurers will decide to purchase liability insurance. On the other hand, it is important to say that the

9. The situation obviously changes if victims are not fully compensated for losses. See, for instance, §10.4.3.

10. The reader may note that this argument serves to establish as well that liability insurance must be beneficial in the previous case, where liability insurers were assumed to be able to ascertain injurers' levels of care.

type of policy risk-averse injurers will purchase will protect them primarily against being found negligent through some type of error or lapse. The policy will not protect injurers so broadly as to induce them definitely to act negligently. The policy might exclude certain intentional acts, for example, but not behavior that injurers are unable to control or that courts are unable to assess accurately (see §8.2.4). The policy will be so structured because, as noted above, one that induced injurers definitely to act negligently would not be purchased because the premium would be too high. I believe that it can also be argued, again along the lines of what was said about strict liability, that the availability of liability insurance will be socially desirable.

*9.4.3 Summary.* Three points about liability and insurance will summarize the analysis of this part. First, since liability insurers pay for some or all of the losses for which injurers are found liable, the manner in which liability rules alter injurers' behavior is to a significant degree indirect, being associated with the terms of their liability insurance policies (with the connection between premiums or the payment of claims and injurer behavior, and with whether the level of coverage is complete).[11]

Second, the availability of liability insurance is socially desirable. The particular arguments demonstrating this result depended on the form of liability and insurers' information about insureds' behavior. The arguments were, roughly, based on the following considerations.[12] The availability of liability insurance increases the welfare of risk-averse injurers because it protects them from risk and meliorates the problems that they would otherwise take excessive care or be discouraged from engaging in desirable activities. Moreover, the availability of liability insurance does not necessarily dilute injurers' incentives to reduce risk; and where it does do that, the dilution of incentives will be moderate, for policies that would substantially increase risks would be so expensive that they would not be attractive for purchase.

This is hardly to deny the existence of circumstances where liability insurance might be socially undesirable, and some such circumstances will be discussed later (see §10.4.3). But it is to say that thinking about the social desirability of liability insurance should proceed from the understanding that in the basic model of liability studied here, the insurance is socially desirable.

11. Other possible terms, though not discussed here, are the link between loss history and premiums and the future right to insure.

12. The reader should note that a consideration that did not enter into the arguments here but that is often mentioned as a socially desirable aspect of liability insurance is that it supplies victims with a source of compensation. This factor was not of concern here because it was assumed that injurers' assets were sufficient to pay for harm done. The case where injurers' assets are insufficient is treated in §10.4.

Third, the availability of accident and liability insurance limits the importance of the allocation of risk as a factor to be considered in evaluating liability rules. For example, the fact that in some areas of accidents the typical injurers might be large, essentially risk-neutral firms and the victims risk-averse individuals will not constitute an argument in favor of imposing liability to the extent that the individuals are insured against their losses.

*9.4.4  Remark on the cheaper insurer.* Although the availability of insurance limits the importance of the allocation of risk in the evaluation of liability rules, it is relevant to consider whether victims or injurers can more cheaply insure because of administrative cost advantages. In this regard, two cautionary points should be borne in mind. First, it is sometimes argued that since a firm need purchase only one liability insurance policy, a firm can more cheaply insure than the many individual victims the firm may harm. But victims ordinarily purchase insurance policies protecting them against *generally* described risks (such as loss of life due to *any* cause). Hence it is not necessary for victims to purchase additional policies protecting them against each new risk they bear; for victims to be insured against additional risks does not mean that additional administrative costs must be incurred. Second, even if injurers can insure more cheaply than victims can, it may still be administratively cheaper for victims to bear their losses. This is because administrative costs must be incurred by victims in obtaining awards or settlements from liable injurers (see §11.1).

*9.4.5  Actual use of accident and liability insurance.* The ownership or public provision of accident insurance and of liability insurance is today widespread, with the major fraction of victims' losses being compensated by their insurers or by injurers' liability insurers. The only real exception is the Soviet Union, where liability insurance is not allowed because of the fear that otherwise the deterrent of liability would be dulled.[13] Historically, similar worries

---

13. See generally Tunc 1974, secs. 90–93, for a summary of the situation in different countries; Rudden 1966 on the situation in the Soviet Union; and Fleming 1983, chap. 19, and *Prosser and Keeton on Torts* (Keeton, Dobbs, et al. 1984), chap. 14, on the Anglo-American situation. Except for the Soviet Union, most socialist countries permit the sale of liability insurance, at least to individuals (state enterprises may still be forbidden from purchasing it). It is interesting to note that the Soviet courts enjoy the discretion to reduce damages below the level of losses caused where hardship to the injurer would otherwise result. This I had said, at the end of §9.3.1, is desirable in theory, in that it furnishes an implicit kind of liability insurance to the injurer. (Ostensibly, the victim obtains the balance of his losses from accident insurance or another source.) See Tunc 1974, secs. 89 and 92. It is also significant that the private ownership of automobiles in the Soviet Union is limited. When more Soviet citizens come to own automobiles, one would expect pressure to grow for them to be able to purchase liability insurance.

were expressed by the legal community about liability insurance in Western countries, and in some cases there was considerable resistance to its sale.[14]

*9.4.6 Note on the literature.* In Shavell (1982a), I demonstrated the results presented here in an analysis of liability and insurance. Related discussions of the subject are contained in James (1948), in chapter 4 and (interspersed) in other chapters of Calabresi (1970), in chapters 10 and 12 and sections 3 and 4 of chapter 23 of Atiyah (1980), in McNeely (1941), and in Williamson, Olson, and Ralston (1967).

# Mathematical Appendix

The role of liability in allocating accident risks among possibly risk-averse parties as well as in creating incentives for them to reduce risks will be examined here both in the absence and in the presence of insurance. As in the text, the analysis will, for convenience, be of the unilateral model of accidents. It will be assumed that injurers' care $x$ alone affects the risk $p(x)$ of victims' suffering losses of $l$, and that the risks of different victims' suffering losses are independent. Let

$U$ = utility function of injurers, who are risk neutral or risk averse;
$u$ = initial wealth of injurers;
$V$ = utility function of victims, who are risk neutral or risk averse;
$v$ = initial wealth of victims.

For parties who are risk neutral, the utility of wealth will be assumed without loss of generality to equal the amount of wealth.

Before liability is studied, the socially ideal solution to the accident problem and the situation in the absence of liability will be briefly considered.

## 9A.1 The Socially Ideal Solution to the Accident Problem

The socially ideal solution to the accident problem is the solution that would be obtained by a dictator who could choose in a Pareto optimal way

14. Tunc 1974, sec. 90, writes "At the beginning of the nineteenth century, liability insurance would have been unthinkable. It would have been considered as immoral." He notes the resistance to sale of liability insurance in France and in the Scandinavian countries, where the leading jurists opposed it. *Prosser and Keeton on Torts* (Keeton, Dobbs, et al. 1984), p. 585, also mentions early uncertainty about the desirability of liability insurance.

levels of care and levels of wealth contingent on the occurrence of accidents, subject to a resource constraint.[15] Denoting by $v_n$ the wealth of a victim if he is not involved in an accident, $v_a$ his wealth if he is, and similarly for $u_n$ and $u_a$, the dictator would

(9.1)   $\displaystyle\max_{x, v_n, v_a, u_n, u_a} EV = [1 - p(x)]V(v_n) + p(x)V(v_a)$

subject to

(9.2)   $EU = [1 - p(x)]U(u_n) + p(x)U(u_a) = k,$

where $k$ is a constant, and subject to

(9.3)   $[(1 - p(x))v_n + p(x)v_a] + [(1 - p(x))u_n + p(x)u_a]$
$+ [p(x)l + x] = u + v.$

Constraint (9.3) states that expected resource use equals the available resources. (The justification for writing the constraint in terms of an expected value equation is that the risks are independent.) Given any $x$, a necessary and sufficient condition for Pareto optimality of $v_n$, $v_a$, $u_n$, and $u_a$ is that they satisfy Eqs. (9.2) and (9.3), that $v_n = v_a$ if the victim is risk averse, and that $u_n = u_a$ if the injurer is risk averse. This may be shown by essentially the steps used in proving Proposition 8.1. Thus we may assume that $u_n = u_a$ (if the injurer is risk neutral, this does no harm) and call their common value $\mu$; similarly we may assume that $v_n = v_a$ and call their common value $\gamma$. The problem of maximizing $EV$ subject to Eqs. (9.2) and (9.3) is therefore equivalent to

(9.4)   $\displaystyle\max_{x, \gamma, \mu} V(\gamma)$

subject to

(9.5)   $U(\mu) = k$

15. Were we to maximize any social welfare function depending positively on parties' expected utilities, the optimum would have to be Pareto optimal. Thus in finding the characteristics of Pareto optimal outcomes, we are determining what must be true of social welfare optima.

and subject to

(9.6)    $\gamma + \mu + p(x)l + x = u + v.$

Constraint (9.5) determines a value, say $\bar{\mu}$, of $\mu$, so that Eqs. (9.5) and (9.6) reduce to

$$\gamma = (u + v - \bar{\mu}) - (p(x)l + x).$$

Hence, the problem becomes that of maximizing $V(u + v - \bar{\mu} - (p(x)l + x))$ over $x$; equivalently the problem is to choose $x$ to minimize $p(x)l + x$. This $x$ will be denoted $x^*$ and will be assumed to be positive. In summary, we have shown the following proposition.

PROPOSITION 9.1    A socially ideal Pareto optimal solution to the accident problem will be achieved if and only if (a) risk-averse parties—be they injurers or victims—are left with the same level of wealth regardless of whether accidents occur; and (b) the level of care minimizes expected accident losses plus the costs of care ($p(x)l + x$).

*Remarks.* (1) The explanation for this result is, of course, that the dictator can fully insure risk-averse parties. It therefore becomes desirable for him to maximize total expected resources, which means minimizing expected accident losses plus the costs of care.

(2) Suppose that injurers are allowed to make a choice whether to engage in an activity. It is then clear that according to a Pareto optimal solution, injurers will engage in an activity if and only if the utility they will obtain exceeds $p(x^*)l + x^*$.

## 9A.2    The Accident Problem in the Absence of Liability

The following proposition is obvious.

PROPOSITION 9.2    In the absence of liability, the outcome will not be socially ideal because injurers will take no care. But victims will bear no risk if insurance is available.

*Remark.* If in the absence of liability injurers are allowed to choose whether to engage in an activity, they may decide to do so when they should not. They will engage in an activity as long as the utility they will obtain is positive, rather than only when it exceeds $p(x^*)l + x^*$.

### 9A.3   The Accident Problem Given Liability Alone

We will be interested here in determining the Pareto optimal solution to the accident problem given that injurers are subject to liability and that insurance is not available (to injurers or to victims). Specifically, we will want to solve

(9.7)      max $EV$

subject to

(9.8)      injurers choose care $x$ to maximize $EU$, given the liability rule; and

(9.9)      $r$ is such that $EU = k$.

Here

  $r$ = lump-sum amount paid (before an accident might occur) by victims to injurers.[16]

The maximization of $EV$ will be over (among over variables) the magnitude of liability and, under the negligence rule, the standard of due care. Let

  $d$ = magnitude of liability;

$d$ may in principle be different from the level of losses.

*9A.3.1   Strict liability.* In the present section we will show the following.

PROPOSITION 9.3   Under strict liability, suppose that injurers are risk neutral. Then according to a Pareto optimal solution to the accident problem, (a) the magnitude of liability will equal a victim's losses ($d = l$); and (b) a socially ideal outcome will result. If, however, injurers are risk averse, then under a Pareto optimal solution, (c) liability will be less than a victim's losses ($d < l$) and (d) a socially ideal outcome will not be achieved.

---

16. If the lump-sum amount $r$ is negative, it would be interpreted as a lump-sum tax paid by injurers. The reason that we are interested in Pareto optima allowing for an ex ante payment $r$ is that this allows us to abstract from considerations of income redistribution. Were we not to allow for such a payment, then the results would be hard to interpret because they would implicitly reflect redistributional goals. For instance, if the magnitude of liability turned out to be high at an optimum, we would not know whether the purpose was to transfer more wealth to victims or to provide stronger incentives for injurers to reduce risk.

*Remarks*. (1) Parts (a) and (b) plainly hold: if injurers are risk neutral, we know from the Appendix to Chapter 2 that making them pay $l$ when they cause losses will induce them to act optimally, and we know that their bearing of risk will not matter to the optimal allocation of risk. Also, victims will not bear risk under strict liability. Parts (c) and (d) are true for the reasons suggested in the text: were $d$ to equal $l$, injurers would be exposed to "excessive" risk, with the consequence that they would have to be compensated excessively (through increases in $r$) for bearing the risk or for exercising excessive care. Thus it becomes desirable to lower $d$.[17] Part (d) is true because if $d$ is positive (as one would expect), injurers will bear risk, and if $d$ is 0, injurers will choose $x = 0$, which is not ideal.

(2) Were injurers' decision to engage in an activity to be considered, the proposition would still hold.[18] (In this case, the explanation for (d) would include the point that were $d$ to equal $l$, injurers might be undesirably discouraged from engaging in an activity or would need to receive implicit compensation to do so.)

(3) The result (c) that $d < l$ means that in the familiar model of (so-called Pigouvian) externalities, the harm done should not be completely "internalized" if the generator of the externalities is risk averse (and cannot purchase insurance).

To prove the proposition, assume first that injurers are risk neutral. If a socially ideal outcome will be achieved when $d = l$, certainly $d = l$ must be a Pareto optimal solution of the problem put forth in Exps. (9.7)–(9.9).[19] We shall therefore assume that $d = l$ and shall show that a socially ideal outcome will result. If $d = l$, injurers will select $x$ to maximize

$$(9.10) \quad EU = [1 - p(x)](u + r - x) + p(x)(u + r - x - l)$$
$$= u + r - (x + p(x)l).$$

---

17. It is true that if $d < l$ the possibly risk-averse victims will bear the risk $l - d$. But the first-order effect on the expected utility of victims of the imposition of risk will be zero if they begin from a position where they do not bear risk—which is their situation if $d = l$. This is why it is Pareto optimal that they bear some risk. (Of course, how much risk it is Pareto optimal that they bear depends on, among other factors, victims' degree of risk aversion relative to injurers'.)

18. This will be the case for other results below, but I will not mention it again.

19. More precisely, it is obvious that $EV$ given the constraints of Exps. (9.8) and (9.9) cannot be higher than $EV$ in the solution to the dictator's problem given by Eqs. (9.1)–(9.3). Therefore, if when $d = l$, $EV$ given Exps. (9.8) and (9.9) equals $EV$ in the solution to Eqs. (9.1)–(9.3), then $d = l$ must solve the problem of maximizing $EV$ given Exps. (9.8) and (9.9).

They will therefore select $x$ to minimize $x + p(x)l$. Moreover, since victims (who might be risk averse) will receive $l$ whenever there is an accident, their wealth will be constant. Thus if $r$ is such that Eq. (9.10) equals $k$, Proposition 9.1 implies that a socially ideal solution will be achieved. This proves parts (a) and (b).

If injurers are risk averse, they will choose $x$ to maximize

$$EU = [1 - p(x)]U(u + r - x) + p(x)U(u + r - x - d).$$

Victims' expected utility will be

$$EV = [1 - p(x)]V(v - r) + p(x)V(v - r - l + d).$$

The problem given by Exps. (9.7)–(9.9) therefore becomes

$$\max_{d,r,x} EV$$

subject to

(9.11)    $EU_x = 0$

and to Exp. (9.9). These constraints determine (let us assume, uniquely) $r$ and $x$ as functions of $d$. Thus the problem may be written

(9.12)    $$\max_{d} EV(d) = [1 - p(x(d))]V(v - r(d))$$
$$+ p(x(d))V(v - r(d) - l + d).$$

Observe that[20]

(9.13)    $$EV'(d) = -p'x'[V(v - r) - V(v - r - l + d)]$$
$$- r'(1 - p)V'(v - r) + p(1 - r')V'(v - r - l + d).$$

To show that $d < l$, we shall verify that $EV'(l) < 0$. (A similar series of steps would verify that $EV'(d) < 0$ for $d > l$.) From Eq. (9.13), we see that $EV'(l) = (p - r')V'(v - r)$, so it needs to be shown that $r' > p$. To do this, differentiate Exp. (9.9) with respect to $d$ to obtain

$$EU_x x'(d) + EU_r r'(d) + EU_d = 0,$$

20. For convenience, I omit the arguments of certain functions here and, occasionally, below.

and using Eq. (9.11), solve for $r'$ to find that

$$(9.14) \quad r'(d) = \frac{-EU_d}{EU_r}$$

$$= \frac{p(x)\,U'(u + r - x - d)}{[1 - p(x)]U'(u + r - x) + p(x)U'(u + r - x - d)}$$

$$= \frac{p(x)}{[1 - p(x)]\dfrac{U'(u + r - x)}{U'(u + r - x - d)} + p(x)}.$$

It is clear from Eq. (9.14) that $r' > p$ for any $d > 0$, and thus for $d = l$. This establishes part (c); part (d) is clear from Remark 1.

*9A.3.2  Negligence rule.* Here we will establish the result stated below.

PROPOSITION 9.4    Under the negligence rule, suppose that victims are risk neutral. Then, according to a Pareto optimal solution to the accident problem, (a) the standard of due care will equal the ideal level of care ($\bar{x} = x^*$) and (b) a socially ideal outcome will be achieved. However, if victims are risk averse, then under a Pareto optimal solution (c) the standard of due care will generally be different from the ideal level and (d) an ideal outcome will not be achieved.

*Remark.* Parts (a) and (b) are true because if $\bar{x} = x^*$, injurers will find it in their interest to choose $x = \bar{x}$. Thus injurers, who might be risk averse, will bear no risk; and as victims are risk neutral, their bearing of risk will not matter to the optimal allocation of risk. But when victims are risk averse, their bearing of risk will matter; in this case an ideal outcome will not be achieved, and it may be desirable that $\bar{x} > x^*$ so as to further reduce the risk of accidents.

To prove (a) and (b), it will suffice to show that when victims are risk neutral, a socially ideal outcome will result if $\bar{x} = x^*$ and $d = l$. To demonstrate this, note first that if injurers choose an $x \geq x^*$, it clearly must be that they choose $x = x^*$. On the other hand, if injurers choose an $x < x^*$, then, since they will be found negligent if involved in accidents,

$$(9.15) \quad \begin{aligned} EU &= [1 - p(x)]U(u + r - x) + p(x)U(u + r - x - l) \\ &\leq U(u + r - x - p(x)l) < U(u + r - x^* - p(x^*)l) \\ &\leq U(u + r - x^*). \end{aligned}$$

(The first inequality here follows from Jensen's inequality,[21] and the second from the fact that $x^*$ minimizes $x + p(x)l$.) Thus injurers will in fact be better off choosing $x^*$, will do this, and will not be found negligent if involved in accidents nor bear risk. Since victims are risk neutral, Proposition 9.1 therefore implies that a socially ideal outcome will be achieved.

Now suppose that victims are risk averse and consider only $\bar{x}$ such that injurers will choose $x = \bar{x}$. (Even if we restrict attention to the case where $d = l$, the set of such $\bar{x}$ properly includes $[0, x^*]$ since Ineq. (9.15) contains a strict inequality.) For such $\bar{x}$, $EV = [1 - p(\bar{x})]V(v - r) + p(\bar{x})V(v - r - l)$ and $EU = U(u + r - \bar{x})$. The problem stated in Exps. (9.7)–(9.9) is therefore to maximize $EV$ over $r$ and $\bar{x}$ subject to $EU = k$. But from the latter constraint, it follows that $r$ and $\bar{x}$ are determined by $r = \hat{k} + \bar{x}$, where $\hat{k}$ is an appropriate constant. Thus, the problem reduces to

$$(9.16) \quad \max_{\bar{x}} [1 - p(\bar{x})]V(v - \hat{k} - \bar{x}) + p(\bar{x})V(v - \hat{k} - \bar{x} - l).$$

If $V$ were linear, the solution to this problem would be $\bar{x} = x^*$, but since $V$ is concave we would expect the solution to exceed $x^*$; it is possible, however, that the solution would be $\bar{x} < x^*$. In any event, since victims are risk averse and bear risk, Proposition 9.1 implies that an ideal outcome will not be achieved.

## 9A.4  The Accident Problem Given Liability and Insurance

We will now assume that victims can purchase insurance against accident losses, that injurers can purchase insurance against liability, and that the insurance policies they choose to purchase are those that maximize their expected utility. (Thus the policies are those that would be sold in a competitive insurance market; see generally §8A.2.) The Pareto optimal solution to the accident problem is therefore found by maximizing Exp. (9.7) subject to Exps. (9.8) and (9.9) and to the following constraints:

(9.17)    victims choose an accident insurance policy to maximize $EV$;

(9.18)    injurers choose a liability insurance policy to maximize $EU$; and

(9.19)    insurers' premiums equal their expected costs.

21. See De Groot 1970, p. 97.

*9A.4.1   Strict liability.* Here we will prove that the following holds.

PROPOSITION 9.5   Under strict liability, according to a Pareto optimal solution to the accident problem, (a) the magnitude of liability will equal a victim's losses ($d = l$), (b) government interference with the sale of liability insurance will not be socially desirable, and (c) a socially ideal outcome will be achieved unless injurers are risk averse and liability insurers cannot observe their levels of care.

*Remarks.* The argument establishing the proposition may be summarized as follows. If injurers are risk neutral and liability insurers cannot observe their levels of care, injurers will decide against purchase of liability insurance. Hence the situation will be as in Proposition 9.3(a) and (b) and a socially ideal outcome will be achieved. (The issue of interference with the sale of liability insurance will be moot since injurers will not purchase it.)

If injurers are risk neutral and liability insurers can observe their levels of care, injurers will be indifferent as to whether and in what amount to purchase liability coverage. Also, if $d = l$, injurers will be induced to choose $x^*$ by their exposure to liability or by the terms of their insurance policies, if they purchase them. In addition, since victims will bear no risk, Proposition 9.1 implies that a socially ideal outcome will be achieved and, thus, that government interference with the sale of liability insurance could not be desirable.

If injurers are risk averse and liability insurers can observe their levels of care, injurers will purchase full coverage against liability, will therefore not bear risk, and, if $d = l$, will be induced by the terms of their policies to choose $x^*$ (see Proposition 8.3). Thus, Proposition 9.1 again implies the claimed result.

If injurers are risk averse and liability insurers cannot observe their levels of care, injurers will purchase incomplete liability coverage, as explained in Proposition 8.4. If, as in §8A.2, $q$ denotes the level of coverage, this means that injurers will bear a positive risk of $d - q$ and a socially ideal outcome will not be achieved. (Also note that because injurers bear the risk $d - q$, there is no reason to expect them to take optimal care, although they will generally exercise positive care.) *If* it is optimal to set $d$ equal to $l$, interference with the sale of liability insurance will not be desirable for essentially the reason given in §9.4.1. Specifically, if $d = l$ victims' expected utility will be unaffected by injurers' behavior (there will be no "externality"), since victims will be fully compensated for losses. Hence one would not think there would be scope for socially beneficial government intervention. *Why* setting $d$ equal to $l$ should result in a Pareto optimal outcome given the sale of liability insurance is difficult to explain, however; the reader will have to study the proof to understand fully the result. In this connection it should be pointed out (and it will be shown at the end of the proof) that in the case under discussion, where liability insurers cannot observe levels of care, an equivalent Pareto optimal outcome can also be achieved if the government bans the sale of liability insurance and reduces the magnitude of liability from $l$ to $l - q$, leaving risk-averse victims to purchase accident insurance coverage of $q$.

Let us now proceed with the proof. Suppose that, if injurers are risk neutral and liability insurers cannot observe $x$, injurers purchase coverage $q > 0$. In this case they will select $x$ to maximize $u + r - \pi - x - p(x)(d - q)$, where, as in §8A.2, $\pi$ is the premium. If the solution to this problem is denoted by $x_1$, then $\pi$ must equal $p(x_1)q$. Consequently, the expected wealth of injurers will be

$$(9.20) \qquad u + r - p(x_1)q - x_1 - p(x_1)(d - q) = u + r - x_1 - p(x_1)d.$$

On the other hand, if injurers do not purchase coverage they will select $x$ to maximize $u + r - x - p(x)d$. If the solution to this is denoted by $x_2$, injurers' expected wealth will be

$$(9.21) \qquad u + r - x_2 - p(x_2)d.$$

Because, as is easily verified, $x_1 < x_2$, and because $x_2$ maximizes $u + r - x - p(x)d$ and is unique (for $p(x)$ is strictly convex), the expected wealth given in Exp. (9.21) will be larger than that in Eq. (9.20). Hence injurers will not purchase liability insurance coverage and we may appeal to the argument proving Proposition 9.3(a) and (b) to establish Proposition 9.5 in the present case.

If injurers are risk neutral, $d = l$, and liability insurers can observe $x$, then whatever level of coverage injurers select (they will in fact be indifferent among all levels of coverage, including none), they will be induced to choose $x^*$. This follows because their premium for coverage $q \geq 0$ will depend on $x$ and equal $p(x)q$, so that they will choose $x$ to maximize

$$u + r - p(x)q - x - p(x)(l - q) = u + r - x - p(x)l.$$

Because injurers will choose $x^*$ and victims will bear no risk, Proposition 9.1 implies the result stated in Proposition 9.5.

If injurers are risk averse and liability insurers can observe $x$, what was said in the Remarks supplies the argument for the result.

For the situation in which injurers are risk averse and liability insurers cannot observe $x$, we shall use a two-part argument to establish (a) and (b).

First, we shall consider the outcome if decisions are made by a dictator whose goal is Pareto optimality and whose powers are limited by inability to observe $x$ and, therefore, by inability to set $x$ directly. Then we shall show in a series of steps that the same outcome will result under strict liability if $d = l$ and liability insurance is sold. (Thus, clearly, a Pareto superior outcome to this cannot be achieved—else the dictator could achieve it.)

The problem of the dictator is

(9.22)     $\max\limits_{u_n, u_a, v_n, v_a} EV = [1 - p(x)]V(v_n) + p(x)V(v_a)$

subject to

(9.23)     $EU = [1 - p(x)]U(u_n - x) + p(x)U(u_a - x) = k;$

(9.24)     $EU$ is maximized over $x$; and

(9.25)     $[(1 - p(x))v_n + p(x)v_a] + [(1 - p(x))u_n + p(x)u_a] + p(x)l = u + v.$

Here the variables are defined as in Eqs. (9.1)–(9.3), except that now $u_n$ and $u_a$ are gross of the costs of care, $x$. Constraint (9.24) is introduced because injurers are free to select $x$. As in the proof of Proposition 9.1, we may assume that $v_n = v_a$ and will set $\gamma$ equal to their common value. The dictator's problem thus becomes

(9.26)     $\max\limits_{u_n, u_a, \gamma} V(\gamma)$

subject to constraints (9.23) and (9.24) and to

(9.27)     $\gamma + [1 - p(x)]u_n + p(x)u_a + p(x)l = u + v.$

Next let us show that the above problem is equivalent to the following one: find a Pareto optimal outcome assuming that liability is strict with $d = l$; that liability insurance is sold; and that the government (rather than the competitive insurance market) determines the extent of coverage $q$. Formally, this problem is

(9.28)     $\max\limits_{q, \pi, r} V(v - r)$

subject to

(9.29)    $EU = [1 - p(x)]U(u + r - \pi - x)$
$+ p(x)U(u + r - \pi - x + q - l) = k;$

(9.30)    $EU$ is maximized over $x$; and

(9.31)    $\pi = p(x)q.$

Under the change of variables $\gamma = v - r$, $u_n = u + r - \pi$, and $u_a = u + r - \pi + q - l$, direct substitution shows that the problem stated in Exps. (9.28)–(9.31) is, as claimed, the same as the problem stated in Exps. (9.26), (9.23), (9.24), and (9.27).

Now write the problem in Exps. (9.28)–(9.31) in the equivalent form

(9.32)    $\max_{q,\pi,r} EU = [1 - p(x)]U(u + r - \pi - x)$
$+ p(x)U(u + r - \pi - x + q - l)$

subject to Exps. (9.30) and (9.31) and to

(9.33)    $V(v - r) = t,$

where $t$ is the optimal value of $V$ in Exps. (9.28)–(9.31). Observe that Eq. (9.33) alone determines $r$. Thus, the problem stated in Eq. (9.32) subject to Exps. (9.30), (9.31), and (9.33) reduces to

$\max_{q,\pi} EU$

subject to Exps. (9.30) and (9.31). This is exactly the problem that is solved by the liability insurance market (see §8A.2.3). Hence we have completed the proof of (a) and (b) for the case in which injurers are risk averse and liability insurers cannot observe $x$. Part (c) also follows because liability coverage will generally be partial (and if it were not, injurers would choose $x = 0$).

Finally, consider the claim made in the Remarks about the banning of liability insurance. Suppose that liability insurance cannot be purchased and let $\hat{d} = l - q$ and $\hat{r} = r - \pi$, where $r$, $q$, and $\pi$ are the values from the Pareto optimal solution when liability insurance can be purchased and liability insurers cannot observe $x$. The reader may easily verify that injurers will then select the same levels of care and enjoy the same expected utility as in the Pareto optimal solution with the purchase of liability insurance allowed. The same is true of victims, who, if risk averse, will buy accident insurance, paying $\pi$ for coverage of $q$.

*9A.4.2 Negligence rule.* Finally, we have the next proposition.

PROPOSITION 9.6    Under the negligence rule, according to a Pareto optimal solution to the accident problem, (a) the standard of due care will equal the socially ideal level of care ($\bar{x} = x^*$), (b) government interference with the sale of liability insurance will not be socially desirable, and (c) a socially ideal outcome will be achieved.

*Remarks.* (1) As in Proposition 9.4, if $\bar{x} = x^*$ injurers will choose $x = \bar{x}$, but now this will be true despite their opportunity to act negligently and to protect themselves by purchasing liability insurance, for they will not purchase such insurance. Also, although victims will bear risk, they can purchase accident insurance. Thus a socially ideal solution will be achieved and government interference with the sale of liability insurance cannot be desirable.

(2) Injurers might well purchase liability insurance if there is uncertainty over the determination of negligence (see the discussion in §9.4.2). In this case an ideal outcome will not be achieved, and I conjecture that interference with the sale of liability insurance will still not be desirable.

To prove the proposition, it will suffice to show that liability insurance will not be purchased, since then an argument virtually identical to that used to show parts (a) and (b) of Proposition 9.4 may be employed to show (a) and (c) here, and (b) follows from (c). Let us therefore assume that when $\bar{x} = x^*$ injurers will purchase coverage and show that this leads to a contradiction. If injurers purchase coverage, it must be that $x < x^*$ (for otherwise injurers will never be found negligent and will have no reason to insure). Thus injurers' premiums must be $p(x)q$, so that

$$
\begin{aligned}
EU &= [1 - p(x)]U(u + r - p(x)q - x) \\
&\quad + p(x)U(u + r - p(x)q - x + q - l) \\
&\leq U(u + r - x - p(x)l) < U(u + r - x^* - p(x^*)l) \\
&\leq U(u + r - x^*).
\end{aligned}
$$

(The first inequality follows from Jensen's inequality, the second from the fact that $x^*$ minimizes $x + p(x)l$.) But this is a contradiction, since it means that injurers would prefer to choose $x^*$ and be nonnegligent.

*9A.4.3    Note on the literature.* This appendix largely follows Shavell (1982a), in which I first incorporate insurance into the model of liability and take into account risk aversion.

# 10 | Liability, Risk-bearing, and Insurance: Extensions to the Basic Theory

This chapter continues the previous analysis by considering insurance against nonpecuniary losses; the possible divergence between liability awards that are optimal for purposes of compensation and awards that are optimal for purposes of deterrence; the rule determining whether victims' receipts of collateral insurance benefits are to be set off against liability; injurers' inability to pay for harm done; and the structure of a system of pure accident insurance.

## 10.1 Nonpecuniary Losses and Insurance

*10.1.1 Nonpecuniary losses and the utility of money to an individual.* In many cases, suffering a nonpecuniary loss will not alter an individual's need for money or, more exactly, the utility he would derive from receiving additional money. If, for example, an irreplaceable family portrait with great sentimental value but no market value is destroyed, there is no obvious reason to believe that the owner's need for money will increase, however much he regrets the loss; the utility he would obtain from having more money to spend would be whatever it was beforehand. Similarly, if a person loses a small toe in an accident, then aside from requiring some money for medical treatment, he might well place the same value on having additional money as he had prior to losing his toe.

In some cases, though, events with adverse nonpecuniary consequences will result in a person attaching a higher value to money. An individual who is crippled by an accident may value money more, even after being compensated for medical expenses and forgone income, because of a desire to obtain household help, special transportation services, and the like.

It is also possible that suffering a nonpecuniary loss will lower the utility of money to an individual. The individual who is crippled by an accident could turn out to value money less because venturing forth to spend is less pleasurable and more difficult. Perhaps the most important example of valuing money less because of a nonpecuniary loss involves death. The value of money in that contingency is, in effect, the value to a person of knowing that his survivors will receive a bequest, and this will often be less than the value to the person of having money while he is alive.

*10.1.2 Optimal insurance coverage for nonpecuniary losses.* The amount of insurance coverage against nonpecuniary losses that an individual will wish to purchase will clearly depend on whether such losses will affect the utility he would derive from receiving additional money.

If nonpecuniary losses will not result in a person valuing money more, then under the expected utility maximizing insurance policy he will not arrange for coverage against the nonpecuniary losses; coverage will be restricted to pecuniary losses, if any. Thus a person might not insure against the loss of his family portrait and might limit coverage against loss of a toe to medical expenses. The following numerical example demonstrates the point.

EXAMPLE 10.1 Suppose that a person's utility is the sum of the utility he derives from money, as specified in the graph in Figure 8.1, and the utility he derives from nonpecuniary elements.[1] Suppose also that his initial wealth is 30,000 and that he faces a 10 percent risk of an accident that would involve a pecuniary loss of 10,000 and a nonpecuniary loss of 25 units of utility.

Calculations will show that this person will be best off purchasing coverage against only the pecuniary loss of 10,000—even though he can purchase higher coverage sufficient to compensate him in terms of utility for the nonpecuniary component of loss. If the person arranges for coverage of only 10,000, his premium will be 1,000, and his wealth will be 29,000 regardless of the occurrence of an accident. Hence his utility will be 994.49 if an accident does not occur and 994.49 − 25 if an accident does occur. His expected utility will therefore be 90% × 994.49 + 10% × 969.49 = 991.99.

On the other hand, suppose the person purchases 15,270 coverage. This is the amount necessary to compensate him for the 10,000 pecuniary loss plus the nonpecuniary loss of 25 units of utility. In particular, if he buys the 15,270 coverage, his premium will be 1,527, his wealth if there is no acci-

---

1. Since utility is this sum, a nonpecuniary loss will not affect the marginal utility of money. The increment to utility due to having extra money will be determined by the rise of the curve in Figure 8.1 and will thus be independent of the occurrence of a nonpecuniary loss.

dent will therefore be 28,473, and his utility from wealth will thus be 991.36. His wealth if there is an accident will be 33,743 (that is, 28,473 − 10,000 + 15,270), and his utility from wealth will be 1,016.36. Hence, in the event of an accident the utility he will gain from having an extra 5,270 in insurance coverage will be 1,016.36 − 991.36 = 25, which will compensate him exactly for his nonpecuniary loss of 25. But if the person purchases 15,270 coverage, his expected utility will be 991.36; this is less than 991.99, so he will indeed be worse off than if he purchases just the 10,000 coverage against pecuniary losses.

Notice that since it will be optimal for a person to insure only against pecuniary losses when a nonpecuniary loss will not alter the utility of money to him, optimal insurance coverage will not make the person "whole" if he suffers an accident, that is, just as well off as if he does not suffer an accident.

If the value a person will place on money will increase as a result of a nonpecuniary loss, optimal insurance coverage will exceed pecuniary loss. Thus a person may purchase greater coverage against the possibility of being crippled than an amount equal only to the costs of medical treatment and forgone earnings. It is unlikely, however, that he will purchase coverage sufficient to make him whole (if this is even possible).

If the value a person will place on money will decrease as a result of a nonpecuniary loss, expected utility maximizing insurance coverage will be less than pecuniary losses. A person who has little desire to leave a bequest will rationally purchase little or no life insurance, despite the possibility that the earnings forgone by his death will be large.

In the discussion so far it has implicitly been assumed that the risk of losses is fixed. If the risk is influenced by the behavior of insureds, then, as was discussed in Chapter 8, ownership of insurance may dull insureds' incentives to take care. But this problem is reduced in importance where the risk includes nonpecuniary elements. Because it is generally not in an individual's interest (and in any event may be impossible) to purchase enough coverage against a nonpecuniary loss to make himself whole, he will be made worse off by the occurrence of a nonpecuniary loss even after having received his insurance coverage. Hence he will have a reason to lower risk. A person who has purchased optimal coverage against loss of a toe or of his life will still have a very strong motive to avoid injury.

*10.1.3   Actual insurance coverage against nonpecuniary losses.* Insurance coverage against loss of property does not ordinarily seem to reflect its sentimental value, only its market value or replacement cost. Coverage against personal injury usually approximates only direct medical expenses and forgone earnings. Insurance against death is ordinarily bounded by lost earnings;

if a person (such as an unmarried or elderly individual) has no dependents, he normally possesses little or no coverage; parents do not often carry significant coverage on the life of their children. Evidently, insurance coverage is intended mainly to remedy pecuniary needs created by losses, not to compensate for the disutility due to losses.

*10.1.4   Note on the literature.* Arrow (1974), Zeckhauser (1973), and Cook and Graham (1977) first developed the theory of insurance for nonpecuniary losses.

## 10.2   Awards Optimal for Compensation versus Awards Optimal for Deterrence

Here I wish to make the general point that the size of the award that is best for a victim to receive, in view of the theory of insurance, may be less than the amount that is best for an injurer to pay, in order that injurers' incentives to reduce risk be appropriate. I will begin with, and stress, the case where the possibility of nonpecuniary losses causes such a divergence between awards optimal for compensation and awards optimal for deterrence, but I shall also mention other reasons for a divergence.

*10.2.1   Nonpecuniary losses and the socially ideal solution to the accident problem.* As emphasized in §10.1, the amount of insurance an individual would wish to purchase against nonpecuniary losses—and therefore the amount of money he will receive under the socially ideal solution to the accident problem—will be based on the value he will place on money if he suffers nonpecuniary losses; the amount he will receive will not generally make him whole.[2] By contrast, the socially optimal level of care taken by injurers (and their level of activity) will reflect the nonpecuniary elements of accident losses as well as the pecuniary (recall the discussion in §6.4). Thus, for instance, it will be best that injurers take substantial care to reduce the risk of accidentally killing children even though their deaths may not impose an economic burden on their parents[3] and consequently, in the ideal, may not call for the parents to receive significant amounts in compensation.

*10.2.2   Socially ideal solution cannot be achieved under the liability system when there is a divergence between awards optimal for compensation and awards optimal for deterrence.* Since under the ideal solution to the accident problem, injurers will take a degree of care reflecting both nonpecu-

2. The noneconomist will have to take it largely on faith that under the socially ideal solution to the accident problem (see §§10A.2.1 and 9A.1), a victim will receive in compensation the same amount that he would have decided to purchase from an insurer.

3. Indeed the death of their children may financially benefit parents, since they will save on childrearing and educational expenses.

niary and pecuniary components of victims' losses, the magnitude of payments injurers make under liability rules must reflect both these components of losses for injurers to be led to take optimal care. But if injurers' payments are this high, then the amount victims receive will exceed optimal compensation, which will usually approximate only pecuniary losses. On the other hand, if injurers' payments equal only optimal compensation, injurers' incentives to take care will be inadequate. Thus the socially ideal outcome cannot be achieved under the liability system.[4] The magnitude of liability will inevitably result in a compromise between awarding victims correctly and creating appropriate incentives for injurers to reduce risk.

*10.2.3  Divergence for reasons other than nonpecuniary losses.* It was noted before (see §6.8.5) that where liable injurers will not always be identified as responsible for harm done, the amount they pay if they are identified and sued must be raised for their incentives to reduce risk to be maintained at the correct level. Where, for instance, the likelihood is 50 percent that a liable injurer will be successfully sued, the amount he pays if so sued must be on the order of twice the victim's losses. Optimal payments by injurers may therefore exceed optimal compensatory awards by a substantial factor.

It was also explained before (see §§6.8.1 and 6.8.3) that where a party obtains socially illicit benefits from an act or incurs socially illicit utility costs when exercising care it will be desirable for him to pay an amount greater than the harm sustained by the victim. Thus, again, optimal payments by injurers may exceed optimal compensatory awards.

Another reason why optimal payments by injurers may be greater than optimal awards concerns taxes that would have been paid on income forgone by accident victims. It was argued previously (see §6.6.9) that for injurers' incentives to reduce risk to be proper, they must pay an amount based on before-tax income forgone by victims. Yet the amount of money that victims will in fact lose, and thus the amount that will constitute the optimal compensatory award, is after-tax forgone income.

An additional reason why optimal payments by injurers may exceed optimal compensatory awards is that victims may receive insurance benefits or gifts (see §§6.6.7 and 10.3). In this case, optimal compensatory awards will

---

4. This is true as long as victims actually receive awards under the liability system. Under a perfectly functioning negligence rule, however, the socially ideal outcome can be achieved, since under that rule injurers will always take due care and never be found negligent; hence victims will bear their losses and can and will optimally insure for amounts less than what injurers would have to pay were they liable. But if, as is realistic, findings of negligence occur, then the optimal outcome cannot be achieved because victims will in fact receive awards.

equal only the shortfall between victims' receipts and their losses, but injurers must pay victims' entire losses to be adequately deterred.

*10.2.4   The case for fines as a supplement to liability.* An improvement over the situation under the liability system may be achieved under a regime in which liability is supplemented by fines collected by the state. With the use of fines, the total amount that injurers are made to pay can be raised to the point that their incentives to reduce risk are appropriate, while at the same time liability can be held to the lower level equal to optimal compensatory awards. Thus under the contemplated regime injurers would pay fines reflecting nonpecuniary losses, the probability of escaping suit, taxes on victims' forgone earnings, and so forth, whereas victims would usually receive in liability awards payments reflecting only their otherwise uncompensated pecuniary losses.

One way to understand why individuals may find a regime with supplemental fines advantageous is to recognize that their taxes can be lowered since the state may use fine revenues to replace tax revenues. Specifically, individuals will find a regime with fines advantageous if they would prefer a savings in taxes to collecting higher liability judgments, or, equivalently, if they would not be willing to pay the insurance premium necessary to purchase coverage in the amount of the fine. Parents should thus find advantageous a regime with fines for the wrongful death of their children and with correspondingly lower taxes if the parents do not choose to insure their children's lives.

*10.2.5   Remarks on supplemental fines.* (1) It would ordinarily be best for the fines used as a supplement to liability to be insurable. The general argument made in Chapter 9 that it is desirable to allow risk-averse injurers to purchase coverage against liability can be employed to demonstrate this result.[5]

(2) The use of supplemental fines would tend to resolve certain tensions arising from application of standard principles of tort law to calculate liability. It is frequently observed, for instance, that if damages for wrongful death are based on the present value of forgone earnings, payments for the death of children or the elderly may be negligible, an uncomfortable result. But although liability awards for the death of children or the elderly may properly be low, optimal supplemental fines could well be significant.

The receipt by tort victims of punitive damages or of large awards for pain and suffering presents different issues. One sometimes encounters uneasiness

5. This is discussed in §10A.2.3. It should be mentioned, however, that if fines are not employed, then in principle it could be advantageous to set liability at a level approximating optimal compensation and to limit purchase of liability insurance, so as to induce injurers to take more care.

over the "windfall" character of punitive damage awards and over victims' incentives to exaggerate pain and suffering. Such incentives would be diminished, and there would be no windfalls—no "inappropriate allocation of risk," in the terminology of economics—if pain and suffering and punitive damage awards were incorporated into fines paid to the state.

(3) To calculate optimal fines for nonpecuniary losses, one can use as a guide extrapolations from the amount optimally insured individuals would be willing to pay for a small reduction in the probability of suffering nonpecuniary losses. Suppose, for instance, that an individual who has the insurance he desires against the medical expenses and forgone income that would result from losing his left arm would be willing to pay $1,000 for a 1 percent reduction in the likelihood of that event. Then the optimal fine for causing the loss of his arm would be approximately 100 × $1,000 or $100,000.[6] Information about persons' willingness to pay for reductions in risk could in theory be obtained by survey or, in some cases, perhaps, by attributing wage differences to differences in risks of accidents.[7]

*10.2.6   Remark on liability of firms to customers.* To the extent that firms will be liable for—or would have to pay a supplemental fine for—nonpecuniary losses of customers caused by their products or services, and to the extent that customers do not wish to insure against these losses, customers will be undesirably discouraged from making purchases, other things equal. This is because prices will reflect firms' expected liability. Consider, for instance, the price of sending a child to camp, supposing that camps will be liable for large losses if children die in accidents. The price of camp will then have to include a component to cover its large liability insurance premiums. Thus in paying for camp, parents will in effect be purchasing substantial life insurance on children, a form or amount of insurance that they may well not wish to carry. It is possible that such forced purchase of life insurance will discourage parents from sending children to camp when it would be best that the children go to camp.

In theory, a two-part scheme can be employed to avoid this problem of socially undesirably discouraging purchases, while at the same time providing firms with proper incentives to reduce risks and supplying customers with optimal insurance coverage. First, let fines supplement liability, as in §10.2.4, so that firms' incentives will be appropriate even though optimal compensa-

---

6. More precisely, and as shown in §10A.2.3, this is the optimal fine assuming that injurers are risk neutral or, if risk averse, that their liability-fine insurers can observe their levels of care; otherwise, the optimal fine would be different.

7. On the latter, see Viscusi 1983. See also Danzon 1984, which discusses how such data can be used to calculate supplemental fines.

tion for customers may be low. Second, let the state pay a *rebate* to customers when they make purchases, where the rebate per unit equals the expected fine revenue collected per unit. This rebate will lower the effective price to customers, and they thus will not be undesirably discouraged from making purchases (see §10A.2.5).

*10.2.7 Note on the literature.* Spence (1977) originally demonstrated the desirability of employing fines in addition to liability in a study of firms' liability for accidents causing nonpecuniary losses.

## 10.3 Victims' Collateral Insurance Benefits and Injurers' Liability

As noted earlier, the payments victims receive under insurance policies against accident losses are often called collateral benefits because they are different from, and potentially augment, what victims receive from liable injurers. When a victim is insured against accident losses—here assumed to be only pecuniary—and an injurer is liable, two legal rules may apply: a rule under which a victim is allowed to collect both his collateral insurance benefits and a judgment from a liable injurer—so that the victim may receive in total an amount exceeding his losses; and a rule under which a victim can collect in a judgment only the difference, if any, between his losses and his insurance benefits. The first rule will be called the "no-subtraction rule" (since collateral benefits are not subtracted from judgments) and the second, the "subtraction rule." These rules were discussed briefly before (in §6.6.7). They will be reconsidered here, along with related issues, in light of the theory of insurance.

*10.3.1 Subrogation.* Before I examine the two rules, the insurance arrangement known as "subrogation" must be defined. Under this arrangement, an insurer will pay a victim for his losses, but the insurer rather than the victim will then have the right to sue and collect from a liable injurer. The insurer will, however, have to return to the victim any excess in the judgment over the victim's coverage. In practice, there may be such an excess if the victim is not fully covered against losses under his policy (or if the judgment includes damages for pain and suffering or punitive damages). But in the analysis here, the victim's coverage will be full.

*10.3.2 Socially optimal outcome regarding victims' receipts and injurers' liability.* Subrogation and the rules concerning subtraction of collateral benefits will be evaluated below with reference to the socially optimal outcome regarding victims' receipts and injurers' liability. The socially optimal outcome will have two characteristics. First, a liable injurer will pay an amount equal to a victim's losses, for that is necessary to maintain injurers' incentives to reduce risk. Second, a risk-averse victim will receive from his insurer and a liable injurer together an amount equal to—but not more than—his losses, for that is an aspect of optimal risk bearing (see §§8.2.2 and 9.1).

Notice that the outcome if victims' insurance policies involve subrogation arrangements will have both these characteristics: a liable injurer will pay an amount equal to the victim's losses to the victim's insurer; the victim will not collect more than his losses since the insurer will keep the judgment (or an amount equal to the victim's insurance benefits). Therefore the outcome will be optimal.

*10.3.3    The outcome under the no-subtraction rule.* Under this rule victims will prefer to purchase insurance policies involving subrogation arrangements and the outcome will thus be socially optimal. Victims will in principle prefer to purchase policies involving subrogation arrangements for two reasons. The first is in essence the point from §8.2.2 that risk-averse parties will generally prefer purchasing policies giving them full coverage to purchasing, at a greater cost, policies giving them more than full coverage. Here the interpretation of the point is that victims will generally prefer purchasing policies where insurers have subrogation rights to purchasing for higher premiums policies where insurers do not have these rights and where, under the no-subtraction rule, victims would collect both from their insurers and from liable injurers. (Of course, premiums will be higher for policies without subrogation rights because insurers will not be able to collect judgments from injurers.)

EXAMPLE 10.2    A victim with initial wealth of 30,000 and utility of wealth as in Figure 8.1 faces a 10 percent risk of suffering losses of 10,000 for which no injurer will be liable and a 10 percent risk of suffering the same losses for which an injurer will be liable. Suppose that the victim purchases an insurance policy giving him full coverage and allowing the insurer subrogation rights. The victim will then receive exactly 10,000 if he suffers losses, whether or not an injurer is liable, and the insurer will bear an expense of 10,000 only when there is no liable injurer. Hence, the premium for the policy will be only $10\% \times 10,000 = 1,000$; since the victim's wealth will be 29,000 for sure, his utility will be 994.49.

If the victim purchases a policy under which the the insurer does not have subrogation rights, the victim will receive 10,000 if he suffers losses and there is no liable injurer; the victim will receive 10,000 plus a judgment of 10,000 if an injurer is liable; and, because the insurer will bear an expense of 10,000 whenever the victim suffers a loss, the premium for the policy will be 2,000. Thus, the victim's wealth will be 28,000 with probability 90 percent and 38,000 with probability 10 percent. His expected utility will therefore be $90\% \times 988.40 + 10\% \times 1,028.85 = 992.44$, which means that he will be worse off under the policy without subrogation and will not purchase it.

The second reason why insurance policies will in theory be expected to involve subrogation rights is that since victims would otherwise collect both insurance benefits and judgments and thereby profit from suffering losses, undesirable incentives for victims actually to cause losses or to fabricate them would be set up. That in turn would lead to high premiums and consequently to policies that would be unattractive for purchase. (See §8.2.3.)

*10.3.4 The outcome under the subtraction rule.* Under the subtraction rule the outcome will be identical to that under the no-subtraction rule. Victims will again purchase policies involving subrogation arrangements, and the outcome will therefore be optimal. The reason that victims will prefer to purchase policies giving insurers subrogation rights is plain. If a policy does not include subrogation rights, then a victim will be compensated by his insurer yet will not, because of the subtraction rule, also be able to collect from a liable injurer. If a policy does include subrogation rights, a victim will again be compensated only by his insurer, but his insurer will be able to collect from a liable injurer;[8] this will reduce the insurer's costs and result in lower premiums. Hence victims will prefer policies with subrogation arrangements.

EXAMPLE 10.3   If the victim of the last example purchases a policy with full coverage under which the insurer has subrogation rights, then, as noted, the victim's premium will be 1,000 and his wealth will be 29,000 for sure. If, however, the victim purchases a policy without subrogation rights, his premium will be 2,000 and his wealth will be only 28,000 for sure. He will therefore decide to purchase the policy with subrogation rights.

*10.3.5 Departures from theoretically predicted outcomes.* It has just been argued that in theory victims will decide to purchase policies giving insurers subrogation rights and thus that under the no-subtraction rule victims will not collect both insurance benefits and judgments from injurers. Yet this may not be true in fact, for there may be legal constraints against subrogation; or victims may be covered by social insurance plans allowing them both plan benefits and recovery from liable injurers; or victims may possess coverage from multiple insurers and, owing to difficulties of coordination among the insurers, may simply find that they are able to collect both insurance benefits

---

8. It is assumed, as is the case in fact, that the subtraction rule will not apply to the insurer and prevent him from collecting from the injurer.

and judgments. Another possibility is that victims may fail to understand the nature of their insurance coverage or consider the chance of recovering from liable injurers so low that they give little or no thought to whether their policies allow them to collect simultaneously from injurers.

*10.3.6   Comparison of the no-subtraction and subtraction rules.* To the extent that, for the reasons just mentioned, victims may collect more than their losses under the no-subtraction rule and that injurers' liability may be reduced under the subtraction rule, it will matter which rule is chosen. The no-subtraction rule will be the better rule if it is more important to maintain injurers' incentives to reduce risk than to avoid overcompensation of victims.[9]

*10.3.7   Remarks on constraints on subrogation.* Constraints on subrogation seem to be against the interests of insureds. As has been emphasized, insureds should prefer to give insurers subrogation rights and pay lower premiums. A failure to take into account this beneficial effect of subrogation on premiums (or disbelief in the effect) is apparently what lies behind the commonly heard argument that subrogation is detrimental to insureds.

A different argument against subrogation that is occasionally advanced is that its use increases the volume of suits. This is surely true, and prohibiting subrogation may be an effective device for preventing suits. But if it is felt desirable to prevent suits in an area of accident, that will be due to factors particular to the area of accident. It would be peculiar to view the matter as one concerning some general defect of subrogation.[10]

*10.3.8   Repayment arrangements.* A type of insurance arrangement resembling subrogation but under which victims retain their right to sue injurers should be mentioned. According to this arrangement, a victim must repay his insurer for insurance coverage received if he sues and collects from an injurer.[11] Thus if the victim sues and collects, the eventual result will be the

---

9. But recall from §10.2.4 that the following rule will in theory be superior to either the no-subtraction or the subtraction rule: Do not subtract victims' insurance benefits from what liable injurers pay, but do not allow victims to obtain insurance benefits plus judgments. Instead, have the state keep all of the judgment beyond that necessary to compensate the victim optimally (or, perhaps, beyond that necessary to compensate him plus to give him an incentive to bring suit).

10. See Kimball and Davis 1962 for a discussion of constraints against subrogation.

11. Under a virtually equivalent arrangement, a victim who sues an injurer will not receive insurance benefits until a judgment or settlement has been made. At that time the victim will receive the difference between his insurance coverage and what, if anything, he obtained from the injurer. This arrangement suffers from the same drawback as the repayment arrangement (that it provides little incentive for victims to bring suit) and also the disadvantage that the victim must wait until his case is concluded to be compensated.

same as under subrogation; the victim will obtain only his losses, and the insurer will break even.

Under a repayment arrangement, however, a victim will often have little motive to bring suit, since he will have to return to his insurer most or all of his award.[12] Therefore suits will usually not be brought, meaning that insurers' costs and premiums charged will be higher than those under policies with subrogation arrangements. As a consequence, it is not surprising that policies with subrogation arrangements greatly predominate over policies with repayment arrangements.[13]

*10.3.9 Actual relationship between victims' insurance benefits and injurers' liability, and the nature of victims' insurance policies.* The United States is one of few countries in which the general rule is that a victim's insurance benefits are not subtracted from a liable injurer's judgment.[14] Nevertheless, the situation turns out to be similar in the United States and in other countries in certain important areas of insurance. This is because there are exceptions made to the general rules that result in a like pattern of use, or of denial of use, of subrogation. For example, in regard to property insurance, subrogation rights are nearly universal.[15] In the areas of life and personal injury insurance, subrogation is prohibited, or at least not encouraged, and victims' insurance benefits are not subtracted from judgments.[16] In respect to workers' compensation, the usual outcome, though reached in various ways, is that victims collect only once and that their insurers may seek reimbursement from liable parties.[17]

In other areas of insurance, however, the situation differs substantially

---

12. He will not have to return all of the award if the award includes damages for pain and suffering or a punitive component, or if insurance coverage was partial.

13. See §10.3.9. Indeed, where policies with repayment arrangements are employed, it is often apparently only because there are legal restrictions against the use of subrogation; see Fleming 1971, secs. 24, 58–61.

14. See Fleming 1971, sec. 9.

15. In Anglo-American law, this is a nonstatutory privilege and need not be mentioned in the property insurance contract; in France, Germany, and the Soviet Union, it is a privilege guaranteed by legislation. See Fleming 1971, sec. 22.

16. In Anglo-American, French, and (apparently) Soviet law, subrogation in life insurance and personal injury insurance is usually prohibited; in German law, subrogation is allowed only if expressly mentioned in the insurance contract. Moreover, in England, France, the Soviet Union, Germany, and, according to the general rule, the United States, victims' insurance benefits are not subtracted in calculating injurers' liability. See Fleming 1971, secs. 12, 23. Hence, in all these countries, the situation is again approximately the same.

17. The situation is complex, in part because liable parties may be either employers or third parties. See Fleming 1971, secs. 31–35.

among countries. This is the case, for example, with regard to private medical insurance and social security.[18]

## 10.4  Injurers' Inability to Pay and Liability Insurance

In this part I first discuss the effect of injurers' inability to pay fully for harm done on their decisions to purchase liability insurance and on their incentives to reduce risk. I then consider regulation of liability insurance.

*10.4.1  Diminished motive to purchase liability insurance.* If injurers' assets are lower than the harm they may cause, a portion of the liability insurance premium they would pay for full coverage would in fact pay for losses that they would not bear if they did not insure. It follows that risk-averse injurers may rationally decide against purchasing full coverage, and may even decide to buy none, as is illustrated by the following example.

EXAMPLE 10.4   Suppose the risk-averse injurer described in Chapter 8 has assets of 30,000 and faces a 20 percent risk of being found liable for 100,000. If he does not purchase coverage, he will enjoy his 30,000 with probability 80 percent and lose his 30,000 (for that is all he can possibly pay) with probability 20 percent. Hence his expected utility will be $80\% \times 1,000 + 20\% \times 0 = 800$. If, on the other hand, the injurer purchases full coverage of 100,000, his premium will be $20\% \times 100,000 = 20,000$ (of which 14,000 will pay for the 70,000 of losses that he would not bear if he does not insure). His wealth will therefore be 10,000 with certainty, giving him utility of 665.24. In other words, he will be worse off with full coverage than with none at all. Indeed, it can be shown he will be worse off with any positive amount of coverage than with none at all.[19]

18. In the United States medical insurers usually do not have rights of subrogation (but there is an increasing tendency to permit subrogation or repayment of judgments to insurers if provided for in insurance contracts). By contrast, in France and Germany medical insurers often do have rights of subrogation. See Fleming 1971, secs. 25–27. In regard to social security, the situation is again mixed. In the United States the social security fund does not ordinarily have rights of subrogation and victims may collect both insurance and judgments. In England the fund does not have rights of subrogation, but victims must give credit to liable parties for a major portion of the social security benefits the victims receive. In most other countries the social security fund does have a right of subrogation. See Fleming 1971, secs. 28–30.

19. He will not wish to purchase coverage in an amount less than 70,000, for then his assets will still be exhausted if he is found liable—the coverage will do him no good. For instance, if he purchases 50,000 coverage and is found liable, the coverage plus his assets will not be enough to pay the 100,000, so the coverage will do him no good. Hence only an amount of coverage of at least 70,000 will do him good, and calculations demonstrate he will be worse off with such coverage than with no coverage.

Although in this example the injurer prefers not buying any coverage, injurers will often decide to purchase positive, though less than complete, coverage and, in particular, to purchase policies with ceilings on coverage. For instance, if in Example 10.4 there is a possibility of liability of 10,000 as well as of 100,000, the injurer may decide to purchase a policy with a ceiling of 10,000.

The likelihood that parties will not purchase much coverage will depend on the magnitude of their assets in relation to the harm they might do and on their degree of risk aversion. For example, an individual with assets of $20,000 might wish to buy automobile accident-liability coverage on the order of $200,000 if he were fairly risk averse, but an almost-risk-neutral electric utility company with assets of $500 million might well decide not to purchase $1 billion liability coverage against the possibility of a catastrophic accident at its nuclear power plant.

*10.4.2 Functioning of the liability and insurance system.* It was emphasized before, in the discussion of the risk-neutral setting without liability insurance (see §7.2), that injurers' inability to pay for harm done dilutes their incentives to take care and leads to too high a level of risky activity. This point remains largely unchanged where risk-averse injurers choose not to purchase liability insurance.

If, however, injurers do decide to purchase insurance coverage, the point must be qualified. Injurers' purchase of coverage will result in their bearing more of the expected losses with which their activity is associated, and thus will tend to reduce their levels of activity desirably. If, for instance, injurers buy full coverage and are strictly liable, they will make correct decisions about engaging in risky activity. If the electric utility were to purchase full coverage, it would not build or operate a nuclear facility unless the benefits outweighed the full expected losses.

On the other hand, whether injurers' incentives to take care will be altered for the better by their purchase of liability coverage depends on the ability of insurers to determine levels of care and to link the premium (or other policy terms) to it. When an insurer can do this (when it can tell if the utility has installed needed safety devices in the nuclear plant) and injurers purchase complete coverage, then they will be induced to take adequate care. But when insurers cannot determine levels of care (how the utility selects and trains its staff, whether pipes in the plant have been properly welded), then injurers' care will be further diluted by their having purchased coverage. In other words, the initial problem of injurers' exercising too little care because of limited assets will be exacerbated.

Finally, injurers' incentives aside, it should be observed that victims will rationally purchase insurance coverage against the risk that liable injurers will be unable to pay for the losses they cause.[20]

*10.4.3    Regulation of insurance.* It has been seen that injurers' inability to pay fully for losses creates two types of problems: their incentives to take care and to engage in risky activity may be incorrect; and because they may choose not to purchase adequate liability coverage, they may bear risk.

Consider first the effect on these problems of a requirement to purchase complete liability insurance coverage. Such a requirement will eliminate the problem of injurers' bearing risk, and it will also alleviate the problem of their excessive engagement in risky activity. If liability insurers are unable to determine injurers' levels of care and injurers possess full coverage, however, they will exercise no care at all. Hence it is not clear that a requirement to purchase coverage will be socially desirable.

On the other hand, prohibiting the purchase of liability insurance will increase the problem of the bearing of risk by injurers, for their entire assets will be at stake. Yet just because this is so, barring coverage may reduce injurers' levels of activity from an initially excessive level. If such a reduction is moderate, it could be beneficial; but it could also be disadvantageously large. Likewise, prohibiting liability insurance may turn out to have either a desirable or an undesirable effect on injurers' exercise of care. Prohibiting liability insurance will tend to increase levels of care in the case where the purchase of coverage would dull incentives, that is, where insurers would not be able to observe levels of care. But prohibiting insurance might reduce levels of care where insurers would be able to observe care.

Whether requiring purchase of liability insurance, prohibiting it, or not regulating it, then, will be best will depend on the situation. Where insurers can observe levels of care, requiring purchase of coverage will be the superior policy; where insurers cannot observe care, requiring coverage may be less preferable than not regulating coverage or, conceivably, than prohibiting coverage.

*10.4.4    Remark on compensation for victims.* The problems considered in this part did not include what is often viewed as the main problem with injurers' inability to pay—namely, that victims might not be compensated by liable injurers for their losses. This did not arise as a problem in the analysis because, as noted in §10.4.2, risk-averse victims were assumed to decide to purchase insurance coverage against not being compensated by injurers. In reality, of course, victims may not purchase such coverage for a variety of

---

20. There is, however, a possible exception. A victim will have a diminished motive to purchase insurance against medical expenses if these expenses may substantially exceed his assets and will be publicly borne if his assets are exhausted.

reasons. Hence, in fact, requiring purchase of liability insurance would help to solve victims' problem; but so would requiring that victims purchase their own coverage or establishing a social insurance fund for victims.

*10.4.5 Note on the literature.* Calabresi (1970, p. 58) observed that the motive to purchase insurance will be diminished where parties' assets are less than the losses for which they may be held responsible; Keeton and Kwerel (1984) and Huberman, Mayers, and Smith (1983) first investigated the point formally; and in Shavell (1986) I studied the implications of the point for the functioning of the liability system and the regulation of liability insurance.


## 10.5  Structure of a System of Pure Accident Insurance

I briefly consider here the nature of a system in which risk-averse victims insure against accident losses but do not enjoy the right to sue injurers. (As will be explained in subsequent chapters, such a pure accident insurance system may be justified even though the liability system, having been eliminated, will no longer provide injurers incentives to avoid doing harm.)[21] The main question to be investigated concerns the connection between the cause of a victim's loss and his coverage under an optimal insurance policy. I will address this question first assuming that victims do not influence the risk of suffering losses, and then that they do.

*10.5.1 Optimal coverage where victims cannot influence risks.* If victims cannot influence risks, coverage under an expected utility maximizing insurance policy will depend only on the losses the victim suffers, not on how they come about. A victim will thus receive the same amount of coverage if his house burns because it was struck by lightning as he will if it burns because a fire was negligently allowed to spread by his neighbor. That only the magnitude of a loss, and not its cause, should influence insurance coverage may seem obvious to the reader. (The reader probably says to himself that the only thing that matters to a victim is the size of his loss, so the victim should have no reason to arrange for different coverage on account of the loss arising from one or another cause.) But the point does seem worth justifying. The reader will recall that it was demonstrated in §8.2.2 that where victims cannot influence risk, expected utility maximizing insurance coverage will equal the loss suffered. It follows that if a loss of some amount, say, 1,000, can come about either through cause A or cause B, optimal coverage will be the same,

---

21. On the one hand, elimination of the tort system will conserve on administrative costs; see Chapter 11. On the other hand, society can and does employ means other than tort liability to control risk, such as safety regulation and the injunction; see Chapter 12.

namely, 1,000, whether the cause of the loss is A or B. In other words, and as claimed, optimal insurance coverage will not depend on the cause of losses.[22]

There are also administrative cost advantages to policies under which coverage does not depend on the cause of losses. Under such policies insurers need not expend resources in investigating the cause of losses; hence the cost of supplying insurance will be lower. Furthermore, victims themselves need not make efforts to establish the cause of losses.

*10.5.2   Optimal coverage where victims can influence risks.* If victims can influence risks, it may be the case that coverage under an expected utility maximizing insurance policy will depend on the cause of losses. Suppose, for example, that a victim's house can burn not only because of lightning or his neighbor's negligence, but also because of the spontaneous combustion of oily rags left in his basement—a risk that the victim can lower by removing the rags. Then it may be optimal for a victim to receive only partial coverage if a fire is caused by oily rags, in order to give victims an incentive to remove them. (See §8.2.3.) By contrast, it will not be optimal for a victim to receive partial coverage if a fire is caused by lightning, because making victims bear some of their losses in that event will not create any beneficial incentives.

The general point illustrated by this example is that it may be optimal for coverage to depend on the cause of losses if victims have greater influence on accident risks that come about through certain causes than through other causes.

*10.5.3   Remarks on causation and optimal coverage.* (1) In view of the foregoing, it is clear that the causes of losses that may in principle be relevant to optimal insurance coverage range widely. For example, it may be relevant whether the cause of a person's lung cancer is his smoking habit or a carcinogen the exposure to which was beyond his control, since making coverage lower in the former instance may induce individuals not to smoke. It may even be relevant whether the cause of an accident was an injurer's fault (as determined by an accident insurer), for where injurers fail to take care it may be that victims are unable to avoid harm.[23]

The question is sometimes asked whether it is desirable for distinctions in (especially social) insurance coverage to be made between losses caused by disease versus those caused by accidents.[24] The answer is that it may be

22. This can be demonstrated to be true under quite general circumstances, for example, when there are nonpecuniary losses.

23. Compare automobile accidents in which a victim's vehicle is struck from behind by another driver from accidents in which that is not the case. Allowing full coverage when vehicles are stuck from behind, since it will not compromise incentives, may characterize expected utility maximizing insurance policies.

24. See, for example, Atiyah 1980, p. 377.

optimal for a distinction to be made if the distinction pertains to a victim's ability to reduce risk. To illustrate, suppose that a person can lose an arm either because of a disease that he cannot prevent or in a type of accident that he can do something to avoid. Then optimal coverage may well be less for losing an arm due to an accident than due to the disease.[25]

(2) The degree to which it will be desirable for insurance coverage to depend on the cause of losses will depend not only on the incentives thereby created, but also on the feasibility and cost of determining causation. Under optimal insurance policies (private or social), coverage will have to depend on broad categories of fairly easily ascertained causes.


# Mathematical Appendix


### 10A.1   Nonpecuniary Losses and Insurance

The theory of insurance as discussed in §8A.2 will be reconsidered here assuming that accidents involve a nonpecuniary component. Specifically, let

$W_n(w)$ = utility of wealth $w$ if there is no accident; $W_n'(w) > 0$; $W_n''(w) < 0$; and

$W_a(w)$ = utility of wealth $w$ if there is an accident; $W_a'(w) > 0$; $W_a''(w) < 0$; $W_a(w) \leqq W_n(w)$.

If, for example, an accident will involve a nonpecuniary loss of $z$ units of utility and will alter the marginal utility of wealth by the factor $s$,[26] then $W_a(w) = sW_n(w) - z$. Individuals will be assumed to suffer pecuniary losses of $l$ in the event of accidents along with nonpecuniary losses. Thus an individual's utility if an accident occurs will be $W_a(w - l)$, exclusive of any insurance benefits.

*10A.1.1   Situation in which insureds cannot influence risk.* If the probabil-

---

25. If, however, accidents are of a type that victims cannot avoid, optimal coverage of losses due to an accident would be the same as coverage of losses due to the disease. It is also possible that optimal coverage for disease could be less than that for an accident. This might be the case if victims can prevent losing their arms from a disease by seeking treatment early on but cannot prevent accidents.

26. See §10.1 for a discussion of why the marginal utility of wealth may be affected by a nonpecuniary loss.

ity $p$ of an accident is fixed and an individual purchases coverage $q$, his expected utility will be

$$(10.1) \quad (1 - p)W_n(w - \pi) + pW_a(w - \pi + q - l),$$

where the premium $\pi = pq$, since it must equal the expected cost of coverage. Substituting for $\pi$ and differentiating Exp. (10.1) with respect to $q$, we obtain the first-order condition

$$(10.2) \quad W_n'(w - pq) = W_a'(w - pq + q - l),$$

which states that the marginal utility of wealth must be the same regardless of whether there is an accident. In the case in which $W_a(w) = W_n(w) - z$, that is, when the marginal utility of wealth is not affected by an accident, Eq. (10.2) implies that $q = l$; it is best to insure against the pecuniary losses. Hence the utility of the optimally insured party will decline by $z$ in the event of an accident. In the case in which $W_a'(w) < W_n'(w)$, Eq. (10.2) implies that $w - pq > w - pq + q - l$ (since $W_n''$ and $W_a''$ are negative), which implies that $q < l$. Here the optimally insured party will again be made worse off by the occurrence of an accident. In the case in which $W_a'(w) > W_n'(w)$, Eq. (10.2) implies that $q > l$. It would be expected in this case too that the optimally insured party will be worse off in the event of an accident, but there is a possibility that he will not.[27]

PROPOSITION 10.1    Under the expected utility maximizing insurance policy, (a) coverage will equal pecuniary losses where the marginal utility of wealth is unaffected by an accident; coverage will be less than pecuniary losses where the marginal utility of wealth is reduced by an accident; and coverage will exceed pecuniary losses where the marginal utility of wealth is increased by an accident. (b) Given optimal insurance coverage, utility will fall as a result of an accident (the individual will not be "made whole") in the first two cases and will be expected to fall in the third case.

*10A.1.2    Situation in which insureds can influence risk.* Here an insured's expected utility will be

$$(10.3) \quad [1 - p(x)]W_n(w - \pi - x) + p(x)W_a(w - \pi - x + q - l),$$

27. For simplicity, I will not consider cases in which over some $w$, $W_a'$ exceeds $W_n'$ and over other $w$ it is less then $W_n'$.

where $x$ is his level of care. The premium must obey $\pi = p(x)q$. Hence the highest expected utility an insured can possibly derive is obtained by maximizing Exp. (10.3) over $q$ and $x$ subject to $\pi = p(x)q$. This is the expected utility an insured will derive if insurers can observe $x$ and charge $p(x)q$ as the premium. In particular, substituting $p(x)q$ for $\pi$ in Exp. (10.3) and setting the derivatives with respect to $q$ and $x$ equal to 0, we find that the $q$ an insured will choose will satisfy Eq. (10.2) with $p = p(x)$ and that the $x$ he will choose will satisfy

$$(10.4) \qquad [1 + p'(x)q]W_n' = -p'(x)(W_n - W_a),$$

where, by Eq. (10.2), $W_n' = W_a'$.[28] The left-hand side of Eq. (10.4) is the marginal cost of taking care, net of the premium reduction in which it results. The right-hand side is the saving in expected utility due to the reduction in the probability of an accident. Assuming that $W_n > W_a$, it follows from Eq. (10.4) that the chosen $x$ will exceed the $x$ that would minimize the premium plus the cost of care: from Eq. (10.4) we have $1 + p'(x)q = -p'(x)(W_n - W_a)/W_n' > 0$; and since $p''(x) > 0$, we know that $x$ exceeds the $x$ for which $1 + p'(x)q = 0$.

PROPOSITION 10.2   Suppose that insurers can observe the care taken by insureds. Then under the expected utility maximizing insurance policy, (a) the level of coverage will be as described in Proposition 10.1. Also, (b) the level of care will be determined by Eq. (10.4) and will exceed that which would minimize the premium plus the cost of care.

If insurers cannot observe levels of care, the analysis is analogous to that in §8A.2.3. The main point worth adding is that in the present case the optimal policy may involve close to the ideal level of coverage, as determined by Eq. (10.2). For even if coverage against pecuniary losses is nearly full, the disutility caused by nonpecuniary losses may provide insureds a substantial incentive to take care.

*10A.1.3   Note on the literature.* Arrow (1974), Zeckhauser (1973), and Cook and Graham (1977) developed the theory of optimal insurance for fixed risks of nonpecuniary losses.

## 10A.2   Awards Optimal for Compensation versus Awards Optimal for Deterrence

As pointed out in the text, there may be a divergence between the amount that risk-averse victims should receive when accidents occur if risk-bearing is

---

28. Here and occasionally elsewhere I omit arguments of functions for convenience.

to be optimal and the amount that injurers should pay if they are to be induced to reduce risk optimally. The reason for a divergence that I will focus on below is the possibility that victims will suffer nonpecuniary losses, but several other reasons will also be briefly noted.

10A.2.1    *Nonpecuniary losses and the socially ideal solution to the accident problem.* When accidents suffered by victims involve nonpecuniary losses as well as pecuniary losses, as described in §10A.1, a socially ideal Pareto optimal solution to the accident problem is, following §9A.1, determined by

(10.5)    $\max_{x, v_n, v_a, u_n, u_a} EV = [1 - p(x)]V_n(v_n) + p(x)V_a(v_a)$

subject to

(10.6)    $EU = [1 - p(x)]U(u_n) + p(x)U(u_a) = k$

and

(10.7)    $[(1 - p(x))v_n + p(x)v_a] + [(1 - p(x))u_n + p(x)u_a]$
$$+ [p(x)l + x] = u + v.$$

As before, it is easy to show that $u_n$ must equal $u_a$ if injurers are risk averse (and we may assume $u_n = u_a$ if injurers are risk neutral). Denote $u_n = u_a$ by $\mu$, where $U(\mu) = k$ so that Eq. (10.6) is satisfied. Hence the optimal choice of $x$, $v_n$, and $v_a$ is given by maximizing $EV$ over those variables subject to

(10.8)    $[(1 - p(x))v_n + p(x)v_a] + [\mu + p(x)l + x] = u + v.$

The solution is obtained by setting equal to zero the partial derivatives of $EV - \lambda[(1 - p(x))v_n + p(x)v_a + \mu + p(x)l + x - (u + v)]$ with respect to $x$, $v_n$ and $v_a$. From this we easily obtain that

(10.9)    $V_n'(v_n) = V_a'(v_a),$

and that $x$ must satisfy

(10.10)    $[1 + p'(x)(v_a + l - v_n)]V_n' = -p'(x)[V_n - V_a].$

Thus, the situation here appears similar to that described in §10A.1.2 on optimal insurance. Indeed, it is easy to show that the problem of maximizing $EV$ subject to Eq. (10.8) is equivalent to the insurance problem. Define $\pi$ and $q$ implicitly in terms of $v_n$ and $v_a$ by $v_n = w - \pi - x$ and $v_a = w - \pi - x + q - l$, where $w$ is the constant $u + v - \mu$. Then $EV$ may be written $[1 - p(x)]V_n(w - \pi - x) + p(x)V_a(w - \pi - x + q - l)$ and the constraint stated in Eq. (10.8) may be verified to be equivalent to $\pi = p(x)q$. Hence choosing $x$, $v_n$, and $v_a$ to maximize $EV$ subject to Eq. (10.8) is equivalent to choosing $x$, $q$, and $\pi$ to maximize the expected utility of insureds subject to $\pi = p(x)q$. We therefore know from §10A.1.2 that, at the optimum, $q$ satisfies

$$(10.9') \qquad V_n'(w - \pi - x) = V_a'(w - \pi - x + q - l)$$

and that $x$ satisfies

$$(10.10') \qquad [1 + p'(x)q]V_n' = -p'(x)[V_n - V_a].$$

In summary, we have the following proposition.

PROPOSITION 10.3    Assume that victims suffer nonpecuniary losses in accidents. Then a socially ideal Pareto optimal solution to the accident problem will be achieved if and only if (a) risk-averse injurers are left with the same level of wealth regardless of whether accidents occur; (b) risk-averse victims are left with levels of wealth such that the marginal utility of wealth is the same regardless of whether accidents occur; (c) injurers' levels of care are determined by Eq. (10.10). Also, (d) victims' levels of wealth and injurers' levels of care may be interpreted as those that would be chosen by victims were they optimally insuring against accident losses and were they to choose and bear the costs of injurers' levels of care, as described in Proposition 10.2.

To illustrate, suppose that losses are solely nonpecuniary and do not affect the marginal utility of wealth. That is, $l = 0$ and $V_a(w) = V_n(w) - z$. Then Eq. (10.9') implies that $q = 0$—victims do not obtain any compensation—and Eq. (10.10') implies that $V_n' = -p'(x)z$—the level of care $x$ is such that the marginal cost of care equals the marginal reduction in the expected nonpecuniary disutility due to an accident.

*10A.2.2 Nonpecuniary losses and inability to achieve the socially ideal solution under the liability system.* That the socially ideal solution cannot be achieved under strict liability is apparent. Consider the situation in which injurers are risk neutral. For them to be induced to choose the ideal $x$, $x$ must satisfy Eq. (10.10'), which is equivalent to

$$(10.11) \quad 1 + p'(x)\left[q + \frac{(V_n - V_a)}{V'_n}\right] = 0.$$

But this implies that liability must equal

$$(10.12) \quad q + \frac{(V_n - V_a)}{V'_n},$$

for only then will injurers choose $x$ to minimize $x + p(x)[q + (V_n - V_a)/V'_n]$. Yet, as discussed in §§10A.1.1 and 10A.1.2, it would be expected that $V_n > V_a$. If so, Exp. (10.12) will exceed $q$, which is the amount that is optimal for victims to receive. It is clear that this same problem will exist more generally, when injurers are risk averse and when they might purchase liability insurance.[29]

PROPOSITION 10.4a    A socially ideal Pareto optimal solution to the accident problem cannot be achieved under strict liability, because the amount injurers must pay to be induced to take the optimal level of care exceeds the amount that is optimal for victims to receive.

In view of this problem, it is apparent also that the best (that is, Pareto optimal given the constraint of strict liability) magnitude of liability will generally be between $q$ and $q + (V_n - V_a)/V'_n$.

It should be noted too that intervention in liability insurance markets may be desirable. To see why, consider the situation in which liability insurers of risk-averse injurers can observe $x$. Then, as we know from the Appendix to Chapter 8, injurers will purchase full coverage and will choose $x$ to minimize $x$ plus their expected liability. But if their liability is below $q + (V_n - V_a)/V_n'$— in order that victims not be overcompensated by too much—injurers' incentives to take care will be less than ideal. Preventing injurers from purchasing full liability coverage may therefore be advantageous, since it could induce the injurers to take greater care.[30]

29. Here and in the rest of §10A.2, some of the details establishing claims will not be supplied. For the most part, the claims will follow in a straightforward way from what has already been shown and from the analysis in the Appendix to Chapter 9.

30. Note that in the present situation, unlike in §9A.4.1, there is an externality that the liability insurance market does not take into account: victims here are made worse off by the occurrence of accidents even though they will receive payments from injurers, since the payments will not make them whole. In view of this, it is not surprising that intervention in the liability insurance market could be desirable.

Consider now the negligence rule. If liability for negligence equals $q + (V_n - V_a)/V_n'$, then the usual proof shows that injurers will be induced to take due care if it is set equal to the $x$ satisfying Eq. (10.11) and if there is no uncertainty surrounding the negligence determination. Hence victims will never collect from injurers; instead, victims will optimally insure and receive $q$ from their insurers if an accident occurs. If, however, there is uncertainty over the determination of negligence (see §4A.3), the points made above about strict liability become relevant because injurers will sometimes be found negligent, in which case victims will receive more than $q$.

PROPOSITION 10.4b   A socially ideal Pareto optimal solution to the accident problem can be achieved under the negligence rule if the rule is perfectly functioning, but not if there is uncertainty over the determination of negligence leading to actual findings of negligence.

*10A.2.3   Nonpecuniary losses and the desirability of fines as a supplement to liability.* A socially ideal outcome can be achieved under strict liability when injurers are risk neutral or when they are risk averse and liability-fine insurers can observe $x$. In particular, suppose that liability equals $q$ and the fine equals $(V_n - V_a)/V_n'$. Then injurers will choose $x$ to satisfy Eq. (10.11): they will clearly do this if they are risk neutral; and they will do this if they are risk averse, since they will purchase full coverage and the terms of their insurance policies will lead them to do so. Moreover, since coverage in the latter case will be full, injurers will be protected against risk. In either case victims will receive $q$. For similar reasons, use of liability supplemented by a fine will be Pareto superior to use of liability alone even where, because liability insurers cannot observe $x$, an ideal outcome cannot be achieved.

PROPOSITION 10.5a   Under strict liability the optimal use of fines paid to the state as a supplement to liability will be Pareto superior to the optimal use of liability alone.

Regarding the issue of intervention in liability-fine insurance markets, it is clear that intervention will be undesirable if injurers are risk averse and insurers can observe $x$, for then, as explained, an ideal outcome will be achievable, whereas without coverage injurers would bear risk and their level of care might not be ideal. It can be shown also that even if liability-fine insurers cannot observe $x$, intervention in insurance markets will not be desirable, but the fine will generally be different from $(V_n - V_a)/V_n'$.[31]

Under a perfectly functioning negligence rule, an ideal outcome can be achieved with fines—as it can be without fines. But if there is uncertainty over the determination of negligence, use of fines will offer a positive advantage because it will make it possible for injurers to pay more than the amount that it is optimal for victims to receive.

PROPOSITION 10.5b    Under the negligence rule, if there is uncertainty over the determination of negligence leading to the occurrence of negligence, the optimal use of fines as a supplement to liability will be Pareto superior to the optimal use of liability alone.

It was stated in the text (see §10.2.5) that to determine $(V_n - V_a)/V_n'$— the optimal fine when injurers are risk neutral or liability insurers can observe $x$— one can ask optimally insured victims how much they would be willing to pay for a reduction in the probability $p$ of an accident. To verify this, consider

$$(1 - p)V_n(v) + pV_a(v + q - l)$$
$$= (1 - p + s)V_n(v - h) + (p - s)V_a(v - h + q - l).$$

Here $s$ is the reduction in the probability of an accident and $h$ is the willingness to pay for the reduction. The equation determines $h$ as a function of $s$. Differentiating it with respect to $s$, we obtain

$$(10.13) \quad 0 = V_n(v - h) - V_a(v - h + q - l)$$
$$- h'(s)[(1 - p - s)V_n'(v - h) + (p - s)V_a'(v - h + q - l)].$$

Since insurance coverage is assumed to be optimal at $p$, $V_n'$ is equal to $V_a'$ at $s = 0$ and, by definition, $h(0) = 0$. Hence Eq. (10.13) implies that $h'(0) = [V_n(v) - V_a(v + q - l)]/V_n'(v)$, as claimed.

*10A.2.4  Reasons other than nonpecuniary losses for a divergence between awards optimal for compensation and awards optimal for deterrence.* The possibility that a party will escape suit means, as noted before (see

---

31. The reason that intervention will not be desirable, despite the externality in the insurance market (see n. 30), is that the fine can generally be made sufficiently high to offset any dilution in incentives created by the purchase of insurance. This, in turn, is true because the insurance policy purchased will generally not involve complete coverage and thus will leave injurers exposed to some risk. For reasons analogous to those mentioned in the discussion of Proposition 9.5, however, an equivalent outcome to that under an insurance market can be achieved if the government bans fine-liability insurance.

§6A.6.3), that for incentives to be appropriate liability must be higher than victims' losses (which are here assumed to be only pecuniary). For instance, if $g < 1$ is the probability of suit, then liability must equal $l/(1 - g) > l$ for risk-neutral injurers to be induced to act appropriately under liability rules. But if this is so, then risk-averse victims will receive more than the optimal amount $l$ from liable injurers. Hence use of fines will be desirable: liability equal to $l$ supplemented by a fine of $lg/(1 - g)$ will create proper incentives for injurers and result in optimal compensation of victims.

The possibility that injurers will obtain socially illicit benefits or incur socially illicit costs of care implies (see §§6A.6.1 and 6A.6.2) that injurers must pay an amount exceeding victims' harm in order that injurers' incentives be appropriate. This again means that victims will receive more than optimal compensation and that liability equal to victims' losses plus a fine equal to the illicit benefits will be desirable.

The possibility that a victim will lose wage earnings as a result of an accident presents similar issues. As noted before (see §6A.4.5), for injurers' incentives to be optimal they must pay the before-tax wage losses. But for risk-averse victims to be appropriately compensated, they must receive only after-tax wage losses (since that is their financial loss). One way to achieve this result is for injurers' liability to equal before-tax wage losses and for victims to receive this amount but be taxed on it. Another is for injurers' liability to equal after-tax wage losses, for injurers to pay in addition a fine equal to what would have been the taxes on the wages, and for victims not to pay any tax on what they receive from injurers.

Finally, victims' receipt of collateral insurance benefits[32] provides another reason why it will be advantageous to employ fines as a supplement to liability. Liability should equal the difference between a victim's losses and his insurance benefits; the fine should equal the victim's insurance benefits. Thus the sum of the liability payment and the victim's insurance benefits will equal his losses, and the sum of the liability payment and the fine will also equal the victim's losses.

In the last two cases and in the first case, it will be desirable to allow injurers to insure against fines as well as against liability; the reasons are now familiar. In the case where illicit benefits or costs of care are the reason for the fine, however, it may be desirable to prohibit or limit purchase of insurance against liability and fines, but this issue will not be pursued here.

*10A.2.5 Remark on liability of firms to customers.* Suppose that firms will have to pay for nonpecuniary losses caused by their products and suffered by

---

32. See also §10A.3 on this subject.

customers. If customers do not wish to insure against these losses, customers may be undesirably discouraged from purchasing products.

To illustrate, suppose for simplicity that the risk $p$ of an accident due to a product is fixed and is known to risk-averse customers; that an accident will cause a pecuniary loss of $l$ and disutility of $z$, that is, $V_a(w) = V_n(w - l) - z$; that the production cost of the product is $c$; and that the utility of the product to the customers is $b$. Then, since optimal insurance coverage will be $l$, it will be optimal for customers to purchase the product whenever[33]

$$b + V_n(v - c - pl) - pz > V_n(v).$$

But if firms are strictly liable for an amount more than $l$, say, for $l + z'$, then since the price under competition will be $c + p(l + z')$ customers will purchase the product when

$$b + (1 - p)V_n(v - c - p(l + z'))$$
$$+ pV_n(v - c - p(l + z') + z') - pz > V_n(v).$$

This inequality holds less often than the former one, because, by Jensen's inequality,[34] $V_n(v - c - pl) > (1 - p)V_n(v - c - p(l + z')) + pV_n(v - c - p(l + z') + z')$. Thus customers may not purchase the product when it will be optimal that they do. Note, however, that customers will purchase the product whenever that is optimal if the firm is not liable and the customer insures himself for $l$, paying a premium $pl$, or if the firm is strictly liable only for $l$.

From this case it should be clear that, generally, imposition of liability in an amount exceeding optimal insurance coverage will tend undesirably to discourage the decision to purchase products. Moreover, although use of fines as a supplement to liability will solve the overinsurance problem discussed in previous sections, fines will hardly solve the present problem because use of fines will not lower product price. It is obvious, however, that fines combined with rebates (equal to the expected fine) on the purchase price will allow an optimal outcome to be achieved.

*10A.2.6   Note on the literature.* Spence (1977) first showed that fines paid to the state may be a desirable addition to liability. He studied a model of strict liability of firms for losses to customers involving a nonpecuniary component. The reason for his conclusion is essentially that given here in §10A.2.3.

33. Here the optimal outcome is that which maximizes a customer's expected utility subject to the constraints that he pays the production cost of a product if he purchases it plus a premium for insurance coverage equal to its expected cost.

34. See De Groot 1970, p. 97.

## 10A.3  Victims' Collateral Insurance Benefits and Injurers' Liability

The effect of the legal rule governing whether a risk-averse victim's insurance benefits will or will not be subtracted from what a liable injurer must pay him if he brings suit will be studied here. It will be sufficient to examine the case in which there is a fixed probability $p$ that victims will suffer a (pecuniary) loss of $l$ for which an injurer will be liable and a fixed probability $t$ of suffering a loss of $l$ for which no injurer will be liable.[35]

Before proceeding, let us define an insurance policy under which the victim's insurer has a right of *subrogation*. Under such a policy, the victim will receive his coverage $q$ from his insurer when he suffers a loss $l$. The insurer will then have the right to sue and collect $l$ from a liable injurer;[36] the insurer will retain $q$ of $l$ and will return $l - q$ to the victim. Thus when an injurer is liable, the victim will receive a total of $l$ from his insurer and the insurer will break even.[37]

We have

PROPOSITION 10.6   The rule under which victims' insurance benefits are subtracted from injurers' liability will result in the *same* outcome as the rule under which victims' insurance benefits are not subtracted. Namely, under both rules (a) victims will decide to purchase insurance policies providing full coverage and giving insurers subrogation rights. Therefore, (b) victims will always receive exactly their losses and injurers will pay (to victims' insurers) an amount equal to victims' losses.

As discussed in the text, the reason that (a) is true is, in essence, that subrogation saves insurers money, and thus results in lower premiums, while guaranteeing that victims will receive full coverage for their losses.

To prove (a), from which (b) follows by definition of subrogation, consider first the subtraction rule. Under a policy with subrogation, a victim will

35. If the size of the losses in the two circumstances is different, the result we will show will still hold.

36. This is true whatever would be the rule regarding subtraction of insurance benefits if the victim rather than the insurer were to sue.

37. Notice that this means that a policy involving subrogation is equivalent to a policy not involving subrogation and not giving coverage when an injurer is liable; under the latter policy, a victim would obtain $l$ directly from suing the injurer. I nevertheless choose to discuss policies involving subrogation, because, for reasons going outside the model, we would expect policies involving subrogation to be preferred by victims over alternative, seemingly equivalent policies. Moreover, as discussed in §10.3.8, policies with subrogation are what are usually observed in fact.

receive $q$ from his insurer whenever he suffers a loss and an injurer is not liable; a victim will receive $l$ from his insurer when an injurer is liable; and a victim's premium will be only $tq$ (as the insurer will keep $q$ from a liable injurer). Thus a victim's utility will be $(1 - t)V(v - tq) + tV(v - tq - l + q)$, from which it follows that he will choose $q = l$, so that his expected utility will be $V(v - tl)$. Under a policy without subrogation and $q > 0$, a victim will receive $q$ from his insurer whether or not an injurer is liable; a victim's premium will therefore be $(t + p)q$, and he will receive $l - q$ from a liable injurer. Thus a victim's expected utility will be $(1 - t)V(v - (t + p)q) + tV(v - (t + p)q - l + q)$, which is less than $(1 - t)V(v - tq) + tV(v - tq - l + q)$, which, by Jensen's inequality, is less than or equal to $V(v - tl)$. Hence a victim will prefer to purchase the policy with subrogation and $q = l$ over a policy without subrogation.[38]

Now consider the no-subtraction rule. Under a policy with subrogation, a victim's situation will be the same as above, so he will choose $q = l$ and his utility will be $V(v - tl)$. Under a policy without subrogation and $q > 0$, a victim will receive $q$ from his insurer when he suffers a loss and an additional $l$ from a liable injurer. A victim's premium will be $(t + p)q$ and his expected utility will be $(1 - t - p)V(v - (t + p)q) + tV(v - (t + p)q - l + q) + pV(v - t + p)q + q)$, which, by Jensen's inequality, is less than $V(v - tl)$. Hence a victim will again prefer to purchase the policy with subrogation and full coverage, establishing Proposition 10.6.

Note that the proposition implies that both the subtraction and no-subtraction rules not only result in the same outcome, but also in a Pareto optimal outcome: under both rules liable injurers pay an amount equal to the losses that they cause and victims receive an amount equal to (but not greater than) their losses.[39] If, however, victims' insurers do not have subrogation rights for some reason (see §10.3.5), the two rules will not result in the same outcome. Under the subtraction rule there will be a dilution in injurers' incentives to take care (and excessive incentives to engage in risky activities), whereas under the no-subtraction rule there will be overcompensation of victims, that is, inefficient bearing of risk. Hence the no-subtraction rule will be preferable if the problem of inadequate incentives is more important than that of overcompensation.

38. But the reader is reminded that a policy with subrogation and full coverage is equivalent to a policy without subrogation and giving no coverage when there is a liable injurer; see n. 37.

39. As shown in the Appendix to Chapter 9, this will result in a Pareto optimal outcome, assuming that injurers can purchase liability insurance.

### 10A.4 Injurers' Inability to Pay and Liability Insurance

In this part I will first discuss a party's decision concerning the purchase of insurance where the amount of his "loss" $l$ will exceed his assets $w$. Then I will examine the functioning of the liability system and the regulation of liability insurance.

*10A.4.1 The decision to purchase insurance.* Suppose initially that the risk $p$ of loss is fixed. If a risk-averse party purchases coverage $q$ and a loss does not occur, his wealth will be $w - \pi$; if a loss does occur, his wealth will be max $(0, w - \pi + q - l)$. In addition, since $\pi = pq$, the highest $q$ the party can purchase is $w/p$. Hence the party will choose $q$ in $[0, w/p]$ to maximize his expected utility

$$(1 - p)W(w - pq) + pW(\max(0, w - pq + q - l)).$$

The solution to his problem is described by the following proposition.

PROPOSITION 10.7    Suppose that the probability $p$ of a risk-averse party's suffering a loss $l$ is fixed. Then there is a critical level of assets below which he will not purchase any coverage and above which he will purchase full coverage. The critical level of assets exceeds $pl$ and is less than $l$.

To show this, observe that if the party chooses $q > 0$, it must be that $w - pq + q - l > 0$—his net wealth if he suffers a loss will be positive—for otherwise the coverage will not do him any good. Hence if $q > 0$, the party's expected utility must be $(1 - p)W(w - pq) + pW(w - pq + q - l)$. Therefore, if $q > 0$, $q$ will be determined by the usual first-order condition (since $q = w/p$ is obviously not optimal). Hence $q$ must equal $l$, and the party's utility will be $W(w - pl)$.

On the other hand, if $q = 0$, the party's utility will be $(1 - p)W(w) + pW(0) = (1 - p)W(w)$. (Assume for simplicity the normalization $W(0) = 0$.) Hence the party will not buy coverage when

(10.14)    $(1 - p)W(w) > W(w - pl)$;

otherwise, he will buy full coverage. At $w = pl$ Ineq. (10.14) will hold; and by Jensen's inequality, at $w = l$ Ineq. (10.14) will be reversed. Also, clearly, $(1 - p)W'(w) < W'(w - pl)$. It therefore follows that the claimed critical $w$ exists, completing the proof of Proposition 10.7.

It should be observed that in a model with multiple levels of losses, the proposition would be altered: the party might well decide to purchase positive but less than full coverage.

If we assume that the risk of loss is $p(x)$ where $x$ is the level of care, the following result holds.

PROPOSITION 10.8    Suppose the probability of a risk-averse party's suffering a loss is influenced by his level of care. Then (a) if insurers can observe levels of care, parties will purchase no coverage if their assets are less than a critical level; otherwise they will purchase full coverage and take optimal care. Also, (b) if insurers cannot observe levels of care, parties will purchase no coverage if their assets are less than a (different) critical level; otherwise they will purchase positive but less than complete coverage and their levels of care will generally not be optimal.

This result can be proved along the lines of the previous argument and by analogy to §8A.2.3.[40]

*10A.4.2   The functioning of the liability and insurance systems.* As was discussed previously (see §7A.2), risk-neutral injurers' inability to pay for harm done will dilute their incentives to take care and will induce them to engage too much in risky activities. If we assume here that injurers are risk averse and may purchase liability insurance, we may expand on this point in light of Proposition 10.8. There are three possibilities to consider. First, injurers may not purchase liability insurance coverage. In this situation the previous argument about dulling of incentives is likely to be unaffected.[41] Second, injurers may purchase coverage when insurers are able to observe their levels of care. In this case coverage will be full and injurers will be led by the policy terms to take optimal care. Third, injurers may purchase coverage when insurers are not able to observe their levels of care. In this instance coverage will not be full and injurers will take less care than they would have in the absence of coverage. Thus the problem of inadequate incentives to take care is likely to be worsened. Whenever injurers purchase coverage, however, there will be an improvement in their choice over levels of activity, since they will then bear a greater portion of the expected losses associated with their activity.

40. See Shavell 1986, in which I give the proof and also the details of the arguments sketched in the next two sections.

41. But injurers' risk aversion means that there may be less dulling of incentives than there is in the risk-neutral case.

The possibility that injurers may not purchase insurance means that the allocation of risk will be imperfect relative to the ideal.

Victims will insure against the possibility that liable injurers will not be able to pay them for their losses.

*10A.4.3   Regulation of liability insurance markets.* From the foregoing discussion we may arrive at the following conclusion.

PROPOSITION 10.9   Compelling purchase of full liability insurance coverage may or may not be desirable.

Specifically, if liability insurers can observe levels of care, compulsory coverage will be desirable, since under their policies injurers will not bear risk and will be led to take optimal care (as well as to choose optimal levels of their activity); but if insurance is not compulsory, injurers might not purchase coverage. On the other hand, if liability insurers cannot observe injurers' levels of care, compulsory coverage will lead injurers not to take care, whereas otherwise they will take a positive level of care (either they will not purchase coverage, in which case their entire assets will be at stake, or else they will purchase partial coverage, so that they will have some assets at stake).

The following result also holds.

PROPOSITION 10.10   Prohibiting purchase of liability insurance may or may not be desirable.

If insurers can observe levels of care, barring coverage will not be desirable, since if injurers purchase coverage they will be led to take optimal care and will not be exposed to risk. But if insurers cannot observe levels of care, then forbidding purchase may be desirable, for then injurers' assets will be at stake and they might take substantial care, whereas if they will otherwise purchase coverage, their exposure to risk and their level of care might be lower.[42]

*10A.4.4   Note on the literature.* Keeton and Kwerel (1984) and Huberman, Mayers, and Smith (1983) analyze the purchase of insurance against losses exceeding assets, and in Shavell (1986) I extend their analysis, taking into account the effect of care on the probability of losses and the functioning of the liability system.

---

42. This argument does not take into account the fact that prohibiting liability insurance will result in an undesirable allocation of risk. But the added incentive to take care could be the more important effect.

## 10A.5   Optimal Insurance and Causation

This part will consider the connection between optimal insurance coverage and the cause of losses, and will verify the points made in the discussion in §10.5 about a pure accident insurance system.

*10A.5.1   Optimal coverage where insureds cannot affect risks.* Suppose here that there are two possible causes, $A$ and $B$, of losses of $l$; that the probabilities of $l$ occurring due to $A$ and to $B$ are $p_A$ and $p_B$, respectively; and that the levels of insurance coverage for losses due to $A$ and to $B$ are $q_A$ and $q_B$. Then $\pi = p_A q_A + p_B q_B$ and the optimal $q_A$ and $q_B$ will maximize expected utility

$$
\begin{aligned}
EW = {} & (1 - p_A - p_B)W(w - p_A q_A - p_B q_B) \\
& + p_A W(w - p_A q_A - p_B q_B + q_A - l) \\
& + p_B W(w - p_A q_A - p_B q_B + q_B - l).
\end{aligned}
$$

Setting the partial derivatives of $EW$ with respect to $q_A$ and to $q_B$ equal to zero, one obtains the first-order conditions,

$$
\begin{aligned}
& - p_A(1 - p_A - p_B)W'(w - p_A q_A - p_B q_B) \\
& + p_A(1 - p_A)W'(w - p_A q_A - p_B q_B + q_A - l) \\
& - p_A p_B W'(w - p_A q_A - p_B q_B + q_B - l) = 0
\end{aligned}
$$

and

$$
\begin{aligned}
& p_B(1 - p_A - p_B)W'(w - p_A q_A - p_B q_B) \\
& - p_B p_A W'(w - p_A q_A - p_B q_B + q_A - l) \\
& + (1 - p_B)p_B W'(w - p_A q_A - p_B q_B + q_B - l) = 0.
\end{aligned}
$$

These conditions are satisfied when $q_A = q_B = l$. Thus, we have the following.

PROPOSITION 10.11a   If insureds cannot affect the risk of losses, optimal insurance coverage will not depend on the cause of losses.

It is straightforward to show that this result generalizes; it holds if there are more than two causes, multiple levels of loss, nonpecuniary losses, and so forth.

*10A.5.2   Optimal coverage where insureds can affect risks.* Consider the case described above, except that $p_B$ is a function $p_B(y)$ of the care $y$ taken by insureds. Suppose also that $y$ cannot be observed by insurers. Then the optimal insurance policy is found by maximizing

$$EW = (1 - p_A - p_B)W(w - \pi - y)$$
$$+ p_A W(w - \pi - y + q_A - l)$$
$$+ p_B(y)W(w - \pi - y + q_B - l)$$

subject to $\pi = p_A q_A + p_B(y)q_B$ and to $EW_y = 0$. The determination of $q_B$ is similar to that of $q$ as described in Proposition 8.4 and may thus be less than $l$ and different from $q_A$. The explanation, recall from §10.5.2, is that to supply insureds incentives to take care to reduce $p_B$, it may be beneficial to make them bear a portion of $l$ if $B$ is the cause of losses; but making them bear a portion of $l$ if $A$ is the cause of losses will not tend to induce them to take a more desirable level of care.[43] This explanation makes it clear that, more generally, if $p_A$ is also a function of $y$, or of a different variable, $q_A$ and $q_B$ will generally be different; the implicit incentive problems will generally be solved by different exposures to risk under the two causes. Summarizing, we have the following proposition.

PROPOSITION 10.11b   If insureds can affect the risk of losses, optimal insurance coverage will generally depend on the cause of losses.

---

43. Actually, altering $q_A$ will have a subtle influence on $y$ because $q_A$ affects wealth through $\pi$. Thus, the optimal $q_A$ will generally be different from $l$, but one would expect it to be closer to $l$ than is the optimal $q_B$.

# 11 | Liability and Administrative Costs

Administrative costs are the various expenses borne by parties in resolving the disputes, or the potential disputes, that arise when harm occurs. Administrative costs thus include the time and effort spent by injurers, victims, and their legal counsel and insurers in coming to settlements and in litigation, as well as the publicly incurred operating expenses of the courts. In this chapter I will first discuss several factors determining the magnitude of administrative costs. Then I will contrast victims' incentives to make use of the liability system with the social interest in their doing so, given that that now involves administrative costs.

## 11.1 Factors Determining Administrative Costs

*11.1.1 Total administrative costs.* When a victim is harmed by an injurer, the victim will decide for or against making a claim. If a victim does make a claim, he will either settle with the injurer or he will go to trial. Total administrative costs will equal the number of claims settled multiplied by the administrative cost per settled claim, plus the number of litigated claims multiplied by the cost per litigated claim. Equivalently, total administrative costs will equal the total number of claims multiplied by the average cost per claim, the average being calculated over both settled and litigated claims.

*11.1.2 Remarks on administrative costs.* (1) A detailed description of the determination of administrative costs would, of course, distinguish among claims settled at different stages (after this or that amount of negotiation, after the filing of certain motions, after discovery) and would allow for the possibility that a victim will abandon his claim. Moreover, it would take into account expenses incurred by insurers.

(2) Because the costs of coming to a settlement may be important and because the frequency of settlement is high (apparently over 90 percent),[1] the proportion of total administrative costs associated with settlement may be significant. It would be a mistake to attribute administrative costs mainly to the costs of trials.

(3) Existing data suggest that in the United States the administrative costs of the liability system are substantial. Many studies find that administrative costs, averaged over settled and litigated claims, approach or exceed the amounts received by victims.[2] It is not clear, however, to what extent these administrative costs should be viewed as intrinsic to the liability system or as a feature of the particular system that has developed.[3]

(4) By contrast, the administrative costs associated with provision of accident insurance are often on the order of from 1 percent to 15 percent of what victims receive.[4] The administrative costs of accident insurance are relatively low because accident insurers have much less need than courts to inquire into the cause of losses or about injurers' behavior, because accident insurers have adopted comparatively simple procedures for verifying the magnitude of

1. For example, Conard et al. 1964, p. 155, found that over 99 percent of automobile accident victims did not press their claims to trial; Ross 1980, p. 1979, reports that slightly more than 95 percent of claims in an insurance company's files were settled or dropped; and Danzon 1985, p. 42, states that over 90 percent of a sample of cases of medical treatment–related injuries were resolved short of trial over medical malpractice. Atiyah 1980, pp. 296–297, cites various studies suggesting that perhaps 99 percent of claims are settled without trial in the United Kingdom.

2. In the area of medical malpractice, Munch 1977, p. 87, discusses estimates of victims' share of the liability insurance premium dollar that range from 18 cents to 40 or 50 cents, and Danzon 1985, p. 187, discusses an estimate of about 60 cents; in the area of product liability, Munch 1977, p. 27, reports best estimates of 38 and 42 cents for victims' share. In the area of litigation over asbestos, Kakalik et al. 1983 estimate victims' share of dollars paid by injurers to be about 37 cents. Keeton et al. 1983, p. 891, review studies implying that victims of bodily injury in automobile accidents obtain 44 cents per premium dollar. Trebilcock 1986, p. 15, cites a study claiming that victims' share of dollars paid by injurers in all torts in the United States is only 25 cents. Atiyah 1980, p. 511, reports evidence that in the United Kingdom victims receive 55 percent of payments by injurers.

3. I can readily imagine much less complex systems (for example, employing tabular schedules to decide damages). Also, I do not have information about the costs of the liability systems in France, Germany, and the Soviet Union; perhaps they are much lower than in the United States.

4. For example, the cost of administering the federal Old Age and Survivors Insurance Program is about 1 percent of total expenditures and that of the Disability Insurance Program is about 3.5 percent; see *Social Security Bulletin*, January 1986, p. 17. The cost of administering workers' compensation, however, is said to be about 38 percent; see Munch 1977, p. 70. Yet Atiyah 1980, p. 522, states that the cost of administering the analogous "industrial injuries" system in the United Kingdom is approximately 12 percent.

insureds' claims, and because accident insurers are not in an adversarial relationship with insureds.[5]

*11.1.3    Administrative costs under strict liability versus under the negligence rule.* Administrative costs under strict liability may usefully be compared with those under the negligence rule by considering, on one hand, the total number of claims and, on the other, the average administrative costs per claim.

The total number of claims is likely to be larger under strict liability than under the negligence rule. Under strict liability a victim will have an incentive to make a claim whenever his losses exceed the costs of making a claim (assuming that he can credibly establish that the injurer was the cause of harm and that he was not contributorily negligent). Under the negligence rule a victim will not have an incentive to make a claim so often because he will also be concerned about establishing the injurer's negligence. If a victim and an injurer both believe that a court will find the injurer free of fault, the victim will be unlikely to make a claim under the negligence rule.

Although the volume of claims should be greater under strict liability, the average administrative cost per claim should be higher under the negligence rule. Under the negligence rule it is more probable that a claim will be litigated than under strict liability, for under the negligence rule there is an additional element of dispute—that of the injurer's negligence—and hence more room for disagreement leading to trial. Since the probability of trial should be greater under the negligence rule and since trials will usually be more costly than settlements, we have one reason for saying that average administrative costs per claim are likely to be larger under the negligence rule. A second reason is that the costs of trial itself are likely to be higher under the negligence rule than under strict liability because the issue of negligence must be adjudicated under the former rule.

In sum, then, the comparison of the size of administrative costs under the two forms of liability is ambiguous as a theoretical matter. One would predict that a greater number of claims will be made under strict liability, but one would expect the average cost of resolving claims to be higher under the negligence rule because of both a higher propensity to go to trial and a higher cost per trial.

*11.1.4    The role of insurers and the comparison of administrative costs*

5. While there may, of course, be disagreement between insureds and insurers, it is unlikely to be as serious as that between victims and injurers. In part this is because insurers have an interest in honoring their policies: private insurers will want to maintain their reputations; social insurers are presumably strongly motivated to serve insureds in any event.

*under the two rules.* Consideration of the role of insurers appears to diminish the importance of the factors determining differences between administrative costs under strict liability and the negligence rule. First, the significance of the point that under strict liability there will be more claims made against injurers than under the negligence rule is lessened when one takes into account claims made by victims against their accident insurers. That is, when victims do not make claims against injurers under the negligence rule, victims will generally seek to collect from their accident insurers, with accompanying administrative costs. Second, the significance of the point that under strict liability there will be no need for a legal determination of injurers' negligence is lessened when one takes into account the behavior of liability insurers. Liability insurers may well wish to ascertain injurers' negligence, or something like it, so as to provide injurers with incentives to reduce risks (see §8.2.3).

## 11.2  The Private Motive to Make Claims versus Their Social Desirability

*11.2.1  In general.* Suppose that administrative costs are included with other costs in the measure of social welfare. Then it will be socially desirable for victims to make claims against injurers if and only if the associated social benefits will outweigh the administrative costs. Yet whether victims will in fact decide to bring claims will depend on the quite different "private" comparison that they make between their own benefits and costs. Specifically, a victim's private benefit from making a claim will be the expected settlement or judgment he will receive. As shall be seen, this private benefit may be higher or lower than the social benefit. A victim's own cost of making a claim, however, will be lower than the administrative costs caused by his claim, assuming that the victim will not bear the injurer's costs of defense or the costs to courts themselves. Although this factor suggests that victims may have too great a motive to make claims, it can well turn out that victims have too small a motive to make claims, since their private benefits from making claims may be less than the social benefits.

*11.2.2  A simple model.* To gain an understanding of the circumstances under which the number of claims will be socially excessive or will be undesirably low, and to see what policies might solve these problems, I will examine a simple version of the unilateral model of accidents. In this model I will assume that parties are risk neutral, that victims will bear a cost if they make a claim, that injurers will bear a defense cost if claims are made against them, and that if injurers are found liable they will pay victims an amount equal to their losses.[6] The social goal will be to minimize total costs, defined as expected accident losses, plus costs of care, plus costs due to the making of claims. The situations under strict liability and under the negligence rule will be examined separately, since there are differences between them relevant to the issues of present interest.

*11.2.3   The private motive to make claims versus their social desirability when liability is strict.* A victim's private motive to make a claim under strict liability is clear in the above model: a victim will make a claim if and only if his cost of doing so will be less than the losses he suffered, since this is the amount he will receive from an injurer. It will be socially desirable that victims make claims, however, if and only if their costs of making claims plus injurers' defense costs are less than the social benefits inhering in the incentives to reduce risk that will result from claims. The next example illustrates the possibility that the difference between the private motive to make claims and their social desirability may lead victims to make claims when it would be best that they did not.

EXAMPLE 11.1   Suppose that the losses victims will suffer in accidents are 1,000; that the probability of accidents will be 5 percent if injurers do not take care and 4 percent if they take care, at a cost of 8; and that a victim's cost of making a claim will be 300 and an injurer's cost of defending, 200.

Victims will then make claims whenever accidents occur, for making a claim will cost a victim only 300 and he will obtain 1,000 in damages. It follows that injurers will be induced to exercise care: this will cost an injurer 8 yet will reduce his expected liability and defense costs by a greater amount, namely, by $1\% \times (1,000 + 200) = 12$. Because if care is taken the probability of accidents will be 4 percent, total costs will be $8 + 4\% \times (1,000 + 300 + 200) = 68$.

From the social perspective, this outcome is undesirable. Although it is true that if victims did not make claims injurers would have no incentive to take care and the accident risk would consequently be 5 percent, total costs would be only $5\% \times 1,000 = 50$.

Making claims is not socially desirable in the example because the incentives toward safety that are created by the claims do not reduce accident losses plus the costs of care by as much as the administrative costs caused by the claims. This fact is of no moment to victims, however. They have no reason

---

6. For simplicity, this model does not distinguish between trial and settlement; the cost of making a claim may be interpreted as some average of the cost of settling and of going to trial. Also, the public expenses associated with the operation of courts are not considered.

to take into account that the incentives created by claims are small; they are concerned only with the judgments they obtain.[7]

The following example demonstrates the opposite possibility, that victims may not make claims even though it would be desirable that they do.

EXAMPLE 11.2 The losses victims will suffer in accidents are 100, and an expenditure of 1 by injurers will reduce the probability of accidents from 10 percent to 1 percent. The costs of making and defending against claims are as in the previous example.

In this case victims will not make claims, since doing so will cost a victim 300 but yield him a judgment of only 100. Hence injurers will have no reason to take care to reduce risk, and total costs will be $10\% \times 100 = 10$.

It would be desirable for victims to make claims, however. If they did, injurers would be led to lower risk to 1 percent, and total costs would be only $1 + 1\% \times (100 + 300 + 200) = 7$.

Here the making of claims would be socially worthwhile because of the significant reduction in accident losses that would result. (And observe that this is true despite the fact that the social resources that would be expended in making a claim, namely, 500, exceed a victim's losses of 100.) But victims do not take the social benefits of making claims into account. Each victim looks only to his own gain from making a claim, which is small.

*11.2.4 Corrective policy.* If a social authority has information sufficient to know whether the private motive to make claims will lead to an undesirable outcome, the authority can remedy the situation. The authority can simply ban suit if victims would make claims when that would be undesirable. Alternatively, the authority can raise the cost to victims of making claims to discourage them from doing so; or, in some cases, it would be enough for the authority to insist that victims pay the total administrative costs of making claims.[8] Conversely, the authority can subsidize the making of claims if victims would otherwise fail to make claims when it would be desirable that they did, or it can shift victims' costs of making claims to injurers (use the "British" system) to encourage claims.

---

7. To illustrate the point further, consider the extreme case where there is absolutely *no* incentive created by having injurers pay for losses because there is nothing they can do to reduce risk. In this case it is clearly undesirable for there to be any claims made, but victims will proceed with their claims if their losses exceed the costs of making claims.

8. In Example 11.1, however, making victims pay total administrative costs will not work. If victims have to pay 500 to make claims, they will still, undesirably, choose to make claims.

While a social authority can therefore act to improve social welfare, it is obvious that the authority's appropriate choice of policy depends on whether the problem faced is one of too few claims or too many. There is no policy that will correct automatically for both types of problem.[9] Shifting costs to liable injurers, for instance, will hardly be helpful if the problem is that victims make too many claims.[10]

*11.2.5  The private motive to make claims versus their social desirability under the negligence rule.* Assume initially that if injurers take due care they will not be found liable by mistake and that victims know this. Then it will be socially desirable for victims *to be willing* to make claims against negligent injurers however great the administrative costs would be. If victims stand ready always to make claims against negligent injurers, injurers will be induced never to act negligently. Thus there will never turn out to be any claims made and no administrative costs will be borne.[11] Although it will be socially desirable for victims always to be willing to make claims against negligent injurers, victims will not do so if the cost of making claims will exceed their losses. Therefore, a policy to encourage the making of claims, such as a subsidy or the shifting of victims' claims costs to negligent injurers, may be desirable.

Now assume, more realistically, that because of errors and misperceptions, victims may make claims even if injurers take due care. Victims may make claims because, for example, they erroneously believe that nonnegligent injurers were negligent, or because they correctly believe that the courts would erroneously find nonnegligent injurers negligent, and so forth. For such reasons administrative costs will in fact be borne under the negligence rule and the situation will be qualitatively similar to that under strict liability: there may be too many claims as well as too few, calling for corrective policy either to discourage or to encourage the making of claims.

9. It is shown in the Appendix that there is no cost-shifting, tax, or subsidy scheme that always will function to correct the difference between the privately-motivated and socially optimal use of the liability system. Whether a particular scheme will correct the difference will depend on the direction and nature of the difference.

10. In this regard it is interesting to consider the argument that costs "should" be shifted to liable injurers—after all, it is sometimes said, liable injurers were "wrong" under the law. This argument ignores the fact that such shifting of costs means that making claims becomes free for victims even though claims are socially costly and even though they may result in small social benefits.

11. Consider, for instance, Example 11.1, where it was undesirable for victims to make claims under strict liability. If victims are willing to make claims for negligence, then injurers will be led to take care. Therefore the accident risk will fall to 4 percent and—unlike under strict liability—no claims will be made, since when accidents occur victims will see that injurers took due care.

*11.2.6  Remarks on the foregoing.* (1) Not only does the presence of administrative costs mean that the socially appropriate versus the privately motivated use of the liability system becomes an issue, it also introduces a new consideration into the determination of optimal levels of care: accidents are socially more expensive if they involve administrative costs in addition to victims' direct losses, so optimal levels of care should be higher on account of administrative costs (see §11A.2.5).

(2) It should be clear from the initial discussion and from the logic of the arguments made in the analysis of the simple model that the main conclusion—that the private motive to make use of the legal system may lead to either too many or too few claims—will apply in more general models. The conclusion will apply in models incorporating the various complexities of the litigation process and social benefits of litigation (such as the creation of precedent and compensation of the uninsured) in addition to its incentive effects.

(3) The difference between the privately motivated and the socially appropriate use of the liability system may well be significant; it may constitute a serious reason for social intervention.

On one hand, because the administrative costs of the liability system seem to be large (as noted in §11.1.2), the incentives toward safety created by the liability system must be substantial to warrant its use. Yet these incentives may not always be very strong, especially when account is taken of factors other than liability that operate to reduce risk. In the area of automobile accidents, for instance, criminal liability, enforcement of traffic laws, and the fear of being injured in accidents already provide incentives toward accident avoidance. Where the added incentives created by the liability system are not sufficient to justify its use, we have seen that it may still be very much in the private interest of victims who have sustained large losses to bring suit. Hence some sort of social intervention may be required to reduce use of the liability system. Indeed, certain observed social attempts to limit litigation (for example, passage of no-fault statutes, shifting of legal fees to losing plaintiffs) might be explained in part in this way, that is, as a necessarily collective solution to the problem that the costs of the liability system outweigh its benefits.

On the other hand, there undoubtedly exist areas in which the private motive to bring suit is socially inadequate. This may be true where the cost of bringing suit will typically exceed the magnitude of losses and where injurers, realizing that they will not be sued, fail to behave appropriately even though it would be cheap for them to do so. What, for instance, would be the incentive of a restaurant not worried about its reputation (say it is located on a super-highway and its customers will usually visit it only one time) to avoid causing minor cases of food poisoning? Where the private motive to sue is small and injurers take advantage of this, social intervention to encourage suit may be desirable. And, again, certain social efforts to affect litigation, here to promote it (for example, through establishment of small claims courts, availability of the class action), might be explained in part in the light of the present theory.

*11.2.7   Note on the literature.* In Shavell (1982b) I first examined the contrast discussed here between the socially desirable and the privately motivated use of the legal system in view of its costs; Menell (1983) and Kaplow (1986) further analyzed the issue. See also the related work of Ordover (1978).

# Mathematical Appendix

As discussed in the text, the administrative costs associated with use of the liability system are victims' costs of making claims, injurers' costs of defense, and the public expenses of operating the courts. Making a claim will be understood to mean taking an action that results either in settlement or in trial.

I will first discuss a simple formula determining total administrative costs. Then I will analyze the privately motivated versus the socially optimal use of the liability system given administrative costs.

## 11A.1   Formula Determining Total Administrative Costs

Let

$s$ = number of claims that are settled;
$t$ = number of claims that go to trial;
$a_s$ = administrative costs per settled claim; and
$a_t$ = administrative costs per claim that goes to trial; $a_s < a_t$.

Total administrative costs will be

$$(11.1)\quad sa_s + ta_t = (s + t)\left[\frac{s}{s + t}a_s + \frac{t}{s + t}a_t\right],$$

the total number of claims multiplied by the expected administrative cost per claim.

Total administrative costs under strict liability and under the negligence rule may be compared, with reference to the right-hand side of Eq. (11.1), using the assumptions in the text. Specifically, suppose that the total number of claims is greater under strict liability than under the negligence rule, but that the frequency of trial, $t/(s + t)$, and administrative costs, $a_s$ and $a_t$, are greater under the negligence rule, so that expected administrative costs per claim are greater under that rule. The comparison of administrative costs under the two rules will then be ambiguous.

It should be remarked that the number of claims and the frequency of settlement versus trial will be endogenous variables in a complete model of parties' behavior.

## 11A.2   The Private Motive to Make Claims versus Their Social Desirability

*11A.2.1   In general.* When the administrative costs of use of the liability system are included as costs in the measure of social welfare, it becomes optimal for victims to make claims if and only if the resulting social benefits—here the incentives toward safety that would be generated—exceed the administrative costs.[12] On the other hand, it will be in a victim's interest to make a claim if and only if his expected award will exceed his own cost of making a claim. A victim's own cost of making a claim will be less than administrative costs, for these include also the injurer's defense costs; this suggests that victims will tend to make claims too often. But a victim's award will bear no necessary relationship to the social benefits resulting from the making of claims. Hence the socially optimal and the privately motivated use of the liability system may diverge in either direction, as will be seen below, first in a simple model in which care is a discrete variable and then, briefly, in the usual model in which care is a continuous variable.

*11A.2.2   A simple model.* Consider the unilateral model of accidents with risk-neutral parties and assume that injurers choose between two actions, taking care or not. Let

$p$ = probability of accidents if injurers take care;
$p_o$ = probability of accidents if injurers do not take care; $p_o > p$;
$x$ = cost of taking care; $x > 0$; and
$l$ = loss caused by an accident; $l > 0$.

---

12. In a more general model than that considered below, the social benefits could include the compensation of uninsured risk-averse victims and other elements as well.

Furthermore, let

$c_v$ = cost to a victim of making a claim; $c_v \geqq 0$;
$c_i$ = cost of defense to an injurer if a claim is made against him; $c_i \geqq 0$.

Assume that if a victim suffers a loss and the injurer is liable, the victim will make a claim if his cost $c_v$ is less than $l$ and he will then collect $l$.[13] Assume also that the criterion of social welfare is minimization of total costs, that is, expected accident losses plus costs of care and the costs to parties of making claims (administrative costs). Let us now analyze the situation under strict liability and the negligence rule.

*11A.2.3   The private motive to make claims versus their social desirability under strict liability.* If injurers are strictly liable, victims will make claims when

(11.2)    $c_v < l.$

When Ineq. (11.2) holds, injurers will take care if

(11.3)    $p_o(l + c_i) > p(l + c_i) + x,$

in which case total costs will be

(11.4)    $p(l + c_v + c_i) + x;$

otherwise total costs will be

(11.5)    $p_o(l + c_v + c_i).$

If Ineq. (11.2) does not hold, victims will not make claims.[14] Therefore injurers will not take care and total costs will be $p_o l$.

Let us now compare victims' incentives to make claims with what would be socially optimal, that is, with what a social authority would command if the authority had control over whether victims would make claims (but not direct control over whether injurers would take care).

It would be socially optimal for victims to make claims if and only if the effect of claims would be to reduce total costs to a level below $p_o l$. If Ineq.

---

13. In a more general model the victim might settle for an amount different from $l$, but as will be seen this would not affect the qualitative nature of the results.

14. I adopt the convention that victims will not make claims if $c_v = l$ and will adopt similar conventions below.

(11.3) does not hold, that is, if injurers will not be led to take care if,victims make claims, it will clearly be undesirable for victims to make claims, for if Ineq. (11.3) does not hold and victims make claims total costs will be as stated in Exp. (11.5), which exceeds $p_o l$.

If Ineq. (11.3) holds, it will be socially desirable for victims to make claims if Exp. (11.4) is less than $p_o l$ or, equivalently, if

(11.6)     $(p_o - p)l > x + p(c_v + c_i)$.

But Ineq. (11.6) implies Ineq. (11.3), for Ineq. (11.6) implies $(p_o - p)l > x - (p_o - p)c_i$, which is equivalent to Ineq. (11.3).

We conclude that it will be socially desirable for victims to make claims if and only if Ineq. (11.6) holds. Note that the interpretation of this inequality is that $(p_o - p)l$, the savings in expected accident losses due to the incentives created by the making of claims, exceeds the cost of care *plus* the expected administrative costs associated with claims.

It follows that claims will be made when they are undesirable if Ineq. (11.2) holds and Ineq. (11.6) does not—and that claims will not be made when it would be desirable that they be made if Ineq. (11.2) does not hold and Ineq. (11.6) does hold. That both cases are possible is obvious and is illustrated by the examples in the text. Moreover, the explanation given in §11A.2.1 for the difference between victims' and society's interest in the making of claims is reflected by Ineq. (11.2) and the following inequality, which is equivalent to Ineq. (11.6):

(11.6')     $c_v + c_i < \dfrac{(p_o - p)l - x}{p}$.

In Ineq. (11.2) we saw that in deciding whether to make a claim, a victim compares only his own cost $c_v$ with his loss $l$, whereas in Ineq. (11.6') we see that society compares the total administrative cost $c_v + c_i$ with the savings in expected accident losses, net of costs of care, due to the incentives created by the making of claims.[15]

Let us now consider whether a social authority can ensure that claims will be made if and only if they are desirable. If the authority can compute Ineqs. (11.6) and (11.2) and adopts a policy depending on them, the authority can ensure the proper making of claims: when Ineq. (11.6) does not hold, the authority can simply forbid the making of claims; and when Ineq. (11.6) does hold but Ineq. (11.2) does not, the authority can subsidize claims or make

15. The savings are multiplied by the factor $1/p$ because administrative costs are borne only with probability $p$.

injurers pay victims' costs. It should be observed, however, that a scheme that does not depend on Ineq. (11.6) cannot induce victims to make claims if and only if that would be socially desirable. In particular, having victims pay the total administrative costs $c_v + c_i$ may not work, for when Ineq. (11.6′) holds, $c_v + c_i > l$ may also hold; shifting victims' costs to injurers will not always work, for then victims will always make claims, yet Ineq. (11.6′) may not hold; and so forth.

PROPOSITION 11.1   Under strict liability, (a) victims may make claims when the making of claims is socially undesirable or they may fail to make claims when it would be socially desirable that they did. (b) A social authority can remedy this problem only by taking into account what the effect of the making of claims would be on incentives and thus on total costs. (c) No scheme of shifting the costs of making claims or of increasing or reducing the cost of making claims will solve the problem if the application of the scheme does not depend on knowledge of the incentive effect of claims on total costs.

*11A.2.4    The private motive to make claims versus their social desirability under the negligence rule.* Assume to begin with that the negligence rule is applied without error; that is, injurers will be found negligent if and only if they failed to take care, provided that

(11.7)    $x + pl < p_o l.$

Assume also that a victim can determine when an injurer is not negligent and will not make a claim in that case. Then it will be socially desirable for victims always to be willing to make claims against negligent injurers—no matter how high are $c_v$ and $c_i$—for if victims will be willing to make claims, injurers will, by the familiar argument, be induced to take care when Ineq. (11.7) holds. Hence no claims will be made and total costs will be $x + pl$; but were victims not willing to make claims against negligent injurers, injurers would not take care and total costs would be $p_o l$.

On the other hand, victims will in fact be willing to make claims against negligent injurers only if Ineq. (11.2) holds. If Ineq. (11.2) does not hold and Ineq. (11.7) does hold, injurers will not take care even though they could have been induced to do so at no administrative cost. To solve this problem arising from victims' unwillingness to make claims against negligent injurers, a social authority could shift victims' costs to negligent injurers, for then victims would always be willing to make claims against negligent injurers.

If we now introduce into the model uncertainty over the determination of negligence (along the lines described in §4A.3), then even if injurers take due care or attempt to do so there will be some claims made for negligence and administrative costs will actually be borne. For example, if courts might erroneously conclude that an injurer who took due care did not, and if the victim could predict this, the victim would, if Ineq. (11.2) held, make a claim. Hence it is clear that the results under strict liability would carry over to a degree under the negligence rule.

PROPOSITION 11.2   Under a perfectly functioning negligence rule, (a) victims will never have a socially excessive incentive to make claims, but they may not be willing to make claims when that would be socially desirable. (b) The shifting of victims' costs to negligent injurers will solve this problem. However, (c) if, as is realistic, there is uncertainty over the determination of negligence, the conclusions about strict liability stated in Proposition 11.1 will apply under the negligence rule.

*11A.2.5   The model with care continuously variable.* Assume now that care $x$ is continuously variable, where $p(x)$ is the probability of an accident, and restrict attention to strict liability (the situation under negligence will be clear from what will be said and from §11A.2.4). Victims will make claims when Ineq. (11.2) holds, in which case injurers will choose $x$ to minimize

(11.8)    $x + p(x)(l + c_i)$.

In other words, they will choose $x^*(l + c_i)$, where $x^*(z)$ denotes the $x$ that minimizes $x + p(x)z$. Total costs if Ineq. (11.2) holds will therefore be

(11.9)    $x^*(l + c_i) + p(x^*(l + c_i))(l + c_v + c_i)$.

On the other hand, if Ineq. (11.2) does not hold and victims do not make claims, then injurers will not take care and total costs will be $p(0)l$.

For essentially the reasons given in the simple model, it is possible that victims will make claims when that is socially undesirable—Ineq. (11.2) may hold when Exp. (11.9) exceeds $p(0)l$. It is also possible that victims will not make claims when they should—Ineq. (11.2) may not hold when Exp. (11.9) is less than $p(0)l$.

There is also a third possible type of suboptimality, concerning injurers' level of care. (This did not arise in the simple model because there was only one positive level of care.) If victims make claims, total costs will be $x + p(x)(l + c_v + c_i)$, which means that the socially optimal level of care will be

$x^*(l + c_v + c_i)$. Injurers, however, will take care of only $x^*(l + c_i)$ since they do not bear the victims' costs $c_v$.

It follows that what is socially best given administrative costs is for victims to make claims if $x^*(l + c_v + c_i) + p(x^*(l + c_v + c_i))(l + c_v + c_i)$ is less than $p(0)l$, and if victims make claims, for injurers to take care of $x^*(l + c_v + c_i)$.

If it is best for victims not to make claims, then, as in the simple model, the making of claims can, if necessary, be forbidden or taxed at a prohibitive level. If it is best for victims to make claims and they would not do so, then, as before, they can be induced to do so by use of a subsidy or by shifting their costs of making claims to injurers. Shifting victims' costs to injurers is superior because it will induce injurers to take optimal care of $x^*(l + c_v + c_i)$.

*11A.2.6  Note on the literature.* In Shavell (1982b) I make most of the points presented in this part; the argument here is extended in Menell (1983) and Kaplow (1986). See also the related work of Ordover (1978).

# 12 | Liability versus Other Approaches to the Control of Risk

Having analyzed the functioning of the liability system, I believe it will prove helpful and furnish perspective for us now to consider the variety of other ways in which society may control risk. In this chapter I will first enumerate and briefly discuss the other approaches to the control of risk and will then study their relative appeal.

## 12.1 The Different Approaches to the Control of Risk

*12.1.1  The approaches described.* One approach in addition to imposition of tort liability that society may employ to control risk is, of course, the direct regulation of safety. Under this approach, parties must adhere to certain standards if they are to be permitted to engage in their activities. Sellers of canned food, for instance, must prepare and seal products in designated ways; electric utilities must build and operate nuclear power plants in conformity with a multitude of requirements; owners of stores and other buildings open to the public must clearly mark fire exits; and so forth.

Another approach available to society makes use of the injunction. According to this approach, a party who establishes that he is in substantial danger of suffering harm may obtain an injunction against, or "enjoin," the potential injurer. The victim may enlist the power of the state to prevent the potential injurer from carrying on his activity until or unless the danger has been reduced. For example, individuals living near a factory's dam that is in danger of collapse from an accumulation of sludge may enjoin the factory from continuing to operate as long as the dam is not reinforced or the sludge is not removed.

A third method by which society may control risk is to levy "corrective" taxes on parties equal to the expected harm in which their actions will result.

*Table 12.1*   Approaches to the control of risk

| How initiated | When applied | |
| --- | --- | --- |
| | Ex ante | Ex post |
| Privately initiated | Injunction | Liability |
| State initiated | Corrective tax; safety regulation | Fine for harm done |

In the classic example, a firm that releases a pollutant into the atmosphere will pay a tax equal to the expected losses caused by the discharge.[1]

A fourth approach is for society to impose fines for harm actually done.[2] As with tort liability, these fines might be imposed either on a strict basis or only if fault is found.

Finally, society may resort to use of the criminal sanction. For simplicity, this sanction shall be identified here with imprisonment.

*12.1.2   The approaches distinguished.* With the exception of the use of the criminal sanction, on which I shall comment at the end of this section, the approaches may be seen to differ in two dimensions (see Table 12.1). First, the approaches may be ex ante in nature—they may apply before, or at least independently of, the occurrence of harm—or else they may be ex post in character—they may be triggered only by the occurrence of harm. Liability and the fine for harm done are by definition ex post approaches, whereas safety regulation, the injunction, and corrective taxes are ex ante devices for the control of risk.[3]

Second, the approaches may be either privately initiated or state initiated. An approach is of the former type if it is employed only after a victim, or potential victim, takes some legal action or reports his situation to a social authority. Liability and the injunction are privately initiated since they apply only where a party has sued for damages or has brought an action to enjoin another. On the other hand, an approach to control risk may be employed by

---

1. I will not consider the approach under which an injurer would be compelled to pay potential victims (rather than the state) the expected losses.

2. Fines for harm done (such as for losses due to fire) should not be confused with penalties paid by parties for violation of safety regulations (such as for failure to install fire exit signs).

3. This distinction, like the others to be made below, is not a perfect one. For example, a regulatory authority may be prompted by the occurrence of an accident to make an inspection. Nevertheless, because the distinction captures an important difference between the approaches to the control of risk, it is a useful one to make, and for expositional reasons I will not qualify it.

the state at its discretion. Safety regulation, the corrective tax, and the fine for harm done are state initiated since they apply regardless of any actions taken by, or notification received from, victims or potential victims.

As noted, the use of criminal sanctions may not be distinguished from the use of the other approaches on the basis of the two factors under discussion. Criminal sanctions may be imposed if no harm is done or conditional on its occurrence, and they may be imposed as a result of private or state initiative. What will be of interest here about criminal sanctions is that their imposition will be assumed to be socially more costly than the imposition of monetary sanctions. The motivation for this assumption is that imprisonment involves significant social expense (associated with the building and operation of prisons and with forgone production), whereas the imposition of monetary sanctions is socially cheap since it may be viewed largely as a transfer of purchasing power.

*12.1.3 How the approaches are to be compared.* In the next several parts I will compare the different approaches by making implicit use of the following social welfare criterion: the value of parties' activities less the costs of care, expected losses, administrative costs, and, where relevant, the costs of imposing criminal sanctions. The comparison, it should thus be noticed, will not take into account compensation of risk-averse victims. Of course, this is not because compensation of the risk averse is considered unimportant; rather, it is because compensation can be accomplished independently of the approach employed to control risk, for risk-averse individuals can purchase insurance coverage or, if necessary, be provided with social insurance.

We will proceed by examining factors bearing on the desirability of ex ante versus ex post approaches to the control of risk, then factors relevant to the appeal of privately versus state-initiated approaches, and then factors influencing the desirability of use of criminal sanctions. This way of organizing the analysis will enable the reader to see the advantages and disadvantages of the different approaches in a general light.

## 12.2 Factors Bearing on the Appeal of Ex Ante versus Ex Post Approaches

*12.2.1 Inability of injurers to pay for harm done.* Where injurers are unable to pay fully for harm done, the incentives to control risk created by ex post approaches will be dulled. As discussed in previous chapters (see §§7.2 and 10.4), the prospect of liability may not generate adequate incentives to reduce risk if injurers' assets are less than the losses they might cause because losses exceeding their assets will impose on them liabilities only equal to their assets; and the same will clearly be true with respect to fines for harm done. Thus the canner of foods or the utility that owns the nuclear power plant might not be led by the threat of ex post payments to take needed precautions if its assets are substantially less than the harm that could be caused by accidents injuring many individuals.

Under ex ante approaches to the control of risk, however, injurers' inability to pay for harm done will be irrelevant if they will be made to behave in desirable ways as a precondition for engaging in their activities. That the canner or the utility will be unable to pay for the losses it might cause will not be of concern if it can be made to obey safety regulations. Likewise, that a firm will not be able to pay for the full harm that the pollutant it releases may do will not matter if it can pay the often much smaller corrective tax equal to the expected harm, for paying this tax will lead the firm to take needed risk-reducing steps; or that a factory will not be able to pay for the harm the sludge building up behind its dam may do will be of no consequence if the factory can be enjoined from continuing its operations.

Although inability to pay for harm done therefore constitutes a general advantage in favor of ex ante modes of control of risk, a qualification needs to be mentioned. Namely, if monetary penalties are relied on to enforce regulations or the other ex ante approaches, injurers' levels of assets set effective bounds on the size of penalties. This may make enforcement difficult.[4]

*12.2.2   Inability to assign responsibility for harm to parties.* If responsibility for harm done cannot be satisfactorily assigned to injurers and they escape having to pay damages or fines, their incentives to reduce risk will be diluted (see §§5.3 and 6.8.5). For example, if a pollutant cannot easily be linked to harm done because of difficulties in establishing causation, the threat of liability or of fines may not create adequate incentives for polluters to reduce risk.

Such problems with ex post approaches can in some cases be ameliorated by altering the way in which they are applied. If a polluting firm will escape having to pay for losses a fraction of the time, the amount it pays when it is found responsible can be raised by an appropriate amount above the level of losses it causes (see §6.8.5). But this strategy raises problems of its own, including that injurers may not have assets sufficient to pay the higher amounts. Another type of solution to the problem of inability to assign definite responsibility for harm done is, recall, to make injurers pay in proportion

---

4. For example, a system of enforcement of safety regulation that involves only occasional checks on compliance and large penalties for noncompliance will be unworkable if injurers cannot pay the penalties. Such problems will not arise, however, where the state can enforce safety regulations directly through exercise of its police powers (by locking the gates to the canning plant, by preventing a truck with dangerous cargo from passing the toll booth at a tunnel entrance).

to the likelihood that they were responsible for harm (see §5.3.2). This solution, however, is limited to contexts in which the universe of possible injurers is not too numerous and can be identified fairly readily.

In any event, it is clear that possible problems in tracing harms to responsible parties do not impede the use of ex ante approaches to the control of risk. The ability to regulate polluters, to enjoin their operations, or to tax them has nothing to do with how hard it would be to establish after harm is done a connection between a particular harm and a particular polluter.

*12.2.3  Injurers' versus a social authority's information about risk and the cost of reducing risk.* If injurers have better information about the nature of risk and the costs of reducing risk than a social authority has, the appeal of ex post approaches to the control of risk will be increased, because under these approaches it will be the injurers who decide what steps to take to reduce risk. To illustrate, contrast the use of strict liability with safety regulation or a corrective tax, assuming that injurers have perfect information about risk and its cost of reduction and that a regulator or tax authority has poor information. Under strict liability injurers will be led to balance risk against the costs of its reduction in a desirable way, other things equal, whereas a regulator or tax authority will be likely to err.

If, on the other hand, it is a social authority that possesses the better information, the desirability of ex ante methods of control will be enhanced. If injurers have little knowledge about risk, they will not be induced by the threat of liability or fines to act desirably; regulating their behavior on the basis of superior information, or enjoining or taxing them, will therefore be advantageous.

Who in fact will be likely to possess the better information about risk and the cost of reducing it, injurers or a social authority? The answer, it seems, is that injurers should usually enjoy a natural advantage in knowledge, for it is they who actually engage in the risky activities. A homeowner, for example, will probably be more able than a regulator to determine the risk of damage to his neighbors' house that will be created by cutting down a tree in his backyard. The homeowner will know the size of his tree, the distance between it and his neighbor's dwelling, and so forth. Moreover, the homeowner may be better able to ascertain the time and effort that will be required to cut down the tree or whether it would be worth his while to hire a private contractor.

Yet in certain contexts information about risk will not be an obvious byproduct of engaging in activities but rather will require effort to develop or special expertise to evaluate. This might be true, for instance, of information concerning the toxic properties of certain pesticides and, more generally, of information concerning many health-related and environmental risks. A social authority may learn about such risks by committing resources to the task (for example, by gathering epidemiological information), whereas injurers may have an insufficient motive to obtain information for well-understood reasons: an individual party who generates information may not be able to capture its full value since others will often learn of it without paying the party; and a joint effort by parties to obtain information may be stymied by the problem of inducing all to lend their support. Consequently, a social authority may be in a superior position to obtain information. In addition, the information may be difficult for a social authority to communicate to injurers because, say, of its technical nature. (How well could the epidemiological analysis of a pesticide risk be understood by the staff of a small exterminating firm?) Thus one can point to situations where a social authority may possess superior information about risk and cannot easily transmit it to injurers, even if the usual expectation is that injurers will possess superior information.

*12.2.4  Administrative costs.* Under ex post modes of control of risk, administrative costs are, by definition, borne only if harm is done. Where an activity will not cause harm in the great majority of instances (something that is true of cutting down a tree in one's backyard and, indeed, of most activities), the savings that can be achieved by limiting the bearing of administrative costs to those occasions when harm does occur may be substantial.

Under regulation and other ex ante approaches, by contrast, administrative costs are borne whether or not harm occurs. Even if, for example, the chance of harm is entirely eliminated through regulation, corrective taxation, or the injunction, administrative costs will have been borne in the process. Thus ex ante approaches seem to suffer from an underlying administrative cost disadvantage relative to ex post approaches when the likelihood of harm is low. In assessing the magnitude of administrative costs under ex ante approaches, one must take into account, among other elements, whether the concern is with verifying the presence of safety features (lifeboats, fire extinguishers), for such verification may not necessitate very costly or very frequent monitoring; or whether the concern is with determining aspects of easily modified behavior (speed on the road), for verification of this will ordinarily call for frequent monitoring; and, if the concern is over behavior, whether the desirable behavior is sensitive to changing circumstance, for this too will increase the need for monitoring.

*12.2.5  Conclusion.* To summarize, the possibilities that injurers will be unable to pay fully for harm done or will escape responsibility for it tend to favor ex ante approaches over ex post approaches, while the factors concerning the locus of information about risk and administrative costs usually, but not always, point in the opposite direction.

### 12.3 Factors Bearing on the Desirability of Privately Initiated versus State-Initiated Approaches

*12.3.1 Dispersion of harm.* The dispersion of harm is a factor that reduces the effectiveness of privately initiated approaches to the control of risk. Victims of dispersed, individually small harms (such as the more-frequent peeling of paint because of pollution) may have little incentive to bring suit, in view of its cost (although use of the class action can lower the cost of suit). Similarly, potential victims of dispersed harms may have little reason to seek injunctions against parties creating dangers of such harms. Consequently, the state-initiated approaches of fines for harm done, regulation, or taxes may be needed to control the risk of widely dispersed harms.

*12.3.2 Victims' versus a social authority's information about risk or the occurrence of harm.* Where victims are likely to possess information about the prospect or the occurrence of harm that is superior to a social authority's, the attractiveness of privately initiated approaches will be enhanced. In many typical instances of nuisance (a neighbor's vicious dog) and, generally, in situations where a danger is recognized mainly by those in close proximity to its source, potential victims may seek an injunction, whereas a regulatory or tax authority might not realize the need for control.[5] Furthermore, in many if not most instances of the actual occurrence (as opposed to the risk) of harm, victims will be in possession of information superior to that of a social authority. A victim will ordinarily be aware of the fact that he has been harmed, and he will often know the identity of the responsible party as well as have observed his behavior, whereas a social authority may have little independent knowledge of these things. (Would a social authority necessarily learn by itself of the fact that my car was damaged, that the damage was done by X rather than by some unknown person, that X was driving at 50 miles per hour, and that the accident occurred at dusk?) In consequence, use of the privately initiated approach of liability, which rewards victims for supplying information about harm, has obvious appeal over use of the fine.

On the other hand, where a social authority will be expected to possess, or to be better able to acquire, superior information about risk or the occurrence of harm, state-initiated approaches will become attractive relative to privately initiated approaches. Where risks are not apparent to potential victims (suppose a holding tank for a dangerous, volatile chemical can be seen only from inside the area of a plant), regulation may be needed, for no one will bring an injunction. Also, even where risks are suspected by potential victims, they

---

5. Unless such an authority is notified by individuals and asked to act; but this, in essence, amounts to use of the injunction even if it is not called that.

may not be able to arrange a proper inquiry about the risks. A social authority may be best suited to do that and, in addition, may take advantage of economies of scale in organizing an investigative body (a corps of inspection agents). Finally, a social authority may sometimes find itself in a better position than victims to detect the actual occurrence of harm or its source. For instance, the Coast Guard may be better able than individuals to spot over-fishing and to determine who is guilty of it. In such cases use of fines will be advantageous, for suits will not be brought.

## 12.4    Factors Bearing on the Appeal of Nonmonetary, Criminal Sanctions

*12.4.1    Assets of injurers.* When injurers' assets are not sufficiently high, it may be difficult to control their behavior adequately through any of the approaches that have been discussed, assuming that the approaches involve use of monetary sanctions alone. It was stated in §12.2.1 that if injurers' assets are less than the harm they might do, they might not be induced by the threat of liability or fines to reduce risk appropriately, and it was then suggested that employing ex ante approaches may alleviate the problem. While it is true that use of the ex ante approaches of regulation, the injunction, or corrective taxes may, and often will, go a significant distance toward solving the problem, it is also true that they may not. As had been noted in qualification, enforcement of regulation may not be automatic but rather require use of sanctions. If the needed monetary sanctions are higher than the assets of injurers, regulation cannot be enforced well by the threat of monetary sanctions only. A similar difficulty may be associated with enforcement of an injunction, and there is also a possibility that an injurer will not be able to pay a corrective tax. To the extent that these problems arise under the various approaches employing solely monetary sanctions, the use of criminal sanctions will be appealing.

*12.4.2    Likelihood that injurers will escape a social authority's notice.* The greater the chance that injurers would escape the notice of a social authority, the higher is the monetary sanction necessary to control their behavior. In particular, we know that when an injurer does not escape notice, he must make a payment approximating the victim's losses multiplied by the reciprocal of the probability of being noticed; if an injurer will be held liable for harm done only one-third of the time, for example, he will have to pay the victim's losses multiplied by about three. Such increases in the payment necessary to induce proper behavior make it more likely that the required payment will exceed an injurer's assets and therefore that use of criminal sanctions will be needed.

*12.4.3    Possibility that injurers' benefits are considered socially illicit.* The benefits parties derive from committing certain acts may be regarded as socially illicit (see §6.8.3). Notably, if the benefits parties derive inhere in their enjoyment of the harm suffered by others (as when parties intentionally injure enemies), the benefits may not be counted in the social calculus. It is optimal to deter acts whose benefits are considered socially illicit, but deterrence is often made especially difficult because the magnitude of the benefits is very high. This, like the previous factors, tends to make it less probable that use of monetary sanctions alone will be enough to deter.

*12.4.4  Probability and severity of harm.* The greater are the probability and the magnitude of harm resulting from injurers' acts, the greater are the consequences of failure to control them adequately. Where, for example, parties act with the purpose of causing harm, the likelihood and severity of harm will typically be high; similarly, where parties behave recklessly risks will also be high. Because in such situations failure of monetary sanctions to control behavior will result in large expected losses, it may become socially worthwhile to resort to criminal sanctions despite the greater social costs attending their use.

## 12.5  Concluding Observations

*12.5.1  Conditions under which liability best controls risk.* It is apparent from the above discussion that a useful way to locate liability among the different approaches to the control of risk is to recognize that liability can be characterized as an approach that relies on monetary as opposed to criminal sanctions, that is ex post in nature, and that is privately initiated. From this perspective it should be clear that liability will be most valuable relative to other approaches when the following conditions hold. (1) Injurers' assets are not low in relation to the harm they may do and injurers will not often escape responsibility for harm. (This means that criminal sanctions will not be needed, and it suggests that ex ante approaches will not be advantageous.) (2) Injurers' knowledge about risk is superior to that of a regulatory or other social authority, and there will be a significant savings achieved from the bearing of administrative costs only when harm is done. (This supplies affirmative arguments for use of an ex post over an ex ante approach.) (3) Victims must be induced to supply to the state information about harm because the state's independently acquired information would be poor. (This implies that the privately initiated approach of liability will be superior to the state-initiated approach of the fine.)

*12.5.2  Joint use of the approaches.* To the degree that the conditions favoring use of liability do not hold, it will generally be desirable to employ other approaches along with liability; there is no reason to view the different approaches as alternatives to one another. For example, suppose that liability cannot solely be relied upon to control risk because some parties' assets are very low, while safety regulation cannot solely be relied upon because the regulatory authority's information about risk is imperfect. Then joint use of regulation and liability will be advantageous. Specifically, it will be desirable for parties to satisfy minimal safety standards and also to face possible liability. Insisting on minimal safety standards—those that the authority can be reasonably confident are needed (such as for hotels to install fire extinguishers) despite its imperfect information—will ensure that at least certain precautions will be taken even by parties who, because their assets are low, would not be led to meet the standards by the threat of liability. On the other hand, the threat of liability will induce parties whose assets are not low to take additional precautions that they, but not the regulator, recognize will reduce risk (such as to avoid storing flammable furniture polish near a heating pipe in a supply closet).

This example should serve to illustrate the desirability of taking into account the possibilities for joint use of the different approaches to the control of risk.

*12.5.3   Note on the literature.* Although there does not seem to exist work that considers together the five different approaches for controlling risk that were discussed here, there are a number of papers that deal mainly with pairs of approaches: see Calabresi and Melamed (1972), considering (among other issues) the injunction versus liability; Polinsky (1980a), also considering the injunction and liability; Weitzman (1974), comparing regulation and corrective taxation; Shavell (1984a), studying regulation and tort liability; and Posner (1985) and Shavell (1985a), discussing criminal law and tort liability.

# Mathematical Appendix

This appendix will compare liability, fines for harm done, corrective taxes, safety regulation, and the injunction as means of controlling accident risks.

## 12A.1   The Model

Consider the unilateral model of accidents with risk-neutral injurers and assume that injurers differ in their costs of exercising care and in the losses they might cause. Specifically, suppose as usual that $x$ is the level of care, $p(x)$

is the probability of an accident, $l$ is the magnitude of losses if an accident occurs, and, as in §4A.1, $k$ is the per-unit cost of exercising care, so the cost of exercising care of $x$ will be $kx$. Assume that both $k$ and $l$ are fixed for any particular injurer; but that $k$ is distributed across the population of injurers according to the probability density $f(k)$, where $f$ is positive only on $[k_1, k_2]$, where $k_1 > 0$; and that $l$ is distributed according to the density $g(l)$, where $g$ is positive only on $[l_1, l_2]$, where $l_1 > 0$. Assume too that $k$ and $l$ are independent random variables, so that their joint density is the product of $f$ and $g$.

Suppose that each injurer knows his own $k$ and $l$ and that the social authority knows the functions $p(\cdot), f(\cdot)$, and $g(\cdot)$, that it can observe $l$ if an accident occurs, and that it may also possess other information (as specified). Finally, suppose that all injurers have the same level of assets $a$ and that the social authority knows $a$.

The social welfare criterion will be minimization of expected total costs,

(12.1)    $\int_{l_1}^{l_2} \int_{k_1}^{k_2} [kx + p(x)l] f(k) g(l) \, dk \, dl,$

where it is understood that $x$ may depend on $k$ and on $l$. If $x$ could be chosen freely to minimize Exp. (12.1), it would clearly be chosen to minimize $kx + p(x)l$ for each $k$ and $l$. Hence $x$ would be determined by

(12.2)    $k + p'(x)l = 0.$

Denote this first-best $x$ by $x^*(k, l)$, and observe that it is decreasing in $k$ and increasing in $l$.[6]

## 12A.2   Behavior under the Different Approaches

Injurers' behavior under the different approaches to the control of risk will now be examined, supposing that each approach will be employed alone. Assume that liability and the fine will be applied only if accidents occur; they are thus ex post approaches. And suppose that corrective taxation, safety regulation, and the injunction will be applied before accidents have a chance to occur; they are therefore ex ante approaches to the control of risk. Also, assume that

$q$ = probability that an approach to the control of risk will be applied.

---

6. Implicit differentiation of Exp. (12.2) with respect to $k$ gives $1 + p''(x)lx'(k) = 0$, so that $x'(k) = -1/p''(x)l < 0$; that $x'(l) > 0$ follows similarly.

This probability will depend on the particular approach for the reasons discussed in the text. To distinguish among $q$ under the different approaches, subscripts will be used (*li* for liability, *f* for the fine, and so on). The level of care of an injurer of type $(k,l)$ will be denoted by $x(k,l)$.

*12A.2.1  Liability.* Under strict liability an injurer will choose $x$ to minimize

(12.3)    $kx + q_{li}p(x)\min[a,l]$.

Thus, as is known from previous analysis (see §7A.2), if $q_{li} < 1$ or if $a < l$, then $x(k,l) < x^*(k,l)$; and $x(k,l)$ is increasing in $q_{li}$ and in $a$ (if $a < l$). To apply strict liability, courts need only observe $l$.

Suppose that under the negligence rule courts can ascertain $k$ and observe $x$, so that they can calculate $x^*(k,l)$, make this the due care level, and compare it with $x$. Then, again, it is known from before that injurers will choose $x^*(k,l)$ unless $q_{li}$ is sufficiently less than 1 or $a$ is sufficiently less than $l$, in which case $x(k,l)$ will equal what it would under strict liability and be less than $x^*(k,l)$.

*12A.2.2  Fines.* Under this approach, assume that injurers will have to make payments to the state for harm done either on a strict basis or only if negligence is found.[7] Hence, the determination of injurers' care levels is as described under liability but with $q_f$ replacing $q_{li}$.

*12A.2.3  Corrective taxes.* Under the corrective tax an injurer who does not come to the attention of the tax authority will pay no tax and will therefore take no care; this will occur with probability $1 - q_t$. An injurer who does come to the attention of the authority will be assumed to pay a tax to the authority equal to the expected losses that he will cause—as perceived by the authority—given $x$, which the authority is assumed to be able to observe. Thus, if the authority can determine $l$ ex ante, the expected losses perceived by the authority and the tax will be $p(x)l$. An injurer will therefore choose $x$ to minimize $kx + \min[a,p(x)l]$, so that he will choose $x^*(k,l)$ assuming that $a > p(x^*(k,l))l$. If the authority cannot observe $l$, the expected losses perceived by the authority and the tax will be $p(x)E(l)$. An injurer will thus choose $x$ to minimize $kx + \min[a,p(x)E(l)]$, so that he will choose $x^*(k,E(l))$ assuming that $a > p(x^*(k,E(l)))E(l)$. Note that $x^*(k,E(l))$ will exceed $x^*(k,l)$ for $l < E(l)$ and fall short of $x^*(k,l)$ for $l > E(l)$.

7. Although it is assumed that the magnitude of the fine (and, for that matter, the magnitude of liability) will equal the harm done, this assumption will not affect the qualitative nature of the conclusions that will be reached about the comparison of approaches. The reasons are that the level of injurers' assets $a$ would place a limit on the possible magnitude of the fine and that courts' inability to observe $k$ or $x$ may hamper use of the fine.

*12A.2.4 Safety regulation.* Under safety regulation an injurer who does not come to the attention of the regulatory authority will not have to satisfy a regulatory standard of care and will therefore take no care; this will occur with probability $1 - q_r$. If an injurer does come to the attention of the authority, his level of care, which the authority is assumed to be able to observe, will have to satisfy the regulatory standard. The standard will be set at the level the authority perceives to be optimal given its information. If the authority can determine $k$ and $l$ ex ante, then it can calculate $x^*(k,l)$ and compel an injurer to take this level of care. If the authority cannot ascertain $k$ but can determine $l$, the authority will set the standard to minimize $\int_{k_1}^{k_2} [kx + p(x)l] f(k)dk = E(k)x + p(x)l$, so that it will set the standard equal to $x^*(E(k),l)$. This will exceed $x^*(k,l)$ if $k > E(k)$ and fall short of $x^*(k,l)$ if $k < E(k)$. Similarly, if the authority cannot determine $l$ but can determine $k$, it will set the standard equal to $x^*(k,E(l))$; and if the authority cannot determine either $k$ or $l$, it will set the standard equal to $x^*(E(k), E(l))$ for all injurers.

*12A.2.5 The injunction.* Where the injunction is employed, courts will make an injurer who is brought to their attention take the level of care that they perceive to be optimal. Thus courts will set $x$, given their information, in the way described in §12A.2.4.

*12A.2.6 Comparison of approaches.* Depending on the values of the variables and the information available to the social authority, any of the approaches to the control of risk may be best. To illustrate, let us note conditions under which each of the approaches will alone lead to the first-best outcome. (A complete characterization of the conditions under which each of the approaches will be best (rather than first-best) would not be difficult to supply.)

1. Strict liability alone will result in the first-best outcome. Assume that $q_{li} = 1$ and $a > l_2$ (thus strict liability will result in a first-best outcome); that $x$ or $k$ is not observable ex post (thus the negligence rule cannot be perfectly applied); that $q_f < 1$ (thus the fine will not result in optimal care); that $q_t < 1$ or $l$ is not observable ex ante (thus corrective taxes cannot be perfectly applied); that $q_r < 1$ or $k$ or $l$ is not observable ex ante (thus regulation cannot be perfectly applied); and that $q_i < 1$ or $k$ or $l$ is not observable ex ante (thus the injunction cannot be perfectly applied).

2. The negligence rule alone will result in the first-best outcome. Assume that $q_{li}$ is slightly less than 1 and $a > l_2$ (thus the negligence rule will result in the first-best outcome, but strict liability will not); otherwise, assume as in 1.

3. A strict fine alone will result in the first-best outcome. Reverse the roles of $q_f$ and $q_{li}$ in 1.

4. A negligence-based fine alone will result in the first-best outcome. Reverse the roles of $q_f$ and $q_{li}$ in 2.

5. Corrective taxation alone will result in the first-best outcome. Assume that $q_{li} < 1$ or $a < l_2$ (sufficiently so that not only strict liability but also the negligence rule will not result in the first-best outcome); that $q_t = 1$, $l$ is observable ex ante, and $a > p(x^*(k_2, l_2))l_2$; that $q_r < 1$ or $k$ is not observable ex ante; and that $q_i < 1$ or $k$ is not observable ex ante.

6. Regulation alone will result in the first-best outcome. Assume as in 5 that $q_{li} < 1$ or $a < l_2$; that $q_t < 1$ or $a < p(x^*(k_2, l_2))l_2$; that $q_r = 1$ and $k$ and $l$ are observable ex ante; and that $q_i < 1$.

7. The injunction alone will result in the first-best outcome. Assume as in 6, except reverse the roles of $q_i$ and $q_r$.

As discussed in the text, a more complete analysis of the above approaches to the control of risk would include the possibility of their joint use and would also take into account administrative costs. In addition, the potential advantages of imposing nonmonetary (criminal) sanctions, notably imprisonment, would be investigated.

*12A.2.7   Note on the literature.* The following articles examine models in which some of the approaches to the control of risk are compared:[8] Weitzman (1974), considering regulation versus corrective taxation; Wittman (1977), studying ex ante versus ex post methods of control; Polinsky (1979), analyzing mainly liability and injunctions; and Shavell (1984b), examining liability and safety regulation.

---

8. These articles consider certain elements that are different from those examined here. For instance, in analyzing the injunction Polinsky 1979 stresses bargaining between injurers and victims.

# 13 | Critical Comments

In this concluding chapter I will attempt to answer a variety of questions that I think are likely to be raised about the analysis of accident law as presented in the book. Moreover, in doing so I hope to respond to certain commonly heard criticisms of economic analysis of law.

## Predictive and Normative Analysis

*Of what value is the analysis of the book for predicting and understanding behavior?* It seems to me self-evident that the analysis should be of value for these purposes, as it seeks carefully to determine the decisions that calculating actors will make given the rules of liability and opportunities to insure. How much value the analysis will have will depend on whether the assumptions studied capture important elements of reality, on the degree to which the analysis helps to organize thought about the effects of liability and the insurance system, and on the extent to which the analysis identifies effects that the reader does not consider obvious. With regard to the latter, the reader should ask himself, for example, whether he had recognized at the outset that under error-free application of the negligence rule, the calculating actor will necessarily, and not just sometimes, be led to take due care; whether he had appreciated that uncertainty surrounding the determination of negligence may lead systematically to the exercise of excessive, defensive, precautionary measures; whether he was well aware of the manner in which the terms of insurance policies are influenced by the ability of insurers to obtain information about insureds; whether he had focused on the point that individuals are unlikely to insure against many nonpecuniary losses; or whether he had realized that the rule regarding treatment of collateral benefits in the computation of liability is unlikely to have much effect. I trust that, on reflection, many readers will agree that their understanding of the working of the liability and insurance systems has been enhanced by the analysis presented here.

*Does the prospect of liability really deter? Was undue importance attached to this issue in the analysis?* It is, of course, an empirical question how much the threat of liability affects behavior, and given the relative lack of statistical study of the question, one must rely mainly on intuition in coming to an answer.[1] One may surmise, first of all, that the possibility of liability may significantly affect the actions of business enterprises in view of their habits of calculation and the magnitude of the harms they may cause. One also must not discount the influence of potential liability on individuals. Even if, as I suspect, some readers believe that the number of times an individual's potential liability will impinge on his behavior is small, this does not mean that the effect of the liability system on the accident rate will be negligible. (The decision of a homeowner to fence in a backyard swimming pool for fear of liability may be made only once in his lifetime, but the fence may significantly reduce the risk of a drowning.) In addition, although it is often said that the ownership of liability insurance undoes the deterrent effect of liability, this view is oversimple. As I have emphasized, insurance policies contain many features that create incentives to safety (the homeowner may fence his pool to obtain a reduction in his liability insurance premium). It thus seems that there is ample reason for theoretical study of the effect of liability on behavior—though I doubt many would seriously have argued against this in the first place.

What may have troubled some readers, however, is the level of detail at which I examined the effects of liability on behavior. My reaction to such a concern is twofold. First, obviously, it is intellectually unsatisfactory not to provide complete answers to questions, however complicated the answers may be. Second, it is worthwhile tracing out fully the rational behavior of parties because effects of liability on behavior that at one time are empirically unimportant may become empirically important later owing to changed circumstances. For example, in discussing uncertainty over causation, I explained that deterrence will be dulled to the extent that parties will escape liability on account of not being identified as the probable cause of losses.

1. The studies of which I am aware include Bruce 1984, a survey of evidence on deterrence of automobile accidents; Landes 1982, an empirical investigation of the same; Chelius 1976, a statistical examination of deterrence of industrial accidents in the past; and Higgins 1978, a statistical study of deterrence of product-related accidents. While these articles suggest that the incentives created by liability are, perhaps, stronger than many may think, they are too few to constitute a real corpus of work, and confident assertions about the facts cannot yet be made.

This point must have been empirically unimportant for most of the history of tort law since uncertainty over causation must have been an unusual occurrence. Today, however, the point may be empirically important because, as I noted, many environmental and health-related harms involve substantial uncertainty over causation.

*What is the normative value of the analysis?* The analysis should be of aid in assessing the desirability of legal rules, presuming as I do that the criterion of social welfare in which the reader is interested will reflect the value to parties of engaging in their activities, the costs of taking precautions, the losses due to accidents, compensation of risk-averse parties, and administrative costs. How much help the analysis will offer in answering normative questions will depend, as was true in respect to predictive questions, on the degree to which the analysis leads to conclusions that were not fairly clear in the first place. In considering this, the reader should again pause to review some of the conclusions that were reached. For example, he should recall the point concerning the advantage of strict liability over the negligence rule in controlling injurers' levels of activity; the argument showing that the sale of liability insurance is socially beneficial; the discussion of the possible gains to be had from accompanying liability by fines where achieving optimal deterrence requires that injurers pay more than it is optimal for victims to receive; and the examination of the privately motivated versus the socially optimal use of the liability system given administrative costs. I believe that most readers will not have found all the conclusions of the book familiar and that the analysis will have helped to clarify thinking.

*What consistency is there between observed and theoretically optimal liability law?* One can point to many instances of approximate agreement between liability law as observed and theoretically optimal liability law, that is, the law that appears best given the measures of social welfare that were examined here and certain guesses about the actual effects of liability on behavior. I suggested, to mention an important example, that the observed use of strict liability in areas where risks are apparently high is consistent with the theoretically optimal use of strict liability. Indeed, I indicated throughout the first seven chapters of the book how desirable incentives are created by this or that feature of tort law. (Recall, for instance, the discussions of the reasonable man and of prior precautions, the analysis of causation, and the treatment of the subject of damages.)

On the other hand, one can readily adduce examples of apparent disagreement between observed and theoretically optimal law. Supplemental fines, for instance, are generally not used despite the strong advantages they offer. One can also find instances where what constitutes theoretically optimal law is not clear. It was shown in the basic analysis of Chapter 2, for example, that use of the defenses of contributory negligence and of comparative negligence will result in the same, and optimal, behavior; no persuasive theoretical arguments were offered indicating the desirability of one defense over the other.[2] One can find as well instances where the law differs among countries in ways that cannot plausibly be explained on the basis of the factors studied here. In this regard the defenses of contributory and comparative negligence again afford an example. It is not apparent why, on the theory in this book, contributory negligence should sometimes be employed in the United States but only comparative negligence in England, France, Germany, and the Soviet Union. Likewise, it is not easy to see why, on the theory in the book, the liability of drivers toward pedestrians should be governed in this country by the negligence rule but usually by a strict theory elsewhere.

Thus, not only does there seem to be considerable consistency, but there also seems to be substantial ambiguity and inconsistency between the liability system that we observe and the regime that is best given the criteria of optimality and the models examined here.[3]

*Where there is consistency between observed and theoretically optimal liability law, can it be said that observed law is explained?* There are plainly a variety of factors going beyond the ones studied in this book that shape the law—the power of interest groups, the particular histories of legal institutions, the opinions of influential jurists and commentators, widely held notions of fairness, and so forth. The mere fact of consistency between observed law and what is here identified as theoretically optimal, therefore, hardly means that observed law is explained. For example, in the brief discussion in Chapter 2 of justifications actually given by courts and scholars for use of strict liability, I noted that little mention is made of incentives; it does not seem that the use of strict liability can be primarily attributed in a direct way to a perception that without such liability the number of accidents would grow too large. Nevertheless, contemplating the matter further, I think it is more than possible that if we discussed with people why they thought strict liability

2. Only rather subtle advantages of each of the defenses with regard to deterrence were discussed in §4.4.4. With regard to administrative costs, the defense of contributory negligence has an advantage in that it should lead to fewer claims and, perhaps, to less complicated proceedings. With regard to risk spreading, comparative negligence is superior in that losses are divided when both injurer and victim are at fault (but if each is insured, this feature does not matter). Taking all into account, there does not seem to be a decisive theoretical case for either rule over the other.

3. The question whether one says that, on balance, the law is or is not consistent with the theory is, I think, not especially fruitful for reasons of vagueness. No one knows what "on balance" means. Two individuals could agree about the areas in which observed law is and is not consistent with the theory but differ in their summary statements about the theory's goodness of fit. On the theme that tort law and economically optimal liability law are consistent, see generally Landes and Posner 1981a.

fair and desirable, we would be able to elicit from them statements indicating the importance of generating incentives to reduce participation in risky activity. It is also likely, in my opinion, that the desirability of the incentives created by strict liability would be recognized explicitly, and perhaps given prominence (in legislative hearings, in the press, if not in judicial opinion), if the number of accidents in an area governed by the negligence rule were to become high.

In any event, there are many examples of rules that are clearly understood to include among their major justifications those discussed in this book. For instance, the rule that an injurer need not pay a victim's entire losses if the victim failed to take reasonable steps to mitigate them I observed to be desirable because it gives victims incentives to limit the magnitude of their losses. This reasoning is also recognized by commentators to be an important justification for the rule.[4]

I conclude, therefore, that the interpretation of consistency between theoretically optimal and observed legal rules will depend on the rule in question. Sometimes consistency will signify very little or reflect mainly an implicit connection to the theoretical considerations studied here. Other times consistency will reflect a close and explicit connection.

*Of what normative significance is the omission from the analysis of consideration of principles of fairness?* One must be cautious in assessing the normative significance of this omission for two reasons. First, principles of fairness may to an important degree encapsulate the goal of maximizing the measures of social welfare studied here, mainly because adherence to principles of fairness often leads to behavior that reduces risk. An obvious example is that adherence to the principle that it is unfair to hold parties liable unless they acted negligently will lead parties to act nonnegligently. To determine the independent importance of a principle of fairness, one must therefore be careful not to count the consequences for behavior of adherence to the principle.[5]

Second, in evaluating the importance of adherence to a principle of fairness, one must recognize the fact that a liability insurer, not the injurer himself, will often be paying the award decided by a court, that the recipient

4. For instance, McCormick 1935, p. 127, says "it is important that the rules . . . be such as to discourage even persons against whom wrongs have been committed from passively suffering economic loss which could be averted by reasonable efforts . . . The machinery by which the law seeks to encourage the avoidance of loss is by denying to the wronged party a recovery for such losses as he could reasonably have avoided."

5. To test his attitude about the importance of the principle that there should be no liability without fault, the reader should ask himself, for example, how many additional accidents he would be willing to countenance in the area of ultrahazardous activities in order to have the negligence rule rather than strict liability decide liability.

of the award may not be the victim but rather his subrogated insurer, and that litigants may be faceless corporations rather than individuals with moral selves. These factors may well alter, and attenuate, the significance of adherence to notions of fairness for many readers.

In any event, readers can modify the conclusions reached here in light of the values they do attach to principles of fairness.[6]

*Of what importance is the omission from the analysis of considerations of income distribution?* This omission appears to be of small importance from the normative perspective. On the one hand, there already exists a social institution with an overtly redistributive function, namely, the income tax system. It reaches virtually all individuals and is, by comparison to the liability system, administratively inexpensive.

On the other hand, there are serious problems with the liability system as a device for accomplishing the redistribution of income. First, it does not reach all individuals, only those who are involved in litigation. Second, legal rules and decisions are likely to affect in a uniform way groups that are quite dissimilar in their need for money or ability to pay awards. The group of victims of automobile accidents, for instance, includes a wide spectrum of individuals categorized by income type, as does the group of negligent drivers. To take another example, a corporate litigant is really comprised of its stockholders, and that group—who may enjoy ownership through pension funds or life insurers' investments—will usually include a diversity of individuals, many of whom will not be well off. Third, liability awards are unlikely to be coordinated with redistribution carried out by other means, such as rent control and food stamp programs. Yet awards would have to be linked to litigants' participation in these programs for redistribution to be appropriate.[7] In all, the liability system appears to be an ineffective tool to employ to redistribute income. Consequently, had I introduced this factor into the analysis, and had I posited a socially desirable income tax structure, I would have concluded, in the main, that redistributional considerations should not influence the choice of liability rules or the size of awards.[8]

From the descriptive perspective, my omission of redistributional considerations seems somewhat more important, but I do not believe that significant redistribution of income is taking place through the tort system. While there may be a tendency today toward generosity in deciding cases and in making

6. For analysis of issues in tort law focusing on principles of fairness, and drawing a contrast with economic analysis, see Epstein 1973 and Fletcher 1972.

7. For example, other things equal, an accident victim who happened to be benefiting from rent control ought to obtain a lower award than a victim not so benefiting.

8. On economic analysis of the question whether legal rules (other than those concerning the income tax) should be used to redistribute income, see Polinsky 1983, p. 110, and Shavell 1981.

awards where the accident victims are poor and the defendants are well-to-do or are firms, it is also true that these defendants will usually have engaged superior legal counsel. Moreover, firms may be able to raise prices to cover liability costs, dulling the redistributive effect of their liability (such as it is; recall the remark about stock ownership). Finally, since the principles of tort law do not allow liability to be based openly on the relative wealth of litigants, the opportunities for redistribution are limited.

## Purpose and Future of Accident Liability

*What is the purpose of accident liability?* The answer to this question depends, in the first place, on the interpretation given to the word "purpose." Suppose that by the purpose of accident liability we mean what most participants in the legal system (or some wider class) *say* the purpose is. Then I would have to admit that the purpose of accident liability prominently includes the compensation of victims; it is my strong impression that the great majority of legal scholars, lawyers, and judges would state that the fair compensation of victims is an important (if not the important) purpose of accident liability.[9]

Another interpretation of "purpose," however, refers to the difference that the presence of the liability system makes to actual outcomes. According to this *functional* definition, which I now adopt, compensation of victims cannot be said to be an important purpose of accident liability, since in its absence victims would probably be about as well compensated as they now are (certainly they could be). Compensation would be accomplished by private and social accident insurance. The main difference the presence of the liability system does make, therefore, is that it creates incentives toward safety. This, then, must be said to be the chief purpose of the liability system today.[10]

It is worth noting, though, that the purposes of accident liability were different in the past. Before the development of insurance markets, liability furnished victims a source of compensation that presumably would not otherwise ordinarily have been forthcoming. Tort law thus served to an important degree the dual purposes of compensation and deterrence. Moreover, in early times before criminal law and tort law had emerged as separate branches of law, a significant additional purpose of the making of money payments for harm was the maintenance of social order. Without the system of money

---

9. See, for example, *Prosser and Keeton on Torts* (Keeton, Dobbs, et al. 1984), pp. 5, 6, and Fleming 1983, pp. 6–14.

10. Contrast this statement with, for example, the statement of Fleming 1983, pp. 7–8, that "in the core area of tort—accidents— . . . it is being increasingly realized that human failures in a machine age exact a large and fairly regular toll . . . which is not significantly reducible . . . through the operation of tort law."

payments, private vengeance would often have followed the doing of harm.[11] Evidently, the purposes of liability have changed over the years.

*What should be the purpose of accident liability?* The principal justification for use of accident liability today should not be compensation of victims because this can be accomplished with our well-developed and comparatively cheaply operating insurance system. Hence, if liability is to be employed in some area of accident, the major justification should be that liability creates incentives toward safety.[12]

Whether liability can be so justified for a particular area of accident is a question that will merit careful consideration in view of the opportunity to employ safety regulation and other approaches for controlling risk, in view of the administrative costs of the liability system, and especially in view of the difference between the social and the private interest in using the liability system (as I stressed, victims may quite rationally decide to bring suits even where the resulting change in injurers' incentives to reduce risk is small).

*What is the future of the liability system?* Although in some areas of accident regimes of insurance, perhaps coupled with enhanced safety regulation, may turn out to replace the liability system,[13] I believe that there will remain an important role for the system in the future. Considerable scope probably exists for reducing the administrative costs of the liability system through its simplification. Moreover, as we saw in the discussion of alternative methods for the control of risk, liability possesses unique advantages where a regulatory authority will not be expected to have good information about risk or the occurrence of harm, and where the deterrent inherent in liability will not be seriously weakened by injurers' inability to pay for harm or the possibility that they will escape suit. It is likely that these conditions will hold, and continue to make the system of liability for accidents socially valuable, in a large domain.

11. See Berman 1983, p. 55.

12. More precisely, I mean that creation of incentives together with other goals different from compensation (such as providing a forum for victims and society to express disapproval of certain acts) must serve as the main justifications.

13. New Zealand enacted legislation in 1974 displacing the tort system in the entire area of accidents causing personal injury. A similar approach was studied seriously, but not adopted, in the United Kingdom. In the United States, many states have passed no-fault statutes partially eliminating victims' right to sue for losses suffered in automobile accidents. Also, as was noted in Chapter 3, in most countries, accidents suffered by workers are compensated under workers' compensation plans, not under the tort system. See generally the descriptions in Atiyah 1980, chaps. 14, 15, and 25; Fleming 1983, pp. 369–377 and 491–496; and Keeton et al. 1983, chap. 19, and references cited therein. The tort system is increasingly criticized on account of its expense, and proposals for reform abound; for a recent example, see Sugarman 1985.

References
Index

# References

Arrow, Kenneth. 1971. Insurance, Risk, and Resource Allocation. In *Essays in the Theory of Risk-Bearing*. Markham, Chicago.

———— 1974. Optimal Insurance and Generalized Deductibles. *Scandinavian Actuarial Journal,* 1–42.

Atiyah, Patrick. 1967. Negligence and Economic Loss. *Law Quarterly Review* 83:248–276.

———— 1980. *Accidents, Compensation and the Law,* 3rd ed. Weidenfeld and Nicolson, London.

Barry, Donald. 1979. Soviet Tort Law and the Development of Public Policy. *Review of Socialist Law* 5:229–249.

Becht, Arno, and Frank Miller. 1961. *Factual Causation.* Washington University Press, St. Louis.

Becker, Gary, and Isaac Ehrlich. 1972. Market Insurance, Self-insurance, and Self-protection. *Journal of Political Economy* 80:623–648.

Berman, Harold. 1983. *Law and Revolution.* Harvard University Press, Cambridge, Mass.

Bishop, William. 1982. Economic Loss in Tort. *Oxford Journal of Legal Studies* 2:1–29.

Borch, Karl. 1962. Equilibrium in a Reinsurance Market. *Econometrica* 30:424–444.

Brown, John. 1973. Toward an Economic Theory of Liability. *Journal of Legal Studies* 2:323–350.

Bruce, Christopher. 1984. The Deterrent Effects of Automobile Insurance and Tort Law: A Survey of the Empirical Literature. *Law & Policy* 6:67–100.

Burrows, Paul. 1982. Idealised Negligence, Strict Liability and Deterrence. *International Review of Law and Economics* 2:165–172.

Calabresi, Guido. 1961. Some Thoughts on Risk Distribution and the Law of Torts. *Yale Law Journal* 70:499–553.

———— 1965. The Decision for Accidents: An Approach to Nonfault Allocation of Costs. *Harvard Law Review* 78:713–745.

———— 1970. *The Costs of Accidents*. Yale University Press, New Haven.

———— 1975a. Concerning Cause and the Law of Torts. *University of Chicago Law Review* 43:69–108.

———— 1975b. Optimal Deterrence and Accidents. *Yale Law Journal* 84:656–671.

Calabresi, Guido, and Jon Hirschoff. 1972. Toward a Test for Strict Liability in Torts. *Yale Law Journal* 81:1054–1085.

Calabresi, Guido, and Douglas Melamed. 1972. Property Rules, Liability Rules and Inalienability: One View of the Cathedral. *Harvard Law Review* 85:1089–1128.

Calfee, John, and Richard Craswell. 1984. Some Effects of Uncertainty on Compliance with Legal Standards. *Virginia Law Review* 70:965–1003.

Chelius, James. 1976. Liability for Industrial Accidents: A Comparison of Negligence and Strict Liability Systems. *Journal of Legal Studies* 5:293–310.

Coase, Ronald. 1960. The Problem of Social Cost. *Journal of Law and Economics* 3:1–44.

Conard, Alfred, James Morgan, Robert Pratt, Charles Voltz, and Robert Bombaugh. 1964. *Automobile Accident Costs*. University of Michigan Press, Ann Arbor.

Cook, Philip, and Donald Graham. 1977. The Demand for Insurance and Protection: The Case of Irreplaceable Commodities. *Quarterly Journal of Economics* 91:143–156.

Cooter, Robert. 1982. Economic Analysis of Punitive Damages. *Southern California Law Review* 56:79–101.

Craswell, Richard, and John Calfee. 1986. Deterrence and Uncertain Legal Standards. *Journal of Law, Economics, and Organization* 2:279–303.

Danzon, Patricia. 1984. Tort Reform and the Role of Government in Private Insurance Markets. *Journal of Legal Studies* 13:517–549.

———— 1985. *Medical Malpractice*. Harvard University Press, Cambridge, Mass.

DeGroot, Morris. 1970. *Optimal Statistical Decisions*. McGraw-Hill, New York.

Diamond, Peter. 1974a. Accident Law and Resource Allocation. *Bell Journal of Economics* 5:366–405.

———— 1974b. Single Activity Accidents. *Journal of Legal Studies* 3:107–164.

Easterbrook, Frank, and Daniel Fischel. 1985. Limited Liability and the Corporation. *University of Chicago Law Review* 52:89–117.

Eisner, Robert, and Robert Strotz. 1961. Flight Insurance and the Theory of Choice. *Journal of Political Economy* 69:355–369.

Eörsi, Gyula. 1975. *Private and Governmental Liability for the Torts of Employees and Organs*. Chap. 4 of vol. 11 (*Torts*) in *International Encyclopedia of Comparative Law*. Mouton, The Hague.

Epple, Dennis, and Artur Raviv. 1978. Product Safety: Liability Rules, Market Structure, and Imperfect Information. *American Economic Review* 68:80–95.

Epstein, Richard. 1973. A Theory of Strict Liability. *Journal of Legal Studies* 2:151–204.

——— 1980. *Modern Products Liability Law.* Quorum, Westport.

——— 1982. The Social Consequences of Common Law Rules. *Harvard Law Review* 95:1717–1751.

Fleming, John. 1971. *Collateral Benefits.* Chap. 11 of vol. 11 (*Torts*) in *International Encyclopedia of Comparative Law.* Mouton, The Hague.

——— 1983. *The Law of Torts,* 6th ed. Law Book Company, Perth.

Fletcher, George. 1972. Fairness and Utility in Tort Theory. *Harvard Law Review* 85:537–573.

Grady, Mark. 1984. Proximate Cause and the Law of Negligence. *Iowa Law Review* 69:363–449.

Green, Jerry. 1976. On the Optimal Structure of Liability Laws. *Bell Journal of Economics* 7:553–574.

Green, Leon. 1927. *The Rationale of Proximate Cause.* Vernon, Kansas City, Mo.

Grossman, Sanford. 1981. The Informational Role of Warranties and Private Disclosure about Product Quality. *Journal of Law and Economics* 24:461–483.

Haddock, David, and Christopher Curran. 1985. An Economic Theory of Comparative Negligence. *Journal of Legal Studies* 14:49–72.

Hamada, Koichi. 1976. Liability Rules and Income Distribution in Product Liability. *American Economic Review* 66:228–234.

Hart, Herbert, and Tony Honoré. 1985. *Causation in the Law,* 2nd ed. Clarendon, Oxford.

Henderson, James. 1981. The New Zealand Accident Compensation Reform. *University of Chicago Law Review* 48:781–801.

Higgins, Richard. 1978. Producers' Liability and Product-Related Accidents. *Journal of Legal Studies* 7:299–322.

Holmes, Oliver. [1881] 1963. *The Common Law.* Harvard University Press, Cambridge, Mass.

Holmström, Bengt. 1979. Moral Hazard and Observability. *Bell Journal of Economics* 10:74–91.

Honoré, Anthony. 1971. *Causation and Remoteness of Damage.* Chap. 7 of vol. 11 (*Torts*) in *International Encyclopedia of Comparative Law.* Mouton, The Hague.

Huberman, Gur, David Mayers, and Clifford Smith. 1983. Optimal Insurance Policy Indemnity Schedules. *Bell Journal of Economics* 14:415–426.

James, Fleming. 1948. Accident Liability Reconsidered: The Impact of Liability Insurance. *Yale Law Journal* 57:549–570.

——— 1952. Social Insurance and Tort Liability: The Problem of Alternative Remedies. *New York University Law Review* 27:537–563.

Jolowicz, J. 1976. *Procedural Questions.* Chap. 13 of vol. 11 (*Torts*) in *International Encyclopedia of Comparative Law.* Mouton, The Hague.

Kakalik, James, Patricia Ebener, William Felstiner, and Michael Shanley. 1983. Costs of Asbestos Litigation. Report R-3042-ICJ, Rand Corporation, Santa Monica.

Kaplow, Louis. 1986. Private versus Social Costs in Bringing Suit. *Journal of Legal Studies* 15:371–386.

Kaye, David. 1982. The Limits of the Preponderance of Evidence Standard: Justifiably Naked Statistical Evidence and Multiple Causation. *American Bar Foundation Research Journal*, 487–516.

Keeton, Robert. 1963. *Legal Cause in the Law of Torts.* Ohio State University Press, Columbus.

Keeton, W. Page, Dan Dobbs, Robert Keeton, and David Owen. 1984. *Prosser and Keeton on Torts,* 5th ed. West, St. Paul.

Keeton, W. Page, Robert Keeton, Lewis Sargentich, and Henry Steiner. 1983. *Tort and Accident Law.* West, St. Paul.

Keeton, William, and Evan Kwerel. 1984. Externalities in Automobile Insurance and the Underinsured Driver Problem. *Journal of Law and Economics* 17:149–181.

Kimball, Spencer, and Don Davis. 1962. The Extension of Insurance Subrogation. *Michigan Law Review* 60:841–872.

Kornhauser, Lewis. 1982. An Economic Analysis of the Choice between Enterprise and Personal Liability for Accidents. *California Law Review* 70:1345–1392.

Kraakman, Reinier. 1984. Corporate Liability Strategies and the Costs of Legal Controls. *Yale Law Journal* 93:857–898.

Landes, Elisabeth. 1982. Compensation for Automobile Accident Injuries: Is the Tort System Fair? *Journal of Legal Studies* 11:253–259.

Landes, William, and Richard Posner. 1980. Joint and Multiple Torts: An Economic Analysis. *Journal of Legal Studies* 9:517–556.

———— 1981a. An Economic Theory of Intentional Torts. *International Review of Law and Economics* 1:127–154.

———— 1981b. The Positive Economic Theory of Tort Law. *Georgia Law Review* 15:851–924.

———— 1983. Causation in Tort Law: An Economic Approach. *Journal of Legal Studies* 12:109–134.

Le Gall, Jean-Pierre. 1976. *Liability for Persons under Supervision.* Chap. 3 of vol. 11 (*Torts*) in *International Encyclopedia of Comparative Law.* Mouton, The Hague.

Limpens, Jean, Robert Kruithof, and Anne Meinertzhagen-Limpens. 1979. *Liability for One's Own Act.* Chap. 2 of vol. 11 (*Torts*) in *International Encyclopedia of Comparative Law.* Mouton, The Hague.

Luce, R. Duncan, and Howard Raiffa. 1957. *Games and Decisions: Introduction and Critical Survey.* Wiley, New York.

McCormick, Charles. 1935. *Damages.* West, St. Paul.

McGregor, J. 1972. *Personal Injury and Death*. Chap. 9 of vol. 11 (*Torts*) in *International Encyclopedia of Comparative Law*. Mouton, The Hague.

McKean, Roland. 1970. Products Liability: Implications of Some Changing Property Rights. *Quarterly Journal of Economics* 84:611–626.

McNeely, Mary. 1941. Illegality as a Factor in Liability Insurance. *Columbia Law Review* 41:26–60.

Malone, Wex. 1958. Ruminations on Cause-in-Fact. *Stanford Law Review* 9:60–99.

Mangasarian, Olvi. 1969. *Nonlinear Programming*. McGraw-Hill, New York.

Marshall, D. 1975. Liability for Pure Economic Loss Negligently Caused— French and English Law Compared. *International and Comparative Law Quarterly* 24:748–790.

Menell, Peter. 1983. A Note on Private versus Social Incentives to Sue in a Costly Legal System. *Journal of Legal Studies* 12:41–52.

Munch, Patricia. 1977. Costs and Benefits of the Tort System if Viewed as a Compensation System. Paper P-5921, Rand Corporation, Santa Monica.

O'Connell, Jeffrey. 1975. *Ending Insult to Injury: No-fault Insurance for Products and Services*. University of Illinois Press, Urbana.

Oi, Walter. 1973. The Economics of Product Safety. *Bell Journal of Economics* 4:3–28.

Opoku, Kwame. 1972. Delictual Liability in German Law. *International and Comparative Law Quarterly* 21:230–269.

Ordover, Janusz. 1978. Costly Litigation in the Model of Single Activity Accidents. *Journal of Legal Studies* 7:243–267.

Osakwe, Christopher. 1979. An Examination of the Modern Soviet Law of Torts. *Tulane Law Review* 54:1–76.

Polinsky, A. Mitchell. 1979. Controlling Externalities and Protecting Entitlements: Property Right, Liability Rule, and Tax-Subsidy Approaches. *Journal of Legal Studies* 8:1–48.

———— 1980a. Resolving Nuisance Disputes: The Simple Economics of Injunctive and Damage Remedies. *Stanford Law Review* 33:1075–1112.

———— 1980b. Strict Liability vs. Negligence in a Market Setting. *American Economic Review* 70:363–370.

———— 1983. *An Introduction to Law and Economics*. Little, Brown, Boston.

Polinsky, A. Mitchell, and William Rogerson. 1983. Product Liability, Consumer Misperception, and Market Power. *Bell Journal of Economics* 14:581–589.

Posner, Richard. 1972. A Theory of Negligence. *Journal of Legal Studies* 1:28–96.

———— 1973a. *Economic Analysis of Law*. Little, Brown, Boston.

———— 1973b. Strict Liability: A Comment. *Journal of Legal Studies* 2:205–221.

———— 1985. An Economic Theory of the Criminal Law. *Columbia Law Review* 85:1193–1231.

———— 1986. *Economic Analysis of Law*, 3rd ed. Little, Brown, Boston.

Pratt, John. 1964. Risk Aversion in the Large and in the Small. *Econometrica* 32:122–136.

Priest, George. 1981. A Theory of the Consumer Warranty. *Yale Law Journal* 90:1297–1352.

Rabin, Robert. 1985. Tort Recovery for Negligently Inflicted Economic Loss: A Reassessment. *Stanford Law Review* 37:1513–1538.

Raiffa, Howard. 1968. *Decision Analysis*. Addison-Wesley, Reading.

Rea, Samuel, 1981. Lump Sum versus Periodic Damage Awards. *Journal of Legal Studies* 10:131–154.

——— 1986. The Economics of Comparative Negligence. University of Toronto. Mimeo.

*Restatement (Second) of Torts*. 1965. American Law Institute, St. Paul.

Rizzo, Mario. 1982. A Theory of Economic Loss in the Law of Torts. *Journal of Legal Studies* 11:281–310.

Robinson, Glen. 1982. Multiple Causation in Tort Law: Reflections on the DES Cases. *Virginia Law Review* 68:713–770.

Rosenberg, David. 1984. The Causal Connection in Mass Exposure Cases: "Public Law" Vision of the Tort System. *Harvard Law Review* 97:849–929.

Ross, H. Laurence. 1980. *Settled out of Court*. Aldine, New York.

Rudden, Bernard. 1966. *Soviet Insurance Law*. Law in Eastern Europe Monograph no. 12. Sijthoff, Leyden.

——— 1967. Soviet Tort Law. *New York University Law Review* 42:583–630.

Savage, Leonard. 1972. *The Foundations of Statistics*, 2nd ed. Dover, New York.

Schwartz, Gary. 1978. Contributory and Comparative Negligence: A Reappraisal. *Yale Law Journal* 87:697–727.

——— 1979. Foreword: Understanding Products Liability. *California Law Review* 67:435–496.

Seavey, Warren. 1927. Negligence—Subjective or Objective? *Harvard Law Review* 41:1–28.

Shavell, Steven. 1979. On Moral Hazard and Insurance. *Quarterly Journal of Economics* 93:541–562.

——— 1980a. An Analysis of Causation and the Scope of Liability in the Law of Torts. *Journal of Legal Studies* 9:463–516.

——— 1980b. Strict Liability versus Negligence. *Journal of Legal Studies* 9:1–25.

——— 1981. A Note on Efficiency vs. Distributional Equity in Legal Rulemaking: Should Distributional Equity Matter Given Optimal Income Taxation? *American Economic Review* 71:414–418.

——— 1982a. On Liability and Insurance. *Bell Journal of Economics* 13:120–132.

——— 1982b. The Social versus the Private Incentive to Bring Suit in a Costly Legal System. *Journal of Legal Studies* 11:333–339.

——— 1983. Torts in Which Victim and Injurer Act Sequentially. *Journal of Law and Economics* 26:589–612.

—— 1984a. Liability for Harm versus Regulation of Safety. *Journal of Legal Studies* 13:357–374.

—— 1984b. A Model of the Optimal Use of Liability and Safety Regulation. *Rand Journal of Economics* 15:271–280.

—— 1985a. Criminal Law and the Optimal Use of Nonmonetary Sanctions as a Deterrent. *Columbia Law Review* 85:1232–1262.

—— 1985b. Uncertainty over Causation and the Determination of Civil Liability. *Journal of Law and Economics* 28:587–609.

—— 1986. The Judgment Proof Problem. *International Review of Law and Economics* 6:45–58.

Simon, Marilyn. 1981. Imperfect Information, Costly Litigation, and Product Quality. *Bell Journal of Economics* 12:171–184.

Skogh, Göran. 1982. Public Insurance and Accident Prevention. *International Review of Law and Economics* 2:67–80.

Spence, Michael. 1977. Consumer Misperceptions, Product Failure, and Product Liability. *Review of Economic Studies* 64:561–572.

Stewart, Richard, and James Krier. 1978. *Environmental Law and Policy,* 2nd ed. Bobbs-Merrill, Indianapolis.

Stoll, Hans. 1972. *Consequences of Liability: Remedies.* Chap. 8 of vol. 11 (*Torts*) in *International Encyclopedia of Comparative Law.* Mouton, The Hague.

Stone, Christopher. 1980. The Place of Enterprise Liability in the Control of Corporate Conduct. *Yale Law Journal* 90:1–77.

Stone, Ferdinand, 1972. *Liability for Damage Caused by Things.* Chap. 5 of vol. 11 (*Torts*) in *International Encyclopedia of Comparative Law.* Mouton, The Hague.

Sugarman, Stephen. 1985. Doing Away with Tort Law. *California Law Review* 73:555–664.

Summers, John. 1983. The Case of the Disappearing Defendant: An Economic Analysis. *University of Pennsylvania Law Review* 132:145–185.

Sykes, Alan. 1981. An Efficiency Analysis of Vicarious Liability under the Law of Agency. *Yale Law Journal* 91:168–206.

—— 1984. The Economics of Vicarious Liability. *Yale Law Journal* 93:1231–1282.

Trebilcock, Michael. 1986. The Insurance-Deterrence Dilemma of Modern Tort Law. University of Toronto Law School. Mimeo.

Tribe, Laurence. 1971. Trial by Mathematics: Precision and Ritual in the Legal Process. *Harvard Law Review* 84:1329–1393.

Tunc, André. 1974. *Introduction.* Chap. 1 of vol. 11 (*Torts*) in *International Encyclopedia of Comparative Law.* Mouton, The Hague.

Tversky, Amos, and Daniel Kahneman. 1974. Judgment under Uncertainty: Heuristics and Biases. *Science* 185:1124–1131.

Varian, Hal. 1978. *Microeconomic Analysis*. Norton, New York.

Viscusi, W. Kip. 1983. *Risk by Choice: Regulating Health and Safety in the Workplace*. Harvard University Press, Cambridge, Mass.

Von Mehren, Arthur, and James Gordley. 1977. *The Civil Law System*. Little, Brown, Boston.

Weir, Tony. 1976. *Complex Liabilities*. Chap. 12 of vol. 11 (*Torts*) in *International Encyclopedia of Comparative Law*. Mouton, The Hague.

Weitzman, Martin. 1974. Prices vs. Quantities. *Review of Economic Studies* 41:447–491.

Williamson, Oliver, Douglas Olson, and August Ralston. 1967. Externalities, Insurance, and Disability Analysis. *Economica* 34:235–253.

Wittman, Donald. 1977. Prior Regulation versus Post Liability: The Choice between Input and Output Monitoring. *Journal of Legal Studies* 6:193–212.

———— 1981. Optimal Pricing of Sequential Inputs: Last Clear Chance, Mitigation of Damages, and Related Doctrines in the Law. 1981. *Journal of Legal Studies* 10:65–92.

Zeckhauser, Richard. 1973. Coverage for Catastrophic Illness. *Public Policy* 21:149–172.

Zweigert, Konrad, and Hein Kötz. 1977. *An Introduction to Comparative Law*. Vol. 2, *The Institutions of Private Law*. North Holland, Oxford.

# Index

Accident insurance, 208, 210, 212, 214, 217, 227, 242; pure system of, 243–245, 260–261; administrative costs and, 263–265. *See also* Insurance; Liability insurance

Accidents: unilateral, 6–7; total costs of, 7; bilateral, 9–10

Activity, level of, 5, 21

Administrative costs: insurance and, 198, 263–265; liability and, 262–264, 270–271; motive to bring suit and, 265–276; alternatives to liability and, 282

Arrow, Kenneth, 2n, 118n, 199n, 202n, 231, 247

Atiyah, Patrick, 52n, 140n, 215, 244n, 263n, 298n

Becker, Gary, 202n
Bishop, William, 140, 156
Borch, Karl, 200n
Brown, John, 21, 40, 40n
Bruce, Christopher, 292n

Calabresi, Guido, 20, 20n, 114, 114n, 215, 243, 286

Calfee, John, 83, 99

Care: level of, 5; dimensions of, 9, 17, 36, 40; error in determining, 79–81, 93–96; momentary level of, 81–83, 96–97. *See also* Due care level

Causation: but for, 110; cause in fact, 110; cause sine qua non, 110; adequate, 114; uncertainty over, 115–118, 123–126. *See also* Coincidence; Necessary cause

Cheaper insurer, 214

Chelius, James, 292n

Coase, Ronald, 20n

Coincidence, 110–112, 121–122; restriction of liability and, 113–114, 122–123. *See also* Necessary cause

Collateral benefits, 142–143, 157–158, 235–240, 255–256

Comparative negligence rule, 15–16, 18, 39–40, 85, 103–104, 210, 294, 294n

Compensation vs. deterrence, 144, 231–235, 247–254

Conard, Alfred, 263n

Contribution, 164n, 165n, 167. *See also* Multiple injurers

Cook, Philip, 231, 247

Cooter, Robert, 151, 163

Craswell, Richard, 83, 99

Criminal sanctions, 278–279, 284–286

Damages. *See* Magnitude of liability

Danzon, Patricia, 234n, 263n

Diamond, Peter, 21n, 40, 77, 83, 91, 99, 101n

Discounting, 141–142, 157

Dispersion of harm, 283

Division of liability. *See* Comparative negligence rule; Strict division of liability
Due care level, 8; individual differences and, 73–77, 86–91; uncertainty about, 82, 97; anticipated error in, 83, 97–98; misperception of, 83, 99. *See also* Care; Negligence; Negligence rule

Easterbrook, Frank, 177, 177n
Ehrlich, Isaac, 202n
Epple, Dennis, 62n
Epstein, Richard, 63n, 296n
Equilibrium, 10, 33
Escape from suit: magnitude of liability and, 148, 161–162; alternatives to liability and, 280–281, 284, 289–290
Exemplary damages, 150. *See also* Magnitude of liability: losses exceeded by
Expected utility, 2

Fairness, 295–296
Fines: as supplement to liability, 233–234, 251–252, 254; as alternative to liability, 278–284, 288–290
Fischel, Daniel, 177, 177n
Fletcher, George, 296n

Grady, Mark, 115
Graham, Donald, 231, 247
Green, Jerry, 101n
Grossman, Sanford, 61n, 72

Hamada, Koichi, 63, 72
Higgins, Richard, 292n
Hirschoff, Jon, 20n
Holmes, Oliver, 76n
Holmström, Bengt, 202n
Huberman, Gur, 243, 259

Inability to pay judgments: effects of, 167–168, 179–182; solutions to problem of, 168–170; insurance and, 240–243, 257–259; alternatives to liability and, 279–280, 284, 289–290
Income distribution, 296–297
Indemnity, 166. *See also* Multiple injurers
Inflation, 141–142, 157
Information about risk: customers', 54–56; negligence rule and, 56–57, 78–79, 93; ' private vs. social, 281–284

Injunction, 277–284, 286, 289–290
Injurers, 5
Insurance: where insureds unable to affect risks, 193–194, 203; where insureds able to affect risks, 194–197, 203–205; other features of, 197–199; administrative costs and, 198, 263–265; nonpecuniary losses and, 228–231, 245–247; causation and, 243–245, 260–261. *See also* Accident insurance; Collateral benefits; Liability insurance
Interest, 141–142, 157

James, Fleming, 215
Joint tortfeasors. *See* Multiple injurers
Judgment proof problem. *See* Inability to pay judgments

Kakalik, James, 263n
Kaplow, Louis, 270, 276
Kaye, David, 116n
Keeton, Robert, 114n
Keeton, William, 243, 259
Kornhauser, Lewis, 175, 185n
Krier, James, 51
Kwerel, Evan, 243, 259

Landes, Elizabeth, 292n
Landes, William, 21n, 32, 115, 150, 163, 167, 179, 294n
Least-cost avoider, 17
Liability, 1; purpose of, 297–298; future of, 298. *See, generally,* Negligence rule *and* Strict liability. *See also* Magnitude of liability; Scope of liability; Vicarious liability
Liability insurance, 210–215, 222–227; inability to pay judgments and, 240–243, 257–259; regulation of, 213, 224, 226, 242, 259; administrative costs and, 263–265. *See also* Accident insurance; Collateral benefits; Insurance
Liability of firms: to strangers, 48–51, 65–66; to customers with perfect information, 52–53, 66–69; to customers with imperfect information, 53–54, 66–69; problems in applying liability rules and, 56–57; strict liability vs. negligence and, 57–58; warnings and, 60–61; warranties and, 61–62, 69–70; form of competition and, 62; actual use of, 63. *See also*

Liability of firms (*continued*)
Information about risk; Strict liability for product defects
Limited liability, 175–177
Losses: level of, 127–128, 151–152; probability of, 128–131, 152; uncertainty over, 131–132, 152–153; pecuniary vs. nonpecuniary, 133–135, 153–154; economic, 135–140, 154–156; mitigation of, 144–146, 158–159

Magnitude of liability: characteristics of losses and, 127–132, 151–152; types of losses and, 133–140, 153–156; special elements in computing, 140–144, 156–158; mitigation of losses and, 144–146, 158–159; losses exceeded by, 146–151, 159–163
Market power, 62
Mayers, David, 243, 259
Melamed, Douglas, 286
Menell, Peter, 270, 276
Models, 1–3
Moral hazard, 195. *See also* Insurance: where insureds able to affect risks
More likely than not criterion, 115. *See also* Threshold probability criterion
Multiple injurers, 164–167, 177–179
Munch, Patricia, 263n

Necessary cause, 105–106, 119; restriction of liability and, 107–110, 120–121. *See also* Causation; Coincidence
Negligence, 8; actual determination of, 19–20; explanation for findings of, 83–84, 99. *See also* Due care level
Negligence rule: unilateral accidents and, 8, 34–36; bilateral accidents and, 14, 38–40; activity level and, 23–24, 28, 42–43; defect in, 25–26; firms and, 48, 50–53, 56–57, 65–69; heterogeneity and, 73–77, 85–91, 102–104; prior precautions and, 78–79, 92–93; causation and, 108, 113, 120, 122; multiple injurers and, 165–166, 178–179; risk aversion and, 210, 221–222; insurance and, 212–213, 227; administrative costs and, 264–265, 268, 271, 274–275. *See also* Comparative negligence rule; Due care level; Strict liability

Negligence rule with the defense of contributory negligence, 14–15, 18, 28, 39–40, 85, 102–104
Nonpecuniary losses, 133–135, 153–154, 231–235, 247–254; insurance and, 228–231, 245–247
Normative analysis, 1, 3, 293

Oi, Walter, 63, 72
Olson, Douglas, 215
Ordover, Janusz, 270, 276

Pain and suffering, 233–234
Pareto optimality, 182, 200, 215
Polinksy, A. Mitchell, 51, 62n, 72, 286, 290, 290n, 296n
Posner, Richard, 20, 21n, 32, 32n, 51, 77, 115, 118, 150, 163, 167, 179, 286, 294n
Predictive analysis, 1–3, 291–295
Priest, George, 61n
Prior precautions, 77–79, 91–93. *See also* Care
Probability of losses, 128–131, 152
Product liability. *See* Liability of firms; Strict liability for product defects
Proportional liability, 116–118, 125–126. *See also* Causation: uncertainty over
Proximate cause, 114. *See also* Coincidence
Punitive damages, 150. *See also* Magnitude of liability: losses exceeded by

Rabin, Robert, 140n
Ralston, August, 215
Raviv, Artur, 62n
Rea, Samuel, 101n, 102n
"Reasonable man," 74–76. *See also* Due care level: individual differences and
Regulation of safety, 277–286, 289–290
Repair vs. replacement, 140–141, 157
Risk allocation, 190–192, 199–202
Risk aversion, 186–190, 199; social welfare and, 190–192, 199–202; liability rules and, 209–210, 218–222
Risk neutrality, 6, 32–33
Rizzo, Mario, 140, 156
Robinson, Glen, 118n
Rogerson, William, 62n
Rosenberg, David, 118
Ross, H. Laurence, 263n

Schwartz, Gary, 59n
Scope of liability, 105, 118–119. *See also* Coincidence; Necessary cause
Setoffs, 140–141, 156–157
Shavell, Steven, 32, 46, 51, 64, 68n, 72, 101n, 114, 118, 123, 126, 170, 182, 202n, 205n, 215, 227, 243, 258n, 259, 270, 276, 286, 290, 296n
Smith, Clifford, 243, 259
Social goal, social welfare, 3
Spence, Michael, 61n, 64, 72, 235, 254
Stewart, Richard, 51
Stone, Christopher, 177
Strict division of liability, 11–12, 37, 164–165, 177–178, 210
Strict liability: unilateral accidents and, 8, 34–36; bilateral accidents and, 11, 37, 40; activity level and, 23, 42–43; firms and, 48–50, 59–60, 65, 68; causation and, 107–108, 113, 120–123; multiple injurers and, 164–165, 177–178; risk aversion and, 209, 218–221; insurance and, 210–212, 223–226; administrative costs and, 264, 266–267, 271–274. *See also* Negligence rule
Strict liability for product defects, 58–60, 71–72
Strict liability vs. negligence: unilateral accidents and, 9, 36; bilateral accidents and, 16–17, 40; activity level and, 24–25, 29, 30–32; firms and, 57–58; miscellaneous factors and, 84–85, 99–100; risk aversion and, 210; administrative costs and, 264–265, 271

Strict liability with the defense of contributory negligence, 12–13, 18, 27–28, 37–38, 40; firms and, 48, 52–54, 57, 66
Strict liability with the defense of relative negligence, 14, 18, 38, 40
Subrogation, 235, 255. *See also* Collateral benefits
Successor liability, 176
Sugarman, Stephen, 298n
Summers, John, 170, 182
Sykes, Alan, 175, 185n

Taxes: magnitude of liability and, 143–144, 158; as alternative to liability, 277–284, 288–290
Threshold probability criterion, 115–118, 124–125. *See also* Causation: uncertainty over
Trebilcock, Michael, 263n
Tribe, Laurence, 118

Utility, 2n. *See also* Expected utility

Vicarious liability, 170–175, 182–185
Victims, 5
Viscusi, W. Kip, 234n

Warnings, 60–61
Warranties, 61–62, 69–70
Weitzman, Martin, 286, 290
Williamson, Oliver, 215
Wittman, Donald, 146, 159n, 290
Workers' compensation, 51–52n, 298n

Zeckhauser, Richard, 231, 247